Law without Precedent

LAW
WITHOUT
PRECEDENT

Legal Ideas in Action in the

Courts of Colonial Busoga

LLOYD A. FALLERS

The University of Chicago Press

Chicago and London

KRK
F3x

Standard Book Number: 226–23681–1

Library of Congress Catalog Card Number: 77–86135

THE UNIVERSITY OF CHICAGO PRESS, CHICAGO 60637
THE UNIVERSITY OF CHICAGO PRESS, LTD., LONDON

To Margaret and Joseph

Contents

Preface

This book represents for me the end of a fifteen-year quest for understanding. As I explain in chapter 1, I did not go to Busoga in 1950 with the purpose of studying law. My subjects were politics and administration—closely related matters, to be sure—but I was quite unprepared for legal research. I had long been fascinated, however, by the mysterious process by which authoritative normative judgment emerges from the courtroom debate and had enjoyed the close friendship of law students and lawyers. When, therefore, I discovered the intense preoccupation of Basoga with litigation and the excellence of their court records, I collected as much material as I could, without really knowing what I would do with it. Since 1953, I have been trying, in relation to this material, to discover just what it was that so fascinated me about the law. One major theme of this study is the implicitness of Soga legal reasoning; I think I now understand my own—previously implicit—reasons for finding law so interesting.

Or perhaps I have discovered new ones. At any rate, it now seems to me that a theory of law occupies an especially strategic place in sociocultural studies, because, to do any sort of justice to its subject matter, one must take very seriously both ideas and social relations, as well as the connections between them. A thoroughgoing reductionism, either social or cultural, seems to be particularly incapable of dealing with legal data of any richness. However, to explain these remarks would involve a superfluous recapitulation of the argument of the book, so I shall acknowledge my debts and pass on quickly to the business at hand.

First of all, to the Fulbright program in the United Kingdom and to the East African Institute of Social Research I owe the opportunity to work in Uganda. Both provided financial resources and the Institute, then under the very able directorship of Dr. A. I. Richards, also provided a stimulating setting for the discussion of research in progress. Later, while I was writing the book, I presented parts of it in the seminar of the Committee for the Comparative Study of New Nations of the University of Chicago, where I received much helpful comment and criticism.

In Busoga I was especially fortunate to receive the hospitality, friendship, and intellectual companionship of Oweek. E. T. Wako, Zibondo, and Omw. Sitanule W. Wandira, then subcounty chief Ssaabawaali, Kigulu, in each of whose courtyards I was allowed to live for several months. Both were judges of many years' experience and I am most profoundly in their debt for discussions of legal questions. Omw. Zefaniya Nabikamba, successively county chief, Kigulu, and county chief, Bugabula; Omw. Yonasani Waibi, county chief, Bulamogi; Omw. E. B. Mwami, subcounty chief Ssaabawaali, Bulamogi; Omw. J. W. Mukama, subcounty chief, Ssaabagabo, Bulamogi; and Omw. Mukamedi Isiko, subcounty chief Ssaabaddu, Bulamogi were also very helpful in this respect. For the careful copying of case records and other important services I am indebted to my paid assistants: J. Mugadu, H. J. Kagoda, M. Magola, D. Wabulembo, S. Kamusala, S. Mukupya, E. Nyende, G. W. Mugadya, E. Ngatia, Z. Kalireko, J. Isoba, S. Walugyo, H. Sajabbi, Y. Kagona, K. Mutaka, and J. Ntende.

Throughout my stay in Busoga I was helped immeasurably by Mr. R. F. Roper, who was successively assistant district commissioner and then district commissioner, Busoga. Besides introducing me to the political and legal authorities in the district and giving me access to administrative and legal records, he was my "guide, philosopher, and friend."

I must also acknowledge the help of many lawyers, academic and nonacademic, who have instructed me in their craft. Prof. Max Rheinstin has given generously of his vast comparative legal and historical learning; Prof. Soia Mentschikoff has shared her ideas about forms of dispute settlement; while Prof. William Twining has given me the benefit of his lawyer's perspective on African customary law. With Prof. Allison Dunham, Prof. D. V. Cowan, and Prof. Kwamena Bentsi-Enchill I had the good fortune in 1962 to share an investigation of land tenure in Basutoland at the invitation of that country's ruler—an experience which provided both comparative perspective and a thorough saturation in lawyers' talk. Ralph Gibson, Q.C., and Mr. Robert Kasanoff, practicing advocates in the courts of England

and New York, respectively, personify for me the finest qualities of the Anglo-American bar; they have taught me what the law is *for*. I hope that my account of the Soga courts has been sufficiently faithful so that they may recognize a kinship with the amateur judges and self-advocates who plead and deliberate in those courts.

Finally, I am especially indebted to those who have read all or portions of the manuscript and given helpful criticism: Dr. Audrey Richards, Prof. Alexander Nekam, Mrs. Shirley Castelnuovo, Prof. William Twining, Prof. David Schneider, Prof. Clifford Geertz, and Mrs. Margaret Fallers. My debt to the last two is quite special: Clifford Geertz has for a decade generously shared with me his own thoughts about the nature of the legal and of human society and culture in general. He also suggested the book's title. Margaret Fallers, who shared the Uganda experience with me, saw before I did that there was a book to be written from the material I had gathered on Soga law. She patiently, but firmly, insisted that I write it. Its shortcomings are of course my own responsibility.

Luganda words are written in the orthography used in Mulira and Ndawula, *A Luganda-English and English-Luganda Dictionary*. Lusoga lacks an authoritative orthography, but I have followed the common practice of literate Basoga in writing words unique to their language. Readers will, I believe, find it easier to distinguish the African names and phrases that appear from time to time if they learn to pronounce them. This is quite simple: pronunciation is essentially as in Italian, except for the double letters. These represent the same sounds as single letters, but should be held twice as long. Thus the double *i* in *lukiiko* ("court") sounds like the adjacent *e* and *e* in "be evil." The double k in *katikkiro* ("prime minister") sounds like the adjacent *ck* and *c* in "black cat."

Material from H. L. A. Hart, *The Concept of Law* (Oxford: Clarendon Press, 1961) is quoted by permission of the publisher.

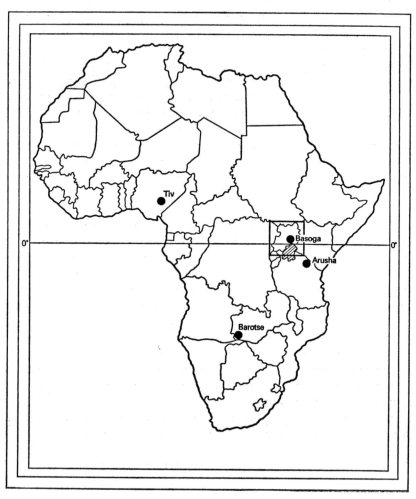

Map 1

BUSOGA AND EASTERN BUGANDA
1952.

Map 2

The social sciences are not staked out like real estate.
Even in the law, the sanctions for trespass
are not heavy.
—Karl Llewellyn

In their zeal not to be bureau-ridden, the American
people achieved the other extreme of being court-
ridden.
—Roscoe Pound

1   An African Legal System in Comparative Perspective

Karl Llewellyn, a legal scholar of restless intelligence, liked to think of jurisprudence as, among other things, a social science. Devoted as he was to the improvement of advocacy and adjudication as practical arts in the service of justice, he also felt it useful, from time to time, to step back from the role of teacher of professional craftsmen to that of observer and analyst and to view the advocate, the judge, the litigant, and the law itself as sociocultural phenomena, inextricably bound up with, influenced by, and influencing their environing society and culture. He even felt it worthwhile to look beyond his own tradition to the lawlike institutions of American Indians in search of a more adequate conception of things legal. His "realistic jurisprudence" involved putting the insights thus obtained to work in the interest of more effective advocacy and adjudication.

However excessively expansive this view of the field may appear to some, it continues a dialogue between jurisprudence and the social sciences that has persisted since the beginnings of the modern scientific study of society and culture, among whose founders lawyers—from Maine to Weber—were prominent. The dialogue is a natural one because lawyers work professionally with normative or moral concepts

—concepts of a sort which are also central to the study of society and culture. Whatever else law is about, it concerns the major institutionalized values of societies, the values to which people are sufficiently committed to be willing to impose them upon themselves in an authoritative manner. Such values are "cultural" in the sense that they form elements in the interrelated system of ideas shared by a people; and they are "social" in the sense that commitment to them underlies the mutuality of expectations upon which ordered social life rests.[1] An interest in legal institutions leads quite naturally into a concern with the culture of which the values they uphold form a part and with the social system out of which the disputes which they exist to prevent and settle arise. And of course, vice versa.

My own interests were drawn to legal matters because the Basoga, whom I had visited with the intention of studying the politics of the colonial situation, give great attention to legal institutions.[2] Like many other African peoples, they go to court readily and frequently; they admire and cultivate the arts of litigation and adjudication and they take great pleasure in discussing legal affairs. This common African characteristic has sometimes drawn unfavorable comment, as if "litigious" necessarily meant "quarrelsome"; but of course that implication may be quite unjustified, as it is, I think, in the case of the Basoga. To a sympathetc American observer, whose own society has made maximal use of the law court as an arbiter of social order, they seem not unduly contentious, but simply virtuously law-regarding. Indeed, as a product of such a system (though no lawyer), I may perhaps accept too uncritically the Soga tendency to try to solve all problems by litigation. At any rate, it is a fact that the Basoga, like the Americans, pour a great deal of their energy and talent into legal activity. Approaching the study of their society and culture, one is quickly drawn into legal concerns; and the study of their courts and law provides a particularly good point of departure for investigating other aspects of their society and culture.

Law, I am suggesting then, whether or not it is in some sense a feature of all human societies, is one to which societies may give varying degrees of prominence and value. This book concerns the legal institutions of a people who regard it highly and cultivate the skills associated with it. Only on one level, however, is it "about" the law of

1. Talcott Parsons and Edward A. Shils, eds., *Toward a General Theory of Action,* part 2; Clifford Geertz, "Ritual and Social Change: A Javanese Example."
2. I have analyzed politics and administration in colonial Busoga in my *Bantu Bureaucracy.*

the Basoga. Like most anthropologists, I write in the hope that my intensive study of a particular sphere of life in one society may have some significance for the understanding of that sphere in some other societies and even—just possibly—in societies generally. I hope, that is to say, to contribute something to the comparative study of legal systems.

The Soga legal system is one among several ethnic or "tribal" systems which exist together within the national legal system of Uganda. Therefore the most obvious comparative context for the institutions with which I shall be concerned is that of the historically recurrent phenomenon to which the term "customary law" has usually been attached. Customary law is not so much a kind of law as a kind of legal situation which develops in imperial or quasi-imperial contexts, contexts in which dominant legal systems recognize and support the local law of politically subordinate communities.[3] Like the peasant community with which it is so often associated, it is characterized by its relation to a wider, more learned, and politically more powerful system.[4] Usually, what is called customary law is unwritten, but it is significant that those who write about law that is unwritten but yet has not been in some sense "received" into a superordinate system, tend not to use the term; Barton writes simply of "Ifugao law," Pospisil of "Kapauku law."[5] Customary law is folk law in the process of reception.

Soga legal institutions find earlier counterparts in the Roman and Islamic empires and in the medieval empires and kingdoms of the West.[6] Today, similar institutions exist throughout much of the "Third World," wherever the new national states retain arrangements—often inherited from European colonial empires—for receiving diverse systems of local, ethnic law. The future of these institutions is an important question for the new states and for students of their development, for it is often through them—especially in Africa, where litigation is so highly regarded as a means of social control—that governments impinge most intimately upon the lives of ordinary people. I shall, therefore, within the limits imposed by a case study, pay some attention to the future of customary law within the modern African political context.

I also hope to add something to the continuing interdisciplinary

3. Charles Sumner Lobingier, "Customary Law."
4. A. L. Kroeber, *Anthropology*, p. 284; Robert Redfield, *Peasant Society and Culture*.
5. Roy Franklin Barton, *Ifugao Law;* Leopold Pospisil, *Kapauku Papuans and Their Law*.
6. Lobingier, "Customary Law."

exploration of the legal dimension in human societies in general. Again, this is a case study and not a general treatise, but even a case study, if it rises above the most mindless description, must proceed within a comparative perspective. This is especially true when one writes about institutions which are not one's own, for an audience to whom they are also exotic. At the very least, one must translate with some self-conscious care observations drawn from one language and social milieu into another and for this purpose one needs a conceptual place to stand. I shall, therefore, while analyzing Soga institutions, have to consider some aspects of the general concept "law" and related notions.

Finally, this study will involve some discussion of the relationship between thought and social relations in human affairs. The argument concerning their relative influence has been a dominant—perhaps *the* dominant—theme in social science and related areas of philosophy for more than a century, despite the repeated attempts by reductionists to bring it to an end by assigning one element or the other to epiphenomenal status. Today the issue is again a lively one, especially in anthropology (though of course the movements concerned run far beyond the boundaries of any one discipline); functional, evolutionary, and ecological perspectives, often in combination, contend with a variety of new emphases upon the primacy of thought, of which "formal semantic analysis" and the "structuralism" of Lévi-Strauss are the most prominent. Since all the reductionisms seem to me unhelpful, I view much of the argument as misconceived and will try to demonstrate, through the analysis of legal institutions, the utility of a view which gives both thought and action their due.

Most of the discussion of these larger themes will be left for chapter 8 when the Soga material, having been analyzed, will be available for reconsideration and for juxtaposition with other bodies of data. Here it is necessary only to indicate the framework within which the analysis will proceed.

Law and the Logic of Comparative Inquiry

Most of the concepts used in analyzing social and cultural phenomena are, in their origins, Western "folk concepts"—concepts used by Western people in thinking and speaking about their own institutions. We begin with words like "religion," "family," "government"—and "law"—words denoting particular Western sociocultural phenomena in all their complexity. When we attempt to use such words to describe and analyze the institutions of other societies, we find, naturally, that they do not suit the material at all precisely and we are faced with the problem of finding a conceptual place to stand that will allow us to take account of the distinctiveness, and yet recognize the basic commensurability, of diverse societies and cultures.

One response to these difficulties is, of course, that of Fielding's Mr. Thwackum, who, when called upon by his colleague, Mr. Square, to recognize certain similarities among the world's religions, declared:

When I mention religion, I mean the Christian religion; and not only the Christian religion, but the Protestant religion; and not only the Protestant religion, but the Church of England.

This sort of conceptual ethnocentrism will not do, of course, for it involves abandoning the comparative enterprise altogether, but the remedy is not as obvious as it is sometimes thought to be. On the one hand, a thoroughgoing relativism is of little use. Describing and analyzing other societies and cultures entirely "in their own terms," merely substituting other sets of folk concepts for our own, tends to leave us with an array of incommensurable, particular phenomena. On the other hand, it is difficult, perhaps impossible, to spin off from our own imaginations a fully developed set of culturally neutral concepts for analyzing societies comparatively. A "comparative science of society" is not, in my view, something which can be constructed in a burst of conceptual creativity; instead it is a process in which the intensive investigation of the particular case and reflection upon as much of the human experience as one has access to engage in a kind of dialogue.[7] One must, inevitably, begin one's investigation with a general rubric, like "law," which is "culture-bound" by virtue of its origin. This procedure is dangerous or misleading only if it remains unrecognized and intellectually undisciplined.

Recognizing that "law" does not, and cannot, have a universal, "culture-free" meaning because the intellectual millenium has not yet arrived, one adopts what strikes one as the most adequate conception of it—the product of others' reflections upon it, perhaps modified by one's own. One then "tries it out" on what appears to be the analogous phenomenon in the society under study. The ways in which it fails to "fit" are enlightening in two respects: First, they lead one to ask revealing questions about the case under study. The concept of law with which one began "made sense" in the sociocultural context from which it was drawn; one understood how such a system worked—both the legal system and the wider sociocultural system of which it was a part. One understood what "law" meant to people within the system, in the context of their values and beliefs, and one understood the

7. Lloyd A. Fallers, "Societal Analysis."

consequences of legal and other institutions for each other in that setting. If, now, "law" in the new society differs in these and these ways, then it must mean something different to people in relation to somewhat different beliefs and values; legal and other institutions must have somewhat different consequences for each other. One pursues these questions until one is able to give an account of this new system that, again, "makes sense." One is led, then, to the second consequence of the lack of fit: the general concept "law" may be modified to embrace the new data, or new analytic distinctions may be made within it. If the work has been convincing, the next investigator will begin from a somewhat different starting point. Thus, the case-by-case form of comparative inquiry serves both the generalizing and the clinical aspects of social science.[8]

Today, of course, "law" is far from remaining a folk concept. Both jurisprudential scholars and social scientists have worried and worked over it with more or less penetration and erudition for a very long time. One begins with all this at one's back and one may choose from an array of available concepts of law that which seems most adequate or useful for the task at hand. But any *general* concept of law is, in any case, only a starting point—an orientational framework within which more particular comparisons may be carried out. In this study, comparisons with other African legal systems are, of course, appropriate, and will be pursued at a number of points. The literature here is unusually rich and there is good reason to believe that many of black Africa's peoples are closely related historically; their institutions, including their legal institutions, may be regarded as variations upon common themes—subjects for what Eggan has called "controlled comparison."[9] The common emphasis upon litigation as a means of social control, mentioned earlier, is one manifestation of this.

I shall also make use of still another sort of particular comparison. As will be explained shortly, I shall be particularly concerned with the way in which the Basoga manipulate legal concepts in a system in which the law is uncodified and this suggests comparison with Anglo-American law. There is a rich literature concerned with the ways in which Anglo-American lawyers and judges manipulate normative concepts to arrive at "rules of law." Perhaps more than most developed legal traditions the Anglo-American one, and more especially its American branch, has been particularly concerned with the *process* of adjudication—in part, one supposes, because of the peculiarly prominent role of uncodified "common law" in this tradition. A system

8. Ibid.
9. Fred Eggan, "Social Anthropology."

which so often asks the lawyer and the judge to "discover," rather than merely to "apply," the law has about it a mystery which has attracted inquiry by particularly able minds. When, therefore, one sets out to try to understand the legal process in another tradition, particularly one which makes even less use of authoritative codes, the comparison with what Anglo-American legal scholars have said about that process in their own system is particularly inviting.

There are also historical and practical reasons why the comparison is particularly apt. For seventy years, from 1892 to 1962, the Basoga were under British administration within the political framework of the Uganda Protectorate. During this period, Soga courts, manned by Basoga, continued to administer Soga law, but meanwhile there grew up alongside, and for appellate purposes over, these courts a set of British imposed courts, manned by British judges and lawyers and administering a body of British-inspired law. A group of British-trained African lawyers developed. Thus the Soga legal system, together with those of the other African peoples of Uganda, operates within a legal environment dominated by these men and institutions.

This environment, as will be explained, has exercised a certain influence upon Soga law in the past; but, rather paradoxically, its influence promises to be even more important in the postindependence period. The pattern of legal pluralism inherited from the period of colonial control, in which a national body of law and hierarchy of courts sits atop a welter of local court systems administering diverse bodies of ethnic "customary" law, is one that many African leaders find unsatisfactory. To such leaders, striving to develop in their countrymen a sense of national unity, this fragmentation is simply the legal manifestation of the vexing problem of "tribalism"; and in Uganda, as in the many other African countries where this pattern exists, schemes for the unification of courts and law are presently being developed.[10] Whatever form the resulting programs of unification and reform may take, they seem likely to involve a still more intimate contact between African and British-type legal systems, with the latter tending to dominate and absorb the former. For it is the national legal system, with its British-influenced bench and bar, that represents national unity in the struggle with "tribalism."

It is therefore relevant, for quite practical reasons, to examine Soga legal institutions in the light of an Anglo-American model and to raise the question of means by which the two might be made more compatible. The issues here are complex, and I do not intend to offer a

10. William Twining, "The Place of Customary Law in the National Legal Systems of East Africa."

prescription for the future. But the present study may, perhaps, contribute to the discussion of these issues by illustrating the rather remarkable efficiency and intelligence with which at least one local court system copes with the problems that modern African life brings before it and by raising some of the questions to which unification schemes, involving drastic modification of the local courts, will have to seek answers: Can unification of law be pursued without destroying the sense of familiarity and confidence that at present recommends the local courts to ordinary Africans? Will more be gained than lost in replacing an amateur bench with a professionalized one and in admitting advocates to courts in which, traditionally, the litigant has been assumed to know his rights and to be competent to argue his own case? Perhaps most important of all, can the local courts be equipped with the tools to enable and encourage them to adapt to changing circumstances, including greater national unity, or must they be simply swept away by wholesale legislated unification?

As these questions indicate, the standpoint from which this study views the practical legal problems of the new African state is that of the "grass roots"—that of the village litigant who is the average consumer of African justice. The legal reformer commonly looks at these problems from a different standpoint, and for good reason. From his position in the legislature, the high court, the attorney general's office, or the law school, he sees the discontinuities, both in substantive law and in court practice, that legal pluralism brings. He sees the "unequal justice" experienced by differently placed citizens of the same nation, the conflict-of-laws problems created by the persistence of ethnic jurisdictions, the apparent incompetence with which untrained judges sometimes respond to unfamiliar circumstances. These problems are all too real. I wish only to suggest that the reformer, in his pursuit of national legal progress, might well take cognizance of the virtues that the local courts possess in satisfying the ordinary African's demand for justice.

I begin, then, with certain notions about law in general, African customary law, and Anglo-American law.

Whatever else is true of it, law clearly has to do with social control. Legal institutions are guardians or reformers of moral order—establishers or upholders of what members of a society regard as proper standards of conduct. However, with the possible exception of Malinowski,[11] writers on the subject have rejected the idea that law is

11. Bronislaw Malinowski, *Crime and Custom in Savage Society.*

simply synonymous with values or customs—that all institutions that uphold moral order are legal institutions. Since the very notion of "institution" involves mutuality of expectation resting upon shared values, such a view would imply that society is simply one great legal institution—a *possible* view, of course, but one that leaves the inquiry precisely where it was before. Nor will it do to define law as a sphere of custom more serious, or supported by more severe sanctions, than the rest. It would make little sense to say that overtime parking is more serious and more severely punished than cowardice or sacrilege. In Busoga, similarly, one may be taken to court for allowing one's goats to trample a few of one's neighbor's cotton plants, but not for incest—a far more outrageous act. Clearly, the distinctive qualities of law and legal institutions are not to be found along this path.

Bohannan has sought to differentiate law as binding rights and obligations which have been "doubly institutionalized" and legal institutions as the vehicles for this "reinstitutionalization." [12] Values governing the responsibilities of, for example, parents toward their children and contracting parties toward each other are institutionalized once in the family and the business world respectively and again in the legal system. This is of course quite unexceptionable, as far as it goes, and no useful conception of the subject can ignore it, but it is not only institutions that one feels comfortable calling "legal" that provide for this kind of institutional backstopping. Religious ritual, for example, insofar as it has moral content, also undergirds the normative basis of other institutions, often quite explicitly; so also, of course, does education.

I press this point not in order to belabor Bohannan, for his further discussion of the subject suggests that he recognizes additional differentia of law of the sort I want to suggest,[13] but rather to underline a point made earlier: some societies, including that of the Basoga, make a great deal more use of what I would call the *legal mode* of social control than do others. In relation to Bohannan's ideas, I should put it that some make more use of the legal mode of reinstitutionalization. A number of east Asian peoples, for example, whose cultures are rich in quite formal codes of norms or precepts, seem to have an attitude toward litigation which is quite the opposite of that exhibited by most African peoples. Beardsley, Hall, and Ward speak of the Japanese ". . . aversion to judicial process in any form." [14] Clifford Geertz illustrates a similar Balinese attitude with a folk tale in which two

12. Paul Bohannan, "Law and Legal Institutions."
13. Ibid.
14. Richard K. Beardsley et al., *Village Japan*, p. 393.

villagers are quarreling over a piece of meat. The legal system, in the guise of a hawk, swoops down between them and snatches it away, pointing up the moral that, right or wrong, successful or unsuccessful, one can only lose by going to court.[15] Much the same attitude seems to prevail in China; Schurmann remarks of courts in communist China that ". . . formal law plays a much smaller role than it does in the Soviet Union," [16] while Fei's account of precommunist village government devotes less than a sentence to anything akin to legal institutions.[17] Courts, of course, exist in these societies, but ordinary people make as little use of them as possible. Reinstitutionalization seems, among these peoples, to be accomplished primarily in other ways.

Another way of differentiating things legal, favored by Nader and others, makes "dispute-settlement" their central characteristic.[18] This view further circumscribes the field, for while the reiteration of moral ideas in ritual is unquestionably a form of reinstitutionalization, it is not, or not necessarily, a means of settling disputes. The latter involves moral reiteration through institutions for applying moral ideas to social events after the fact—"cleaning up social messes," or "trouble cases" as Llewellyn and Hoebel put it.[19] Now this may, of course, be a useful topic for comparative study, as indeed may social control and reinstitutionalization, but I feel that it still casts the net too widely to serve as an adequate conception of law. Significantly, those who write on the east Asian societies mentioned earlier often couple their statements about the hostility to "judicial process" or "litigation" with remarks to the effect that "mediation" or "arbitration" is preferred.[20] Disputes occur in these societies, but the writers want to tell us that these are dealt with, wherever possible, by arbitration or mediation *as contrasted with* something else—something which I want to distinguish as legal process. In part, the attitude reported by these writers seems to be associated with village solidarity and a desire to avoid drawing extravillage authorities into local affairs, but it also, I gather, involves a dislike of litigation and adjudication as such, since if these were approved means of handling disputes they would be provided for locally, as they commonly are in Africa.

Again, one might, of course, define "law," "litigation," and "adjudication" broadly enough to embrace "mediation" and "arbitration," but these writers sense an important distinction and it seems to me to be

15. Personal communication.
16. Franz Schurmann, *Ideology and Organization in Communist China,* p. 188.
17. Hsiao-Tung Fei, *Peasant Life in China,* p. 106.
18. Laura Nader, ed., *The Ethnography of Law,* p. 23.
19. K. N. Llewellyn and E. Adamson Hoebel, *The Cheyenne Way,* p. 20.
20. See especially Beardsley, et al., *Village Japan.*

one worth preserving. Not all the categories used in comparative inquiry need apply uniformly to all societies; indeed if they did so, comparative inquiry would become much simpler (and less instructive) than it can be. The anthropological study of law has, I think, suffered from a reluctance to recognize that some societies make little, if any, use of law, as if this would somehow be a matter for reproach. But mediation is no less useful a procedure for not being "legal"; indeed, from some moral standpoints, or for some purposes, it may well be superior. A familiar strain of critical thought in Western countries has long held that legal or (more pejoratively) "legalistic" modes of dispute settlement have been overworked in those countries. The fact that much of this criticism has been the work of the "legal profession" does not mean, of course, that the alternatives suggested are, in an analytical sense, "legal."

For a view of law more congenial to my purposes, I turn to the work of H. L. A. Hart. For Hart, law involves the combination of "primary rules of obligation" with "secondary rules."[21] The primary rules are norms of social life which are supported not only by institutionalization and internalization in the society at large—by conscience and public opinion—but also by institutions which apply secondary rules. Secondary rules are rules *about* the primary rules. But the secondary rules do not merely reiterate primary rules; they "specify the ways in which the primary rules may be conclusively ascertained, introduced, eliminated, varied, and the fact of their violation conclusively determined."[22] "Rules of recognition" specify means of determining which norms will be treated legally; "rules of change" specify the means by which rules may be introduced, eliminated, or altered; while "rules of adjudication" specify the means for determining whether or not a particular rule has been violated on a particular occasion. Hart has relatively little to say about the institutional embodiment of these rules, beyond speaking of them as being applied by "officials," but he would argue that some organizational structure for their application is necessary to the specifically legal mode of "double institutionalization."

Now it is important, I think, that Hart talks about *rules* and *rules for applying rules*. The legal mode of social control requires that values with respect to human conduct be reduced to normative statements which are sufficiently discrete and clear so that it may be authoritatively determined *whether or not* in a particular case a particular rule has been violated. This way of looking at situations of

21. H. L. A. Hart, *The Concept of Law*, pp. 77–96.
22. Ibid., p. 92.

social conflict—in terms of violation of rule—may usefully be contrasted with two others. First, such situations may be regarded as conflicts of *interest*—as what are commonly called "political" conflicts. In this perspective, the parties are not regarded as having violated (or not violated) rules, but rather as pursuing conflicting policy goals. Rules enter, of course, as means of confining conflict to orderly bounds, and values in a more general sense are appealed to in mustering support. Also, legal rules may be the *subjects* of political conflict. But political conflict is precisely about "open questions"—questions which have not (or not yet) been reduced to rules. Law, of course, does not *completely* reduce to rules the questions with which it deals. It deals with recurrent, relatively stereotyped conflicts, but because conflicts are never *precisely* the same, the law always retains a degree of "open texture." And as Pospisil and many others have pointed out, there is a range of intermediate phenomena in which the political shades off into the legal; it is within this spectrum that one finds some of the phenomena referred to as "mediation" and "arbitration"—for example in international, labor, and commercial relations. These resemble legal process in that they are precipitated by an event—a "dispute" or "case"; they resemble political process in that justiciable rules are lacking. In connection with industrial arbitration in Australia Goodrich writes: "The choice among rival and conflicting doctrines leaves ample room not only for the 'equity and good conscience' which the Commonwealth act commends to its judges but also for expediency and good policy." [23] And Potter says of international mediation that, even under the best (i.e., most lawlike) conditions, "it still remains nothing more than an attempt to adjust political demands or, even when the demands are allegedly based upon international law, a search for a form of settlement not necessarily cast in terms of accepted law." [24]

Second, the legal mode of assessing situations of conflict may be contrasted with their full moral evaluation. Here common standards may exist, but an attempt is made to take account of the full moral complexity of conflict situations. Morally, human conflict is almost never as simple and straightforward as the phrase "whether or not a rule has been violated" would suggest. A "case" very commonly climaxes a substantial period of association between the parties, in the course of which each has done things to the other of which he ought to be ashamed. Even in "atomistic," "anonymous" modern urban societies, a strikingly large proportion of disputes involve kinsmen, neigh-

23. Carter Goodrich, "Arbitration, Industrial," p. 155.
24. Pitman B. Potter, "Mediation," p. 274.

bors, friends, or work associates, not total strangers.[25] A legal culture cuts into this complex "objective" moral reality in a highly "arbitrary" way. It is characteristic of the legal mode of social control that rules are used to arrive at simple, dichotomous moral decisions—"yes" or "no" decisions that in other contexts would seem intolerably oversimplified morally. The legal process does not ask: What are all the rights and wrongs of this situation—on both sides? Rather, it asks: Is John Doe guilty as charged? John Doe may be utterly depraved—may be shown to have treated Richard Roe abominably—but if he cannot be shown to have violated the rule as charged, he (as far as the legal process is concerned) goes as free as if he were a saint. It is, I think, significant that even in societies that make extensive use of the legal mode of social control, persons often exhibit a certain ambivalence of attitude toward this aspect of it. On the one hand, my own court-ridden countrymen, for example, are often made uncomfortable by their courts' necessity to arrive at such "hair-splitting," "legalistic" (as they say) decisions; on the other hand, they sense that it is, after all, the essence of what they like to call, in admiring moods, the "reign of law" to isolate for adjudication a rather narrow segment of moral reality. They sense that it is really only with respect to such narrow segments that there can be "rules of law."

Again, there is a range of intermediate phenomena; indeed, the pure case of the uncompromising reign of rules probably cannot exist because it would be morally too painful to bear. Even in legalistic England and America its rigor is tempered by such devices as the "degrees" of homicide and larceny, and by variable penalties—as well as, of course, by the fact that only a small part of society's normative structure is treated legally. Toward the other end of the continuum, the "mediators" and "arbitrators" who settle intravillage conflicts in China, Japan, and Bali are perhaps best thought of as the agents of a cultural attitude even less sympathetic to the legalistic application of rules. (The terms "mediator" and "arbitrator" thus have, I think, been used to distinguish from legal process two elements which are analytically quite different: on the one hand, the third party who achieves a compromise between conflicting interests; and, on the other, the one who restores amity, or at least peace, by bringing the parties to recognize the justice of each others' grievances.) The Lozi of Zambia, whose legal institutions have been so ably analyzed by Max Gluckman, exhibit an interesting compromise between legalism and what might be called moral holism. Lozi judges measure conduct against

25. Hans von Hentig, *The Criminal and His Victim*, esp. chap. 12.

rules, clearly enough, but for them the "case" involves the evaluation of a substantially greater amount of interpersonal history than is true among the Basoga. (Thus, the "case" is a culturally variable, not a universal, unit.) They feel no necessity to judge only one party to a dispute at a sitting, and they feel free to alter the cause in the course of the trial. During the consideration of one case, both parties may be judged guilty (or liable) in the light of different rules and additional rules may be invoked as the "facts" unfold.[26] This allows them to deal more holistically with social conflict than do Basoga judges who, as will be seen, resemble Anglo-American judges in taking up rules in a more one-at-a-time fashion. If it comes out in the course of a "civil" trial that a defendant has cause for action against the plaintiff or a third party, the most the Soga court will do is to advise him of this fact.[27] A Lozi court, if I understand Gluckman correctly, may well proceed, on its own initiative, to charge and try the new defendant. The Basoga (and their neighbors) are, I suspect, unusually legalistic, even among Africans. These comparisons will be taken up in more detail in chapter 8.

I shall, then, following Hart, adopt the view of law as a combination of primary and secondary rules. For past conduct to be measured against rules, there must be rules allocating to some institutional structure the authority to decide what segments of morality are to be embodied in justiciable rules—the violations of what norms are to be regarded as causes of action—and there must be rules for applying these rules to sets of "facts." Law thus accomplishes social control, reinstitutionalization, dispute settlement, through this special mode of moral discourse. Legal institutions are institutions in which this mode —this subculture—is institutionalized. Viewing things legal in this way gives a certain shape to the study of any legal system and suggests certain problems for investigation.

First, it calls attention to the relationship between that system and the society and culture in which it is embedded. The secondary rules form a distinct subculture whose internal logic calls for investigation as such, but the prefix "sub" cuts both ways: If courts of law work with "artificially" narrow moral issues, and with a logic of their own, the issues nevertheless remain moral ones. Their decisions pertain to matters about which the everyday, common-sense morality of the society also has something to say—sometimes something rather different. The legal system, since those who participate in it are also members of the society at large, both draws upon and feeds back into

26. Max Gluckman, *The Judicial Process among the Barotse,* 178–81.
27. See *Zakaliya Yande* v. *Amadi Simola.*

the everyday system of morality. To the degree to which the two reach different moral conclusions about the same events, there exists a tension between law and popular morality that may induce change in either or both. Again, the legal system has its own distinct social organization consisting, at a minimum, of the roles of those who apply the secondary rules, but those who occupy such roles are also members of the larger society, in which they occupy other roles as well. Of course the sociocultural differentiation of legal systems varies enormously. In the Soga courts there is no bar and the bench is only semiprofessional. The legal subculture is much less differentiated from popular culture than in modern Western societies. The consequences of these differences, as well as the fact of differentiation itself, require investigation.

The perspective I have adopted also invites attention to the relationship between the logic of ideas and the exigencies of social relations within the legal system and in the society at large. The notion of "applying rules to sets of 'facts'" to reach "decisions" involves, intrinsically, a conception of interplay between moral ideas and social experience which is quite incompatible with either social or cultural reductionism. If either culture or social relationships were simply a reflection of the other—if either were "determinant" and the other "epiphenomenal," as is sometimes argued—such a mode of expression, implying deliberate choice between alternative judgments, would make little sense. Adjudication would become a mechanical process. As Hart puts it:

The necessity for such choice is thrust upon us because we are men, not gods. It is a feature of the human predicament (and so of the legislative one) that we labor under two connected handicaps whenever we seek to regulate, unambiguously and in advance, some sphere of conduct by means of general standards to be used without further official direction on particular occasions. The first handicap is our relative ignorance of fact; the second is our relative indeterminacy of aim. If the world in which we live were characterized only by a finite number of features, and these together with all the modes in which they could combine were known to us, then provision could be made in advance for every possibility. We could make rules, the application of which to particular cases never called for further choice. . . . This would be a world fit for mechanical jurisprudence.[28]

There is, of course, a mechanical element in human social life, and even in adjudication, as anyone who has watched a magistrate "process" routine traffic and drunk-and-disorderly cases knows. Much of social life is quite unreflective and repetitive. Even the more self-con-

28. Hart, *The Concept of Law*, p. 128.

scious forms of social action commonly proceed, for the most part, in stereotyped sequences in which mutual expectations are satisfied by interactions based upon common patterns of belief and value—which is, of course, why such terms as "social *structure*" and "cultural *pattern*" have their uses in social science. But by no means all of social life is captured by such terms. They are perhaps best regarded as conceptualizations of that routine element in social life that provides persons with a place to stand while they decide what to do next. This, no doubt, overstates men's capacity for creativity; choices are usually made between socially and culturally "given" alternatives. But our entire experience of sociocultural change speaks against a conception of human affairs as being *rigidly* governed by either patterns of thought or social structural exigencies. Culture is not *simply* the noise given off by social machines, nor is society *simply* an automaton guided by cultural computers. Such images are seen to be most inadequate in times of social upheaval when different segments of a society's population march to different drummers, but smaller-scale divergences of a similar sort are common. Human beings, both as marchers and as drummers, are continually experimenting with direction and beat. Systems of thought are therefore most usefully seen as consisting of themes with manifold possibilities for variation, social systems as structures open to reorganization. And, since the same human actors are caught up in both the logic of ideas and social commitments to each other, cultural-thematic and social-organizational variations constantly play upon each other. I find it most revealing to view history as "made" neither by social "interests" nor cultural "ideals" but rather by their interaction through the medium of men's choices.

None of this, of course, is peculiar to legal institutions, but in the study of such institutions a view which recognizes a degree of indeterminacy in relations between the part and the whole and between ideas and organization seems particularly useful. The "cases" with which the legal system works spring from "trouble spots" in sociocultural systems—areas of life in which, because of conflicting social demands, divergent value commitments, or "deviant" character organization, persons choose to evade norms declared by the legal system to be justiciable. Or again, especially in times of rapid change or in situations in which the legal subculture is sharply differentiated from popular culture, they may result from uncertainty concerning the law's requirements. In either case, the legal process is one in which, a nonroutine sequence of events having occurred (I neglect here, as *legally* uninteresting, routine litigation of the sort mentioned earlier), a special set of persons conducts an explicit inquiry into the normative status of these events, taking the legal subculture into their hands, so to speak, and using it as a tool for this purpose. Here again choice is involved, but now choice involves attention to the law itself. As Hart says, after noting that in any healthy society most people obey the law most of the time, the ordinary person may obey for any of several reasons: conviction, self-interest, or merely habit. But:

> [The] merely personal concern with the rules . . . cannot characterize the attitude of the courts to the rules with which they operate as courts. . . . Individual courts of the system though they may, on occasion, deviate from these rules must, in general, be critically concerned with such deviations as lapses from standards, which are essentially common or public.[29]

The officials of the legal system are agents of the "rationalization" (as Max Weber would say) of one segment of the culture, as priests and scientists are of others.[30] They are charged with giving self-conscious attention to the coherence of elements of culture that otherwise remain implicit, common-sensical, subject to only ad hoc attention. As Schutz has put it, in contrasting the social scientist's with the participant's perspective on social experience, the events that precipitate a case are not, for the legal official, "the theater of his activities," but "merely the object of his contemplation." [31] The result is not, of course, the pure reign of legal reason, for, as Frank and many others have shown, the legal system has its own sociology and psychology.[32] But the specialized reasonings of legal officials are sufficiently apart from the life to which they are applied that they may serve to sharpen the issues and heighten the tensions between values and social experience, and between different segments of society, that are among the springs of sociocultural change. A crucial problem here, and one which I shall take up in connection with the Soga courts, is that of the relationship between the social role of the judge and the degree of rationalization of the legal subculture. It seems a reasonable hypothesis that the ability of judges to deal with moral issues "legalistically"—that is, to deal with "artificially" narrow moral issues—will depend to an important degree upon the authority and prestige they enjoy.

LAW WITH, AND WITHOUT, PRECEDENT

I have argued that Hart's view of law as an affair of rules about rules implies that legal institutions utilize a mode of normative judgment involving the isolation of rather narrow moral issues for adjudi-

---

29. Ibid., p. 111.
30. Max Weber, *The Theory of Social and Economic Organization*, p. 123.
31. Alfred Schutz, *Collected Papers* 1: 36.
32. Jerome Frank, *Law and the Modern Mind*.

cation. Earlier I suggested that, in attempting to understand how this process works in the Soga courts, a comparison with similar processes in Anglo-American courts is of special relevance. It will be useful, therefore, to examine the process of legal reasoning as seen by a student of Anglo-American jurisprudence in order to gain a clearer understanding of how "rules of law" are handled by judges and advocates in that tradition—how rules of law are "applied" to social events.

In Anglo-American law, much use is made of precedent. In some parts of the law, where there are no statutes, the law is entirely case-law, which is to say, precedent-law. Even where statutes exist, a body of case-law develops in the course of their application. How do rules of law come into play in this process? Edward Levi has suggested that, however much judges and advocates wishing to stress the stability of the law may sometimes try to disguise their arguments as some form of deductive reasoning from fixed rules, in fact they reason from case to case, with a moving system of classification, so that the rules are in fact discovered as they are applied. He describes the three-step process as follows: "similarity is seen between cases; next the rule of law inherent in the first case is announced; then the rule of law is made applicable to the second case."[33] The rule that the judge in the second case draws out of the reasoning of the judge in the first case may be formulated in terms quite different from those the latter himself used, for each judge always faces a somewhat different problem. Cases are never identical. Thus, the doctrine of precedent does not mean, and cannot mean, that general rules, once stated in case decisions, are simply applied mechanically to subsequent cases. Instead it means something closer to the principle that, in deciding particular cases, the judge must have due regard for the coherence and consistency of the law as a whole in the relevant field.

The reason, Levi suggests, why legal reasoning must take this case-by-case form is that it operates in a changing society: "Not only do new situations arise, but in addition peoples' wants change. The categories used in the legal process must be left ambiguous in order to permit the infusion of new ideas."[34] By operating with a moving system of classification in which, by means of the comparison of cases, the framework may be reordered as fresh cases are decided, the logic of the law achieves, simultaneously, a tolerable degree of coherence and predictive coerciveness, and a measure of responsiveness to new circumstances. Thus, the *stare decisis* rule cannot be applied with the

33. Edward H. Levi, *An Introduction to Legal Reasoning*, pp. 1–2.
34. Ibid., p. 3.

rigidity that it is often thought, particularly, it seems, in England, to necessitate. Indeed, since, as Cross indicates, the English rule in its present rigid form is of only late nineteenth or early twentieth-century origin,[35] it would appear to be more in the nature of a cautionary maxim of judicial self-restraint than a rule descriptive or prescriptive of judicial behavior. It is perhaps best interpreted as an ideological statement whose function is to preserve a sense of continuity and certainty in a period when rapid change has made the strain of reconciling fixity with flexibility particularly severe. Thus, a judge in an Anglo-American system does not, strictly speaking, "follow" precedent; rather, he constructs it by formulating a rule that brings the decision in the instant case into logical relation with its predecessors.

Levi is, of course, concerned with the more innovating decisions by appellate courts in difficult cases. The run-of-the-mill "plain" case in the lower courts requires little judicial reflection. Still, the pattern Levi describes is paradigmatic: cases are never exactly the same; the more novel the "facts," the more obvious becomes the process of precedent construction.

Soga law is also case-law in the sense that it makes little use of statutes, but, unlike Anglo-American law, it contains no explicit doctrine of precedent of any sort. Neither judges nor litigants, at any level, ever refer explicitly to previously decided cases as precedents or to any duty on the part of judges to follow precedents. When asked, they reply that, of course, they decide cases as they have been decided in the past, but they are quite uninterested in, and unable to discuss, the process by which this is accomplished; that it *is* accomplished, they simply regard as self-evident. There clearly is order and predictability in Soga law. Litigants go to court with the assurance that their cases will be decided in accord with familiar principles; judges confront the cases that come before them with confidence in their ability to reach decisions consistent with their own, and the litigants', legal experience. Furthermore, in Soga courts, as in Anglo-American courts, litigants and judges reason with the law in a manner that serves to narrow issues to a point at which "rules of law" may be applied to them. If they do not reason in precisely the same way as their Anglo-American counterparts, still they are clearly, on some level, doing the same kind of work—*legal* work. By comparing the two systems it may be possible to isolate intellectual processes common to both of them, and perhaps even to judges and litigants wherever we find institutions that we can reasonably call "courts of law."

35. Rupert Cross, *Precedent in English Law*, pp. 17–30.

This is not meant to suggest, it should now be clear, that all societies
have such institutions. To be useful for comparative purposes, a concept need not have universal application; it need only define an
element of some cross-cultural significance. Clearly many societies
outside the Western world *do* have legal systems in the sense under
discussion here, and I am interested in similarities and differences, in
terms of intellectual processes, among such systems wherever they
exist. Achieving a satisfactory working conception of a generic pattern
of legal reasoning should make it possible to compare things that are
really comparable and to discuss with greater precision the differences
between particular systems, their causes and consequences. It should
yield a clearer understanding of both the similarities and the differences between legal systems, like that of the Anglo-American world,
that have trained judges and advocates, law reports and law schools;
and those like the Soga system that lack these facilities but are,
nonetheless, engaged in what is, on some level, the same kind of
work.

Now in Levi's account of Anglo-American legal reasoning, a key role
is played by the "categorizing concept." [36] Judges, in their search for
"precedents" or "rules," do not look for similarities and differences
among raw cases. They conduct the search, rather, with the aid of
categorizing concepts which are felt to sum up the essence of the
relevant cases—concepts like that of the "inherently dangerous article," whose development Levi traces in his essay.[37] By means of such
concepts, judges, with the help of the arguments of advocates, order
the cases that come before them. They are a guide to the relevant
cases, without which the law would be a jumble of isolated, ad hoc
decisions. They are the tools of "moral oversimplification," of issue
narrowing, the elements in the "moving system of classification" which
Levi sees as characteristic of the law. By means of them, the almost
infinite complexity of circumstances surrounding a particular case may
be reduced, in advocates' arguments and in judges' decisions, to problems of inclusion and exclusion. More fundamentally, they make it
possible to decide whether or not there is an actionable "case" at all,
for unless it can be plausibly argued that the "facts" fall within some
existing categorizing concept, the legal process cannot go to work. Law
courts require that a man be accused of something more specific than
wickedness. To follow Levi's example, advocates and judges do not
have to ask themselves: "Is a storekeeper who sells his customer a
defective lamp liable for injuries suffered by the customer's wife when

36. Levi, *Introduction to Legal Reasoning*, pp. 4–5.
37. Ibid., pp. 7–19.

the lamp explodes?" Rather, they reduce the problem to the questions: "Is the 'inherently dangerous article' concept the proper category for this case?" and "Do the circumstances of this case place it inside or outside the concept?" Of course, not all categorizing concepts are the products of precedent construction; many result from legislation, but here, too, meaning must be construed, and precedent develops upon the legislated base. Nor, of course, is only one categorizing concept invoked in each case. In the course of including or excluding a particular set of "facts" in relation to the concept that forms the cause of action, other, subsidiary, concepts may come into play. The process of inclusion and exclusion, however, remains the same.

Now, Basoga judges and litigants also make use of categorizing concepts. They do not handle them in the same way British or American judges and advocates do, even in difficult cases, for there is no explicit doctrine of precedent and no machinery for case reporting to put such a doctrine into systematic practice. The courts keep excellent records, but there is no provision for selecting precedent-setting cases and bringing them to the attention of the judges. In addition, the concepts themselves are somewhat different—less abstract and generalized. But use is quite clearly made of categorizing legal concepts to order the case experience of judges and litigants. Basoga judges do not, any more than Anglo-American ones, approach each case in a tabula rasa frame of mind. The categorizing concept enables them to place it in a framework that indicates the questions that must be asked and answered if a decision is to be reached. It enables them to decide, to begin with, whether or not there is a case. The argument of this study is that the tribunals of the Basoga are in some degree true "courts of law" because they reason legally, with categorizing concepts that narrow and frame the issues for decision; but that, with their lack of a specialized bench and bar trained in the explicit manipulation of legal concepts, their legal reasoning is both relatively implicit—in that reasoning is seldom spelled out by either litigants or judges—and relatively concrete—in that the concepts used are closely tied to the concrete, stereotyped social situations which commonly give rise to disputes in Soga society. It will be argued that these courts are impressively efficient legal institutions, whose administration of justice in the context of village society gains them the respect and confidence of the Basoga, but that today they are increasingly faced with processes of social change to whose accompanying legal problems their organization and mode of work is inadequate. It will be suggested that, if they are to continue to have a place in the legal structure of the new Uganda nation, they must be given the tools and the personnel to enable them to adapt and apply their law to changing circumstances.

These themes will run through the analyses of the several bodies of case material which form the heart of this study. Before this material can be presented, however, a good deal of groundwork must be laid. I must describe the setting in which the Soga courts work—the society and culture in which they are embedded and with whose problems they must deal. I must describe the courts themselves, their personnel, their place in the total judicial organization of Uganda, and the sources of the law they administer. These are necessary preliminaries, but they inevitably postpone a confrontation with the data upon which this study is based: the arguments of litigants and the questionings and decisions of judges in actual cases. To make these preliminary discussions somewhat more meaningful, it may be helpful to look in on a local court in Basoga as it hears and decides an actual case.

AN EXAMPLE

The courthouse is a long, low, thatched building with whitewashed mud-and-wattle walls, open all around at window level so that those unable to find seats on the rows of wooden benches inside can stand outside and watch. Although the court is not yet in session, dozens of bicycles are stacked against the outer walls, and the room itself is already crowded, for litigation is a preeminently public activity and a popular one, providing ample scope for the people's love of intricate and eloquent rhetoric. Among the majority who have come not to participate but simply to form an appreciative audience are gray-haired elders, who through years of attendance at court have become connoisseurs of the litigious art; wide-eyed boys eager to further their legal education; and nursing mothers for whose infants such days in court will be among their earliest remembered experiences. Chickens wander, clucking, in and out of doorways; and a passing herdsman stops to listen to the proceedings, leaning against a tree while his cattle graze on the courthouse lawn.

For everyone present, the experience will be not merely enjoyable but also instructive, for in this court every man is his own advocate. The judges do most of the questioning, but each of the principals makes an initial statement, setting forth his view of the case, and may question both his adversary and the witnesses, who are summoned at the initiative of the principals. And, since something like one in every ten adult males is likely to appear in court as a principal ("accused" or "accuser," as the Basoga call the litigants) every year, the lessons learned today will find ready application. The audience is therefore attentive as the sub-county chief and his fellow judges, formally attired in their long white gowns and tailored, Western-style jackets, file in and take their places at the table on the dais at the end of the hall. As each speaker—litigant or witness—addresses the bench, he bows respectfully to the judges and speaks with as much gravity and eloquence as he can muster. The frequent vehemence of the arguments is tempered by great politeness and formality; "My friend," a litigant may say, "has lied!"

Yoweri Kibiri v. Yowabu Kabwire: narrowing issues

Today, May 15, 1950, there come before the court a middle-aged peasant, Yoweri Kibiri, the accuser, who lives in the village of Bwa-yuya; and his father-in-law, Yowabu Kabwire, of nearby Nabitende village, who stands accused.[38] The case opens as the court clerk, who will laboriously record the proceedings in longhand, reads out Yoweri's charge, laid a few days before in the subcounty chief's office:

> You are accused of harboring my wife, Kolositina Toko, for six months without giving me a reason for harboring her.

"Harboring a wife" (*kutuuza omukazi*, literally: "causing a wife to settle") is an important Soga legal concept and one whose application I shall explore in some detail in a later chapter. A bit of explanation is required here, however, to make this illustrative case intelligible. Marriage, in Busoga, transfers authority over a woman from her father or guardian to her husband. A consideration, which I shall call "bridewealth," is almost always given in exchange and this is refundable upon dissolution of the marriage. Much litigation arises from marriage contracts, for the relationship between husband and wife is a tension-ridden one. Very often a woman becomes unhappy in her husband's home and runs away, usually taking refuge in the home of her father or guardian. If the latter allows her to stay, he invites a charge of "harboring," for the husband has, through his payment of bridewealth, acquired a right to her presence in his home. It is this offense—a serious one, for which the penalties may be quite severe—with which Yoweri charges Yowabu. As the latter rises to answer it, the chairman of the court asks:

> Do you agree to contest this case, in which Yoweri charges you? Do you think you will win?

Following directly upon the clerk's reading of the charge, this formula formally notifies the accused that he must now answer that charge and gives him an opportunity to acknowledge his guilt or

---

38. A table of cases cited is provided at the end of the book.

liability. Yowabu, however, wishes to contest and so he launches into a circumstantial account of how it was that Kolositina Toko came to leave her husband, the burden being that she did not leave voluntarily but was driven out:

I was at home about eight o'clock one evening when I saw this wife of Yoweri's coming to me and saying: "My husband has sent me away." So I asked her why and she answered: "He had sent us to dig sweet potatoes, but we left off doing that and dug yams instead. Because of that, he accused me of taking his other wife, Jeneti, into the bush so my brother Fudu could lie with her. That's why he sent me away." So I told her to call Esawu (Yowabu's brother) and he came. I said: "Take this daughter of yours back to her home. There's some trouble there; you go look into it." So the four of them went—Fudu and Katono and Esawu, as well as Yoweri's wife. They returned during the night and reported: "Matters are confused there; our in-law is disturbed and he has sent the girl away for good."

Next morning, I saw that Kolositina had also returned. She said: "My husband has sent me away for good. He wouldn't allow me to sleep in the house, so I slept in the kitchen." So then I sent two of my children to call Yoweri so that we might investigate whether or not that boy [Fudu] had attacked Yoweri's wives. . . . Next morning he came and they [husband and wife] argued about their troubles [literally: "litigated their case"]. I gave him his wife, but he refused to take her. So [after he left], I sent two children . . . to escort her to his place, but they met Zakaliya, who shouted: "Don't stay here! Go away!" and in the afternoon they came back. Again, I sent her sister to escort her back, but when Yoweri saw them he took up a stick, intending to beat them. Then they all went to the sub-village headman, who was acting for the village headman. Then Yoweri said: "I don't want that woman now. I want my bridewealth." For that reason—since Yoweri wanted his bridewealth repaid—I went to the parish chief and told him all that had happened.

Some further explanations are now in order. First, these cases, like Russian novels, are frequently difficult to follow because they contain many characters with unfamiliar names. Since it will be necessary to follow the testimony in some detail, I shall, therefore, whenever it seems appropriate, provide a diagram of the following sort showing the genealogical and other relations among the principal characters (see fig. 1).

In this and later diagrams, circles indicate women, triangles men. Deceased persons are indicated by shading. The double line represents marriage, while the order of marriages is shown by superscript numbers. Vertical and horizontal lines indicate parent-child and sibling relationships, respectively.

Two basic institutional features—these will be described in much greater detail later on—must also be explained. On the one hand, the Basoga are divided among patrilineal, or agnatic, descent groups or patrilineages. In certain respects, marriage is a contract not between individuals, but between patrilineages. When the father of the wife dies, for example, his responsibilities under the marriage contract pass to other males in his patrilineage; similarly, when a husband dies, certain of his rights in the wife pass to *his* lineage mates. Lineages also hold certain rights in land corporately and their members tend to be neighbors. All this explains why, although the litigants here are the husband and the wife's father, one has the sense of two patrilineages in conflict. Esawu is Yowabu's "brother," while Zakaliya is Yoweri's "father." I am not certain whether or not these are "real" (in the English sense) brother-brother and father-son relationships, since the Lusoga terms are extended collaterally to patrilineal uncles, cousins,

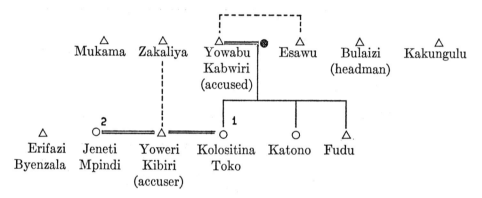

Fig. 1

and nephews (in the English sense). I indicate this by broken lines on the diagram. In the present case, the exact (in the English sense) relationships do not matter. When they do, Basoga make it clear by speaking in terms of who begat (or bore) whom.[39]

On the other hand, Busoga is also divided for political—and legal-jurisdictional—purposes among a hierarchy of territorial units: subvillages, villages, parishes, subcounties, and counties. The heads of the first two I shall call "headmen," the rest "chiefs." Although only subcounty and county chiefs chair formal courts of record, the others hold tribunals which attempt to settle cases before they reach the subcounty level. Indeed I should perhaps include the family as the lowest level in the hierarchy for, as happened in this case, the father of the wife usually attempts at some stage to adjudicate in husband-wife disputes. The same language and gesture of litigation and adjudication

39. Appendix A.

are used throughout the hierarchy of tribunals, from the family to the highest courts.

To return now to *Yoweri Kibiri* v. *Yowabu Kabwire:* Yowabu has defended himself against the charge of harboring his daughter Kolositina, Yoweri's wife, by asserting that he, Yowabu, has done everything in his power to return the woman to her husband, but that Yoweri has refused to take her back. Both he and the headman have "adjudicated" between husband and wife, found Kolositina guilty (or Yoweri innocent—it is not entirely clear who accused whom of what), and tried, unsuccessfully, to reconcile the couple. Finally, Yowabu has reported all this to the parish chief. Notice, now, the preoccupation of the court as it questions Yowabu:

Q: But what evidence is there that Yoweri wanted his bridewealth and not his wife?
A: The headman has the evidence.
Q: At the headman's place, Yoweri said he wanted his bridewealth, but did you make a written agreement with him confirming that?
A: No . . . .
Q: Do you refer to the headman for testimony?
A: Yes . . . .
Q: Besides the headman, do you have any other evidence from Yoweri that he wanted his bridewealth?
A: He himself came to ask for his things and when he met Esawu he said: "Why does your brother continue to struggle with his daughter? Why doesn't he just . . . find another man for her and give me my things?"
Q: But when he agreed in that way to wanting his bridewealth, did you give it to him?
A: I didn't . . . because I didn't have it. When he came back later, I told him: "Your wife hasn't yet found another man. . . . When she has found a man to pay the bridewealth, I'll give it to you."

In this exchange, the court repeatedly returns to the same questions: Has Yoweri asked for the return of his bridewealth? Has Yowabu repaid it? Evidently the answers will be crucial, for as Yoweri rises to testify the court pursues the same theme:

Q: Why did your wife stay at her father's place for six months?
A: Because . . . whenever I went there they refused to give her to me. I went five times, but they just abused me for losing their daughter's amulet.
Q: When you had gone there five times and they didn't give you your wife, what did you do?
A: . . . I came here to accuse him.
Q: You have heard your in-law say that you sent your wife away and that you wanted your bridewealth back?
A: Yes, I've heard, but it's not true.
Q: Do you call upon the headman for testimony?
A: Yes, I call upon him for evidence concerning the dispute with my wife about the amulet. We litigated and I won.

Q: Do you have evidence that you did not ask your in-law for your bridewealth . . . ?

A: I have no evidence for the time before the dispute at the headman's place . . . .

Q: But why did she stay away for six months?

A: First of all, my wife lost her amulet and she thought I had taken it. So she left and stayed at their place until the dispute at the headman's place. We litigated and I won. But then my in-law said: "Even though you have won, my daughter will not return to you."

Q: But didn't you go to him to ask for your bridewealth, as he says?

A: No . . . .

Q: Do you have evidence . . . ?

A: Yes, I have brought Erifazi Byenzala, with whom I went twice to ask for my wife, and not my bridewealth.

Evidence accumulates that this marriage has been disintegrating for some time in a manner which is classical for Basoga. Yowabu's testimony has suggested that Yoweri is jealous of his wives, suspecting them of meeting lovers and of assisting each other in doing so. Yoweri's own testimony reinforces this suggestion: The amulet likely was, or likely was thought by Yoweri to be, a love amulet of the sort worn by young women to increase their sexual attractiveness. Soga marriage is unstable. Especially when, as in this case, the wife is a good deal younger than her husband, she is likely to become lonely and unhappy and to flee to her father. Whether or not she is unfaithful, her husband suspects her of it and abuses her. This in turn increases the likelihood that she will in fact run away, take a lover, or both—and so on, in a vicious circle of deepening estrangement. The sociocultural roots of this pattern will be discussed in chapter 4, but something broadly similar is not unfamiliar in Western societies—the principal difference being, of course, that in Busoga the deteriorating husband-wife relationship involves not just two people, but two descent-groups.

In any case, the point I wish to make is simply that a dispute of this sort does not arise from a single isolated act, but rather represents the culmination of a long history of mutual misbehavior. A "case" is precipitated when one party or the other does or can be alleged to have done something "actionable"—something which Soga law defines as sufficient cause for one to hail the other into court. As was noted earlier, societies differ both in the precision with which their dispute-settling tribunals define causes of action and in the range of moral reality with which, once a case is precipitated, they will deal. Soga courts are relatively legalistic in both respects. The tribunals held by household heads and headmen are more permissive, but the courts of record operate with a limited repertory of causes of action and once a case has been opened under one of these rubrics, the judges concentrate upon finding a yes-or-no answer in terms of that rubric. This is why, in questioning both principals in *Yoweri Kibiri* v. *Yowabu Kabwire*, they keep returning to the question of whether or not Yoweri has asked for his bridewealth. This, it seems, is crucial to the problem of Yowabu's guilt or innocence of the charge of harboring—one of Soga law's actionable offenses. The principals, too, know pretty clearly what the crucial questions are, but they—like advocates in Western courts—often clothe their arguments on these questions in terms of moral recrimination and self-justification, in the process bringing in events with no *legal* bearing on the case. This is one manifestation of the tension between legal institutions and their moral environment: each litigant wants the advantages of both narrow legalism and moral holism. Each tends to argue legalistically when he thinks he has a good case and moralistically when he does not.

The relative economy of Yoweri's argument reflects the far sounder quality of his case. Before going into that, however, it will be well to examine, briefly, the evidence given by the litigants' witnesses, who are now called. Bulaizi, the headman, and Kakungulu, a neighbor, appear for Yowabu:

Bulaizi: . . . the wife of Yoweri came to my place to accuse her husband of losing her amulet. Yoweri won the case. Then Yowabu told his daughter to return to her husband. But Yoweri didn't agree to this; he said: "I don't want the woman. I want my bridewealth."

Q: When Yoweri rejected his wife, what did you do?
A: I told Yowabu to go home with his daughter and collect the bridewealth and give it to Yoweri. That was in March [two months earlier].

Kakungulu: . . . I went to Yowabu's to fetch my fish spears and I found him working in the millet field. When Yoweri came, he found me there. . . . When Yowabu had greeted his in-law, Yoweri said: "Elder, what brought me here is that I want my bridewealth." Yowabu answered: "I don't have it because your wife has not yet remarried." That's all I know.

Q: Do you remember the date . . . ?
A: No . . . .

Yoweri then calls Mukama, Erifazi Byenzala, his "father," Zakaliya, and Jeneti Mpindi, another of his wives. Since their testimony is nearly identical, Mukama may stand for all of them:

The testimony I give concerns the tribunal held by the headman when Yoweri and his wife litigated. The case concerned an amulet. Kolositina said that Yoweri had taken it and Yoweri denied it. The headman decided the case for Yoweri . . . and that finished it. Yoweri asked for his wife, but Yowabu said: You won't take my daughter because you lost her amulet. When it is found, she will return."

Nothing new has been added; the witnesses of both sides have simply supported the stories of their principals. Yoweri, however, is confident of victory and indicates this in a final exchange with Yowabu:

Q: Besides Kakungulu, whom you have brought to say that I asked for my bridewealth, and not my wife, do you have any other evidence . . . ?
A: [no reply]
Q: Do you agree with what your witnesses have said . . . ?
A: Yes . . . .

Yoweri's confidence is well founded. The case is a plain one, and the court's decision is brief:

It has gone against the accused, Yowabu Kabwire, for harboring Kolositina Toko, wife of Yoweri Kibiri, for a period of six months. He has no evidence to take away the fault, although he makes the false excuse that Yoweri sent his wife away. Therefore he must pay twenty-five shillings compensation and ten shillings fine, or two weeks in jail in lieu of the fine.[40] He has thirty days in which to appeal.

The case is plain because Yowabu has brought forward nothing approaching a plausible defense. The language of the decision ("he has no evidence to take away the fault . . .") does not mean that in Soga courts a man is guilty until proven innocent. But Yowabu does not deny that his daughter has been in his home for six months and this, in Soga law, places upon him the burden of justification; for as father of the wife he is responsible to her husband for her continued presence in the husband's household. If she is not there, he must convince the court that his action does not constitute harboring. The decision means that there is a case to answer, and he has not answered it.

He has, of course, offered a defense of sorts: He argues that Yoweri repudiated Kolositina and asked for the return of his bridewealth. If he could satisfy the court that this occurred, it *might* protect him, which is why the court keeps returning to the point. The judges want to offer Yowabu every opportunity to establish the one point that might save him. However, as will be seen in chapter 5, the law is heavily weighted on the side of the husband in these matters. The father must have very strong evidence indeed if he is to succeed. The testimony of Kakungulu and of Bulaizi, the headman, that they had heard Yoweri ask for his bridewealth is not enough, especially in the face of contrary testimony by Yoweri's army of witnesses. Did Yowabu obtain a written agreement to that effect from Yoweri? He did

40. In 1952 one East African shilling was equal to fourteen United States cents. The annual cash income of the average Musoga taxpayer was about four hundred shillings.

not. Worst of all, he has, by his own admission, made no attempt to repay the bridewealth during the six months since Kolositina left her husband. A prudent father, in these circumstances, would press the bridewealth upon the husband and then, if he refused to accept it, would sue him for refusal, citing the wife's grounds for leaving her husband. This is the Soga procedure for divorce on the initiative of the wife.[41] But Kolositina's grievance against her husband, losing her amulet, is trivial—so trivial that Yowabu does not even mention it in his argument. His assertion that he intended to return the bridewealth as soon as he found for Kolositina a new husband who would pay it has a certain plausibility. This sometimes happens when a marriage is dissolved by mutual consent, but it depends entirely upon the husband's acquiescence.[42] As a defense against harboring, when the husband wishes to maintain the marriage, Yowabu's argument is pitiful.

Legally, therefore, Yowabu stands quite naked. Morally, on the other hand, the affair is clearly a great deal less one-sided. Many of those present will have had a good deal of sympathy for Kolositina and her father. The fact that the law strongly protects husbands' authority over their wives does not mean that Basoga approve of inhumane husbands; and there is evidence that Yoweri has been, by Soga standards, difficult to live with. That he is suspicious and jealous has already been suggested, but there is more. Yowabu, who is clearly guilty in law, accepts the decision, but Yoweri, who has won the case and had his wife returned to him, appeals on the ground that Yowabu's fine and the award of compensation are inadequate in view of his loss of Kolositina's labor for six months! In his letter of appeal to the county court he writes:

I appeal because the punishment is very light for my having been cheated for six months. [Yowabu] was fined ten shillings and I was given twenty-five shillings compensation, but I have lost the following: a field of millet yielding twelve bags, each worth twelve shillings; a field of groundnuts which yields nine bags at nine shillings each; a field of sweet potatoes forty-five by sixty yards; a field of cassava thirty by thirty-five yards and some sesame, marrows, and maize . . . . Because of this I place my appeal before you so that you will understand the [lower court's] mistake in this case.

Soga marriage is not, even ideally, a companionate love-match, but neither is it a mere labor contract. This Scrooge-like argument, read out before the county court, will have offended the judges, who now are dealing not with the strictly legal problem of guilt or innocence, but rather with the more moral one of fit punishment and compensation.

41. See chapter 5.
42. See the decision in *Mikairi Magino* v. *Ntumba*.

Yoweri's appeal is quite unique among the many records of harboring cases I have examined. However they may have felt, I found no other aggrieved husband who was mercenary enough to try to measure his loss in terms of agricultural production. The argument was always: "I still love my wife; I want her back." Compensation is thought of, at least publicly, as balm for wounded feelings. The county court is therefore unsympathetic: "It sees that [the compensation awarded by the lower court] is quite enough. It suits the case." Significantly, the chairman, county chief Samwiri Wakoli, is a traditionalist in marriage matters, with little sympathy for such modern ideas as the right of a woman to reject an arranged marriage.[43] He speaks here for a unanimous court with the voice of conservative morality; even by his standards, Yoweri has received all that was due him.

The account of this rather simple case will, I hope, have helped to make clear in a preliminary way the sense in which, and the manner in which, the Soga courts make use of legal concepts. Yoweri does not simply accuse Yowabu of wrongdoing; he accuses him of harboring. And it is in similar terms that Yowabu frames his defense. He cannot be a harborer because Yoweri has repudiated his marriage. The rights against which harboring is an offense, he argues, no longer exist. Again, when the court finds Yowabu guilty, it is in terms of harboring; in their questions and decision, the judges stick closely to what is legally relevant to that charge, ignoring the moral complexities until the amount of the fine and the compensation are at issue.

I have indicated some of the issues—sufficient reason, existence of a valid marriage—that may arise in the application of the concept "harboring." In chapter 5, I shall go on to compare other cases in order to determine the other elements that may enter into the meaning of the concept as used by the courts. It is, however, only by such comparison of cases that an outside observer can determine the meaning of this and other Soga legal concepts. Never do the courts themselves attempt to spell out the meanings of these concepts. Never do they refer to previous decisions as sources for these meanings—though they keep excellent records, which are used when cases go up on appeal and to establish *res judicata*. Nor do the courts even spell out in any detail their reasoning in the case at hand. Their decisions consist, not of a *ratio decidendi*, but simply of a brief statement of conclusions, usually in quite factual terms, with no reference to legal rules. As cases become more difficult, there is some tendency for both litigants' and judges' reasoning to become more explicit, but for the most part one can only

43. See *Maliyamu Kyazike* v. *Samwiri Wakoli.*

follow their reasoning inferentially by observing the way in which they question witnesses and by linking this questioning to the conclusions reached.

And yet the Soga courts engage in legal reasoning—amateur (in the sense of not based upon specialized training), rather concrete, and often implicit legal reasoning, perhaps, but legal reasoning, nevertheless. Legal reasoning, in the sense in which I am using the term, means *the application to the settlement of disputes of categorizing concepts that define justiciable normative issues.* Where legal reasoning is in use, an accuser must lay his case in terms of one or more such concepts and the court must decide the issue in such terms, by inclusion or exclusion. It cannot concern itself with moral questions irrelevant to the concepts—in harboring cases like that of *Yoweri Kibiri* v. *Yowabu Kabwire,* for example, with the question of whether Yoweri had treated his wife so abominably that she found life with him unbearable. (A mistreated wife has a remedy in Soga law, as I have noted, but she may never simply return to her guardian without exposing him to a charge of harboring.) In contrast, where tribunals do not make use of legal concepts, the judge is faced with a welter of blame and counter-blame—with all the moral ambiguity that is present in any situation of interpersonal conflict. "To classify," Karl Llewellyn once wrote, "is to disturb." [44] The legal concept disturbs in order to define an issue that may then be decided simply in terms of inclusion or exclusion.

I have defined legal reasoning rather more broadly than Levi did in his essay. He was concerned to emphasize the role of precedent in the process and to show how it can be that a regard for precedent is reconciled in Anglo-American law with constant change. This is where explicit reasoning by example, from case to case, comes into his argument. By carefully reworking previous decisions in the light of the instant case, the Anglo-American judge may preserve the conceptual framework of the law while making the minimum changes necessary to deal with the matter at hand. Basoga litigants and judges have not needed, and have not been equipped, to do this kind of reworking because the situations that come before the courts have been relatively stereotyped and the legal conceptual system has been relatively simple and stable. The judges have been able, consequently, to reason directly from concept to instant case, without referring back to earlier cases in which the concept has been applied. The Musoga judge, of course, remembers previous cases of a similar kind, but under these conditions, I suggest, he assimilates each case directly to a set of concepts which

44. Karl Llewellyn, *Jurisprudence,* p. 27.

he carries in his mind. A formal doctrine of precedent, together with a reporting system for putting it into practice, externalizes this process —makes it explicit and a matter of record. When change is rapid, this becomes essential. Precedent becomes the guideline that allows the law to follow a consistent course as it changes. Soga law, on the other hand, has until recently operated under conditions of much more gradual sociocultural, and hence legal, change. Under such conditions, the judge need not talk or think explicitly about precedent. He need only act upon past experience encapsulated in a repertory of legal concepts. How far, and in what way, this repertory constitutes a system of ideas, and not simply a collection, it is one of the objects of this study to discover.

THE CASE MATERIALS AND THE CASE METHOD

The analysis in the following chapters of the work of the Soga courts is based in large part upon the written records kept by Basoga court clerks. The account of *Yoweri Kibiri* v. *Yowabu Kabwire* given above is essentially a translation of one such case record. Since this reliance upon the written records of actual cases, supplemented by observation and interviewing, is fundamental to the nature of this study, the remainder of this chapter will be devoted to a discussion of its methodological implications and to a description of the body of material from which the cases to be discussed are drawn.

"Sociologically," Max Weber has written, "the statement that someone has a [legal] right . . . means [that] he has a chance, factually guaranteed to him by the consensually accepted interpretation of a legal norm, of invoking in favor of his ideal or material interests the aid of a 'coercive apparatus' which is in special readiness for the purpose." [45] In this definition, two elements are brought together, of which one is the courtroom encounter, with its acceptance of a cause of action, its litigation and judgment. But to say that the law involves judicial acts is not to say that it is *only* a series of *isolated* judicial acts. The second element in Weber's definition—what "factually guarantees" the litigant's "chance" of obtaining a favorable judgment—is the "consensually accepted interpretation of a legal norm"—by which, I take it, he means roughly what Hart would call a rule rendered justiciable by a "rule of recognition." [46] Judges and litigants (or their advocates) *think* about and with the law; with the aid of legal thought-categories, they knit together their experience of what courts

45. *Max Weber on Law in Economy and Society*, p. 15.
46. Weber's discussion of the nature of legal systems closely parallels Hart's: *Max Weber on Law*, pp. 11–33.

actually do to produce intellectual guides to litigation and judgment and—by no means least important—to the avoidance of litigation. Most lawyers, nowadays, spend most of their time helping their clients so arrange their affairs that the legality of their actions will be less likely to be challenged. In a society like that of Busoga, where there are no professional lawyers, ordinary men perform such services for themselves. Still, litigation is the test; what distinguishes law from other forms of moral culture is the potentiality for measuring actions against its norms through some institutionalized process to determine their legitimacy or illegitimacy. It is with the possibility of litigation in mind that the law user, professional or amateur, thinks and acts.

Thus the analysis of a legal system must stand on two feet: one, the study of litigation; the other, the study of extracourtroom experience which the participants in litigation bring with them. For the first, the requisite data are good case materials—detailed accounts of the exchanges in the courtroom that eventuate in judicial decision. Of course in a larger sense the case does not begin and end in the courtroom. I have already noted the obvious fact that legal systems cut into the full "objective" complexity of social relations in highly "arbitrary" ways. It is only when one party finally decides to sue or complain, and when he can do so in terms of a concept acceptable to the legal system, that a case in the narrow sense is precipitated; but it would be useful to a fuller understanding of the legal institution's place in the larger society to know what took place before and afterward. Is the system really open to the conflicts that plague the society's members? Does it generally deal with them to peoples' satisfaction? Such questions can only be answered by investigation of the events leading up to the courtroom encounter and of its aftermath, and by the study of conflicts which are never litigated. Again, even within the restricted segment of interpersonal history with which the courtroom case deals, the "facts" to which judges apply legal concepts are not "what really happened" but rather the "facts as found"—the "facts" as presented by the litigants and witnesses and evaluated by the judges. Of course "what really happened" is ultimately undiscoverable—indeed, some would consider it a meaningless notion—but, setting aside such deeper epistemological questions, it *is* possible, through interviewing, to learn more than the courtroom arguments tell. The notorious conspiracies in untruth which have been so common in Anglo-American jurisdictions in which adultery has been a principal ground for divorce provide an excellent illustration. To take at face value the "facts as found" in these cases would be misleading indeed. Legal fictions, of varying degrees of self-consciousness, probably play a role in most legal systems, as they do in that of Busoga, and only extracourtroom investigation can reveal their existence and significance.[47]

For the experience brought by litigants and judges into the courtroom, the potentially relevant data are almost limitless. Quite apart from idiosyncratic elements, the whole of the common culture provides material for legal discourse. The repertory of justiciable norms is not co-extensive with everyday morality, but the interplay between them is continuous in the courtroom encounter and becomes especially conspicuous when change accelerates. Nonmoral culture, too, enters intimately into the legal process, especially in the ascertainment of the "facts"—which, of course, is why "absolute truth" is meaningless in this context. Litigants and judges come to court with common assumptions about the physical, biological, and social world, as Gluckman has shown so well for the Lozi,[48] and such common understandings are the ground against which the courtroom argument takes place. Sometimes they may emerge as critical elements in argument and decision, as when a Soga court is required to decide the probable age of the saplings planted on a property boundary [49] or the public symptoms of adultery.[50] The entire sociocultural environment of the courts is full of such "sources of law" whose ethnographic study is relevant to an understanding of the legal process.

Of course not all parts of the extracourtroom environment are equally, and in the same manner, sources of law. In the legal systems most familiar to lawyers, there is an elaborate institutional machinery which mediates between the courts and the rest of the sociocultural system, shaping the interaction between them. Reporters collect, analyze, and publish important cases. Scholars organize legal ideas and legislative and judicial acts into coherent "fields." Philosophers reconsider the moral and intellectual bases of legal thought. Legislatures and appellate judges, from time to time, tidy up sections of the law. Politicians and publicists debate legal principles in the public forum. From all this, one may learn a great deal about the legal process without entering a courtroom or examining a case record. Indeed, this torrent of words and activities *about* the law becomes so vast that Llewellyn feels it necessary to remind the legal profession that ". . . at the very heart [of law] is the behavior of judges." [51] But for the student of a legal system that lacks all this machinery for collect-

---

47. See *Sabasitiano Gavamukulya* v. *Bumali Mawa.*
48. Gluckman, *The Judicial Process,* chap. 3.
49. See *Aminsi Waiswa* v. *Sajjabi Kibba.*
50. See *Bulubutu* v. *Kunya Nyonyi.*
51. Llewellyn, *Jurisprudence,* p. 40.

ing, analyzing, reconsidering, and tidying-up, the situation is very different. On paper, at least, he has only the body of case records, like the one reported above. Where such records are not kept, he must collect his own records. There are no textbooks and no legislative statements. The legal subculture is, to a much greater degree, institutionalized only in the courts and in the society at large. Legal subculture and general common culture interact in the thoughts and acts of the amateur judges and of the general adult population.

Of course, this is an extreme way of stating the contrast. Even in a legal system without professional thinkers-about-the-law, there are sources of information about "consensually accepted interpretations of legal norms" other than actual case decisions. Basoga judges are not professional legal analysts, but they take their judicial work very seriously. They think about it, discuss it among themselves, and are perfectly capable of discussing it with an outside investigator. Indeed, they do so enthusiastically. One may ask them about hypothetical cases and about general principles and receive thoughtful and enlightening answers. This sort of information must be treated with caution; as will be seen—indeed, as the account of *Yoweri Kibiri* v. *Yowabu Kabwire* will perhaps already have made clear—the proceedings in their courts rarely involve the explicit statement of rules, even for the particular case. In a legal system in which so much is left implicit, talk *about* the law outside the context of particular cases is apt to be an even less accurate reflection of courtroom reality than it is in more self-consciously analytic systems. It becomes even more necessary to ground the study of law in case analysis. Still, discussions with judges and litigants can be most enlightening, especially when conducted with particular cases as a point of departure. Indeed, without such discussions, even the most accurate records of court proceedings would often be unintelligible, or at best misleading.

In these past few paragraphs I have been describing essentially what I now, after almost a decade and a half's reflection on my Soga material, believe to be adequate data for the study of a legal system. These are the kinds of data I would collect if I were setting out today to study Soga law. I have all these kinds of data, but I have much less of certain kinds than I would like.

I say this not apologetically, but by way of pointing out a necessary feature of anthropological inquiry which I think has been insufficiently discussed in the profession's literature. Much of an anthropologist's work is serendipitous in the sense that he studies, and then writes about, subjects somewhat different from those he intended to pursue when planning his fieldwork. The reason for this is simply that he very often knows in advance relatively little about the society in which he plans to work. This very lack of information is often among the reasons that lead him to visit that society, for anthropologists generally see it as one of their special tasks within social science to extend the range of comparative inquiry by working in little-known places. One consequence, however, is that the fieldworker often encounters, and becomes interested in, problems for which he is intellectually not well prepared. It is often scientifically justifiable for him—even incumbent upon him—to go ahead anyway and do the best he can with such problems, for he has traveled far and invested in the fieldwork a good deal of other people's money and his own intellectual labor—including the labor of learning a difficult language. No other anthropologist is likely to pass that way again soon. He therefore often works by what a scientistically minded psychologist colleague once scornfully called the "vacuum cleaner method": Besides pursuing the interest with which he came, he also collects such other kinds of data as seem to him scientifically important. Since his anthropological training—in recognition of these very conditions of work—has made of him something of a social scientific jack-of-all-trades, he probably knows *something* about previous work in these other areas. When he returns to the university to write up his material for publication, he fills in the relevant weaknesses in his intellectual background. If the data are, in spite of the inevitable gaps, sufficient to sustain an analysis that contributes something to understanding of the subject, he publishes one.

As the world becomes better known, of course, anthropological fieldwork tends to become more narrowly focused and more closely guided by prior intellectual preparation, but until we know far more than we know today about the world's cultures, this sort of serendipity will remain an inevitable, and useful, characteristic of anthropological inquiry. And reflection upon the resulting imperfections may serve, on the methodological level, the dialogue, mentioned earlier, that seems to characterize comparative inquiry generally: The flaws in one's serendipitous explorations of a subject in the field may prove enlightening to those who follow.

Legal "realists," by critically examining some of the myths of jurisprudence, have helped others to understand how legal institutions "really work." I have here tried to return the compliment by being "realistic" about anthropological fieldwork. As I noted earlier, I went to Busoga in 1950 with the intention of studying politics and administration in a colonial context, and had prepared myself accordingly. It was clear from the literature that the customary law courts were a feature of the Soga political system, but I was quite unprepared to find them so prominent in Soga life and was astonished to discover the treasure house of data that lay in the court records. I had read, somewhat casually, the then classics in the anthropological study of law, but was quite innocent of the literature of jurisprudence. Nevertheless, the subject seemed too important, and too accessible, to neglect; and so, lacking mechanical copying equipment, I hired assistants to hand-copy selected case records. I also attended court on many occasions and followed up some cases by interviewing litigants. As I became more aware of the importance of legal work in the life of the chiefs, whom I was studying anyhow in connection with my major subject, I interviewed some of them about particular cases. All this was accompanied, of course, by a good deal of general ethnographic inquiry on Soga society and culture, which previously had not been well described in the literature. Over a period of some twenty-one months, I studied intensively two groups of villages in different parts of the district and made shorter visits to other areas. Soon after finishing the fieldwork I reported briefly on the courts in my study of Soga politics and administration and in a short article,[52] but it was not until several years later—around 1961—that I began to think seriously about the nature of law and to undertake the analysis that follows.

As a result there are certain gaps. The case records (these are described in Appendix B) provide, I believe, excellent data on what takes place in Soga courtrooms, and my ethnographic inquiries make it possible to relate these data to their general sociocultural setting. But for far too many cases, I know only what the case records tell and what I can infer from my knowledge of the society. In too few cases do I know what happened before and after and I have too few interviews with judges and litigants about particular cases and about law in general. More of such material would have made possible a richer analysis of Soga legal culture and of the relationship between the legal institution and society than I am able to provide.

This study, therefore, focuses upon the courtroom encounter, in which litigants and judges frame legal issues and decide them. Through the analysis and comparison of cases, I try to show that the participants in the encounter work upon recurrent kinds of social disputes with a coherent system of legal concepts. The reader may judge whether the data are adequate to sustain the analysis and whether, together, data and analysis yield a convincing account of the Soga courts at work.

52. Fallers, *Bantu Bureaucracy*, pp. 163–71; Lloyd A. Fallers, "Changing Customary Law in Busoga District of Uganda."

*If you want an order to be obeyed, give
it in Luganda.*
—A subcounty chief

*A native court shall administer and enforce . . . native
law and custom in the area of the jurisdiction of the
court, so far as it is applicable and is not repugnant to
natural justice and morality.*
—Uganda Native Courts Ordinance, 1941

2 The Setting:
The Basoga and Their Courts

This study is not concerned with a purely indigenous African legal system. The Soga courts and the society and culture in which they operate are in important respects products of seventy years of British colonial rule, a rule whose attitude toward indigenous institutions combined, in varying proportions, a respect for tradition and local autonomy with a zeal for modernizing reform. In addition, the Basoga have been strongly influenced by the neighboring kingdom of Buganda, which for at least a century prior to the establishment of British administration was the dominant political force in the area to the north of Lake Victoria and which, by virtue of size, wealth, and a special political relationship with the British, continued throughout the colonial period to set the pattern for African life in much of Uganda. These statements should not, however, lead the reader to think of Soga society and culture as a patchwork of ill-combined elements, for it was one of my firmest impressions, after living and working in Busoga for almost two years, that I had been observing a way of life with a great deal of unity and integrity. Elements of thought and action that one knew *must* have come from the great kingdom to the west of the Nile or from British administrators and missionaries seemed to have been worked into the texture of Soga life with astonishing ease and effectiveness. The result is a social and cultural synthesis perhaps best described as "neotraditional." Basoga have accepted a great deal from the outside, but they have retained a strong sense of identity, unity, and continuity with the past.[1]

The present tense as used in this study refers to the years 1950–52, the period of my observations. Many things have happened in the subsequent fifteen years to challenge the neotraditional synthesis that seemed to have been achieved at midcentury and to make this study, strictly speaking, out of date. The more rapid political evolution of the late 1950s—an evolution that, of course, involved the courts as well as other governmental institutions—was climaxed in October 1962 by the emergence of an independent Uganda state. While the course of social change may be expected to be quite different under these new conditions, it is still too early to see clearly just what the difference will be. The more obvious changes that have taken place, particularly in the legal sphere, will be summarized in the final chapter of this book, but I shall make no serious attempt to assess them. To do so would require an additional period of on-the-spot study—study which will be far more profitable a few years hence when the pattern of postcolonial life in Uganda will have become clearer.

Thus, what I shall describe here is an African legal system at that point in its history when the impact of British rule had been quite thoroughly absorbed and when the new conditions of self-government loomed on the horizon. What is described here is the baseline for a new period of legal development in which the Basoga themselves and their fellow-citizens of independent Uganda will decide what use to make of their neotraditional legal heritage.

Soga Society and Culture at Midcentury

The Basoga are overwhelmingly a rural people, both by circumstance and by choice. Busoga contains only one substantial urban area —the town of Jinja, located in the southwest corner of the district at the point where Lake Victoria spills into the Nile. The site of the Owen Falls dam and hydroelectric plant, Jinja is the administrative and commercial center of the district and contains most of such industry as it possesses. It is not, however, a Soga town. Of the approximately 20,800 residents in 1950, nearly 6,000 were non-African, and of the African population only some 30 percent were born within the district.[2]

1. The development of neotraditional society and culture in Busoga and Buganda is discussed in my *Bantu Bureaucracy,* especially chapters 2 and 6, and in my "Ideology and Culture in Uganda Nationalism."

2. Cyril and Rhona Sofer, *Jinja Transformed,* p. 18.

Jinja is largely the creation of its Indian and European residents, the former owning and managing most of its commercial and light industrial establishments, the latter administering its political life and public services and managing its larger industrial enterprises. To the Basoga, Jinja is an "alien town," as are the numberous smaller trading centers which lie scattered about the district at intervals of fifteen to twenty miles.[3] Basoga come to Jinja to work and shop and to do business with Uganda government officials, but the only institution in the urban area with which they really identify themselves is the headquarters of the African Local Government—a Soga government, manned by Basoga—at Bugembe, a few miles outside the town.

The focus of Soga life is in the countryside where the vast majority of the half-million Basoga make their homes and earn their livelihood. Unlike many West African peoples, the interlacustrine Bantu—the Bantu-speaking peoples of the lake region of east-central Africa among whom linguists and ethnologists classify the Basoga [4]—have no indigenous urban tradition. They are in fact antiurban, and not only in the contemporary context in which the towns are the places of foreigners. In Buganda and Bunyoro, the largest of the interlacustrine kingdoms, the king's palace might be surrounded by some dozens, or even hundreds, of dwellings occupied by his subordinates and retainers; but these agglomerations were not true towns, for they lacked any continuous, self-conscious community identity and were highly transitory.[5] They were more in the nature of royal camps than permanent towns. In the Soga kingdoms, which were much smaller, these court agglomerations were even less townlike. Even the nucleated rural settlements of the sort called to mind by the English word "village" were lacking. I shall, to be sure, use the word, for lack of a better one and because it is current in the literature of the area, to denote the dispersed rural communities of Busoga. These communities are real enough socially and politically, but they are never clusters of dwellings along a street or around a clearing. The Basoga, like other interlacustrine Bantu peoples, prefer to build nearer the soil they cultivate. It is on the *kibanja,* the family landholding with its dwellings surrounded by banana gardens and fields for annual crops, that the Musoga prefers to live. Even elite Basoga, wealthy, well-educated men with high positions in the civil service, whose work may require them to live tempo-

3. Ann Evans Larimore, *The Alien Town: Patterns of Settlement in Busoga, Uganda.*

4. Fallers, *Bantu Bureaucracy,* chap. 2.

5. Lloyd A. Fallers, *The King's Men: Leadership and Status in Buganda on the Eve of Independence,* pp. 104–7; Peter C. W. Gutkind, *The Royal Capital of Buganda,* pp. 9–10.

rarily in town, maintain *kibanja* holdings which they value highly, visit on weekends, and consider their real homes. Urban manual and white-collar workers often do the same.

It is their prosperous agriculture that has enabled Basoga to reconcile their preference for rural life with economic progress. Blessed with ample rainfall and fertile soil, they had developed in precolonial times a subsistence economy based upon the cultivation of the banana, which provides both the staple food, *matooke*—a steamed mash of the green fruit—and the standard beverage, *mwenge*—a beer made from the juice of the ripe fruit.[6] The banana is a perennial, requiring constant care by the women of the household; the *lusuku,* the banana garden, commonly surrounds the courtyard and dwelling houses and forms the spatial and sentimental core of the family holding. On its margins lie the fields for annual crops—sweet potatoes, millet, maize, and sim sim. Cattle, sheep, goats, and chickens provide meat and milk. The district does not provide a uniformly favorable environment for this pattern of farming. In the north and east, which are drier, the emphasis is more upon livestock and the annual crops; banana gardens are fewer and less productive; population is sparser. In the south and west, where bananas thrive, the gardens leave less room for fields of annuals and population densities reach four hundred to the square mile. Over all, however, this agricultural system provides security and abundance. While there are occasional droughts and famines—the fruit of the banana is difficult to store against a lean season—it remains true that the Basoga had, and have, one of Africa's richest subsistence economies.

To it have been added during the decades of British rule three valuable cash crops: cotton, peanuts (ground nuts), and coffee. All three had been introduced in precolonial times, but it was the new cash economy and facilities for export that encouraged their extensive cultivation. In general, the Basoga have been able to add these crops to their subsistence agriculture without serious detriment to food-crop cultivation. Cash income, though small by world standards, has therefore been free for allocation to the new, imported items of consumption that have become standard in Soga households—cotton clothing (replacing the traditional barkcloth), bicycles, factory-made utensils, tea, soap, school fees, and, increasingly, corrugated iron or aluminum roofing (replacing the traditional thatch). With the opportunity to achieve

6. There are, in fact, many varieties of banana, often in the same garden. Some are eaten fresh, some go into beer, while the bulk—the varieties sometimes called "plantains"—are cooked. I shall follow Allan in calling them all "bananas." See William Allan, *The African Husbandman,* p. 161.

a steadily rising standard of living while remaining within the familiar
context of rural life, the Basoga have been reluctant to enter wage
labor, even in their own district; and when they have done so, they
have generally tried to maintain a footing on the land—a small
holding near the town from which they might commute to work, or a
more substantial one farther away to which they might retire in later
life.[7]

The neotraditional society, therefore, remains a rural society, a
society of village communities. I have said that the village is spatially
indistinct, since homesteads are scattered over the holdings that make
up the village area rather than being clustered. Most villages, however,
are at least partially bounded by one or more of the swampy valleys
that crisscross Busoga. The word for village (*mutala*), in fact, also
means "a piece of high ground between swamps"; one lives "on" (*ku*)
a *mutala*, not "in" (*mu*) it. Each village has its headman, whose
position is hereditary within his lineage, and each is divided into
subvillages (*bisoko*, singular: *kisoko*), each with its own hereditary
headman. In a later chapter, when considering cases in Soga land law,
I shall have to discuss in some detail the position of these headmen
vis-à-vis their people. Here it is sufficient to say that they are the
political heads, and their homesteads the social centers, of their
communities.

In addition to being members of these local communities, Basoga are
divided among more than 150 patrilineal clans (*bika*, singular: *kika*),
each of which is in turn divided and subdivided into patrilineal lineages (*nda*, singular: *nda*). Members of a clan are united by "respect" or "fear" for a common totem—usually a plant or animal
species—and are forbidden to intermarry. Both clans and lineages are
named for founding ancestors; one says, for example, in declaring one's
clan membership: "I am a Mwiseigaga": literally, "of the father
Igaga." The clan name is nearly always made up in this way, by
joining the personal prefix *mu* to the word for father, *ise*, and the name
of the ancestor. In speaking of one's lineage, on the other hand, one
says: "I am of the lineage of Idhoba" (*nda ya Idhoba*). Clans are
large and dispersed over Busoga; often members of the same clan in
different parts of the country will be unable to trace the kinship links
between them, or will be unable to agree about the nature of these
links. The lineage is a more intimate and more localized group, among
whose members the links are, in principle, known. The term *nda* may
be used in speaking of any level of group segmentation within the clan.

7. Walter Elkan and Lloyd A. Fallers, "Labor Mobility and Competing Status
Systems."

The word also means "womb" or, in a sexless sense, "the interior of the body." In discussions of lineage, however, the implication is always male, rather as, in the King James Bible, children come from a man's "loins." The other principal meaning of *kika* (clan), on the other hand, is "kind" or "class" or, in a modern commercial context, "brand." The phrase *"nda ya* so-and-so" is often used to indicate the male agnatic ancestor, descent from whom links any two persons or groups. The most important lineage unit for social (and legal) purposes, however, is that which unites members of a clan living in a group of neighboring villages—the group that can come together to engage in corporate action. Somewhat confusingly, the Basoga often speak of such a lineage as "the clan," or use the clan name in referring to it. Thus, when a Musoga speaks of "the Baiseigaga," he usually means the Baiseigaga who live nearby and act together. It is this "local chapter" of his clan that is of greatest interest and importance to a Musoga.

This local unit I shall call the "succession lineage," for it is in connection with matters of succession that the group is most commonly mobilized. When a man dies, the group comes together under the leadership of its hereditary head to choose two successors: one, the "successor of the belt," who assumes responsibility for the deceased's wives and children and in general takes over his kinship responsibilities; and another, the "successor who takes the things," who becomes the heir to the deceased's land and, if he holds one, to his hereditary office. The first is usually a brother or paternal cousin, the latter a son or brother's son. These selections rest with the group in law, as will be seen, as well as in custom, and they are made at the funeral feast that follows a period of mourning for the dead. It is said that such decisions, if they are contested, may be "appealed" to the hereditary heads of lineages of wider span, or even to the clan head, but this rarely happens.[8] In the life of the average Musoga villager, including those matters that most often bring him to court, it is the local succession lineage and its head—usually spoken of in local contexts as the "head of the clan"—that represent institutionalized patrilineal descent-group solidarity and authority.

Village community and patrilineal descent are distinct modes of organization in Busoga, crosscutting one another to form the two principal axes of rural society. As a resident of one's village and subvillage, one is the political subordinate and tenant of one's headman; as a clan member, one is linked in corporate solidarity with other

8. See chapter 6. In this, as in many other ways, Basoga tend to treat Ganda patterns as ideals for Busoga. The Ganda clan system is much more hierarchical. See Fallers, *The King's Men,* chapter 2.

members, descended from a common ancestor, who live in one's own and neighboring villages. But the two modes of organization do not coincide; they are not simply the territorial and genealogical dimensions, respectively, of the same social groupings. The village or subvillage seldom consists entirely of the households of members of a single lineage or clan. Thus, one's headman is usually not one's lineage head, or even a member of one's lineage. Both village and subvillage normally contain members of several lineages of several clans, and the headman's lineage is often not even the largest.[9]

These features of kinship and local organization are traditional institutions that have survived almost unchanged in the neotraditional society of the colonial period; and their persistence, facilitated by a relatively productive agriculture, has been a major factor in maintaining the continuity of Soga life and law. In the religious sphere, continuity has been less marked. Missionary endeavor on behalf of both Christianity and Islam preceded British administration and in both cases struck deep roots in Soga society. Today the Christian and Muslim communities include all Basoga leaders of any significance and a large majority of the population at large. For example, of a total of 491 married men in the five villages in which I carried out complete surveys in 1951–52, 390 (almost 80 percent) claimed to be Christians or Muslims.[10] Of these, 102 (21 percent) were Muslims, 100 (20 percent) were Roman Catholics, and 188 (38 percent) were adherents of the Anglican communion. Both Muslim and Christian communities are largely served by African clergy. Furthermore, the new religions' organizational success has been paralleled by a cultural conquest: religion, along with education, modern medicine, and economic progress, is one of the "good things" of the modern world to which the Basoga have committed themselves; and *ddini*, the word for it, introduced from Arabic via Swahili, the East African lingua franca, applies only to Islam and Christianity, not to the traditional faith. Those who are not Christians or Muslims are now, pejoratively, *bakafiri* (Arabic-Swahili: "pagans"). At the annual national celebration at Bugembe of Kyabazinga's Day, the Soga national holiday, leading Christian and Muslim clergy are given places of honor; no dignitary, however, represents the old religion.

Religion, in the minds of Basoga, is closely associated with educa-

9. See chapter 6; and Fallers, *Bantu Bureaucracy*, chapter 4.
10. The villages surveyed were Budini and Buyodi in the county of Bulamogi, and Bunyama, Wairama, and Bukwaya in the county of Kigulu. Bulamogi is in the drier, less densely populated north of the district, Kigulu in the more fertile and heavily populated south.

tion, for the missions created the educational system and at the time of my observations were still, with the help of government grants, responsible for operating it. The high value which Basoga place upon education is perhaps most clearly demonstrated by the fact that it is the one purpose for which they are always ready to pay more taxes. In 1950–52, the school system was not yet large enough to satisfy the popular demand for a primary education for every Musoga child. Still, the district was at that time served by sixty-four "vernacular primary schools" (schools offering three years of education in the Luganda language), thirty full (six-year) primary schools, four junior (three-year) secondary schools, and one full (six-year) secondary school. There was one teacher-training institution. For a few fortunate Basoga students, higher education was available at Makerere College, the University College of East Africa, in nearby Kampala. Much of this represented recent growth in educational facilities, growth which was not yet reflected in the educational level of the adult population of Busoga. However, in the five villages surveyed, 41 percent of the married men and 14 percent of their wives were literate.

This ready acceptance of the monotheistic religions and western education does not, however, mean that traditional religion has left no trace in contemporary Soga society and culture. There are, first of all, important elements of syncretism in the local expressions of both Islam and Christianity, centering particularly, as one would expect, upon those aspects of belief most closely associated with the continuity and solidarity of the patrilineal descent group. Since this institutional complex underlies many of the legal ideas to be discussed in later chapters, a brief account of its religious side is in order.

In traditional belief, the descent group comprised both the living (*balamu*) and the spirits (*mizimu*) of the dead. The spirits maintained an active interest in the well-being of the group and might express their displeasure by visiting illness or misfortune upon living members. The latter, therefore, acted to secure the good will of the spirits by making offerings of food and beer at shrines built in the family courtyard, and most importantly, by assuring at the death of a member a satisfactory passage from the living to the spirit state. This was achieved through a series of ritual acts making up the funeral complex known as *kwabya olumbe*, "dismantling death." [11] This began with the preparation of the body by a sister's son—a kinsman whose relationship to the deceased was close and affectionate, but disinterested and safe, since he was not a member of the patrilineage and hence not

11. A pavilion is erected to shelter the mourners during the ceremonies. It is the dismantling of this structure upon their completion to which the term refers.

involved in any potential disputes over succession. The sorcerer who, it was assumed, had caused the death was cursed; the successors were chosen by the assembled lineage mates and were made to spear a cow sacrifically beside the grave, usually dug in the banana garden, which thereby took on a sacred character. The spirit was then "released" by the senior widow, who, throwing a handful of soil from the grave into the air, called upon it to "rise up." For a period of several months, the widows, children, and successors mourned by allowing their hair to grow long. Finally, a shrine was built, offerings were made, a funeral feast was held, and the senior widow spent a ritual first night with the "successor of the belt," whose wife she usually became. The damage done to the social fabric of the lineage by death was thus repaired, it was hoped, and harmony between its living and dead members assured.

This complex of ritual acts survives, in some degree, in the lives of most Basoga today although the mourning period is much briefer and the selection of successors and the funeral feast have been combined. For almost all, it is safe to say, the ancestors remain objects of veneration. Even for the majority who no longer build shrines or make offerings, the ancestors' graves in the banana garden give land a sacred quality, as well as conferring important rights in law. And most Basoga Muslims and Christians today take part, without any feeling of contradiction, in funeral ceremonies that involve some combination of *kwabya olumbe* rites with those of the new faiths. Similarly, most find it possible to reconcile Islam and Christianity with features of the traditional kinship system that to an outside observer might seem incompatible with them. Few Basoga Muslims, for example, follow the rules of the *sharia* with respect to succession, most preferring instead to follow general Soga custom; while few Christians, in spite of frequent sermons on behalf of monogamy, feel that it is wrong to have more than one wife. In the five villages surveyed, 24 percent of the Christian men were polygamous, as compared with 34 percent of the Muslims, and only 14 percent of the "pagans," whose lower rate is explained by their relative poverty. Both Christians and Muslims, on the whole, continue to regard women as minors, under the authority of their fathers before marriage and that of their husbands afterward. Thus, the major social institutions that form the matrix for much of Soga law have retained the allegiance of Basoga of all faiths.

There were, of course, other aspects of traditional Soga religion besides the ancestor cult. For nineteenth-century Basoga, the spirit world was intricately differentiated: every prominent feature of the landscape—every river, large tree, or prominent hill—harbored a spirit

(*musambwa*) with which living men might communicate and by whom
their welfare might be affected. At the head of this pantheon were a
series of powerful anthropomorphous spirit figures: Waitambogwe,
Walumbe, Mukama, and many others—several of whom are common
to neighboring Bantu peoples. All were capable of causing illnesses
which could be cured only by yielding to possession by the spirit.
Many Basoga Christians and Muslims believe in the power of these
spirits, as they do in the efficacy of amulets, fetishes, and sorcery,
though they may reinterpret them in terms of Christian and Muslim
theology as manifestations of the devil (*ssitaani*). A remnant of organized "paganism" exists in the form of local cult groups of *basweezi* [12]
—devotees of *musambwa* spirits who meet regularly for seances. Only
regular membership in such a seance group is popularly regarded as
incompatible with Islam and Christianity.

To summarize then, the average Musoga villager and the average
litigant in the Soga courts is a relatively prosperous peasant farmer
with an assured food supply and a bit of money to spend. He is a
Christian or Muslim with little formal education, though quite possibly literate and anxious that his children should be better educated
than himself. He is closely bound, both by complex social ties and by
traditional religious conceptions, to his lineage, his village, and the
land. All this, however, describes only the village level of Soga society.
In addition, there are the governmental institutions through which this
average villager is related to a larger political order; these also represent an amalgam of indigenous elements with features resulting from
external influences.

From Kingdom to Local Government

In the latter half of the nineteenth century, the earliest period for
which the combination of written records and old men's memories
makes it possible to form a reasonably clear picture of political
arrangements, the territory of the present Busoga District was occupied by a dozen or more small kingdoms, ranging in population from a
few thousand to perhaps one hundred thousand. Although the area
lacked political unity, and although at least two distinct dialects were
spoken by its people, it was regarded both by them and by their
neighbors as forming a distinct cultural entity with a common pattern
of political institutions.

Each of the kingdoms was headed by a dynasty, a descent group of
princes which formed a lineage within a royal clan. Although then, as

12. The cult is widespread in the interlacustrine Bantu region, though in other
areas it is the spirits, and not their votaries, who are called *basweezi* or *bacweezi*.

now, most clans were dispersed over Busoga, the same clan was not royal in every kingdom. In Bugabula, Bulamogi, Bukono, Luuka, Kigulu, and Bukoli, the rulers were Baisengobi, while the Baiseigaga ruled in Busiki and Busambira and the Baisemenya in Bugweri. In the many small kingdoms of the south, there were still others. Each dynasty possessed regalia—drums, stools, and spears—which were the inherited symbols of royal authority. Court bards sang of the great deeds of kings and recited their genealogies. In each kingdom, the royal ancestors were the objects of a "national" cult similar to, but more elaborate than, the one practiced by ordinary Basoga in relation to their own ancestors. Government in the kingdoms was not, however, clan or lineage government. Only the ruler's position was, in principle, hereditary; subordinate officials held office at his pleasure, a pattern that served both to centralize authority in the ruler's hands and to open the ranks of the political hierarchy to able commoners. A ruler might appoint his son chief of a section of the kingdom, but it was recognized that this practice amounted to storing up trouble for the future; the prince, sharing the royal blood, might be tempted to assert his autonomy or to usurp the rulership. Even if he himself remained loyal, his descendants might claim independent hereditary authority. Incidents of this kind are recounted in the traditional histories of several of the kingdoms. To strengthen his hand, therefore, a ruler was always careful to balance any princely appointments with able and loyal commoner chiefs, often men related to him by marriage. Such chiefs were entirely dependent upon his favor and were the subordinates upon whom he mainly relied in the exercise of his authority.

The complexity of the chiefly hierarchy varied with the size of the kingdom. In Bulamogi, for example, which was one of the larger states in the north, it consisted of a palace staff headed by a prime minister, the *katikkiro*.[13] A series of chiefs, some princes and other commoners, were in charge of major divisions of the kingdom, while at the local level there were village and subvillage headmen, some of whom were royal appointees, while others were hereditary. In the little southern kingdom of Busambira, on the other hand, the ruler's immediate subordinates, apart from his *katikkiro* and his household servants, were the village and subvillage headmen, some of whom were fellow princes while others were commoners. Everywhere, however, the basic principles were the same: rulership, hereditary within a royal lineage, was exercised through a mixed hierarchy of princely and commoner chiefs headed by a *katikkiro*, who seems always to have been a

---

13. "*Katikkiro*" is probably a Ganda title borrowed, like so much else, by Basoga.

commoner. Each chief was responsible for the collection of tribute and the organization of a militia unit in his area, and each held court as a judge in the disputes that arose among his people.

These little kingdoms were not politically isolated, either from each other or from states outside the borders of Busoga. In their external relations, they were among the smaller units in a regional system of international politics that stretched around the northern and western shores of Lake Victoria from Kavirondo, in what is now the Nyanza Province of Kenya, to Bukoba, in present-day northwestern Tanzania. This whole area was occupied by states broadly similar in structure, all struggling to increase their wealth and extend their territory at the expense of their neighbors. Raids and wars were frequent. The larger kingdoms endeavored to absorb the smaller, both through direct military operations and by intervention in princely struggles over succession, secession, and usurpation. The Soga kingdoms used these tactics against each other, but in the larger struggle for domination over the whole area, none of them was large enough to be a major competitor. Instead, they tended to participate as satellites of the two major contending powers: Bunyoro, which lay to the northwest beyond Lake Kyoga; and Buganda, which bordered Busoga to the west beyond the Victoria Nile. At an earlier period, traditional histories suggest, when Bunyoro was the more powerful of her neighbors, Busoga had been under strong Nyoro influence. The dynasties in several of the northern Soga kingdoms claim descent from the Nyoro royal line. By the middle of the nineteenth century, however, it is clear that Buganda had begun to win out, both in the larger struggle and in dominance over Busoga in particular. By the 1860s and 1870s, when the first written accounts of the area became available, much of Busoga had become tributary to the Kabaka (king) of Buganda, whose authority over the area was exercised through the Ssekiboobo, the chief of the neighboring Ganda county of Kyaggwe. Captain W. H. Williams, representing the Imperial British East Africa Company, which had been chartered in 1888 to look after Britain's interests in the area, wrote to his superiors in January, 1893, characterizing the Ssekiboobo as the "paramount chief" of Busoga.[14]

The British had concluded that Buganda held the key to control of the whole region; during the 1890s, therefore, British officers concentrated upon increasing their influence there in order to establish control of surrounding peoples. In 1894, a formal British protectorate succeeded the administration of the chartered company, and in 1900 an

14. Uganda Government Archives, Staff and Miscellaneous, 1893.

agreement was signed, recognizing the Kabaka as "native ruler of the Province of Uganda, under Her Majesty's protection and over-rule." [15] The word "Uganda," as used then, referred only to the Kabaka's kingdom; it was simply the Swahili form of "Buganda." Gradually, however, "Uganda" came to be used for the larger area under British protection, "Buganda" being reserved for the Ganda kingdom itself. Under the agreement, Buganda relinquished all claims to Busoga and other tributary areas outside her boundaries, but the method of administration thereafter adopted in these areas served to perpetuate, and even deepen, Ganda influence.

Even before Britain achieved political domination over Buganda, the Christian missionaries had concentrated their efforts there. As a result, by the turn of the century there was available in Buganda a substantial corps of young men with a modicum of western education and a knowledge of British ways, ready to serve in surrounding areas as chiefs, teachers, and missionaries. Such men were the principal architects of the neotraditional social order which took shape in Busoga during the first two decades of the present century and they are largely responsible for the strongly Ganda flavor that still characterizes it. [16]

Chief among the Baganda agents of British administration was Semei Kakunguru, an able young man who was made "paramount chief," presiding over a unified council of Basoga rulers. A number of other Ganda chiefs were made "advisers" to Basoga rulers, and through them the political structure of the country, now an administrative district of the eastern province of the Uganda Protectorate, was reorganized on a Ganda model. The larger kingdoms became "counties" (ssaza), while the smaller kingdoms and the major divisions of the larger ones were made "subcounties" (ggombolola). These latter, in turn, were divided into miruka (singular: muluka), or "parishes." Each of these territorial units was governed by a chief, who now owed his appointment, ultimately, to the protectorate government. Within each county and subcounty, heads of subordinate units were given ranked Ganda titles: Mumyuka, Ssaabaddu, Ssaabagabo, Ssaabawaali, Mutuba. The senior subcounty chief within a county became Mumyuka, as did his senior parish chief. These titles are still used in referring to chiefs and to the courts they chair.

In practice, the rulers of areas that had in the past been independent kingdoms were retained at first, but as these men died or reached retirement age, they were replaced by others without hereditary claims, chosen for their ability and education. Similarly, the means by

15. The Uganda Agreement, 1900.
16. A. D. Roberts, "The Sub-Imperialism of the Baganda."

which the chiefly hierarchy was remunerated were gradually modernized. At the beginning of the colonial period, the chiefs were supported through an adaptation and regularization of the traditional tribute system. Each chief's area was divided into *butongole,* the "official" part, which he ruled and taxed on behalf of the protectorate government; and *bwesengeze,* the "benefice," from which he collected tax and tribute labor for himself. Between 1926 and 1936, however, personal tribute was abolished and replaced by a system of taxation, from which chiefs were paid regular salaries. Thus, during the twenties and thirties, the traditional hierarchy of hereditary rulers, princes, and their client-chiefs was gradually replaced by a corps of civil-servant chiefs, appointed on the basis of personal qualifications and serving on civil service terms.

An important element of continuity was provided by the tendency for the chiefly lineages and their kinsmen to fill the schools with their children. The "bright young men" with the best "personal qualifications" turned out in very many cases to be sons or sister's sons of traditional rulers and princes and thus what had been a series of local dynasties, each with its penumbra of officials and matrilateral kinsmen, became a Busoga-wide oligarchy or "establishment," adding to its traditional ascriptive position the new symbols of formal education and money wealth. The chain of legitimacy was never broken.

During the 1930s and 1940s, as Britain began to think more seriously in terms of a future self-governing Uganda, it became the policy to develop these institutions for "indirect rule" into modern local governments. To the administrative bureaucracy, therefore, was added, beginning in 1938, a hierarchy of parish, subcounty, county, and district councils, which gradually became less official and more elective in composition. An ordinance enacted in 1938 gave this local government the right to incorporate.[17] Finally, the African Local Governments Ordinance of 1949 gave the structure the form it exhibited at the time of my observations. With more than one thousand full-time employees and a budget of a quarter of a million pounds, it was served by, in addition to the hierarchy of chiefs and councils, an elected Kyabazinga (President), a central secretariat, a treasury office, an agriculture and forestry department, a police department, and a public works department. Upon these departments of the A.L.G. were gradually devolved many functions formerly performed by central government departments. The county and subcounty chiefs tended to become the coordinators for their areas of these specialist services. At the

17. African Administrations (Incorporation) Ordinance, 1938.

lowest level of political organization, the village and subvillage headmen remained little affected by all this reorganization. Forbidden to collect tribute and unwilling to accept salaries that would, they felt, make them subject to transfer and dismissal by the protectorate government, they formally remained aloof from the official Busoga African Local Government structure and became uniformly hereditary, although, as will be seen, they continued to do much of the work of the local government, including important aspects of its judicial work.

Busoga was not ruled throughout this period of evolution by Baganda chiefs. Kakunguru, the Muganda "paramount," was removed in 1914, and by 1918 all Baganda chiefs had departed. The long period of Ganda influence, however, had left a permanent mark on the district. The Luganda language was doubtless widely used in Busoga in the period of Ganda domination before the coming of the British; it is, in any case, very similar to, in fact mutually intelligible with, the Lusoga dialects. The missionaries, therefore, made their Luganda translations of Bible, prayerbook, catechism, and hymnal the instruments for the evangelization of Busoga, and the close link between religion and education meant that Luganda became the written language of the district. Attempts have been made to develop a standard orthography for Lusoga, but there seems to be little popular demand for this. Basoga quite happily correspond with one another in Luganda and a substantial Luganda press provides them with reading matter. The court clerk, like other officials, works in Luganda quite easily, "translating" as he goes along from the testimony of those—usually the elderly and uneducated—who prefer to address the court in Lusoga, and retaining, in Luganda orthography, the Lusoga words that have no exact Luganda counterparts. *"Omusadha ono akobye nti ow'ekisoko aidhye ewaiffe,"* an old man may say ("This man said that the subvillage headman had come to our home"), and the clerk, without thinking, writes: *"Omusajja ono agambye nti ow'ekisoko azze ewaffe."*

This cultural "imperialism" seems to encounter remarkably little resistance. Unlike some other peoples of Uganda, who resent the Ganda domination of much of the country's life, the Basoga tend to identify themselves with Ganda culture and even with Ganda political interests. Particularly at the upper levels of society, where friendships formed at the elite boarding schools in Buganda are reinforced by a good deal of intermarriage, Basoga have been quite thoroughly "Ganda-ized." At the village level, of course, this is less true. But throughout, Ganda influence has been so pervasive that it is often difficult to distinguish Ganda from indigenous elements in Soga life.

The British influence is, of course, more easily distinguished. The Busoga African Local Government is the end product of a quite explicit policy of building upon, and reforming, indigenous political institutions to produce an English-model local government. The process has been gradual enough, and the rewards to those most directly affected substantial enough, that the reforms have been quite generally accepted. Perhaps the most important factor in this success has been the combination of firmness and restraint with which British officers have dealt with Soga institutions and officials. The district has been administered throughout the colonial period by a handful of British officials headed by a district commissioner. On paper, their authority has been very nearly absolute: "Whenever a provincial commissioner or district commissioner shall consider that, for the proper administration and good government of the area within which any chief has jurisdiction, it is necessary or desirable that any order or orders should be issued . . . he may direct the chief to issue and enforce or may himself issue and enforce such order or orders." [18]

In practice, the policy has been to devolve the maximum responsibility upon Basoga. Basoga officials have generally been treated with respect. In the absence of the racial tensions produced in some other colonial areas by the presence of a European settler population (alienation of land to foreigners was never substantial in Uganda and was halted entirely around 1910 in favor of a policy of developing peasant agriculture), the relationship has been essentially a tutorial one, often carried on over friendly cups of tea. The pupil has often enough felt that the pace of advancement was insufficiently rapid, but the relationship has been amicable enough, and resentment sufficiently offset by admiration, that the innovations introduced have been quite thoroughly institutionalized.

The above sketch will give the reader sufficient initial information concerning the social and cultural context in which the Soga courts operate. These courts, to summarize, form the judicial arm of the Busoga African Local Government, administering Soga customary law and certain statutes in the adjudication of the disputes which arise in the neotraditional society I have described, under the general supervision of a British colonial administration. It will be necessary to enlarge upon some aspects of Soga ethnography from time to time as the analysis proceeds, but for the present I turn to matters more specifically legal: the development of the court system and the sources of the law it administers.

18. African Authority Ordinance, 1919, 8 (1).

THE DEVELOPMENT OF THE COURT SYSTEM

The Soga courts are heirs to a vigorous indigenous legal tradition. As will become quite obvious when I begin to analyze the way in which they approach the task of adjudication, they work with procedures and conceptual tools so coherent and so well developed that they cannot possibly have been acquired during the colonial experience, though they certainly have been influenced by that experience. On the other hand, it is exceedingly difficult to discover the precise shape of indigenous Soga legal institutions and, consequently, the exact nature of the changes in these institutions wrought by British administration. First Ganda and later British influences have been so thoroughly absorbed and so subtly mingled with indigenous tradition as to defy any attempt to clearly separate out the "purely Soga" elements. It is possible, however, from a combination of documentary sources and old men's memories, to reconstruct the precolonial legal situation in rough outline.

So far as I am aware, the documentary record begins on April 23, 1893, with a memorandum from the first British commissioner in Uganda to the newly posted officer in charge of Busoga, suggesting that he "try to settle all land cases locally" and not send them to the still-suzerain Kabaka of Buganda for adjudication.[19] The following year, the officer in Busoga, W. T. Grant, wrote that he had "held a *lukiiko*" (court) of Basoga chiefs to settle cases.[20] These two brief extracts from the Uganda government archives represent the earliest written records of judicial activity in Busoga and they tell not about the Soga courts themselves, but about the passing of appellate jurisdiction over these courts from Ganda to British hands. Unfortunately for the historian, Grant, the first European to have prolonged contact with the Basoga, seems to have lacked the literary urge.[21] His reports to his superiors are spare and practical and he seems to have left no memoirs. From him one learns only that there *were* courts in which chiefs adjudicated disputes among their people.

19. E. J. L. Berkeley to Officer-in-Charge, Busoga, April 24, 1893. Uganda Government Archives, Staff and Miscellaneous, 1893.
20. W. T. Grant to H. Colville, October 17, 1894; Ibid., 1894–2.
21. Grant's memoirs would have made fascinating reading. He married the daughter of a chief in the early years of British administration, when administrators came without wives and there was no European "Society" in Uganda. This phase lasted only a few years, however, and soon there existed a European community whose disapproval forced a separation. The wife was settled on a freehold estate. When I arrived in 1950 and announced my intention to live in a village, it was widely rumored that I was a descendant of Grant, returned to find my mother's kinsmen and to claim rights in the land.

The memories of men still living in 1950–52 tell a little more. All rulers, chiefs, and headmen, I was told, acted as judges, sitting with their subordinates to hear cases. One man recalled that a litigant might keep track of the main points of his argument by holding a bundle of sticks in his hand and throwing them down, one by one, before the bench to mark each point. Very difficult cases, it was said, were settled by resort to an ordeal by intoxicating drug. Some said that certain types of cases—assault and homicide were mentioned—were settled by retaliation or composition between lineages, while others—such as land and bridewealth cases—were tried before a chief. Lineage heads were said to hold judicial proceedings to decide inheritance disputes and to try offenders against the norms governing behavior among lineage mates—as indeed they still do today. The picture that emerges from these memories is very like the descriptions of Ganda legal institutions given by turn-of-the-century Baganda and European writers.[22]

I shall not, however, attempt to repeat for Busoga the remarkable achievement of Llewellyn and Hoebel in reconstructing the indigenous legal order of the Cheyenne Indians from memory data.[23] One reason is that the task seems impossible to accomplish. Soga memories seem to yield less adequate data on these matters than do Cheyenne memories. While the two peoples came under regular European administration at about the same period prior to the two studies—some sixty years—the circumstances and consequences of alien administration in the two cases were quite different. For the Cheyenne, conquest and confinement on a reservation represented a catastrophic end to their former nomadic hunting and warring way of life, but little effort seems to have been made by United States agents, at least during the early years, to influence their legal institutions. In Busoga, the British assumption of control was both less catastrophic in its effects upon life in general and more immediately consequential for legal institutions. There was no military conquest—the British acquired Busoga as a by-product of their ascendancy in Buganda—and the village way of life remained intact, changing only gradually over the years with the development of mission religion and education and a cash economy. Political and legal institutions were guided from the first in accord with British notions of just administration, but this process, too, was gradual, and a deliberate effort was made to preserve the fabric of "customary law." The new political and legal order was sufficiently

22. John Roscoe, *The Baganda*, chapter 8; Sir Apolo Kagwa, *Ekitabo kye Mpisa za Baganda*, chapter 23.
23. K. N. Llewellyn and E. Adamson Hoebel, *The Cheyenne Way*.

like the old so that Basoga have little sense of discontinuity in their recent history. In consequence, they think about their precolonial political and legal order as little different from their present one and their memory of the former is heavily contaminated by their experience of the latter. Thus, while I was able to collect some case material remembered from the precolonial phase, I often felt that this material was being filtered through a screen of present-day experience of the African Local Government courts.

A more important reason for not dwelling unduly upon the exceedingly difficult task of reconstructing precolonial Soga legal life is that, particularly for the kind of analysis I am attempting, present-day case material is so much more rewarding. My central interest is the use made by the courts of legal concepts and an understanding of this process requires the close analysis of bodies of related cases.[24] To assemble such material for the precolonial period would be quite impossible. This sketch of the growth of the court system should therefore be regarded as merely introductory to the central task of analyzing present-day litigation and adjudication.

For these purposes, it is sufficient to know that at the beginning of the colonial period Basoga were familiar with tribunals in which litigants argued their cases before judges and that they readily accepted the jurisdiction of the British-supervised courts over cases of all kinds. This is not to say that Basoga were always enthusiastic about British overrule, but simply that they regarded British supervision over the courts as a natural and inevitable consequence of it. I found no trace in the reports of administrative officers of resistance to the courts' jurisdiction and none was recalled by any Musoga with whom I spoke. On the contrary, administrative officers' reports, which from 1913 include returns of all cases in the "native courts," attest to the positive enthusiasm of Basoga for litigation before judges who were, after all, their familiar chiefly authorities in an only slightly changed guise. In 1913 the county, subcounty, and district courts heard 2,415 cases, or about one for every 85 Basoga. The per capita frequency of litigation subsequently rose slowly over the years to one case for every 45 souls in 1950,[25] but this rise probably reflects an increase in the frequency of certain types of disputes (principally land disputes, as

24. Llewellyn and Hoebel did not attempt this sort of analysis, and probably could not have done so with the sort of data they could obtain.

25. The case returns are taken from the quarterly and annual reports of provincial and district commissioners, on file in the Central Offices, Jinja. Population figures are from the 1911 and 1948 censuses, summarized by Margaret C. Fallers in *The Eastern Lacustrine Bantu*, pp. 20–21.

will be seen) rather than in the legitimacy of the courts. All evidence suggests that courts of law, in the sense developed in the previous chapter, were familiar to Basoga from precolonial times and that the "new" courts represented for them no radical departure.

The structure of the court system seems to have changed relatively little since the early years of the British protectorate. Rulers and their client-chiefs gradually became civil servants, as I have said, but the territorial units, especially at the top and bottom of the hierarchy, remained quite stable; the larger kingdoms, that is to say, became "counties," while the villages and subvillages remained villages and subvillages. At intermediate levels, many "subcounties" represented traditional units, either kingdoms or traditional divisions of kingdoms. And each continued to have its chief or headman, who was also its judge. Through all the changes that transformed the loose collection of autonomous kingdoms into a single, relatively modernized local government, courts continued to be held at most of the same places, and in a recognizably similar manner.

At the beginning, British officers simply assumed supervisory authority and appellate jurisdiction over the judicial functions of the rulers, chiefs, and headmen. It was probably at this time, in the first few years of the present century, that the most important changes in court practice—whatever these were—were instituted. Practices felt by British officers to be, in the words of the Native Courts Ordinance, "repugnant to natural justice and morality," were probably eliminated at this time, before there had been any formal legislation to this effect. Thus, one hears no more of the ordeal, and the punishments a court might inflict were limited to fining, imprisonment, forfeiture, and whipping (though it is interesting to note that the last form of punishment seems to have been more repugnant to Basoga than to their British mentors; though still provided for in legislation in force in 1950–52, I found no recent case in which a Soga court had imposed it). It was perhaps also at this time that such elements as the conventional charge to the parties at the opening of an action and the rule of *res judicata*, both of which *sound* British-inspired, were introduced— though there is no way of knowing for certain that these did not exist in traditional court practice. One element that clearly *was* introduced at this time, perhaps the most important single contribution of British administration to Soga court procedure, was the practice of keeping written records. By 1904, the British officer in charge was keeping a book of "native court cases" which recorded the names of the litigants, a statement of the charge, and an abstract of the testimony in cases appealed to him.[26] By at least 1920, and probably earlier, each sub-county court was keeping such a case book.[27] Thus the courts now had a new and important kind of servant, the clerk.

As the colonial regime began to take on the attributes of a full-scale modern government, these arrangements were formalized through the legislative authority granted, first to the governor and then to the legislative council, by the Uganda Orders in Council of 1902 and 1920 respectively.[28] Beginning in 1905, a series of native courts ordinances recognized and regulated the courts of the county and subcounty chiefs and established a "district native court." At first, the bench was exclusively official; a county chief sat with a group of his subordinate subcounty chiefs, a subcounty chief with his subordinate parish chiefs. Under the ordinance of 1941, however, half the bench at each level was made elective. These "unofficial" members are chosen by the subcounty, county, and district councils, which are themselves largely popularly elected. Decisions are arrived at by majority vote, but the chief-chairman tends to dominate the proceedings. The "courts" held by parish chiefs, by village and subvillage headmen, and by lineage heads have never received legislative recognition, but the official courts have recognized their usefulness and in practice have acted to maintain them. A subcounty chief, for example, usually insists that an accuser first take his case to the headman and the parish chief so that they may attempt to settle it "out of court." A good many disputes are settled this way. The subcounty courts also recognize the jurisdiction of the lineage gatherings over internal lineage disputes—principally disputes over succession—and will enforce their decisions. From the point of view of the average villager, all these tribunals are part of a single judicial system; all are *nkiiko*, with the authority to "cut cases."

This Soga judicial system, manned entirely by Basoga, stands beside, and within, another system, manned by British officials. Legislation, beginning with the Subordinate Courts Ordinance of 1902, has created a series of magistrates' courts and a high court and has provided for appeal to a court of appeal for eastern Africa and to the

26. On file in the Central Offices, Jinja.

27. In subcounty Ssaabawaali, Kigulu, I found a casebook for 1920–23. These must have existed at least from 1913, when district commissioners began including judicial statistics in their reports.

28. The development of the protectorate administration and its courts is well summarized in H. B. Thomas and Robert Scott, *Uganda*, chapters 4 and 17, and Lord Hailey, *Native Administration in the British African Territories* 1: 25–43. The present system is outlined in A. N. Allott, *Judicial and Legal Systems in Africa*, pp. 106–17.

privy council. In general, the allocation of jurisdictions between the two systems is such that the great majority of cases in which both parties are Africans or, in criminal cases, in which the accused is an African, go to the Soga courts (or to similar courts in other districts), while cases involving Europeans and Indians go to the British magistrates' courts. The racial division is not, however, complete. Persons of any race accused of homicide or rape are tried by the high court, while non-Africans "who, having regard to their general mode of life

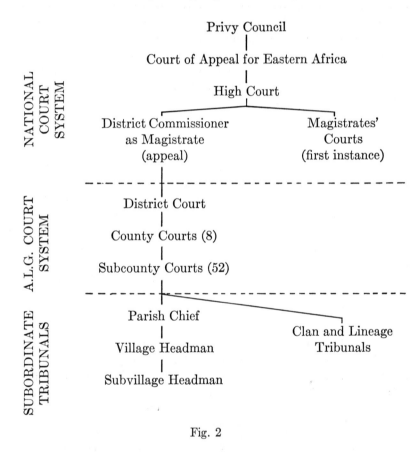

Fig. 2

. . . may be made amenable to the jurisdiction of such court"[29] may be tried in the Soga courts. Furthermore, British administrative officers supervise the work of the Soga courts, principally by inspecting their records, and in their capacity as magistrates exercise appellate juris-

29. Native Courts Ordinance, 1941, 8 (1–2).

diction over them. Appellate jurisdiction is exercised with restraint, especially with regard to the substance of customary law. Partly because the African judges are assumed to know this law better than their British superiors, and partly because the latter recognize the perils of translation (few know Luganda well enough to read a case file), the administrative officer or the high court generally confirms the highest A.L.G. court's judgment—unless, of course, there is evidence of gross procedural irregularity or factual error.

Figure 2 summarizes the judicial structure.

THE SOURCES OF LAW: BRITISH COLONIAL LEGISLATION

In this study, I have adopted a court-centered, case-centered view of law; the law is what judges with the authority to do so say it is when they make decisions with respect to the cases that come before them. By thus centering my attention upon adjudication—upon the judicial act—I do not, as I have indicated, mean to suggest that events occurring outside the courtroom and unrelated to particular cases are irrelevant to law. From the standpoint adopted here, such events—legislative enactments, customary moral and cognitive categories acquired by judges and litigants in the course of growing up, religious injunctions, previous judges' decisions—all these phenomena, and perhaps others, may be *sources* of law.[30] They are sources of the legal concepts employed by judges in the adjudicatory process. The court-centered, case-centered view implies no more than that it is in the courtroom, in the adjudication of actual cases, that these concepts, whose sources may be found in all sorts of extracourtroom social and cultural processes, are made use of for truly *legal* purposes—are woven into the fabric of law by legal reasoning.

At the time of my observations, the overriding source of law for the Soga courts was, in one sense, the commands of the British sovereign, exercised through the governor-in-council. This was the ultimate "rule of recognition," in terms of Hart's scheme. The legislative council has regularly legislated for the national courts, presided over by British judges, and it has the authority to do the same for the Soga and other local African courts. In practice, however, the national legislature has by ordinance severely limited its own legislative functions vis-à-vis the African Local Government courts and has left wide areas of law to be supplied from other sources. The principal such source is "native law and custom," which according to the Native Courts Ordinance of

30. I follow here Rupert Cross's discussion in his *Precedent in English Law*, pp. 147–56.

1941 should govern both the substance [31] and the procedure [32] of adjudication, with certain specified exceptions and limitations.

By "native law and custom," the legislators presumably meant the bodies of legal concepts and procedures in use in the Soga and other African courts prior to the establishment of British rule, but it would be a mistake to think of the law applied by the courts in 1950–52 as a simple persistence of precolonial elements, modified only by the limitations imposed by the national legislature. There has indeed been a continuous Soga legal tradition, but it is quite apparent, from the situation as I have described it, that any attempt to isolate a "purely indigenous" Soga strain in the present practice of the courts would be fruitless. If life for Basoga has not changed catastrophically, as it has for Llewellyn and Hoebel's Cheyenne, it has nevertheless changed very greatly in ways that might be expected to influence legal ideas. The great majority of Basoga have become quite serious Christians or Muslims; almost half the men have become literate. A money economy has come into being and the population of the district has doubled. A dozen warring petty kingdoms have been pacified and incorporated into a much larger political community. The smoothness with which all these changes have been accomplished and the fact that one could still, in 1950, meet an old gentleman who could plausibly claim to have seen "Sipiki" (J. H. Speke), the very first European to enter the district, should not blind one to the magnitude of the legal transformation that must have accompanied them.

Undoubtedly that body of legal ideas and procedures identified by present-day European administrators, and indeed by Basoga themselves, as "Soga customary law" is the product of a process of development in which whatever system of legal concepts that existed in, say, 1890 has been continuously molded by changing conditions. The absence in Busoga of a formal system of precedent and of machinery for case reporting makes it difficult to trace (and, indeed, to discipline) this process, but it quite clearly has occurred. Basoga judges have obviously been faced by substantially changing sets of "facts" which must, inevitably, have induced them to make new distinctions as they applied their received systems of legal concepts. And the judges, being themselves members of a changing society with a changing culture, must have come to look at old sets of "facts" in new ways. Sometimes one can discern at least the outlines of what must have happened. In those aspects of customary law that bear upon the status of women, in and out of marriage, Christian teaching and female education and

31. Section 11(*a*).
32. Section 18.

employment seem both to exert a constant pressure toward emancipation of women and to induce a conscious reaction in men, whose dominance seems threatened. In the field of land tenure, population increase and the resulting appropriation of reserves of unused land, together with the growth of a cash economy, have tended to make land a commodity in a sense in which it was not so before, and this appears to have resulted in an efflorescence of "customary" land law. In both fields, the arguments in present-day cases exhibit ranges of opinion which must reflect these processes of change—or so I shall argue.[33]

"Native law and custom" or, as I call it here, "customary law," is thus best identified simply with that part of the Soga courts' adjudicatory activity that is unencumbered by superordinate legislative authority, that in which the "rule of recognition" is that the courts have the authority to find law. It is the part of Soga law that, whatever its ultimate sources in ancient custom, old and new religion, and new forms of social experience, has been able to evolve freely out of the adjudicatory activity of the courts themselves. While it is with this part of Soga law that the body of this study will be mainly concerned, it is by no means the only source of law administered by the Soga courts. To give an adequate picture of the framework within which the courts work, I must briefly outline the other sources.

First of all, national legislation places certain restrictions upon the application of customary law. The racial limitations upon the courts' jurisdiction and the exclusion of capital offenses from their consideration have already been mentioned. In addition, they are forbidden to apply any customary law which is "repugnant to natural justice or morality" or "in conflict with the provisions of any law in force in the protectorate."[34] The "repugnancy clause" has long since done whatever work was expected of it and has ceased to be a source of legal issues. The "conflict clause" simply states the overriding authority of legislation and creates a potentially shifting borderline between customary and statute law. At the time of my observations, this borderline had for many years been relatively stable. It had been settled policy for the national legislature to refrain from legislating for Africans in a number of fields, while others had been subjected to legislative regulation. A brief outline of the provisions of the Native Courts Ordinance of 1941, the legislation under which the Soga courts were operating in 1950–52, will indicate the extent to which they were controlled by statute.

1. The courts were given the authority to enforce certain statutes,

33. See chapters 5 and 7.
34. Native Courts Ordinance, 1941, 11 (a).

such as the tax ordinances affecting Africans, parts of the Witchcraft Ordinance, and ordinances controlling the marketing of certain kinds of produce.[35] In addition, the African Authority Ordinance of 1919, from time to time amended, gave chiefs the authority to issue, for certain purposes, orders having the force of law, and the courts were given the authority to try cases arising out of disobedience to such orders.[36] Finally, the African Local Government Ordinance of 1949 gave the District Council subordinate legislative authority.[37] However, this authority, though it had existed in some form under earlier legislation since 1919, had not been made use of by Basoga and hence had resulted in no contribution to the law administered by Basoga judges. The district council had discussed much legislation, but had not enacted any.

2. At the same time, the Soga courts were expressly forbidden to apply any other legislation and in particular were forbidden to hear cases concerning matters governed by national land and marriage legislation.[38] These provisions are interesting and worthy of brief comment. Land law has been a subject of much controversy in Uganda. In neighboring Buganda, much of the land was, at an early date, surveyed and allotted to Baganda chiefs under legislation providing for freehold title.[39] Whether, and to what extent, such provisions should be extended to other districts was hotly debated. Basoga chiefs, envious of their Baganda counterparts, were anxious that this should be done in Busoga, while the protectorate administration resisted it. In the event, only a very small area of Busoga was surveyed and registered, the remaining land being left under customary tenure. The express removal of registered titles from the local courts' jurisdiction reflects the desire of the British administration to restrict and control the area of noncustomary tenure. The provisions regarding marriage legislation are designed to prevent a conflict of statute and customary laws. Probably most Basoga are today married by clergymen or Muslim *bawalimu* (from Arabic: *alim*), who are licensed marriage officers, and their marriages are thus regulated by the various national marriage and divorce ordinances. But, in order to prevent the complete suppression of customary law in this field, the Native Courts Ordinance provides that "a claim arising only in regard to bride-price or

35. Section 12.
36. Native Courts Ordinance 11 (*b*); African Authority Ordinance, 1919, 5, 7.
37. Section 6 (4).
38. Native Courts Ordinance, 1941, 10 (*b*).
39. The history of land policy in Uganda is well described in H. B. Thomas and A. E. Spencer, *A History of Uganda Land and Surveys and of the Land and Survey Department.*

adultery and founded only on native law and custom"—which is pretty much the only sort of question about which Basoga litigate in this field—is adjudicable in the local courts and without reference to national legislation.[40] Cases involving this curious dual jurisdiction will be encountered in chapter 4.

3. Finally, the Native Courts Ordinance regulates the procedure of the courts in various ways. It lists the penalties and remedies that may be imposed, provides for the power to summon witnesses and to try for contempt of court, forbids the appearance of advocates, and regulates appeals.[41] It also provides that "no proceedings in a native court and no summons, warrant, process, order, or decree issued or made thereby shall be varied or declared void upon appeal or revision solely by reason of any defect in procedure or want of form" and directs all judges to "decide all matters according to substantial justice without undue regard to technicalities." [42] This last provision is, of course, meant to protect the courts and their law from the intrusion of inappropriate British procedural niceties.

These limitations and injunctions are known and used by Soga judges with little attention to written sources. Many chiefs have one or more volumes of the *Laws of Uganda* in their offices, but they make little use of them. The small part of these volumes' content that concerns them—as judges—has been quite thoroughly absorbed into Soga legal culture and is applied almost as implicitly as are customary law notions.

It would, of course, be naïve to think that the influence of the British-type legal system that envelops the local courts has been limited to formal legislation. Basoga have contact with this system as litigants and witnesses. More importantly, chiefs are often called to serve as assessors in the national courts, where they observe with the keen interest of fellow law-users the work of British judges and advocates. It is, of course, extremely difficult to assess the influence of such experiences upon the work of the Soga courts, but my conversations with chiefs suggest that they deserve to be listed among the, at least potential, sources of contemporary Soga "customary" law.

THE INDIGENOUS SOURCE: LAW IN SOGA CULTURE

Under the British colonial legislation and administrative practice which applies to the Soga courts, then, much is left to "native law and custom." Marriage and land tenure, the two substantive fields with

40. Section 10 (b).
41. Sections 13, 16, 17, 20, 25, 26.
42. Section 27.

which this study is concerned, are very largely governed by law from this source. Actually, as I suggested in chapter 1, one might distinguish here two sources in interaction. Saying that custom is a *source* of law is not the same as saying that custom *is* law. It is not the whole complex of rules of obligation with respect to marriage and land tenure that the courts apply as "native law and custom," but rather a selection from this complex embodied in the legal concepts, such as "harboring," which make up the legal subculture. Some of the rules which are institutionalized in the mutual expectations of everyday life, in the ordinary business of marrying and carrying on family life, taking up and using land are again institutionalized in the courts. Of course where everyone pleads for himself and where judging is only a part-time specialty, the barrier between the general culture and the legal subculture is thin. Competence in the legal subculture is widespread; the judges are only somewhat more expert in it than the litigants who come before them. All parties come to court equipped with both popular moral ideas and the legal subculture and the interaction between them is continuous.

The sociocultural setting of marriage and land tenure and the legal concepts with which disputes in these fields are litigated and adjudicated will be the subject of the chapters that follow. It would be inappropriate to attempt to summarize them here. But in introducing the courts, it is appropriate to say a bit about the place of law and courts in Soga culture.

I have said that the Basoga value highly the legal mode of dispute settlement and the skills which it employs. Perhaps the most telling manifestation of this is the fact that the "rule of law" seems to be indigenous to Soga life. I use the term here to mean not simply the application of legal rules—the appropriateness of that notion to the Soga situation has already been discussed—but rather in the narrower, Anglo-American lawyer's sense: ". . . the judiciary, in ordinary legal proceedings, may pronounce upon the legal validity of the acts of the king's ministers and servants . . ." [43] In the Soga context, this means that the chiefs and headmen are subject to the same courts and law as other Basoga and that when they shirk their duties or exceed their authority they may, upon complaint by an ordinary citizen, be tried by the regular courts, rather than being simply disciplined administratively.[44]

43. Pound, "Rule of Law," p. 463.
44. As Pound notes, this principle is, in the Anglo-American tradition, both ancient and modern. It existed prior to the late medieval development of strong royal administrative organs and then, somewhat later, was reasserted as a check upon these organs. Ibid.

This principle has, of course, been embodied in British colonial practice. A provincial commissioner, who valued administrative "discretion," complained in 1919:

The knowledge that came to the natives through the issue of circular no. 1 of 1919 of the High Court that there were more limitations to the powers of district commissioners than the natives had imagined has had a serious effect on the native mind and, as he has seen that the district commissioners have been unwilling to carry out administrative punishments for offenses that do not come within the letter of the law . . . a decidedly retrograde tendency in administration has resulted which is deplorable.[45]

Basoga may well have been surprised (and pleased) to discover that British administrators were subject to judicial restraint. They cannot, however, have found the idea novel, for there is every indication that they and their ancestors shared it. The early casebooks, as well as present-day ones, are full of cases in which Basoga officials have been brought to trial for malfeasance. In the first such case of which I have a good account, one Azedi Bwami, parish chief Musaale of subcounty Ssaabawaali, Kigulu, was charged with an offense recalling that of King David against Uriah the Hittite: [46]

Zibairi Muwanika v. Azedi Bwami: the rule of law

Zibairi Muwanika brought his case in which he accused Azedi Bwami of Busowoobi of having chosen him to do corvée labor on the road, and when he returned he found Azedi Bwami in his [Zibairi's] house, sleeping with his [Zibairi's] wife. The name of the wife is Asya Nabirye, for whom he paid one cow and one goat as bridewealth. On August 9, 1920, the case was judged and it went against the accused, who was fined thirty-five rupees and assessed fifteen rupees compensation to Zibairi. (Rupees were then the local currency unit.) He was discharged from his chiefship and given ten strokes.

During 1923, in the same court, various chiefs and headmen were tried and convicted for failure to suppress rats, for neglecting the roads, and for wrongfully beating a peasant who had been slow in paying his taxes. King David, of course, being sovereign, could receive justice only from the hands of the Lord, and presumably Soga rulers were in a similar position. But Azedi Bwami and the others were mere public servants, whose acts were subject to judicial scrutiny. Actually, the courts of Busoga and Buganda carried the notion of the rule of law a step beyond anything known to the Anglo-American tradition by holding judges personally responsible for the correctness of their decisions. A decision found, upon appeal, to be incorrect became an offense

45. Report of the Provincial Commissioner, Eastern Province, for the Year Ended 31st March, 1919. Central Offices, Jinja.
46 2 Samuel, 11–12.

on the part of the judge. The procedure for appeal, in pre-British times, was for the unsuccessful litigant to accuse the trial court judge in these terms and to litigate with him, rather than with the unsuccessful litigant, before the appellate judge:

> But if the unsuccessful party in the action was not satisfied with the decision, he would not pay the debt or the court charges but instead would go to the next higher chief having authority over the chief who had decided the action against him and complain as follows: "Such and such a chief has decided my case badly and I complain against him." The chief who decided the case would be called in so that the appellant could plead [against him].[47]

If the appeal were successful, Basoga elders told me, the accused trial court judge might be fined. Although judges whose decisions are overturned are no longer punished, this view of things is retained in the way in which appellate cases are still commonly recorded in casebooks. As in the example shown in Appendix B, the "defendant" is recorded as the trial court, together with what Anglo-American law would call the "respondent." The "cause of action" is "wrongfully finding the appellant liable or guilty"—in this case of adultery.

It may seem paradoxical in view of this rooted attachment to legal process and to the notion that there is an objectively correct solution to every case, that the Lusoga and Luganda languages contain no word corresponding at all closely with the English word "law" and its Indo-European relatives. The compilers of the English-Luganda dictionary list three words: *etteeka, mpisa,* and *Ttawuleeti.*[48] The first, however, means only "enacted rules" or "legislation." It applies in ordinary speech to the rules a man lays down for members of his household as well as to those a political superior issues with respect to his subordinates. The noun is related to the verb *kuteeka* ("to put" or "to place"). Thus, the various councils which in present-day Uganda are empowered to legislate are spoken of as *lukiiko eteeka amateeka:* "council that enacts rules" or "laws." The word is, however, seldom used in the Soga courts. Curiously, its commonest use is in cases in which a litigant loses because he fails to appear in court and the matter cannot therefore be adjudicated on its merits. In such a case, a litigant is said to lose the case *"mu mateeka"* ("in law"). Basoga would agree that the various national ordinances and orders they are empowered to enforce are *mateeka,* but the word is almost never mentioned in cases in which offences against these enactments are alleged. Judges usually do not cite statutes or orders in their judg-

47. Kagwa, *Ekitabo kye Mpisa za Baganda,* p. 238.
48. E. M. K. Mulira and E. G. M. Ndawula, *A Luganda-English and English-Luganda Dictionary.*

ments in such cases, just as they do not cite customary rules in the abstract in cases in which those sources of law are involved. A man is simply accused, for example, of not paying his poll tax on time and the court goes on from there. "Everyone knows" what the relevant legislation requires.

Ttawuletti is simply a Bantuization of Torah and is the work of the missionary translators of the Bible. Its addition to the vocabulary of Baganda and Basoga indicates only that the missionaries, too, who in this part of Africa were often quite scholarly men, were at a loss for a Luganda equivalent of "law."

Mpisa means "custom" in the broad sense. That is to say, it covers morally relatively neutral regularities of behavior and the habitual conduct of individuals, as well as morally sanctioned group norms. Occasionally it may even be extended in conversation to the properties and behavior of nonhuman objects. Thus: "It is the custom of the rain to fall in the afternoon at this time of year." The idea of *mpisa* thus embraces a body of assumptions about the nature of man and the world, assumptions upon which the courts constantly draw in applying their legal concepts to the cases that come before them, but its meaning is far too broad for a satisfactory translation of the English "law." Still, when, very occasionally, litigants and judges *do* talk about rules, this is the term they most often use.

This absence of a clear-cut concept of law as the rules or concepts applied by courts is, perhaps, precisely what one would expect, given the inexplicitness of Basoga about the process by which they manipulate legal concepts. The judges shun the clearly stated *ratio decidendi* in their judgments. They have no machinery for collecting precedent-setting decisions from other courts and do not even refer in judgments to their own personal experience of previous cases. The statutes which they apply are few and well known. Unlike Jews and Muslims, they lack a body of religious scripture from which specialists are enjoined to derive a "law" for the guidance of judges (I neglect here the community of Muslim Basoga, who are of course familiar with the idea of *Sharia*, but who do not make courtroom use of it). Thus it is perhaps not surprising that the product of the central activity in which the courts engage—the result of their work of applying legal concepts to isolate issues for authoritative judgment—has no name in the language of the courts. I shall return to the possible significance of this in chapter 8; in any case, the words "law" and "legal" as used in this study are analyst's words, brought to the study from an external, comparative perspective: they are not native to Soga thought.

There is, however, a rich vocabulary for speaking about what goes on in court—apart from the specifically legal product that results from it. That which brings litigants to court is a *musango,* which means both "case" or "cause" and "fault." A case file is the record of *"musango* number so-and-so, in such-and-such a court, for such-and-such a year." At the same time, one "commits" *(kuzza)* a *musango.* In court, one "defeats" *(kusinga)* or "is defeated by" *(kusingibwa)* a *musango,* depending upon whether one wins or loses. A legal concept which embodies a cause of action, like "harboring," is an *ngeri y'omusango* —a "type of case."

In court the "accuser" *(muwaabi)* and the "accused" *(muwa- abirwa)* "plead" or "litigate" *(kuwoza)* by stating "reasons" *(nsonga)* and by giving "evidence" or "testimony" *(bujulizi).* *Nsonga* also means "grievance"; a complainant goes to the chief with an *nsonga* and the latter decides whether or not it forms a plausible ground for action— an *ngeri y'omusango.* A witness called to give testimony *(kujulirwa)* is *mujulizi.* The judges who meanwhile listen and ask questions are said to "adjudicate" *(kulamula),* a verbal form related to the noun *mula- muzi,* "judge." When all arguments have been heard, they "cut the case" *(kusala omusango)* by delivering their decision, *nsala:* literally, "the cutting."

This whole vocabulary is used for what is, in Soga minds, a special kind of activity. Its use calls forth a clear and well-known image: the standing litigants—passionate, eloquent, and self-righteous—address- ing with elaborate politeness the impassive, seated judges; the judges, questioning the litigants and witnesses with penetrating astuteness; the successful litigant, kneeling before the judges and thanking them effusively while cutting the air with palms pressed together in the customary gesture of gratitude. This vocabulary goes with this activ- ity, but it is not, as I have said, a full-time specialist's activity for either pleaders or judges. Professional advocates are absent and the judges are judges not because they are specialist jurists, but because they are chiefs. In precolonial times, the judicial function was—as it to a great extent remained in 1950–52—simply one aspect of general administrative authority *(bufuzi).* All rulers, chiefs, and headmen were ex officio judges and hence it was natural that the Kabaka of Buganda, and later the British officer in charge of the district, should also judge.

Indeed, this association between judicial and general administrative authority extends beyond the realm of government proper into every social situation in which authority is exercised. A father "cuts cases" among his children, a master among his household servants, a priest among his parishioners, an employer among his employees. I once observed a subcounty chief and his daughter "pleading" before their priest; the girl was due for confirmation, but she had lost her baptismal certificate and this was regarded as an offense. She was "convicted" and the fee charged for a new certificate was treated as a "fine." I myself, as an employer of servants and assistants, was occasionally called upon to fill the role of judge and was expected to know the requirements of the role. All these situations are spoken of in the idiom, and acted out with the gestures, of the courtroom. The Soga courts thus exist in a cultural environment pervaded by a belief in authority and in adjudication as the concomitant of authority.

An analysis of the meaning of the word for "court" makes the same point. In the letter quoted above, the British officer, Grant, says that he "held a *lukiiko* to settle cases." The verb *kukiika* means "to attend upon one's superior," for whatever purpose. The precolonial *lukiiko* was, it seems, a "court" in the old English sense of an assembly before a ruler to transact a mixture of legislative, executive, and judicial business. To be sure, the language recognized quite clearly that adjudication was a special kind of activity for a chief and his *lukiiko;* "cutting cases" was an activity quite different from issuing administrative orders (*kulagira:* "ordering" a specific course of action) or legislating (*kuteeka amateeka:* "laying down general rules"); [49] but just as the ruler or chief was a generalized authority as well as a judge, so the assembly that attended him was structurally undifferentiated with respect to the three classical functions of government.

Today this differentiation has partly taken place. The county or subcounty chief, at the time of my observations, met with his subordinate chiefs to discuss administrative matters, such as tax collection; he met with other groups of differing composition to hear law cases and to discuss local government legislation. The language had developed compounds of the word *lukiiko* to denote these various bodies, but all were still called, simply, "*lukiiko*" in ordinary speech and the chief was still chairman of all of them. One interesting linguistic development was a tendency to use "*lukiiko*" also to denote the Busoga African Local Government as a whole, as a corporate entity. (The British protectorate government was always "*gavumenti.*") Thus, A.L.G. property was "*lukiiko* property"; a messenger was sent on "*lukiiko* business"; the accuser in a criminal case was "the *lukiiko*" or "the *lukiiko,* together

49. In the most famous case of precolonial legislation, Kabaka Mutesa I of Buganda is said to have altered the system of succession and to have been followed in this by Basoga rulers. Today there are two successors: the "successor of the belt," who is a brother or patrilineal cousin; and the "heir of the property," who is ordinarily a son. Before Mutesa's legislation, it is said, the brother or cousin succeeded to both kinship status and property.

with the complainant." Generalized authority, which traditionally had resided in the person of the ruler or chief, had come to reside in a corporate abstraction. Authority was less personalized, but it was still highly generalized.

The place of adjudication in all this may be summed up by saying that, throughout the period under discussion, it was a distinct and highly valued art, with its own vocabulary and techniques, but an art widely diffused through the society and practiced by men who were not specialist jurists, but rather holders of generalized authority and responsibility.

Two more introductory tasks remain before I turn to an analysis of the use made by the courts of legal concepts. First, since the success of the courts in adjudicating disputes depends in large measure upon the character and status of the chief-judges who guide them, I shall say something more about these men. Second, I shall indicate the range of disputes that Soga society presents to its courts for adjudication—a range from which the case data to be discussed represent only a limited selection. Chapter 3 will be devoted to these matters.

I take judge-made law as one of the existing realities of life. . . .
Not a judge on the bench but has had a hand in the making.
—Benjamin Cardozo

The dynamic tensions which lead to law-stuff, feed it and give it material to work on, show up particularly in claims—*claims repudiated or resisted or merely unfulfilled; claims asserted as "right" or "rightful" in the going order of some particular group or entirety.*
—Karl Llewellyn

3 Judges and Dockets

My principal concern in this study is with Soga law and its application to the conflicts that bring Basoga to their courts. But law, like any cultural system, any system of ideas, is not a disembodied force; its influence in human affairs depends entirely upon its capacity to inspire and direct the intelligent action of individual men. More than this, law is a special set of conceptual tools which, though rooted in moral conceptions common to the community at large, is nevertheless, because of its necessity for "legalistic" moral oversimplification, always to some degree in tension with popular morality. If it is to retain both its intellectual integrity and its relevance to the problems of the society, it must be managed by men of ability who enjoy a good deal of legitimate authority in the eyes of their fellows. Basoga judges are not full-time specialist jurists, but they are serious amateur jurists, proud of their skill. The chief whom I knew best, for example, once boasted: "Thirty cases so far this year, and not a single one appealed!" The success of the Soga courts in maintaining and developing their law during a period of profound change and foreign domination is due in great measure to the fact that they have been presided over by men who have earned for themselves, and hence for the law they administer and the courts they serve, the respect of the people of Busoga. It is, therefore, relevant to examine the social backgrounds and social status of these men.

THE JUDGES

The principal custodians of Soga law are the county and subcounty chiefs who chair the bench in the county and subcounty courts. One important effect of British administration has been to make of these chiefs a corps of salaried civil servants, recruited and promoted on the basis of merit. They are therefore, on the whole, young men and relatively well educated. In 1952, there were sixty county and sub-county chiefs. Of the fifty-three whose ages I was able to ascertain, well over half (thirty-one) had not yet reached the age of forty-six.[1] Of the fifty-five for whom educational data were available, nearly half (twenty-six) had had some secondary education, while four had been to Makerere College. As my earlier sketch of the state of education in Busoga indicates, the chiefs are thus among the educational elite of their society. Their educational peers are limited to a small number of senior clergy and schoolmasters and an even smaller number of profes-sional and business men.

One reason these young men are accepted as the legitimate succes-sors of the chiefs of the past is that the "career open to talent" is not something new and unfamiliar in Busoga. The nineteenth-century rulers were hereditary, but most of their subordinates were men chosen from the commoner population for their military and administrative ability and their personal loyalty. Some of the criteria for success—notably education—are new, but social mobility is a familiar and admired pattern and education has been readily accepted as a means to its attainment. Another reason for the security of the chiefs' status is their relative wealth. In a society in which the average yearly cash income is a few hundred shillings, the chiefs may rise, at the top level of the county chiefs' scale, to a salary of 12,000 shillings. They live in official houses of high standard, receive pensions upon retirement, and, at the senior levels, may possess that most valued of all status sym-bols, a motor car. Finally, the new civil-servant chiefs tend to be related by kinship ties—often affinal or matrilateral rather than patri-lineal—to each other and to the traditional royal lineages. Figure 3 shows the kinds of ties that exist among ten county and subcounty chiefs for whom I was able to obtain data of this kind. These men do

---

1. These data were taken from the personnel records in the Uganda Govern-ment Central Offices, Jinja.

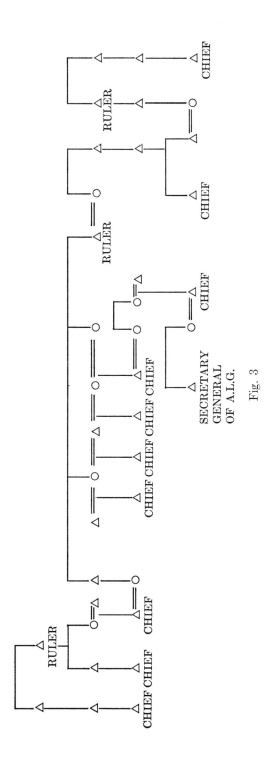

Fig. 3

not form a random sample of the total of sixty, but I have no reason to believe that they are unusual in this respect.

Again, the pattern is a familiar one; rulers often appointed to chiefly office men who were their mother's brothers or sister's sons, and whose loyalty could thus be counted on; and they frequently gave their daughters in marriage to favorite chiefs. Today, as in the past, the chiefs are members of an open, but kinship-interrelated, "establishment," whose legitimacy owes something to traditional ties but which is sufficiently open to attract the ambitious and the able.

One feature of the chiefly hierarchy, however, is I think quite new: its sense of professional solidarity. The nineteenth-century chief was above all a personal servant of his master. The contemporary Busoga African Local Government service is not without its self-serving networks of patrons, clients, and kinsmen,[2] but to an important degree the civil service esprit de corps has taken root among men who work in the full modern bureaucratic milieu of fixed salary scales, files, superior's reports, and regular transfers and promotions. The creation of a single service for the whole district has helped to break down territorial particularism. Of the fifty-seven county and subcounty chiefs in 1952 for whom data were available, 80 percent (forty-six) had been in their present posts less than four years. Few were serving in their home counties. The resulting sense of common calling and solidarity is apparent whenever chiefs meet; the conversation often turns around common problems, such as the difficulty of collecting taxes and the intricacy of land cases, and around the gossip of bureaucratic politics. To a significant degree, the chiefs live in a distinct professional world whose affairs can only be discussed with other chiefs. Thus, while they are not professional judges, they *are* in an important sense professional public servants.

A chief's jurisprudential knowledge and skill are largely learned "on the job" in subordinate posts. Much of this knowledge and skill, of course, is common property in a society in which attending court is a popular pastime and in which every litigant is his own advocate. His formal schooling probably helps a chief more in his other administrative work than in his judging. In recent years, special schools have been established by the Uganda Government to give chiefs short training courses in the various aspects of their work, but those who attend are mostly men who already have had some years of service behind them; the legal content of the courses is slight and is concerned

2. Lloyd A. Fallers, *Bantu Bureaucracy*, pp. 190–96.

more with Uganda-wide standards of procedure than with substantive law. The training courses draw chiefs from all parts of Uganda, while much of the substantive law administered by the courts is ethnic law, peculiar to each district. Such special knowledge of Soga law as a chief has when he first takes the chair in a subcounty court has usually been acquired in the years since he left school, during which period he will probably have served the A.L.G. either as a parish chief or as a court clerk, or both. Of the fifty-seven county and subcounty chiefs in 1952 for whom such data were available, 63 percent (thirty-six) had served as parish chiefs, while thirty-nine percent (twenty-two) had served as clerks. Seventy-two percent (forty-one) had served in one or the other of these capacities, both of which provide useful preparation. The parish chief, while he does not preside over a "court of record," hears many cases and tries to settle them before they reach the subcounty court. He also takes his turn sitting on the "official" side of the subcounty bench, and may preside for the subcounty chief in his absence. The clerk learns much from his work of recording testimony. Chiefs themselves believe that such experience is essential preparation for their judicial work. The minority of men who have been appointed directly to subcounty chieftainships from positions in education or in the Uganda national civil service are sometimes said to be poor judges because they are out of touch with the customary law which is the chief source of legal concepts in the Soga courts.

Such chiefs are not, of course, alone on the bench. Both they and their more experienced colleagues are assisted by subordinate chiefs and by the elected "unofficial members." Having been chosen by the county or subcounty council, these latter are likely to be men of some substance and standing in the community—men rooted in the community and related by kinship ties to many of its members, but a bit above average in terms of education, wealth, and experience. In the subcounty of Ssaabawaali, Kigulu, in 1952, for example, the panel of six unofficial members, from which two were drawn for service each month, consisted of a village headman, a wealthy cattle-breeder, and four farmers of more than average prosperity. One was a veteran of World War II service in the King's African Rifles. All were literate. Such men are extremely useful to the court. While the chiefs on the whole are more knowledgeable about the law, the unofficial members often know more about the "facts" of a case before the court and are often better able to elicit these from witnesses by shrewd questioning. Although the written case records do not indicate the identity of questioner from the bench—questions are simply recorded as coming from "the *lukiiko*"—my own observations of "live" cases showed that unofficial members often take an active part in both questioning and the determination of the judgment.

Still, the chiefs dominate the courts and it is upon their performance, ultimately, that the effectiveness and legitimacy of the Soga legal system rests. In order to acquire a better understanding of the outlook that these men bring to their work, I interviewed ten of them —one-fifth of the county and subcounty establishment. These are the men whose kinship relations are shown on the above diagram. All were questioned concerning their ancestry, their education, and their careers, and were asked to describe and comment upon their work as chiefs. A few extracts from the interviews with two subcounty chiefs, whom I shall call, fictitiously, Abudala Mukama and Samwiri Waiswa, will perhaps help to clothe my rather abstract descriptions of the chiefs and their work with flesh and blood. These two men are not, in any statistically meaningful sense, "representative" of the whole group; although quite different in character and background, both are better-than-average chiefs, having been more than usually successful in the difficult task of simultaneously holding the respect of their people and eliciting the approval of their superiors in the colonial government. Both presided over cases which will be discussed in later chapters.

Samwiri Waiswa is (1952) thirty-nine years of age, a Christian, speaks good English, and has recently taken over his second subcounty chieftainship. He is a small, restlessly vigorous man, articulate about himself and his work. In answer to my questions, he describes his ancestry and early life: [3]

I was born in Bubiri in 1913. My father, Waiswa, was *katikkiro* (prime minister) to the ruler of the area. His father had been a servant of the ruler and his father's father had been *katikkiro*. Waiswa used to go to Buganda with the *katikkiro* on the ruler's business and the ruler noticed that he served well, so when the *katikkiro* died, Waiswa was made *katikkiro*. He was also given a subvillage in which he is still headman.

I went to Iganga Central School in 1925 and stayed until 1932. My father, Waiswa, sent me and paid my fees—twenty-five shillings each year for the first four years, thirty-two shillings for the last three. Then, in 1932, they opened the Health Office and the doctor in charge asked for boys who could speak English. He sent a request around to the county chiefs and my chief chose me. Twelve of us went to take the examinations and four of us passed.

The first Europeans I knew well were Dr. Grant, the district health officer, and Dr. Phillips, the provincial health officer. (The school I went to had only

3. The personal and place names in these accounts have been disguised.

African teachers.) Then there was Mr. MacDonald, the health inspector, and Mr. Barrow, the inspector in Kigezi District, where I was sent in 1934. Mr. Barrow and I invented "Barrow's Disinfector." They had an outbreak of plague there in 1934 and many people were dying. If I had been a European, they would have called it "Waiswa's Disinfector," because I did most of the work. I still have my notebooks that show the experiments I carried out. We tried "cynogas"—that American stuff—but it didn't work. But I had seen our mothers using a Soga device—two baskets, one on top of the other. You put cow dung in the bottom one and burn it. It burns slowly, like a cigarette. The fumes come up into the top basket and the heat and smoke kill the lice. You put the people's clothing in there and they're disinfected. They found that it worked, so they published it, and sent the notice around to schools and prisons.

In 1935, I was called back to Jinja to work with Dr. Allen, the provincial medical officer, and with Mr. Beattie and Mr. Williams, the health inspectors. The doctors never went on *safari* [tour] without me. We inspected prisons and dispensaries and I was interpreter. Then, in 1939, the war came and Dr. Allen and Mr. Beattie were seconded to the army. I was transferred to be a clerk in the hospital in Soroti.

When I was transferred back to Jinja, the district commissioner, Mr. Barberton, already knew me. He had noticed that the medical officers always asked me to do things. He had heard them say, "Samwiri, do this, do that. . . ." Sometimes I had interpreted for him. So one day he met me outside the office and asked me if I wanted to be a parish chief. He said he had just been on *safari* and had discharged most of the parish chiefs. He said he had a list of names for new ones, but that if I liked he would scratch off one of the names and add mine. He said: "Think it over for five minutes!"

So I went to see a friend of mine who was a clerk in the office and asked his advice. He said it was a good opportunity. The D.C. said I might have to take a cut in salary and that he couldn't promise I would become a subcounty chief, but that I would be serving my country, so I agreed.

The D.C. sent my name to Omw. Wambi,[4] the county chief of Kigulu. But Omw. Wambi didn't know me and I knew he would be surprised when he saw my name. So I got on the four o'clock bus and went to see him. I said: "When you get the list of new parish chiefs, you will see a name you don't know." He asked me whose name that would be, and I answered that it would be mine. He said: "That's fine!"

When my master in the health office heard that I was going to be a chief, he didn't want to part with me and complained to the D.C. We had quite a struggle! But the D.C. finally said: "We are here to represent King George. We want to teach these people self-government and we need capable people." So I started as a parish chief on July 1, 1940.

I served in two parishes and then volunteered for the army in April 1942. I served for two years and 185 days as a clerk in the East African Army Service Corps and was discharged as a corporal, first class. When I returned from the army, I became assistant county chief. In May, 1949, I was made a subcounty chief.

4. Omw. is an abbreviation of *omwami*, the traditional word for chief. It still means "chief," but in addition it has come to mean "Mr."

Omw. Waiswa reads two newspapers regularly and takes a lively interest in international affairs. He questioned me closely about the atomic bomb because, he said, "The people have heard it can blow up Busoga and they ask me to explain it to them." The current rise of nationalism and the beginnings of decolonization in Africa had his full sympathy. He was particularly indignant about the temporary return of Somalia to Italian trusteeship because "so many of our brothers [in the East African forces] died liberating it." He was critical of Uganda government schemes for resettling areas formerly depopulated by sleeping sickness because, he felt, they took insufficient account of traditional land rights. In general, he thought, European officials were too out of touch with the people:

My workers are building a camping shelter right near the headquarters so the D.C. won't have to stay in the rest house over on the hill when he comes on *safari*. It's too isolated. But the shelter probably won't do any good. The D.C. will just come, go shooting, eat, sleep, get up, hold a formal meeting, and leave. People won't get to know him any better. In my father's time, before they had cars, the D.C. stayed longer and got to know people much better.

But Omw. Waiswa believes that his work as a chief is essential to the progress and well-being of Busoga:

I attended the chiefs' training course at Bukalasa. We learned the facts about the various government departments, but not much else. Chiefs can't be taught. The work is not technical, like that of a doctor. The great thing is common sense—knowing how to deal with people. You must be able to teach them how to build latrines, how to use good agricultural methods, how to grow cassava for famine reserves. There are rules that say these things *must* be done, but if a chief fined everyone who disobeyed, he'd soon be sacked for not having common sense. He should just fine one or two in each village as an example for the others. Sometimes, if you fine too many, the D.C. returns the fines. Then the people talk about the chief's mistakes and make his position impossible. In the regulations, it says that the chiefs should keep regular office hours, but you can't do that. The chief's job extends to all hours. If people come at odd hours with problems, you must deal with them.

I spent a good deal of time around Omw. Waiswa's courtyard and was in a position to observe what he meant. One evening, after the household had retired, a group of young men came up the path, dragging a young woman and calling for the chief. After he had emerged, seated himself on the veranda, and had a few words with the men, he began to question the girl very sternly. It seems that she had left her husband in Busiki county some two months before. Omw. Waiswa knew of this because the husband had reported it to his own chief and the A.L.G. had sent around a circular. The husband had heard that she was living in a nearby village with one Dauda and had come yesterday to get permission from Omw. Waiswa to search for her. This evening, they had hidden themselves near Dauda's household and when she returned from the well, they had seized her, though Dauda had escaped. This, Omw. Waiswa observed, was foolish of him because "everyone knows him." The girl admitted that her husband had paid bridewealth for her, but claimed that Dauda was a relative, not a lover. Omw. Waiswa told the husband to bring the girl's father to court the next day and ordered the guard, who had meanwhile been fetched, to take the girl to the county jail for safekeeping, since she was a "stranger, who might run away."

On another occasion, we were all awakened in the middle of the night by the drumbeat that indicated someone had died violently. Omw. Waiswa immediately appeared, called his guard, and went off to investigate. It turned out that a young man in a neighboring household had hanged himself because, it was said, his mother had opposed his marriage to the girl of his choice. Omw. Waiswa commented on the "foolishness" of the young man: "Life is the most valuable thing we have and he just threw his away." On this occasion, the chief was up most of the night, for this was a case for the central government courts. The central government police had to be summoned to investigate; meanwhile Omw. Waiswa had to see to it that the body remained undisturbed.

Among the chief's problems is kinsmen who expect special treatment:

I can't let her [his father's sister] come straight to me with the case. She must go through the proper channels—she must go to the parish chief first. Otherwise people will think I let her bring it straight to me because she is related to me. But she can't understand that.

On the tendency of some people to engage in useless litigation:

Some people are born thieves, some are born fornicators, and some are born appealers, like Musa. When he brings a case, it always ends in the high court, and he always loses.

Abudala Mukama is a different sort of man in many ways. He is muscular and forceful—the image of what Basoga call, admiringly, a "real man." A forty-five-year-old Muslim, he has had little formal education and speaks no English. It is perhaps for this reason that his account of himself reflects much more distance from, and uncertainty about, his European superiors.

I was born in Bubanda in 1907. We were the rulers of that area. The last real ruler was my father's father. Then [when British administration was established], the kingdom was divided among several counties. My father was the successor who speared the cow over the grave of my grandfather and was chosen by the clan, but another son was chosen by the clan and the government to act when the kingdom was reunited to form a county. But he was not the real ruler. The important thing is spearing the cow.

For three years, I went to school. Then I learned to play the lyre and went about playing at weddings and funerals. My father was hereditary chief of one part of the kingdom, so he made me a subvillage headman, and later a village headman. I still own them, but I leave them in the hands of a *musigire* [steward]. I worked in my village for one year, and then went to work for an Indian jeweler, who taught me to make rings out of copper coins. After that, I worked for a Muganda, who was a mechanic at the cotton gin at Kaliro. From 1919 to 1940, I worked in many gins in Busoga, Bugisu, Budaka, and Bukedi. Then, in April, 1940, I went to Iganga to be chosen for chieftainship by the D.C., *Bwana* Boyle.

I was sent to Bulopa as a parish chief. Then, in 1945, I was sent to Bulange, but I stayed only two months. In 1946, I was made acting subcounty chief at Namutumba, and in 1948, I was made subcounty chief here. I was well thought of by the D.C.s. They brought me here because there were many unpaid fines here. I soon cleaned them up! I was able to finish up all those fines because I rule with great force! They wanted to transfer me to Kibale for the same reason, but the Kyabazinga refused because the chief there is one of his people [a member of his faction within the A.L.G. service] and it is a good post.

As you can see, I am strong as a lion! What I say need not be repeated! In 1950, an order came from Entebbe [the capital of Uganda] to issue cassava for famine reserve plots to five subcounty chiefs in this county. The agricultural officer sent a lorry to take the cassava around to the subcounty chiefs. They told the subcounty chiefs to get workers to plant the cassava and said their pay would be supplied by the government. After a while, the agricultural officer started going around to inspect the plots. He went to the first subcounty and found nothing. Then he went to the second, and found nothing there. He was angry and wanted to kick the agricultural assistant. Then he went to the third subcounty, and still he found nothing growing. He was *very* angry, and started to drive away in his car, leaving the agricultural assistant to go on foot. But he finally took him in his car and brought him here. When they arrived, they found me away at Bugembe (the A.L.G. headquarters), but my assistant was here. They asked him to show them the plot, and he straightway took them to where the cassava was growing. The A.O. thought it was an excellent garden and asked my assistant: "How did the chief manage to do this so well?" So my assistant explained that I first told the workers to prepare the garden well. Then I had them make holes, in rows, and after planting the cassava, I told them to fill the holes with fertile soil from another place. Finally, he explained that I had them cover each hole with grass so that when the dew came at night it would be caught and held by the grass and help the cassava to germinate. The A.O. was busily writing all this down. Afterward, he asked: "Why do they call this chief to Bugembe when he is so busy helping his people?"

Then they went to the last subcounty and again they found no cassava. The chief explained that he had planted it, but that the weather had been dry and the ants had eaten it. The A.O. replied: "I suppose it rained in Mukama's subcounty!" (just a few miles away) And he went away, angry again.

When the D.C.s are on *safari*, they always eat lunch here. Perhaps it's because my wives prepare the food so well. It's a rule with D.C.s always to stop here for lunch.

Omw. Mukama today feels that he understands Europeans and knows how to deal with them. Certainly he has been successful in this, judging from the high regard in which administrative officers hold him. He recalls, however, that his first real personal encounter with Europeans, when he was nearly thirty, frightened him greatly. He had not yet been made a chief and was leading the agitation of a group of headmen against a proposal to allot part of the land of the district in freehold estates:

The headmen were arguing with the government; they didn't want the land divided into acres. They complained and said that the villages and subvillages were made by God. They said that the swamps are our boundaries and that they didn't want a survey. So the D.C. asked who the leader of the headmen was. They said it was I and so the D.C. called me to his house at nine o'clock in the evening. I went and told the Kyabazinga about it and he said: "Since I have been Kyabazinga, I have never been called to the D.C.'s house at night. You'd better go tomorrow." But I said: "I don't care if they eat me.[5] I must go there and find out why they called me."

So I started out for the D.C.'s place on my bicycle. When I reached Jinja, the police caught me and asked why I was riding in the town at night without a light. I said: "Go ask the D.C.—he's the one who called me at night." They took me to the corporal of the guard, who gave me another policeman to take me to the D.C. When we arrived, the D.C. agreed that he had called me and ordered the policeman to wait until we were finished so he could escort me safely home.

Then they put me in a room in the D.C.'s house. The D.C. ordered his servants to bring me food. Then he left me to eat. After I had eaten, I heard a car outside, and English voices. I didn't understand and thought I was to be eaten. Then a messenger called me to the office where the Englishmen were. On my way, I opened my knife in my pocket in case they tried to kill me! When I arrived, I saw all white faces, and I trembled! I was the only black man. There were ten of them—the police captain, the agricultural officer, the

5. There is a longstanding and widespread myth in Busoga that Europeans are cannibals. Mothers sometimes try to frighten children into obedience by threatening to "feed them to the Europeans." This imagery is not, however, associated exclusively with African-European relations. Throughout much of Bantu Africa, the word for "eating" is used to express a wide range of meanings associated with power and property. In traditional Busoga, a ruler who conquered a neighboring territory was said to "eat it." Today, a man who secures for himself an appointment to chieftainship "eats" the office and an embezzler "eats" the money he misappropriates. When Omw. Mukama recounted the above story he laughed at his fear of being "eaten"; but at the time he was, quite obviously, terrified by the strangeness of the situation.

veterinary officer, and others, but I recognized only the D.C. When I was asked to speak, I said: "I am speaking in the name of the people of Busoga. It's about our land. Long ago, the land was divided by God for our people. The swamps are the boundaries of our villages and subvillages. They were not invented by the people or the government. We don't want our land divided into miles and acres. The idea of dividing the land hurts the hearts of the Basoga. Among you is the provincial commissioner, but I don't know which one he is."

Then the D.C. replied: "Go and prepare a letter in Luganda and English and put there the words you have spoken. I will send it to the P.C., who is in England." The meeting was over and the D.C. put me in his car and took me home. Next day the car came to get me to fetch my bicycle. I had a friend translate my letter and I sent copies to the D.C., the P.C., the Kyabazinga, and the Governor. I signed it. The Governor replied, and I still have the letter.

Omw. Mukama's parting shot to me, following a discussion of the history of Busoga:

> There are two kinds of Basoga: the first loves Busoga, the second loves the protectorate government. The first will tell you one kind of history, the second will tell you another kind. You must judge which is right!

Despite their many differences, both these men illustrate the qualities that have enabled the hierarchy of chief-judges to maintain and develop Soga law as a vigorous system of ideas, legitimate in the eyes of both the Basoga villagers who submit their disputes to it and the British administrators who oversee it. Both men have roots in the traditional elite of rulers and client-chiefs and are deeply loyal to their society. Both are firmly convinced of the importance of their work and of the necessity to approach it with the combination of authoritative self-assurance and imaginative efficiency that will earn for them *kitiibwa*—honor, respect, glory—in the eyes of their people. Both are ambitious and intelligent career civil servants who, by responding to the rather different opportunities open to them, have acquired a good deal of experience of the forces shaping modern Soga life. Both have been able to work with, and learn from, the British administration while remaining sufficiently critical of it to avoid becoming alienated from their own people.

"TROUBLE SPOTS": THE SOCIAL SOURCES OF LITIGATION

The corps of chief-judges, made up of men like these, together with the unofficial members of the benches and the court clerks, represent one locus of institutionalization of legal culture in Soga society. The other is, of course, the rest of Soga society itself, especially those aspects of it which are productive of litigation.

In the chapters which follow, I shall analyze the way in which the

Soga courts make use of their system of legal concepts to adjudicate some of the kinds of disputes that commonly arise in two spheres of Soga life. In order to understand the judges' use of the concepts in actual cases, I shall, in each of these chapters, have to add to the outline account of Soga society given in chapter 2 some additional detail concerning the institutional framework in the spheres of life out of which the cases to be discussed arise. A reasonably complete understanding of this framework is necessary because, while law itself, as I view it here, is a cultural system—a system of ideas with a logic of its own—it is a cultural system which is bound up in a particularly intimate way with the social system—the system of normatively governed social relations—in which the persons who make use of it for litigating and adjudicating participate.

Law is a system of ideas for thinking about and, most importantly, for reaching authoritative moral judgments about, social behavior. But if legal thought and judgment are unquestionably normative phenomena, they are not, as I have argued, coextensive with the everyday morality of the community. Legal thought involves a simplification and rationalization of everyday morality. An accuser is a person who feels he has been treated wrongly by the standards of the commonly accepted norms and he comes to court with the hope that he can persuade the judges that the treatment he has received is illegal, as well as immoral. Thus the legal ideas made use of by judges must provide conceptual tools for distinguishing legal standards from merely moral ones. This distinction, of course, presupposes an understanding of the pattern of common moral standards institutionalized in the social system at large. The judges and litigants, especially in a relatively undifferentiated society, share an implicit understanding of this institutional background to the process of legal debate and judgment, but for the outside observer it must be explicitly grasped if the legal process and the problems it confronts are to become intelligible for him.

This, however, is not all. The wider social system is more than merely the moral environment of the legal process—the source of the moral norms which the legal process reshapes into legal norms by means of legal concepts. It is also the matrix out of which disputes arise—the source of "trouble cases," to use Llewellyn and Hoebel's phrase.[6] Society orders its members' behavior, but it also "disorders" it in typical ways, so that each society seems to produce its own characteristic types of dispute—its own peculiar profile of conflict. At first

6. K. N. Llewellyn and E. Adamson Hoebel, *The Cheyenne Way*, chapter 2.

glance, these statements seem paradoxical. "Society," "social system," "institutional framework," "moral norm"—these terms call to mind harmony, order, predictability in social relations. But social scientists have long since learned that sociocultural systems are not most use-fully regarded as mechanical systems of smoothly articulating parts. The interaction in behavior of the logic of ideas, the drives of personal character and the demands of interpersonal relations results not in complete harmony, but rather in a kind of ordered struggle, in which conflict often plays as great a part as consensus. All sociocultural systems seem to call upon their members to do some things which, because of obligations to others, or because of conflicting beliefs and values, or because of personal psychic needs, they do not wish to do and seek means of avoiding. Both the demands and the resistance to them, being rooted in social, cultural, and personality systems, are patterned. Thus societies have their characteristic "trouble spots" out of which disputes sprout like weeds. In societies whose members take their trouble cases to courts of law, these trouble spots shape the docket—give pattern to the traffic of litigation that flows through the courts. Arising from such troubled areas of social life one may expect to find more frequent—and more interesting (from the point of view of an analysis of legal concepts in action)—litigation.

SOME SAMPLE DOCKETS

In the remainder of this chapter I shall examine the dockets of a number of Soga courts for what they may reveal concerning the trouble spots in Soga society that are most productive of litigation. This is not, of course, to suggest that the sheer frequency with which a particular area of social life produces cases in court is an adequate measure of its interest or importance for the study of the legal process. In Soga courts, as in American ones, some areas of life productive of much court action produce little litigation that is interesting in the sense of revealing much about the problems faced by the courts in applying legal concepts to conflict situations, while other areas, from which relatively little litigation arises, produce case material of much greater significance in this respect. In the United States, minor motor traffic cases are very frequent and are "important" socially in that they perhaps represent the average citizen's commonest contact with the legal process; but the conceptual issues such cases raise are seldom profound. Frequently, indeed, the issues are so insignificant that they are not litigated at all, the accused simply pleading guilty and paying his fine by mail. On the other hand, constitutional cases involving relations between the federal government and the states, which make up only a tiny proportion of the total volume of litigation and involve very few citizens directly as litigants, often raise the most fundamental legal issues.

More revealing of the legal significance of an area of social life than the simple frequency of cases arising from it is the difficulty experienced by the courts in "settling" those cases—in arriving at judgments

TABLE 1

CASES HEARD IN THE SUBCOUNTY COURT OF
SSAABAWAALI, BULAMOGI, DURING 1950

1. *Offenses against the State*	
"Disobedience"	188
Tax evasion	35
Dereliction of duty and abuse of office	10
Contempt of court	—
2. *Breaches of Marital and Sexual Norms*	
Adultery	11
Fornication	3
Harboring	6
"Eating two hens"	4
Wife-beating	5
Bridewealth	19
Refusal to accept repayment of bridewealth	—
Rape	—
3. *Rights in Land*	
Individual holding	7
Subvillage	—
Village	—
4. *Rights in Livestock*	14
5. *Other Debts*	24
6. *Offenses against Persons and Property*	
Damage by straying livestock	15
Other property damage	6
Bicycle accidents	5
Theft	42
Arson	7
Threatening	2
Beating	26
Slander	10
Robbery	—
7. *Other*	4
Total	443

from which the litigants do not feel it necessary or worthwhile to appeal to a higher tribunal. Tables 1, 2, and 3, which summarize the cases heard in an ascending series of Soga courts during the year 1950, provide a crude basis for judging the "difficulty," in this sense, of

TABLE 2

CASES HEARD IN THE COUNTY COURT OF
BULAMOGI DURING 1950

	Appeal	Original	Total
1. *Offenses against the State*			
"Disobedience"	2	5	7
Tax evasion	—	—	—
Dereliction of duty and abuse of office	17	30	47
Contempt of court	1	2	3
2. *Breaches of Marital and Sexual Norms*			
Adultery	3	—	3
Fornication	—	—	—
Harboring	2	—	2
"Eating two hens"	1	1	2
Wife-beating	—	—	—
Bridewealth	5	—	5
Refusal to accept repayment of bridewealth	—	—	—
Rape	—	—	—
3. *Rights in Land*			
Individual holding	7	—	7
Subvillage	—	—	—
Village	—	—	—
4. *Rights in Livestock*	3	—	3
5. *Other Debts*	6	—	6
6. *Offenses against Persons and Property*			
Damage by straying livestock	7	—	7
Other property damage	1	—	1
Bicycle accidents	—	—	—
Theft	10	6	16
Arson	—	1	1
Threatening	2	—	2
Beating	7	2	9
Slander	1	1	2
Robbery	2	—	2
7. *Other*	3	2	5
Total	80	50	130

various types of cases. The subcounty court of Ssaabawaali, Bulamogi (table 1), is a court of "first instance" in the sense that it is the lowest court of record in its area of jurisdiction. As indicated in chapter 2, the cases it hears will normally have previously come before the subvillage and village headmen and the parish chiefs for "arbitration," but none of these officials presides over a court of record recognized by the national legal system. The county court of Bulamogi (table 2) is the court of appeal from Ssaabawaali's court and from the other four subcounty courts of Bulamogi, while the Busoga district court (table

TABLE 3
CASES HEARD IN THE BUSOGA DISTRICT
COURT DURING 1950

	Appeal	Original	Total
1. *Offenses against the State*			
"Disobedience"	2	—	2
Tax evasion	—	—	—
Dereliction of duty and abuse of office	14	1	15
Contempt of court	—	—	—
2. *Breaches of Marital and Sexual Norms*			
Adultery	1	—	1
Fornication	—	—	—
Harboring	2	—	2
"Eating two hens"	1	—	1
Wife-beating	—	—	—
Bridewealth	6	—	6
Refusal to accept repayment of bridewealth	2	1	3
Rape	1	—	1
3. *Rights in Land*			
Individual holding	101	—	101
Subvillage	25	—	25
Village	13	—	13
4. *Rights in Livestock*	11	—	11
5. *Other Debts*	23	—	23
6. *Offenses against Persons and Property*			
Damage by straying livestock	1	—	1
Other property damage	1	—	1
Bicycle accidents	—	—	—
Theft	20	—	20
Arson	1	1	2
Threatening	1	—	1
Beating	6	—	6
Slander	3	1	4
Robbery	4	—	4
7. *Other*	6	—	6
Total	245	4	249

3) is the appeallate court for all the eight county courts of Busoga. In addition, both the county and the district courts are courts of first instance in certain cases, as tables 2 and 3 indicate. The three courts thus provide a "vertical sample section" of the Soga legal system. By comparing the proportions of total cases they make up at the three levels, it is possible to judge the relative difficulty the courts experience in settling the various types of cases.

Two of the commonest types of cases at the lowest, or subcounty, level arise out of accustations of tax evasion and what is known in

Soga court parlance as *butawulira* or "disobedience" (literally: "not listening"). The first is an offense under the national tax legislation which the Soga courts are empowered to administer; the second represents breach of any of a multitude of rules issued by administrative officers and chiefs under the authority of the African Authority ordinance of 1919 and its subsequent amendments. Among such rules are those requiring the burning of cotton plants following the harvest to suppress plant diseases; regulating the time, place, and manner of marketing certain kinds of produce; setting safety standards for bicycles; licensing the brewing of beer; enforcing the construction of latrines; regulating the movement and slaughtering of livestock; requiring the reporting of births and deaths, and in other ways providing for public health, safety, and welfare under modern conditions. Together, the tax and disobedience cases, involving alleged breach of government laws and rules quite unknown to Soga customary law, account for half (223 out of 443) of all cases at the subcounty level. Few of either sort, however, are appealed; the county court heard only 5 such cases (out of 80) and the district court only 2 (out of 243) in 1950. My examination of full case transcripts indicates, furthermore, that such cases are seldom seriously litigated by the accused, who generally admit their guilt and pay their fines without contest upon first hearing in the subcounty court. These are the "minor motor traffic cases" of the Soga courts and they are of little interest to this study.

"Dereliction of duty and abuse of office" is a category of greater interest, and one which I have already mentioned in discussing the "rule of law" in chapter 2. Generally, it includes all those cases arising out of the alleged failure of public servants—members of the African Local Government hierarchy—as well as private persons who, because they have been co-opted for public service or for some other reason, find themselves under direct A.L.G. discipline, to carry out their duties properly, whether out of corrupt self-interest or simple lassitude and indifference. As the rather large number of such cases indicates, the maintenance of discipline within the A.L.G. organization constitutes a rather prominent part of the courts' work, reflecting the relatively undifferentiated structure of government in Busoga and the readiness with which formal court proceedings are resorted to. The court of which a chief is chairman hears allegations of breach of public duty against all officials and citizens who may be under his authority. A parish chief who is insufficiently zealous in urging his people to build latrines or to pay their taxes; a prison warder who, through carelessness, allows a prisoner to escape; and even a prisoner who commits some minor breach of prison rules, such as smoking in a forbidden place—all of these may be formally charged and, if convicted, fined a few shillings. The relatively large number of cases of the last sort (involving prisoners) originating at the county level, incidentally, is for the most part due to the fact that even prisoners convicted by, or awaiting trial in, subcounty courts, are kept in county prisons, under the authority of the county chief, whose court thereby acquires jurisdiction over all breaches of prison discipline, however minor. In one case, for example, the county court of Bulamogi found a prisoner guilty of allowing a goat, for which he was responsible as part of his work on the prison farm, to stray away; found guilty, the accused was fined 9.80 shillings and imprisoned for an additional two weeks.

Not all cases in this category are so trivial, however. Basoga public servants, like their counterparts elsewhere, occasionally succumb to the temptations of corruption. Bribery is not common, I believe, but it sometimes occurs, and when detected may result in charges against both giver and receiver. In 1950, for example, the county court of Bulamogi upheld the conviction in a lower court of a man accused of offering a bribe to the subcounty council to excuse him from poll tax on grounds of senility—an authority given to the council in connection with its responsibility for drawing up tax lists.

Charges of abuse or neglect of authority do not always originate within the A.L.G. hierarchy; the courts also offer redress to ordinary citizens who feel themselves mistreated by public servants. In 1950, for example, the county court of Bulamogi heard a woman accuse a *katikkiro* (deputy chief) of humiliating her, while she was being held for trial in the county prison, by refusing to give her her clothes. She had been arrested in a state of *déshabillé* while meeting her lover. The courts also, of course, hear complaints by public servants falsely accused of malfeasance by private citizens. In 1950, the Busoga district court found another *katikkiro* had been falsely accused of bribery by a citizen and awarded him ten shillings compensation.

One final case, heard in 1950 by the county court of Bulamogi, is worth citing in exemplification of the court's work in maintaining proper standards of government. I noted in chapter 2 that village and subvillage headmen are not officially part of the A.L.G. judicial and administrative hierarchy—they are not, for example, salaried and their adjudicating activities are not recorded. Soga customary law, however, gives them extensive authority over, and responsibility for, their villages and subvillages, and the courts of record acknowledge and apply these customary norms. In the case referred to, a village headman was found guilty of failing to respond to a "hue and cry" raised by neighbors when a thief attempted to break into a house to steal some cotton. In customary law, the headman is required to respond to such alarms, so the court fined him twenty shillings. Likewise, although village and subvillage headmen are not officially members of the A.L.G. organization, the courts of record uphold their right to give orders to private persons in the public interest.

Thus, cases arising out of the exercise of governmental authority constitute a significant part of the traffic in Soga courts and they are sufficiently serious, or difficult to settle, that they appear in the appeal courts in substantial numbers. The same is true of cases arising out of the field of sexual relations and marriage. At subcounty Ssaabawaali in 1950, these formed some 10 percent (48 out of 443) of all cases; the proportion was a bit larger at the county level, smaller at the district level. The commonest cases in this field are those involving accusations of adultery (an offense which, as will be seen in a later chapter, Basoga define in terms rather different from those familiar in western societies) and claims for the payment or repayment of bridewealth. The next commonest charge—"harboring"—has already been encountered in the illustrative case recounted in chapter 1. "Eating two hens" is a form of fraud perpetrated by a father or guardian who accepts bridewealth for his daughter or ward from two men simultaneously. "Refusal to accept repayment of bridewealth" is a form of divorce proceeding—the only form open to a wife in Soga customary law. A woman wishing to divorce her husband must persuade her father to offer to repay the bridewealth. If the husband refuses to accept it, the father may sue for "refusal to accept repayment of bridewealth," citing the wife's grounds for seeking a divorce.

By all odds the most difficult of all cases to settle are those involving claims to rights in land. In the "vertical sample section" of court dockets for 1950, land cases as a percentage of all cases rise from 2 percent at the subcounty level (7 out of 443) to 5 percent at the county level (7 out of 130) to 56 percent at the district level (139 out of 249). In Busoga as a whole, for which in a separate inquiry I gathered data on frequencies of land cases at all levels, the figures for 1950 were 6 percent at the subcounty level (635 out of 9,737), 30 percent at the county level (307 out of 1,019) and, again, since at the highest level the "vertical sample section" corresponds with the district as a whole, 56 percent in the district court. Bulamogi is thus not representative of Busoga as a whole in the frequency of land cases brought before its courts. One reason is that much of the county is relatively thinly populated; there is more uncultivated land available, less competition for already appropriated holdings. This is generally true of northern and northeastern Busoga. In addition, this part of the district has been

more stable demographically. During the early years of the present
century, a series of sleeping sickness epidemics killed many of the
inhabitants of the heavily populated southern and southwestern part
of Busoga and forced the survivors to take up residence elsewhere.[7]
The resettlement of the area, which is still in progress, has been
accompanied by many disputes between new settlers and previous
landholders or their descendants. Finally, the political structure of
Bulamogi is in some respects more traditional than that of many other
counties. The position of the subvillage and village headmen, who are
crucial figures in the institutional structure of landholding, is a good
deal stronger, and the traditional ruler of Bulamogi remains a powerful figure, able to assert his own authority in land matters. All these
factors tend to keep land out of the Bulamogi courts.

As tables 1, 2, and 3 suggest, Basoga classify as "land cases"
disputes over rights to village and subvillage headmanships as well as
those involving individual holdings. The same basic legal concepts
tend to be invoked in all three types of dispute. As will be seen, there is
much evidence to suggest that the proliferation of land disputes appearing before the courts, and in particular the proliferation of disputes over individual holdings, is a relatively recent phenomenon,
stimulated by social and economic changes which have come about in
recent decades. In analyzing land cases, therefore, I shall be dealing
not with a field of settled law, but with one in which law has been
actively developing in response to new conditions.

Cases involving claims to rights in livestock are quite common in
some parts of Busoga—particularly in the north and east, where stock
raising is a major activity.[8] There are, of course, two ways, broadly
speaking, in which claims to rights in livestock may come before a
court. On the one hand, livestock may form a part or the whole of the
consideration in a bridewealth contract or, less commonly, in a contract concerning rights in land; on the other hand, stock raising as an
activity in itself often gives rise to claims and counterclaims as animals are bought, sold, and lent. Only the latter cases are enumerated
under heading 4 in the tables; the others have appeared as land and
bridewealth cases. The customary law concerning rights in livestock is
well developed in Busoga and would reward careful study; its principal interest lies in the special characteristics of animals as a form of
property and the special legal concepts designed to take account of

---

7. H. B. Thomas and Robert Scott, *Uganda*, pp. 299–300. The worst ravages of
the disease occurred between 1901 and 1905.
8. Fallers, *Bantu Bureaucracy*, p. 50.

these. This is not, however, a field to which I will give further attention in this study.

The law with respect to livestock-holding is quite traditional and settled; the general law of debt (*bbanja*), on the other hand, is a rapidly developing one, as Basoga increasingly enter into new kinds of commercial transactions and new forms of enterprise. In the tables, heading 5 excludes debts arising from the more traditional fields of bridewealth contract and land- and livestock-holding; the rather substantial number of the other debt cases at all levels, and particularly in the category of appeals to the district court, suggests the importance of the challenge which new forms of economic action have presented to the courts. This, too, however, is a field I must neglect in order to give adequate attention to the fields of law which have been selected for detailed analysis.

Thus far, this classification of cases has been a sociological one; I have classified disputes in terms of the institutional spheres out of which they arise. The final heading in the tables, "offenses against persons and property," cuts across these social fields and classifies cases in which Basoga are alleged to have damaged each other or each other's property, either deliberately or through want of care, in terms of the means employed. Many of the cases tabulated under heading 6 might, on a strictly sociological classification, be counted under previous headings. A man may beat, slander, or turn his goats onto the fields of his neighbor because of a marriage or landholding dispute. My excuse for employing this mixed form of classification, however, is simply that Basoga themselves do so. The offenses listed under heading 6 are recognized as actionable wrongs quite irrespective of the previous relationship, if any, which may have obtained between the parties. The previous headings pertain to wrongs peculiar to particular forms of social relationship and their associated obligations. One might make the two bases of classification commensurable by describing the wrongs listed under heading 6 as offenses against common membership in Soga society generally—or, since the jurisdiction of the courts is territorial and not ethnic,[9] as offenses against common residence in Busoga.

Since most of the offenses listed under heading 6 are familiar to Western readers, a few brief comments on the peculiarities of the Soga situation will suffice. Particularly in densely settled and intensively cultivated southern Busoga, damage to crops by straying livestock is a

---

9. An exception is the city of Jinja, with its large non-Soga African population. There an ethnically mixed court attempts to apply the customary law of the coming parties before it.

constant problem. As in most agricultural communities, the burden of care is generally upon the grazier, not the cultivator, and the small boys who are usually entrusted with grazing animals are often less than vigilant. Accidents with bicycles are also relatively common and the courts have long since recognized the negligent and harmful handling of them as an actionable offense. Precolonial Busoga lacked wheeled vehicles and draft animals. As soon as cotton cultivation began to produce money income, bicycles were imported in large numbers and became for the Basoga and their neighbors what donkeys are to villagers of the Middle East. Today almost every household owns one and uses it for the transport of goods to market as well as for travel. Motor vehicles are also becoming common on the roads of Busoga, but accidents involving them are handled by the national courts.

Theft is quite common in Busoga, robbery relatively rare. When a Musoga sets out to appropriate his neighbor's movable property—crops, livestock, or bicycle—he generally does so by stealth. Violent confrontations are relatively rare and are usually precipitated by the consumption of alcohol—either the traditional *mwenge* (banana beer) or the modern *walagi* (locally distilled spirit, prohibited by national law). The beer party, a popular form of sociability, is the prelude to many of the complaints of beating. The deliberate, premeditated assault upon a man's person and property is more often accomplished through nocturnal arson—which goes far to explain the eagerness with which Basoga replace their thatched roofs with corrugated iron or aluminum sheets as soon as their financial resources permit it. Another popular means of interpersonal aggression is slander, or "spoiling a man's name," sometimes through quite obscene accusations. Village society, however, deplores and provides means of discouraging physical violence; when it occurs, most villagers recognize the obligation to raise a "hue and cry" (*kukuba endulu*) to bring headmen and chiefs to the scene to restore order. The latter, as I have said, are required by customary law to respond. Of course, not all cases of interpersonal violence come before the Soga courts; those in which death has resulted go to the national courts.

This review of a year's dockets from a vertical sample section of Soga courts has provided a sketch of the kinds of litigation that come before the courts today and of their institutional sources. A glance backward in time to the docket of a subcounty court for the year 1923, when British administration over the courts had been in effect for only a quarter of a century, will provide some indication of change in the traffic of cases over the twenty-seven years prior to my study (table

4). The data come from the subcounty court of Ssaabawaali in the county of Kigulu, the county to the south of Bulamogi, and thus are not directly comparable with those for the subcounty court in my present-day sample. The Kigulu subcounty has a substantially smaller

TABLE 4

CASES HEARD IN THE SUBCOUNTY COURT OF
SSAABAWAALI, KIGULU, DURING 1923

1. *Offenses against the State*	
"Disobedience"	2
Tax evasion	—
Dereliction of duty and abuse of office	8
Contempt of court	1
2. *Breaches of Marital and Sexual Norms*	
Adultery	7
Fornication	3
Harboring	12
"Eating two hens"	—
Wife-beating	—
Bridewealth	1
Refusal to accept repayment of bridewealth	1
Rape	—
3. *Rights in Land*	
Individual holding	—
Subvillage	7
Village	—
4. *Rights in Livestock*	12
5. *Other Debts*	11
6. *Offenses against Persons and Property*	
Damage by straying livestock	—
Other property damage	—
Bicycle accidents	—
Theft	1
Arson	1
Threatening	1
Beating	5
Slander	—
Robbery	—
7. *Other*	2
Total	75

population today (8,023) than the Bulamogi subcounty in the sample (11,503).[10] The difference must have been at least as great in 1923, when the populations of both will have been smaller than they are

10. These figures are from the census of 1948. See *African Population of Uganda Protectorate, Geographical and Tribal Studies,* pp. 20–21.

today.[11] The areas, naturally, differ in other ways as well. Despite the lack of strict comparability, however, certain crude differences and similarities in the two dockets seem worth taking note of.

First, there are few cases of "disobedience" and none of tax evasion, two of the largest categories of cases in the present-day sample. The explanation is simple in both instances. In 1923, the role of the British protectorate administration in promoting economic and social development was still very limited; it saw its task principally as that of maintaining peace and order and collecting sufficient revenue to support itself. The embryonic African Local Government—then known as the "Native Administration"—was similarly limited in its functions, and its courts had not yet been given authority to try cases under national tax legislation. During the period between the wars, however, and particularly after World War II, government became much more activist and many additional functions and powers devolved upon the A.L.G. Among the consequences, if the subcounty of Ssaabawaali, Bulamogi, is anything like representative, has been a doubling of the case load of the subcounty courts. Half its cases in 1950 concerned evasion of the poll tax and breaches of administrative rules.

With respect to cases arising out of alleged breaches of marital and sexual norms, one should perhaps be most impressed by the lack of apparent change during the twenty-seven years prior to the period of this study. While there are differences in the frequencies of various types of case under this heading, it seems quite clear that the tensions between husbands and wives and between husbands and their in-laws which are so productive of litigation in present-day Busoga have been a feature of Soga life for some time and are not the results of recent social change.

In the field of litigation over rights in land, on the other hand, there appear to have been important changes. In 1923, while there were seven cases in which rights in subvillage headmanships were contested, not a single case concerning rights in an individual peasant's holding appears on the docket. During 1950, in the same subcounty of Ssaabawaali, Kigulu, there were five such cases, while in the same year, in the Bulamogi subcounty which forms part of my sample, there were seven. This evidence, admittedly, is less than one would desire. One would like to see other dockets from other years and other subcounties for the early period, but unfortunately I was unable to find others that had withstood the ravages of fire and termites—the two scourges of record keeping in Uganda. Such as they are, however, these data suggest that

11. Between 1911 and 1948, the population of the district more than doubled. See Margaret C. Fallers, *The Eastern Lacustrine Bantu*, pp. 20–21.

changes have occurred in the field of land tenure with the result that rights in individual holdings are claimed in court much more often than formerly.

The final point suggested by a comparison of dockets separated in time by almost thirty years is an apparent general increase over this time span in allegations of offenses against persons and property. Perhaps such acts have in fact increased. Alternatively, as some informants have suggested, some of these offenses may, in precolonial times, have been dealt with outside the courts by retaliation and composition. By 1923, the A.L.G. courts may not yet have exerted effective jurisdiction over all of them.

I shall return to a consideration of the significance of these apparent continuities and discontinuities in the kinds of disputes Soga society brings before its courts in connection with the analysis of particular fields of law. In particular, I hope to probe further into the contrast between the relatively settled nature of the law of marriage and sexual relations and the continued development that seems apparent in the law of landholding.

Thus far I have considered only the kinds of cases that come before the official A.L.G. "courts of record"—the subcounty, county, and district courts. It will be recalled from the discussion of the structure of the court system in chapter 2 that these are not the only tribunals before which disputes are heard in present-day Busoga. Below the official courts are the tribunals of subvillage and village headmen and parish chiefs, in which these authorities attempt to settle by mutual agreement "civil" disputes—those involving claims to property. The same authorities are responsible for bringing to the courts of record "criminal" cases—those involving allegations of offenses in which "punishment" may be appropriate. In such cases, the proceedings of these lower tribunals take on the functions of a preliminary hearing. These tribunals require no further discussion here, for the headmen and parish chiefs very often appear as witnesses in the courts of record, where they report on the proceedings and investigations they have conducted. More will be learned about their activities as cases heard by the official courts are examined.

The tribunals held by clan or lineage authorities, however, require some additional preliminary comment. While evidence of their activities, too, will be encountered in the study of cases before the official courts, these tribunals stand in a somewhat different relationship to the official system. Their "jurisdiction" is limited to internal clan or lineage questions—to matters of succession and breaches of lineage norms. Usually their proceedings are held at *kwabya olumbe* ("dismantling death") funeral gatherings at which successors to the deceased are chosen. The process of choosing the heir to the property and the successor to the deceased's kinship responsibilities may itself take on the aspect of a "trial," conducted in the gestures and idiom of the courtroom, for there may be more than one candidate for either role. On the same occasion, while the lineage is "in session," the group may consider other disputes over succession or allegations of breach of lineage norms, such as contracting an incestuous marriage or failing to hold *kwabya olumbe* ceremonies for a kinsman. In cases of the latter kind, fines may be levied, but these are not enforceable in the official courts. Clan tribunals' decisions regarding succession are, however, recognized by the official courts as binding. Evidence that a man has been chosen by the lineage as heir to another's land or headmanship or as guardian of his children, if accepted, confirms his rights and responsibilities. Thus the activities of the lineage tribunals articulate with official courts in a manner different from those of the headmen and parish chiefs. When the latter fail to settle a case, it is tried "on its merits" before a subcounty court. When a lineage gathering reaches a decision regarding succession to one of its deceased members, a dissatisfied party may take his case to the subcounty court, but that court will not attempt to adjudicate the substance of his claim. It will rather simply endeavor to determine what the lineage gathering has decided and will then enforce that decision.

The finality with which lineage gatherings are able to settle such cases, however, seems to vary a good deal from one part of Busoga to another. The two areas that I came to know best—the former kingdom of Busambira, which today forms the southern portion (subcounty Ssaabawaali) of Kigulu county; and Bulamogi county, whose boundaries correspond with those of the precolonial kingdom of the same name—differ substantially in this respect. In Busambira, succession cases are quite often "appealed" from the lineage tribunals to the subcounty court, even though, as I have said, the role of the subcounty court in such cases is simply to add its authority to what the lineage tribunal has already done. This is true even of cases involving the Baiseigaga clan, the former "royal" clan and the most prestigious one in the area. In Bulamogi, on the other hand, the royal clan (the Baisengobi) in particular seems much more effective in settling its own succession disputes without recourse to the official courts. It also asserts jurisdiction, somewhat less effectively, over land cases of all kinds, including those involving non-Baisengobi. The Baisengobi of Bulamogi operate a county-level "appeal court" which hears cases from all parts of the county and keeps a written record of its proceedings. In 1949, it heard two cases involving the inheritance of subvillage headmanships and five concerning the inheritance of individual holdings. In 1950, it heard three land inheritance cases and fined the clan treasurer for misappropriating clan funds. In 1951, there were six inheritance cases, all involving individual holdings. Entries for earlier years include an allegation of misrule against a headman and a number of rulings on the clan membership of individuals. The Baisengobi of Bulamogi have been able to maintain an effective countywide organization because their head, the heir to the rulership of the traditional kingdom, is a figure of great authority in the area who has served both as a county chief and as Kyabazinga (president) of Busoga. Their situation is clearly exceptional.[12] Throughout Busoga, however, at least at the level of the local succession lineage, descent groups continue to hold tribunals whose decisions in matters of succession have important consequences for the work of the official courts of record.

Having introduced the courts, the setting in which they work, the judges who man them, and the kinds of disputes that Soga society brings before them, I now turn to the main business of this study: the analysis of the manner in which the courts manipulate legal ideas in the adjudication of disputes. I shall begin with the field of sexual relations and marriage.

12. Bulamogi is not, however, unique; a similar situation seems to prevail in Bugabula county.

You ask why the woman is never the accused in adultery cases. But if someone were to steal your shoes, would you accuse the shoes?
—A subcounty chief

4 The Courts at Work:
Husbands and Lovers

Discussion of the kinds of cases that come before the Soga courts has shown that among the important sources of litigation are marriage and, more generally, relations between the sexes. Actually, disputes arising in this field of social life are, as I have noted, responsible for an even larger proportion of cases than the review of sample casebooks would indicate, for the brief summary that appears in the casebook often does not reveal the social locus of the trouble. If the action directly concerns a breach of norms governing sexual relations or marriage, this will be obvious from the casebook summary, as for example when a father accuses a young man of seducing his daughter or a husband accuses his father-in-law of "harboring" his wife. But tensions between husband and wife, or between in-laws, may first emerge into public view not in litigation over marital or sexual norms, but rather in direct interpersonal aggression. An aggrieved son-in-law, instead of accusing his father-in-law of harboring, may instead slander him or give him a beating, in which case the matter will come before the court as an action of "the *lukiiko*" against the son-in-law for assault or slander, with no mention in the casebook summary of the roots of the dispute. In the full transcript of the testimony, of course, all this will come out, but in the summaries, upon which the discussion of frequencies of types of cases has of necessity been based, such affairs tend to boil down to something like: "He is accused of spoiling my name without reason"; or: "I accuse him of beating me three strokes and throwing me down without reason." Thus it is very likely that many of the types of interpersonal aggression mentioned in chapter 3 occur quite often as a result of tension between spouses, lovers, rivals, or in-laws.

That this is so is suggested by the results of a study of homicides and suicides in Busoga which Margaret Fallers and I carried out.[1] Cases in which death has occurred are not within the jurisdiction of the African Local Government authorities; they are investigated by the Uganda national police and come before the national courts in the form of an inquest or a trial for murder or manslaughter. Our study, based upon the records of these proceedings, covered continuous series of one hundred homicides and one hundred suicides occurring between 1947 and 1954. In more than one-third (thirty-seven) of the homicides, the victim was the killer's spouse; in the remaining cases, eight victims were in-laws, five were rivals, and two were lovers, so that in all more than half the cases (fifty-two) directly involved sexual relations or marriage. Of the one hundred suicides, twenty-two seemed to have been precipitated by quarrels with spouses, lovers, or in-laws, and eight by anxiety over impotence. If Basoga, when they kill, so often do so as a result of marital or sexual difficulties, they probably commit other forms of interpersonal aggression, at least some of the time, for the same reason. Thus, behind the attempts of the courts to settle disputes arising out of breaches of marital and sexual norms, lies the threat of violence and death. An examination of the institutional setting of marriage and intersexual relations will make it clear why this area of social life is such a fertile source of trouble for Basoga.

Soga Marriage: The Institutional Background

Marriage is a contract between the bridegroom and the father of the bride in which authority over the bride is transferred from the latter to the former. Although it is the agreement between the two parties concerning the transfer of authority over the woman that concludes the contract, this agreement is almost invariably accompanied by the payment of bridewealth (*mwandu*) and nowadays the terms of the contract, which may involve a schedule of payments over time, are often embodied in a written agreement (*ndagaano*). Bridewealth pay-

---

1. Lloyd A. Fallers and Margaret C. Fallers, "Homicide and Suicide in Busoga."

ments, which are additional to a fixed symbolic gift to the bride's parents of a fowl and a goat, vary from one or two goats, a few fowl and a few shillings, to as much as eight hundred shillings.

The woman herself is not a party to this contract, but rather the object contracted for. While she has means of making her feelings effective in the choice of a mate, in law the deciding voice is that of her father or guardian and the respect in which she customarily holds him gives him much informal influence as well. Women are in many respects perpetual dependents; they may not hold real property and in many kinds of action cannot litigate on their own behalf in the law courts. They pass at marriage from the *patria potestas* of their fathers to that of their husbands. It is this thoroughgoing legal subordination and dependence of the woman, which finds its attitudinal counterpart in the male belief that she tends to be irresponsible and overemotional —a person to be guarded rather than trusted with freedom—that the chief was trying to convey with his analogy of the stolen shoes, quoted at the beginning of this chapter.

It would be wrong, however, to think of the woman as a "chattel." Basoga do, to be sure, use the verb *kugula,* whose nearest English translation is "to buy," in speaking of the way in which a man acquires a wife. But the translation is not an entirely accurate one, for the Lusoga lexicon does not divide the universe of meaning in the same way that English does. The word *kugula* is also used when a person hires the services of a professional specialist. A man with a case in the high court, for example, "buys" a lawyer or "pleader" (*kugula pulida*). Similarly, a man who takes up land upon payment of entry money to a headman "buys" the land (*kugula itaka*) although, as will be seen, this transaction is far from amounting to a "sale" in any English sense of the word. *"Kugula"* is, in fact, used whenever a consideration is exchanged for rights in any good or service and it thus covers a much wider range of meanings than does the English "to buy." The nearest Lusoga translation of "chattel" would be *kintu,* "thing" or "possession." A litigant in a bridewealth case will often, for example, speak of the chickens, goats, money, etc. for which he is litigating as "my things" (*bintu byange*). But no Musoga would think of speaking of a woman received in exchange for bridewealth as a *"kintu";* she is a *"muntu,"* a "person," as much as her husband or father. The fact that Basoga often speak of marriage in the vocabulary of commerce and often pursue what they see as their rights in marriage in a very mercenary way should not blind one to the deeply human quality of relations between men and women in Soga society, however asymmetrical these relations may be with respect to the distribution of authority and however contorted they may become as a result of tension and conflict.

Although marriage is contracted between the bridegroom and the bride's father or guardian as individuals, its consequences involve other members of the two patrilineages. On the side of the bridegroom, lineage mates may assist him in collecting the bridewealth. Soga custom does not lay down fixed rules requiring certain kinsmen of the bridegroom to contribute to it. But it is to his agnates and to a lesser extent to his maternal kin, that a young man is entitled to turn for assistance in assembling the required quantity of money and livestock. For his junior male siblings, who may succeed him in marriage when he dies, his bride is a potential wife. On the woman's side, her male lineage mates are potential successors to her father, upon whom may fall his responsibilities as her guardian under the marriage contract. Her children will be their *baiwa*—sister's or daughter's children, a category of kin for whom Basoga have a particularly warm regard.[2] Her brothers may have been allotted the bridewealth from her marriage in order to contract marriages of their own. Her sisters may well join her as co-wives in her husband's household, for Basoga are very polygynous—frequencies of multiple marriages ranging, in the villages which I surveyed, from 30 to 50 percent [3]—and sororal polygyny is the preferred form. In all these ways, the consequences of marriage tend to reach out from the couple immediately concerned to other members of their respective lineages.

The ceremonial practices which accompany marriage emphasize the importance of the bond thus established between the two groups. The agreement between the bridegroom and the bride's father is arrived at on a highly formal occasion known as "the introduction" (*kwandhula*). Dressed in their best clothes, the bridegroom and his father visit the father of the bride, accompanied by the *mukwenda*, a friend (*not* a kinsman) who will act as a formal witness to the contract. Agreement having been reached, the bride is secluded until the wedding under the care of an elderly woman, who bathes and anoints her and instructs her in the duties of a wife. On the wedding day, the bride is accompanied to the bridegroom's home by her brother and her fathers sister, who remain for one night to assure themselves of the bridegroom's potency and who, on the following day, must be given a token gift to "drive them away." A similar interest in the fertility of the marriage is taken by the bridegroom's actual and classificatory "mothers," who linger about the home on the wedding night amid the drinking, danc-

2. See Appendix A; and Lloyd A. *Bantu Bureaucracy*, chapter 4.
3. Ibid., table 11.

ing, and drumming kinsmen and guests, urging the bridegroom to consummate the union.

Today in many—perhaps most—cases these traditional observances are accompanied by Christian or Islamic ceremonies which, particularly in the case of Christians, emphasize the importance of marital stability. A standard feature of Christian weddings, particularly among the more affluent, is a tea-party reception, following the ceremony in the church. Speeches describing the duties of husband and wife in Christian matrimony are given by the fathers of the bride and bridegroom, and often by the bridegroom himself. Concern for stable marriage is also voiced in the public forum. In April 1950, the district council debated on four successive days the corrosive influence upon marriage of town life in general and the employment of women in particular. On an earlier occasion, in 1942, the council considered means of reinforcing husbands' authority over wives. Being an almost exclusively male body, the council tends to view female weakness as the chief threat to stable marriage.

This explicit concern for the maintenance of the marriage bond on the part of persons and groups external to it is reinforced by the ties between parents and children that are its natural result. The relationship between mother and child is the strongest and most emotion-laden in Soga society. Unlike the father, who is rather distant and authoritarian, the Musoga mother is protective and nurturant. Her complete responsibility for the banana garden makes her the source of sustenance, and she remains its symbol long after infancy. Throughout their lives, most Basoga regard their mothers with deep and unconditional affection. The father-child bond is also strong, but for different reasons; the father is the disciplinarian and the giver of formal status in the patrilineage. Through him are transmitted rights in property. Thus, the tie between husband and wife is strengthened by their common, though rather different, ties with their children. A broken marriage means that a child is separated either from its mother, with whom its affectual ties are strong, or from its father, who gives it social status and whose authority is believed necessary to the proper development of its character.

Nevertheless, the relationship between the two spouses, and between their kingroups, is commonly one of strain and incipient conflict. A man and his wife's agnates call one another *bakoirume* or *bako*, and the relationship is called *buko*. The strain between *bako* becomes apparent at weddings, where the bride's people are quick to resent and to complain about arrangements for the ceremony—these are the bridegroom's responsibility—which they consider inadequate. At one wedding I attended, for example, an open quarrel developed over the adequacy of the motor vehicle which the bridegroom had hired to take the party to the mosque for the religious ceremony. The subcounty chief, who was a guest, had to intervene to save the situation. Often there is a last-minute argument over the bridewealth. After the wedding, the bride's brother and her father's sister, who have accompanied her to the bridegroom's house, make a show of being reluctant to leave her and it is at this point that they must be given money to "drive them away." It is this sort of conflict, which comes to the surface at nearly every wedding, that underlies the belief, held by many Basoga, that traditional marriage consisted of a kind of "theft" of the bride by the bridegroom. Elopement or wife-stealing as a regular practice would, of course, be incompatible with the negotiation of bridewealth prior to marriage, of which so much is made, and at first the contradiction seems puzzling. But observation of a number of weddings made it clear to me that an element of "theft" was, indeed, involved in even the best-arranged marriage. At the last moment the mutual attachment of the bride and her own people bursts forth, and, on some minor pretext, they may angrily accuse the bridegroom's people of "just trying to take our daughter by force."

What is involved here, of course, is a strain between the bond established by marriage and the rather stronger, in Soga society, bond of the unilineal descent group, a strain which splits the conjugal unit and sets *bako* against each other. Partly, it would seem, in order to control the ever-present threat of conflict, relations between *bako* are supposed to be very formal and correct. There is much formal visiting and gift-giving. A man who visits his *muko* should always wear the long white *kkanzu* gown as a sign of respect and should behave with the utmost circumspection and politeness. *Bako* should not touch one another and the father of neither husband nor wife should sleep in the couple's house. Similarly, within the household, wives should submit themselves completely to their husband's authority and should treat them with elaborate deference. Wives may not absent themselves from the home without explicit permission, even, or perhaps especially, to visit their parents.

A common result is that a wife feels oppressed and tries to escape by running away to her father. The latter may accept her, and thus involve himself in conflict, and possibly litigation, with her husband; or, because accepting her would involve repaying the bridewealth, he may force her back into a strife-filled existence in her spouse's home. Husbands, for their part, are sensitive to the fact that their theoretically great authority over their wives is in reality insecure and often flouted. In reaction, many become household tyrants. For both husbands and wives, the sexual act itself tends to become the focus of the conflict. For the rebellious wife, extramarital affairs become an assertion of autonomy against a domineering husband. For the husband whose position is threatened, intercourse with his wife becomes an act of authority. "The jealous man," a proverb says, "does not eat; he just climbs trees"—to spy on his wife, whom he suspects of meeting lovers. When he feels his dominance slipping away, he may imagine himself to be losing his virility (and consequently may, in fact, lose it) as a result of sorcery directed against him by his wife. In the study of homicides and suicides referred to above, a number of cases were discovered in which husbands or wives had killed themselves or their spouses (in a few cases, both) immediately following sexual intercourse. It is most expressive of the obsessive anxieties and discontents that swirl around Soga marriage that the word *buko* (the in-law relationship) also denotes a paralytic disorder and that a *bwa lya buko* ("ulcer of *buko*") is an ulcer of the penis.[4]

Of course the dark picture I have been painting does not portray every Soga marriage. Many men and women live happily together, overcoming the institutional contradictions of their situation. And most couples, when the strain becomes too great, simply separate. In the five villages I surveyed, between one-quarter and one-half of all marriages contracted by the men had failed,[5] and in 90 percent of these cases the bridewealth had been returned. Most fathers, apparently, are willing to assist their daughters in escaping from an intolerable marriage. It is the minority who are unable to make stable marriages and who, when conflict does arise, are unable to settle it amicably, who are the litigants in the cases to be analyzed.

It is now time to pick up the thread of my argument concerning the nature and use of legal concepts by examining a number of the concepts the Soga courts apply in order to reach authoritative decisions regarding the conflicts that arise in this troubled field of sex and marriage.

Such a concept has already begun to shape and narrow the issues by the time the accuser reaches the court with his complaint, for only if he can describe his cause in a word or phrase that corresponds to a wrong recognized by the court will the court summon the accused and allow the action to proceed. Of course, since a knowledge of the system

4. E. M. K. Mulira and E. G. M. Ndawula, *A Luganda-English and English-Luganda Dictionary.*
5. Lloyd A. Fallers, "Some Determinants of Marriage Stability in Busoga."

of legal concepts is common to most adult males, and since most cases have been argued, and the issues sharpened and made more explicit, before headmen and parish chiefs before they reach the lowest court of record, most accusers arrive before the subcounty chief with a plausibly framed complaint. What is at issue, therefore, when the case comes before the court, is the reach of a well-known concept with respect to the "facts" of a given case, as these emerge from the process of litigation.

The accuser need not, however, adhere to an absolutely set verbal formula; the concept pertaining to a recognized wrong need not always be invoked in precisely the same words. The participants in the courtroom encounter are peasant litigants and part-time judges, not learned jurists trained in verbal hairsplitting. Legal language remains very close to everyday language. Thus, a man who alleges that another has wrongfully appropriated his wife or daughter may accuse him of "seducing her away" (*kumubayiza*) or of "being caught with her" (*kukwatibwa naye*) or of "marrying her" (*kufumbirwa naye*), although everyone concerned would recognize that all these accusations might be reduced to *bwenzi* ("adultery" or "fornication"; the one word covers both), as indeed they are in the brief headings commonly used in the casebooks (see Appendix B). A husband who accuses his wife's father or guardian of wrongfully keeping her usually employs the formula *kumutuuza awatali ensonga* ("causing her to stay without reason"), but occasionally one encounters *kumukwekwa* ("hiding her") and even *kumubba* ("stealing her"). Perhaps the best Soga example of specialized language, closely adhered to in invoking a legal concept, is the phrase *kulya enkoko bbiri* ("eating two hens"), invariably used when a father or guardian is accused of accepting bridewealth from two different men for the same woman. The phrase is made up of everyday words, but it is strongly associated in people's minds with the courtroom context and with a particular recognized wrong.

Thus far I have used the term "legal concept" to mean "a wrong recognized by the law"—a wrong for which one man may bring another to court—and have spoken as if the problem for the court were simply to decide whether or not the "facts" of a particular case, as accepted by the court, place it sufficiently within the compass of such a concept to justify a decision in favor of the accuser. As a gross description of the overall task of the court, this is accurate enough. I have been content with it thus far because I have been concerned to isolate, within the general sphere of moral ideas, with all the various forms of social control that support them, the specifically legal concepts by means of which issues are narrowed for authoritative adjudication by courts. It is the necessity, in a society with courts of law and a legal subculture, to frame an accusation in terms of a concept that narrows and frames the issues that brings out most clearly the nature of the specifically legal. But this emphasis upon the concept embodied in the accusation oversimplifies, and may even falsify, the total process of litigation. Thought and discourse always involve the use of concepts, and the thought and discourse involved in litigation and adjudication are far from being exhausted by the bald statement that "the court's problem is to determine whether or not the facts of a case place it within the scope of a given legal concept." In the process of reaching a "yes or no" decision with respect to an accusation framed in terms of what I should now like to call a "concept of wrong" framing a cause for court action, the court must ask and answer to its own satisfaction a number of subsidiary questions, making use, in the process, of subsidiary kinds of legal concepts (Levi calls them "satellite concepts").

On the one hand, the court must determine the "facts" which it will measure against the concept of wrong invoked. Sometimes these are agreed upon, but often the evidence is wildly conflicting. The court must weigh the testimony of litigants and witnesses and for this purpose must make use of concepts of *credibility* which allow it to answer such questions as: Is the witness in a position to know what he says he knows? Are his interests likely to bias his testimony? What is the significance of internal inconsistency in a man's testimony? . . . of inconsistency between his testimony and his other behavior? What can a man be expected to remember, and for how long? What weight is to be given to written evidence? On the other hand, the court must make use of concepts embodying assumptions about the nature of man, society, and the nonhuman world in exploring the *applicability* of a particular concept of wrong to a particular set of facts as determined. It must decide such questions as: "What, for purposes of this particular wrong, is a "father," a "brother," a "wife," an "heir"? What is "marriage"? What is a "goat" given in bridewealth? Is it the particular goat only, or one similar to it, or its money equivalent? Who has "standing" with respect to this particular wrong, so that he may accuse in terms of it? Who may be accused? What constitutes, with respect to this particular wrong, "infancy," "youth," "adulthood," "old age"? What is "force," "intention," "care"?

Like the concepts of wrong, the concepts used in establishing credibility and applicability are expressed in everyday language, not in a specialized, refined legal lexicon. What makes them legal concepts is their use in exploring the scope of specific concepts of wrong. While they are almost never explicit about this in the sense of stating formal definitions, one frequently finds litigants offering, and judges considering for acceptance or rejection, particular concepts of persons, events, and things relevant to the concept of wrong under consideration. Examples of this were encountered in chapter 1 in the case of *Yoweri Kibiri* v. *Yowabu Kabwire,* in which the court and the litigants made use of various concepts subsidiary to that of "harboring." If Yoweri has repudiated Kolositina, is he still her "husband" for purposes of the law of harboring? What constitutes evidence of "repudiation"?

There is, of course, a certain arbitrariness in this distinction between "concepts of wrong" and "concepts of applicability" and "credibility." One might say, with perhaps equal fidelity to the legal process, that the concepts of applicability and credibility simply represent fuller statements of the concepts of wrong. Thus, it might be argued, the phrase "harboring a wife without reason" is really just a shorthand tag for a wrong whose full description would embody a statement of what, precisely, the courts have found the terms "harboring," "wife," and "reason" to mean, together with a statement of all the kinds of testimony the courts have accepted as evidence that such an event has occurred. In a sense, the legal concept of "harboring a wife without reason" comprehends all these things.

But two considerations argue against thus collapsing the whole legal process into concepts of wrong. First, the distinction I have proposed is, I think, a useful analytic device. Particularly in a legal system as inexplicit about its operations as that of the Basoga, one can only discover the fuller meaning of a concept of wrong by comparing cases in which it has been invoked. Examining such cases, one discovers that some are closely contested, while others are quickly brought to an end, often by an admission of guilt or liability. The more closely contested case, as I suggested in chapter 3, is legally more interesting because it reveals more of the logic of the legal process and it is this logic that the distinction between concepts of wrong and subsidiary concepts is meant to capture. I think of the concept of wrong as having a central, or core, meaning surrounded by areas of ambiguity which give the law its "open texture." The core meaning covers the "plain case," the case on whose proper outcome "everyone" would agree. (There are, of course, intransigent litigants who fight on when they are "obviously" wrong, but these are easily spotted: no one takes their arguments seriously.) Cases which are not so plain are "marginal" in the sense that they do not fall clearly into the core meaning but rather involve the surrounding areas of ambiguity. Litigating them and deciding them involves more legal work, work which one may usefully analyze in terms of "subsidiary concepts." However Basoga may view the legal process, then, the comparison of plain and marginal cases is a means of "unpacking" the meaning of concepts of wrong.

Second, and perhaps more important, the distinction between "concepts of wrong" and "subsidiary concepts" seems more faithful to the way in which the Soga courts (and perhaps all courts) actually work. They do in fact *begin* with an accusation embodying a concept of wrong, briefly stated, and *then,* if the case is not a plain one (in which event a decision is rapidly reached without argument), they begin to explore, by questioning litigants and witnesses, the relevant questions of fact and applicability. The judges themselves would not analyze what they do in the terms I have used, perhaps—for they are quite unselfconscious about their work—but these terms seem helpful in capturing the kinds of questions they appear to pursue in answering, "yes" or "no," the larger question of whether, for example, Yowabu harbored Yoweri's wife without reason.

In analyzing this process as it operates in cases arising from the field of sex and marriage, I shall not discuss all the concepts of wrong that may be invoked or all the subsidiary concepts that may come into play, for I am interested primarily in the process, rather than the full substance, of Soga law in the field. My object is not to produce a textbook of Soga law. I shall therefore focus upon a few concepts of wrong and the subsidiary concepts which their invocation commonly causes the courts to employ.

ADULTERY (BWENZI): PLAIN AND MARGINAL CASES

Kunya Nyonyi v. Bulubutu: unlawful possession is adultery; ignorance is no defense

"Adultery," a subcounty chief once told me, "is a serious matter because if we do not punish it severely in court, men will beat and spear one another over it." This perhaps accounts for the vigor with which an accused may defend himself against the charge, even when the case is clearly a plain one, as did Bulubutu of Kanabugo when accused by Kunya Nyonyi of Bunyama on June 27, 1950. Quickly convicted, he appealed, on tenuous grounds, to the county court of Bulamogi, which, after very brief deliberation, upheld the lower court. Bulubutu's is the plain case that brings out rather clearly the core meaning of the concept of adultery in Soga law—a meaning, incidentally, which is sufficiently divergent from that of the English word that one should perhaps hesitate to use "adultery" to translate *"bwenzi."*

Bulubutu is accused of "being found with the woman Mbeiza, wife of Kunya, having put her on his bicycle. He had seduced her away and kept her for five months." Bulubutu knows that he has been caught dead to rights, but he does what he can to defend himself:

Q: Do you agree to argue this case, in which you are charged with putting the woman Mbeiza, wife of Kunya, on your bicycle? Do you expect to win?

A: I won't argue. I know I will lose, because I put that woman on my bicycle at Bulima and we went to Budomero and I was caught and taken to the village headman and the parish chief and they were going to take me to the subcounty chief. I asked the one who caught me, the owner of the wife, to forgive me. He asked 100 shillings of me and I agreed to 70 and asked him to go with me to Alisigula to borrow the money. But he didn't have it, so while we were there Kunya said "write an agreement with me" [promising to pay]. But I said I couldn't write. Then he took my bicycle and left. My friends said I should find the money and take it to him the next morning, but when I went with the seventy shillings, I met Kunya on the road—he said it was impossible to accept it because he had already taken the matter to the subcounty chief. So I returned the money to my friend who had lent it and set out for the subcounty headquarters.

Two points are particularly significant in Bulubutu's defense. First, he admits that he will lose the case because he has been found with the woman on his bicycle. This is enough, as many similar cases confirm, to convict him of "adultery." It need not be shown that he had sexual relations with her, or even that he kept her in his house (though that is alleged in this case). A man with a woman on his bicycle has possession of her and that is sufficient. Is this a matter of evidence—that sexual relations have occurred or are intended—or is it a question of the definition of "*bwenzi*" itself as a concept of wrong? The distinction between "concepts of wrong" and "subsidiary concepts," whether of credibility or applicability, is, admittedly, a slippery one, but the courts' questionings, both here and in other cases, seem to me to provide a rather clear answer. Never, in these cases, do the courts show the slightest interest in proving sexual intercourse, nor defendants in disproving it. Basoga simply assume, as part of the nature of things, that a man will have intercourse with any woman who is in his possession and who is not forbidden to him by virtue of kinship. Having control of such a woman without properly marrying her *is bwenzi,* and not simply prima facie[6] evidence of it. The bicycle, of course, by extending the range and speed of movement in the Busoga countryside, has increased the opportunities for such wrongful possession.

6. "Such as will suffice until contradicted or overcome by other evidence." *Black's Law Dictionary.*

The second point to note is that, while Bulubutu has essentially admitted his own guilt, he has sought to blacken his accuser's character. He says that Kunya took his bicycle and he accuses Kunya of offering to accept compensation in exchange for dropping his intention to take the case to court. This is a serious, even actionable, matter, for, as the court of Bugabula county remarked, in upholding a lower court's imposition of a fine of twenty shillings or one month's imprisonment in a case in which a man was shown to have accepted money to drop a charge of adultery, "People who . . . assume power to demand compensation privately in cases in which the court might punish the offender more severely . . . should not be encouraged." [7] Bulubutu says that Kunya then double-crossed him by going to the subcounty chief before he could pay the money. The charge of asking for compensation out of court is probably false, for no such case against Kunya appears in the records of subsequent months, but such attempts to discredit an accuser by counteraccusations of immorality are common in Soga pleading, particularly when the accused has been made desperate by being caught in a plain case of wrong. In any event, the story told by Kunya, the accuser, is quite different:

Q: When did this wife Mbeiza leave your home?
A: She went on January 27, 1950. I didn't know where she went. When I went to my in-laws' at Bukono, I didn't find her there; my in-law told me to look everywhere for her and said he would do the same. On June 24, I returned to my in-laws' to find out whether she had been seen. When I arrived, my in-law said she had not, so I returned home. Yesterday, June 26, 1950, I was on my way to Budomero to buy salt, together with my friend Wansaja, when we found this man Bulubutu with my wife Mbeiza on his bicycle. We seized them and went to the village headman and the parish chief and were going to the subcounty chief when Bulubutu asked the village headman, Nabikamba, to allow him to go off privately [to relieve himself]. While doing this, he ran away, leaving his bicycle. The woman also ran away. So the village headman brought the bicycle to subcounty headquarters.

Thus, in Kunya's account of what happened on the road to Budomero, nothing is said of settling the matter out of court and Bulubutu abandons the bicycle in his flight from justice. The case is so plain, however, that these side issues are left unexplored. It being agreed that Bulubutu was caught with Mbeiza on his bicycle, the court quickly seals off two possible routes of escape for the accused and moves toward a conclusion:

Q: Where did the woman Mbeiza say she was going and where she was coming from, that you should give her a lift?

7. Court v. *Yafesi Iyunju.*

A: She said she had come from Kigulu [the county to the south] and was going to Gadumire [in northern Bulamogi].

This is to give Bulubutu a chance to claim that Mbeiza had been on some legitimate journey—returning to her husband, perhaps, or to her parents—but Bulubutu sees no help in that direction. Then:

Q: What do you and this woman call each other?
A: There is no clanship.

A claim of kinship might legitimate the fateful bicycle journey, as will shortly be seen in other cases, but again Bulubutu has no argument to make. One final question:

Q: Had you ever seen Mbeiza before?
A: I had never seen her before yesterday.
Q: Now, when Kunya accuses you of the fault of seducing away his wife for five months up to June 26, when he caught you with her, is he correct?
A: Yes, he is correct, but I didn't realize she was his wife.

Bulubutu's flimsy defense has collapsed. The plea of ignorance is brushed aside and the court concludes:

It goes against Bulubutu. He himself admits that he put the woman Mbeiza on the bicycle and that he kept her secretly for five months. Therefore he is assessed 100 shillings compensation, 20 shillings fine, and three months imprisonment.

Particularly in plain cases, the defense often collapses in this card-house manner with an admission of guilt. Even so, Bulubutu, in his desperation to escape the penalties imposed—which are heavy for a Musoga peasant with an annual cash income of two hundred or three hundred shillings—appeals to the county court. In his letter of appeal, he returns to a previous argument—that he hadn't known Mbeiza was married—and adds the allegation that he was not given a fair hearing. Again, however, his defense is short-lived. The clerk of the county court reads out the transcript forwarded from the subcounty court:

Q: Do you agree that the statements just read are those you made and confirmed with your signature in the subcounty court?
A: I signed it, but I was forced. It isn't what I said in the court.
Q: Which words were you forced to sign?
A: . . . that I put Kunya's wife on my bicycle. I didn't know she was a wife.
Q: Do you still insist in this court that you were forced to sign those words and that you didn't say them in the subcounty court?
A: I agree that I said them and confirmed them by signing.
Q: Do you have anything to add that you didn't say in the lower court?
A: I have something to add: My friend there, Kunya, is taking revenge on me. We worked together as tailors at Namwiwa. Because he didn't sew well, the Indian [employer] dismissed him. So he accuses me of seducing his wife

Mbeiza. I know the case goes against me, but I plead with the court to help me by reducing the punishment.

Kunya, the accuser, is also offered an opportunity to speak, but adds only that he himself had intended to appeal against the lower court judgment on the ground that its sentence was too lenient! The county judges, however, simply confirm the previous decision.

From such a plain case as this, one learns relatively little about the logic of Soga law. Something has been learned about the core meaning of *bwenzi*—that it means wrongfully having control over a woman in such a manner that sexual relations are possible, but that actual sexual relations need not be proved. There is also a clear indication that ignorance of the woman's married status is no defense, since the accused's argument on this point is ignored. It is clearly his responsibility to know her marital status. The case has also provided an opportunity to observe the desperate tactics employed by an accused in a situation in which it is clear from the outset that he has no real defense. But, precisely because the case is such a plain one, the margins of *bwenzi* as a concept of wrong are little explored. The behavior alleged to be adulterous—carrying the woman on the bicycle —is admitted from the start, so there is no exploration of the problem of credibility. With respect to the problem of applicability, the accused offers no defense—apart from the weak and futile one of ignorance. He does not, for example, claim, as the court offers him an opportunity to do at one point, that he and the woman are related to one another in a manner that would remove their association on a bicycle from the reach of the concept *bwenzi*. It is when such questions are raised in defense that one can see the court making those more marginal decisions that constitute the real logic of the law.

Abudala Olere v. Gaunye: a "naked" confession convicts

Consider first a case from which something additional may be learned about the problem of credibility in accusations of *bwenzi*. This is also a relatively plain case in which the defense is not a strong one, but it is worth citing because the evidence of adultery is less direct than in the previous one. In that case, the accused was caught, and admitted to having been caught, with the woman. Here, the accused, Gaunye of Kitukiro, denies behavior which might be construed as adulterous. He is accused by Abudala Olere of Kaketa of "seducing away my wife, Tino, and being caught with her." Gaunye defends himself thus:

Q: Do you . . . [admit to] seducing away Tino, wife of Abudala Olere, or will you contest it and hope to win?

A: I agree to contest it and will win . . . because I have never taken this woman, Tino . . . and I have never been caught with her, as is alleged.

Q: Do you have any evidence to show that you have never taken [her] and were never caught with her?

A: Yes, I have, first . . . that of the village headman . . . and also that of the policeman,[8] D. Wamudumire.

Abudala, however, calls upon the same two witnesses in support of his charge:

Q: Do you have evidence to show that you caught Gaunye and your wife, Tino?

A: Yes, I have [that of] the village headman, Y. Kitamirike . . . and the policeman, D. Wamudumire.

Q: What do you call upon [them] to say?

A: I call upon them because they were there when Gaunye agreed that this woman, Tino, was "married"[9] to him, but they can't testify that I caught him with her in his house.

Q: Is it true, then, as Gaunye says, that you did not catch him with your wife, Tino?

A: Yes, that is true, we didn't find the wife in his home, but we saw her afterward in the home of her father, Kagodo.

At this point, the accuser's prospects appear rather bleak. The court seems to be concentrating on the point of "catching him with the wife," and for this Abudala admits to having no evidence. The court, however, decides now to hear the witnesses, starting with Yoweri Kitamirike, the village headman:

Q: Do you agree to give testimony for these litigants, Abudala and Gaunye, who call upon you?

A: Yes. . . . We went to the house of Gaunye and there were no wives there. Then we went into the field and we found there two wives. We asked Gaunye, "How many wives do you have?" and he told us, "I have three wives. Here are two of them. The third is the daughter of Kagodo. She has gone to his home." Hearing that, I . . . sent them here [to subcounty headquarters].

The policeman, Dasani Wamudumire, tells a similar story:

A: Yes, I have testimony. On March 29, I went to the house of the village headman and we accompanied Abudala to Gaunye's house. . . . He said he had three wives, and told us their names. . . . Then I told him that the wife Tino, who was absent, was the wife of this Abudala. He answered, "You have caught me, but I bought that wife from Kagodo." Then we seized Gaunye and brought him here.

Now the court turns back to Gaunye, bearing down:

8. The A.L.G. has its own constabulary, distinct from the national police.
9. That is to say, he was treating her as his wife.

Q: Is this woman, Tino, about whom you spoke with the village headman, the one who is here in court now?

A: Yes.

Q: Do you agree that what your witness, the village headman, says is true?

A: Yes, what he says is true.

Q: You have heard your witness Dasani [the policeman] speak. Is what he says true?

A: Yes, it is true.

The court now has grounds for a decision:

The case has gone against Gaunye because he himself agrees that he took the woman Tino, daughter of Kagodo, and "married' her. The testimony of Y. Kitamirike and D. Wamudumire shows very clearly that he agreed to this when they caught him. He is given punishment of four months imprisonment and a fine of 100 shillings, of which 60 shillings is compensation.

The punishment is harsh, and, as in the previous case, the accused appeals, on the ground that "I paid bridewealth for the woman concerning whom the court accuses me. I have an in-law from whom I bought the woman."

Again, however, it is a reckless argument, born of desperation. If Gaunye had, in fact, contracted a valid marriage for Tino with her father, he would be guiltless, as will be seen. The father would soon be in the dock, charged with "eating two hens." But at the county court he drops this argument, since he doubtless lacks evidence to support it, and abjectly admits defeat: "I withdraw my appeal. I now agree that the case goes against me. I do not contest. I am defeated. The woman I took was a married woman." It remains only for the county court to confirm the decision of the court of first instance.

In this case there has been a contest on the question of evidence and some new information emerges. To prove "adultery," one need not even catch the man and the woman together; one need only establish that the man has verbally claimed her as his own. The problem of evidence might, of course, have been pursued further. The accused might have challenged the credibility of the two witnesses. But in this case he could not do this, for he himself had called upon them, their testimony had agreed, and they were public servants—prestigious witnesses. There are possibilities for an infinite regression in this matter of evidence. If Gaunye had countered Abudala's witnesses with witnesses of his own, Abudala might have challenged *their* testimony with still other evidence. Here, however, the pursuit of "the facts" stopped at a rather early point. What was said when Abudala and the two witnesses visited Gaunye was common ground. It was only the evidential significance of the conversation that was at issue. Apparently, if there is uncontested evidence that a man said he acted wrongly, it is assumed by the court that he did so. A "naked" confession is sufficient to convict.

The problem of credibility will be encountered again and again in more complex form as other kinds of cases are examined. The remaining adultery cases which I shall discuss are more interesting with respect to the other side of the court's problem—that of determining the *applicability* of the concept *bwenzi*. In discussing the concept thus far, I have taken it to mean something like "wrongful possession or control of a woman." In *Kunya Nyonyi* v. *Bulubutu* and in *Abudala Olere* v. *Gaunye,* it is relatively clear from the start that possession of the women in question by the accused would be wrongful. They are other men's wives and the accused, if they have appropriated the women, are assumed to have done so in order to make them sexual partners—a clear violation of the husbands' rights. In the cases to which I now turn, however, the argument takes a different turn. The accused do not deny that they have been caught with the women. This they readily admit. Instead they argue in defense that they are related to the women in such a way that the association with them is legitimate. In two of the cases the accused claim that the women are their "sisters." If it can be sustained, this is a sufficient defense against *bwenzi,* since the courts assume that sexual relations do not take place between siblings. Incest is known, but it is very rare and is a matter for the clan concerned rather than the regular courts. In the other two cases, the accused claim that their association with the women is legitimate because the women are rightfully their "wives." One cannot be convicted of *bwenzi* with one's own wife. In both these types of case, the court, in exploring and deciding upon the reach of the concept *bwenzi,* must take everyday words of relationship—"wife" and "sister"—and determine their legal meaning. Faced with the necessity to make a "yes" or "no" decision about the applicability of the concept *bwenzi* to the association between a particular man and a particular woman, the court must look beneath the ambiguities of everyday language—which uses the words "sister" and "wife" more loosely—and draw a clear line—a line which for the accused will mean the difference between guilt and innocence, between punishment and vindication.

What Is A "Sister"?

Nasani Beka v. *Kibikyo: lineage mates are siblings; the reliability of witnesses*

I shall begin with the cases in which siblingship is alleged. The first concerns a rather feckless youth, Kibikyo of Bugulumbya, Bugabula, and a woman named Kafuko, a veteran of two unsuccessful marriages. Seized in Kibikyo's home and accused of adultery by Kafuko's most recent husband, they claim to be "brother" and "sister," and hence immune from the charge. There is no impropriety in a married woman's visiting her brother's home. If she does so without her husband's permission, the brother might be subject to an accusation of "harboring," but never *bwenzi; that* is assumed not to occur between siblings. The husband argues, however, that they are not so related. While a number of side issues are raised, each party attempting, as usual, to clothe himself in the garments of righteousness, it is clear from the beginning that the central question the court has to decide is whether or not Kibikyo and Kafuko are siblings for purposes of the law of adultery. In part this is a question of genealogical fact—of who begat whom and of the clan membership of the begetter. In part it is a question of the *meaning* of the genealogical facts, once determined to the court's satisfaction, in the context of an adultery charge. Most of the explicit argument concerns the genealogical facts, but implicitly the courts (two are involved, since there is an appeal) must also take a clear position on the question of legal meaning.

The affair begins on April 9, 1950, when Kibikyo is accused of being "seized while having 'married'[10] the woman Kafuko, wife of Nasani Beka, having spent seven days with her." Here, first, is Kibikyo's defense as presented by him, his witness, and the woman Kafuko:

Kibikyo: I do not agree that this case goes against me, because this woman is my sister and she came to my place today to see me because my wife had just died. This Kafuko stays in the house of our father Nabuti. When this Nasani found her at my place, he began to beat her, saying that he had caught her with me and that I had "married" her. Then Kafuko raised an alarm. When Yekemiya Igesa [a neighbor] heard the alarm, he came quickly and found [Nasani] running away, but he caught him and struggled with him and finally brought him here.

Q: In your statement you claim that the woman Kafuko is your sister. Do you have testimony to show that she is your sister?
A: Yes, I have that of her father, Nabuti.
Q: . . . in what way is she your sister?
A: She is my sister in the clan of Baisetoli because [my father] Bakisula died when I was still young and I was taken to Kabukye, where I grew up. When I was grown, I left there and went to Bugulumbya, where I discovered that Nabuti was of my clan. I grew up among the [clan of] Baisemulondo, but my father was buried near Kamuli at Bulagira. Kafuko told me that Nasani was her husband, but I never visited there, nor did she come to my place [before the day Nasani discovered her there].

---

10. Here "married to" (*kufumbirwa*) is a euphemism for "having an affair with" (*kubayiza*). This usage is common and will be encountered again.

Nabuti: I know Nasani Beka; he is my in-law. He married my daughter Kafuko. But his wife left him. He had bought her for fourteen shillings, but I paid them back in 1949 because my daughter was staying at home. When there was a death at Kibikyo's, she went to visit him. When [Nasani] found them, he beat her and seized both of them and took them to the headman. But long before that, Nasani had fought with his wife at my place and it was for that reason that she left him. Kibikyo is my child in the clan of Baisetoli and my brother, Bakisula of Bulonda, begat him.

Q: How long did your daughter Kafuko stay at Kibikyo's?
A: She didn't stay there at all. She was just arriving there the day Nasani caught her, and Nasani did not come to my place before he caught her.
Q: How do you know that Kibikyo is your child in the clan?
A: I found it out at Bulonda, at the funeral of my late brother Bakisula. . . . Kyewalyanga of Naluwoli was the successor.
Q: Since your daughter Kafuko was married to Nasani, did she ever visit Kibikyo with her husband Nasani?
A: They didn't visit there because Kibikyo only recently moved to Bugulumbya. But Kibikyo knows me and I know him and I used to ask him to come visit me at my place.

Kafuko: I admit that Nasani Beka, who was my husband, found me with my brother Kibikyo. He seized me, saying I had "married" [Kibikyo]. But I rejected Nasani long ago. He bought me for fourteen shillings, but they were paid back. His things were paid back a year ago this February. Kibikyo is my brother in the clan of Baisetoli. . . . The day I went there, there were two of us. Nasani told me to come with him and I refused and he began to beat me. Kibikyo stopped him. Then my brother raised an alarm. They seized us and brought us here.

Q: How long did you spend in Nasani's home?
A: I spent three years there. Kibikyo did not visit there, but the way I knew he was my brother was this: Nabuti, my father, pointed him out when we were at a funeral at Nawanende. It was the funeral of Kalongo, my brother. It was in 1949, before I had left the house of Nasani. Before that, I hadn't known him. Since I left Nasani's home, I haven't remarried. This was the third time I had visited Kibikyo.
Q: Who begat Kibikyo?
A: It was Bakisula.

A diagrammatic summing-up of the genealogical situation, as presented by Kibikyo and his witnesses, may prove helpful at this point (see fig. 4).

Nabuti, Bakisula, and Kyewalyanga, then, are said to be "brothers" within the clan of Baisetoli. This does not necessarily mean, in Soga terminology, that they were begotten by the same man or born of the same mother; indeed, the exact genealogical relationships among them are never made clear. The use of the term "brother," however, indicates that they are of the same generation and the fact that they are all Baisetoli means that they are, at some point, linked by descent

from a common ancestor. The fact that Kyewalyanga succeeded Bakisula and that Nabuti attended his *kwabya olumbe* funeral ceremonies
means that they are probably members of a single succession lineage
of a depth of not more than five or six generations.[11] The essential
point, however, is that they are said to be "brothers" by patrilineal
descent. If this is true, Kibikyo and Kafuko are "brother" and "sister"
by patrilineal descent, or, as Soga terminology has it, "siblings of the
opposite sex" (*banhina*). Such persons cannot commit adultery with
each other, no matter how distant the relationship genealogically. (A
fuller description of Soga kinship terminology, indicating the manner
in which all these terms are used, is given in Appendix A. As will be
seen in the case to be discussed next, sibling terminology is also used,

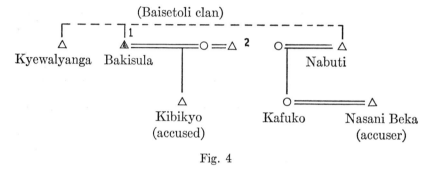

Fig. 4

in some circumstances, between persons not related in the patrilineal
line, with rather different legal consequences.)

Kibikyo and his witnesses have also testified that Kibikyo had not,
as a child, known about the patrilineal links shown in the above
diagram. The story he tells is not entirely implausible. A Musoga
woman whose husband dies ought to marry one of his "brothers,"
preferably his "successor of the belt," in which case her children are
brought up within the lineage of their deceased father. If, as often
happens nowadays, she remarries outside her deceased husband's lineage and clan, her children remain with her while young. Sometime
before puberty, they should return to their father's people. Normally,
however, even under these circumstances, quite young children are
taught their kinship connections, particularly those in the patrilineal
line, for in Busoga, unlike some other African societies, a child acquires his clan and lineage affiliation, with all its attendant rights and
responsibilities, from his begetter, not from his mother's husband. The

11. See Fallers, *Bantu Bureaucracy,* chapter 4.

court will therefore have received Kibikyo's account of his earlier ignorance and recent enlightenment in these matters with a certain surprise, and perhaps skepticism.

So much, then, for the defense. It is time now to hear the testimony of the aggrieved husband, Nasani Beka, and that of his witness. The court questions Nasani:

Nasani Beka: I married the woman for fourteen shillings and have been with her since 1946. But her father called her on about December 12, 1949, because her mother, Nakisige, was ill. He said that her mother wanted to see her. From that time, she has not returned to my home. Then today, while I was walking along, I found her at Kibikyo's and I asked her, "What are you doing here?" And she replied, "This is the place where I am married." Then I told her I was seizing her and I raised an alarm and they caught us and took us to the village chief. [In the process] Kibikyo hurt my hand.

Q: In his statement, the accused Kibikyo claims that Kafuko is his sister. He says that she went there on that day to visit him. Now just how do you know that he married her?

A: I knew that he had married her because, on that same day when I caught him, I had been to see her father Nabuti and he said, "Your wife has disappeared." So I went and seized him [implying that Nabuti's alleged answer was an obvious evasion].

Q: But what is the evidence that shows that Kibikyo is not the brother of the woman, and that he "married" her?

A: I have the testimony of Petero Waiswa. He knows the clan of Kibikyo and knows that Kafuko is not his sister. He lives near Kibikyo. He knows that Kibikyo just "married" her and is not her brother.

Petero Waiswa: I agree to give [evidence] because Nasani calls upon me and because I know the clans of Kibikyo and Nabuti. I myself know that Kibikyo is a Mwisemulondo. His father was Kiwulule and his mother was a Mwisekantu. She came from Namwendwa. That man Nabuti is a Mwisetoli. His wife is a Mwisembupi. Nabuti begat this woman Kafuko, about whom they are litigating. I know that because Nabuti is a neighbor of mine, and I know about Kibikyo because I have a brother named Amaiwa, with whom he used to converse at the home of Temusewo Kyeya at Namwenda. But my brother and he [Temusewo] are dead.

Q: If you are a neighbor of Nabuti and Kibikyo, what do you know about Kafuko's "marrying" Kibikyo?

A: I don't know about his "marrying" her, but the fact that he [falsely] calls her his sister shows that he "married" her [that he has something to hide].

The court has now heard two conflicting accounts of the facts. To be sure, there is much common ground. The various statements about the encounter at Kibikyo's house, while they differ in the way self-interested observer's accounts of the same events usually do, agree in all important respects. All take it for granted that Kibikyo and Kafuko were caught in circumstances which, if they are not siblings, amount to adultery. But on two key sets of facts there is conflict: first, Kibikyo's case asserts, and Nasani's denies, that Kibikyo and Kafuko are lineage siblings;[12] second, Kafuko and her father assert that the marriage with Nasani has been dissolved by repayment of bridewealth, while Nasani denies this. If the marriage has been dissolved, of course, an accusation of adultery cannot be sustained in any case.

In its final round of questioning, the court begins with the latter point, asking Nasani:

Q: How long did your wife, Kafuko, spend in your home?
A: I spent four years with her.
Q: Is it true, as Nabuti says, that the fourteen shillings with which you paid for his daughter were paid back?
A: I was never repaid. When I seized Kafuko, she was still my wife.

This could well become a major issue. The court might call for the witnesses and written agreements that ought to be available if a properly contracted marriage has been properly dissolved. But the court drops the point; it is not, after all, part of Kibikyo's defense. Kafuko and her father have introduced it, probably to forestall an accusation of harboring, which might well succeed even if Kibikyo cannot be convicted of adultery. Kibikyo's case rests on the siblingship argument and it is to this that the court now turns. The court, clearly, has decided that Kibikyo is either a liar or a fool. He has confessed that until recently he did not know Kafuko was his sister, while Nasani's witness on the genealogical issue, Petero Waiswa, sounds confident and well informed. Furthermore, Kibikyo has made some surprising statements about "visiting." Married siblings are expected to visit one another, accompanied by their spouses; such formal visits clarify the pattern of kin relations and help control the tensions that so often develop between in-laws. But Kibikyo denies that such visits have occurred. He knows Kafuko's husband only by hearsay, while Kafuko says she has visited Kibikyo before, presumably alone. The court's suspicions thoroughly aroused, it therefore turns to Kibikyo, thrusting at him questions designed to reveal inconsistencies and weaknesses in his defense:

Q: Do you agree that, as Nabuti says, the man Kyewalyanga of Naluwoli was the one who succeeded your father, the late Bakisula? Is he still living?
A: Yes, I agree. What Nabuti says is the truth. Kyewalyanga was the successor and he is still living and I can bring him if the court wishes.

12. Kibikyo's account of his parentage is not necessarily wholly incompatible with that of Petero Waiswa. Kiwulule, whom Petero names as Kibikyo's "father" may well be the stepfather that Kibikyo has himself spoken of. Both accounts may well have been given in good faith.

A fair offer. Kyewalyanga's testimony would be valuable, but the court has made up its mind and as it relentlessly pursues Kibikyo, further evidence of his unreliability or stupidity is forthcoming.

Q: If you are a member of the Baisetoli [clan], can you call upon the head of the clan?
A: I can't get testimony from any of the clan heads. I might be able to call on an ordinary member, but I don't even know the head for the subcounty in which I live.
Q: Your witness, Nabuti, says that he came to know you at Bulonda—that you were his child—and that he invited you to visit him. . . . But you say that Nabuti only got to know you when you moved to Bugulumbya. Now . . . who is telling the truth?
A: Nabuti has spoken the truth. I was mistaken.
Q: If you are a Mwisetoli, what is your totem?
A: The bushbuck.
Q: When did you begin to visit in the house of your father, Nabuti?
A: I began to visit there in 1948. I moved to Bugulumbya in 1940, but at first I didn't visit [Nabuti]. I knew that Kafuko was my sister when she was still married to Kitosi, before she married Nasani Beka. I knew it from her father, Nabuti.
Q: If you knew Kafuko before the marriage to Nasani, then is [she] right [or wrong] when she says she first met you at Kalongo's funeral at Nawanende in 1949, after she left Nasani?
A: No, she is not right. She has forgotten. I saw her first at Nabuti's and not at the funeral of Kalongo.

The court's doubts having hardened into firm conviction, the decision is given:

The accused, Kibikyo, has lost the case. It appears from the evidence given in this court by Petero Waiswa that he "married" the wife of Nasani Beka . . . . The evidence shows that Kibikyo is not of the clan of Baisetoli but is instead of the Baisemulondo. Although Kibikyo brought the testimony of Nabuti, who begat Kafuko, nevertheless there is conflicting evidence. His evidence is not correct. He is fined 40 shillings and will be imprisoned for three months at hard labor. Compensation of 120 shillings will be given to the owner of the wife, Nasani Beka. The wife [also] is given to Nasani.

Kibikyo is perhaps naïve, but he is persistent, and so, faced with severe punishment, he appeals to the county court, addressing, as is customary, the county chief, the chairman of the court. The formal, highly deferential style is typical of such communications:

Sir, with great humility and honoring your person, I write to you to appeal my case . . . in which I was charged with seducing away Kafuko, the wife of N. Beka, and of spending seven days with her. Sir, the charge against me is not true, for these reasons: 1. That woman Kafuko is not my "wife," but rather my sister. The reason why she was found in my house was that she came to visit me because of a death. Finding her at my house, her husband, my in-law, just wanted to fight. 2. In the case I called upon our father, the father of both of us—myself and my sister Kafuko—to show that she was my sister. And our father gave good testimony to the court . . . but they did not believe it.

Sir, my lord Gabula,[13] do not fail to examine carefully this case in which I am accused in your court. It is a terrible thing when a person brings true evidence and is not believed. Pay particular attention to asking the husband of the wife: "Have you heard the testimony of the witness [Nabuti]? Is it true? Do you know that he is the father of this woman and Kibikyo?". . . It is said that only the head of the [clan] can give true evidence. But it seems to me that [only] if my father says he doesn't know about the relationship [between us] would the charge be true.

Sir, I am your man,
Kibikyo

The county court is more sympathetic. Having heard the lower court record read out by the clerk, it merely asks Kibikyo to confirm his testimony there:

Q: You have heard the statements read. . . . Are they the ones you made in the court of Mutuba VII, and did you confirm them with your signature?
A: I have heard them and I confirm that they are true. I have nothing else to add.

Now Nasani makes use of his right to question Kibikyo:

Q: If you are sure you are the brother of my wife Kafuko, can you call upon one of my wife's sisters' spouses [14] who know you [to say that] you are their brother, even though I am not aware of it?

In the intervening three months, Nasani's confidence seems to have weakened. Perhaps his accusation of Kibikyo was overhasty, the ill-considered act of a suspicious husband. In any case, Kibikyo's self-confidence has correspondingly risen:

A: If I were to call upon your wife's sister's spouses, as you say, their answers would not be better than those of Nabuti, the father of both Kafuko and myself. . . . He has already given evidence in the court of Mutuba VII, and that is enough.

Now it is Nasani who is on the defensive, harried by a bench which remains unconvinced of his case. After hearing him confirm his testimony in the lower court, it asks:

Q: Is Petero Waiswa, about whom we have heard in your evidence, of the same clan as Nabuti?
A: No . . . .

13. "Gabula" is the title of the hereditary rulers of Bugabula, here applied honorifically to the present-day appointed civil-servant chief. This is common whenever the boundaries of present-day political units correspond with those of traditional ones.
14. *Basangi.* See Appendix A.

Q: If [he] is not, as you say, of the same clan as Nabuti, what is it that shows [that is, how can he be sure] that Nabuti is not the father of Kibikyo . . . and Kafuko?

A: I say that P. Waiswa has already given his evidence to the court of Mutuba VII.

Q: Besides Nabuti, the father . . . of Kafuko, is there any other parent [15] of Kafuko whom you can bring to give evidence?

A: . . . there is no other.

Q: Now, if you agree that there is no other parent besides Nabuti, then when Kibikyo says he is of the same clan as she . . . , is he correct?

A: He is not!

Q: When you were going to seize Kibikyo . . . did you first go to the headman in the usual way?

A: I did not . . . . I went straight to his home and caught him and my wife.

Following this last exchange, which suggests that Nasani acted impetuously, the court decides to alter the decision of Mutuba VII, concluding:

The appellant . . . has won the case. It appears that he was not "married" to the woman Kafuko . . . but that she just went to visit him as a sister . . . . The appellant Kibikyo brought Nabuti, the father of the woman Kafuko, and he gave testimony confirming that Kibikyo was his son in their clan of Baisetoli. Because of the testimony of Nabuti . . . the appellant has won the case.

Reversals upon appeal are not uncommon. Of the 189 cases that passed through the Bugabula county court in 1950, for example, more than one-third (67) were reversed by that court; of these, 4 went on to be reversed yet again, and 2 a third time, by higher courts. In 16 cases, punishments or awards of compensation were altered at some stage.

The case of *Nasani Beka* v. *Kibikyo* has been presented at this point because, in the course of deciding it, the court has said something authoritative about the legal meaning of the word "sister." Nowhere, to be sure, has the court set out a formal definition: "A 'sister' is . . . ." But the arguments of the litigants and the questions and decisions of the judges all clearly proceed from the understanding that a man and a woman who call each other "sibling of the opposite sex" by virtue of descent in the patrilineal line from a common ancestor cannot commit adultery. This one case does not, of course, tell one how far, for this purpose, the word "sister" extends collaterally. I do not have the case material with which to test its limits further, though Basoga say that it extends to all members of a clan and thus to persons whose common agnatic descent is no longer traceable in collective memory, but is

15. *Muzaire:* Parent of either sex. See Appendix A. The county court considers that Nabuti's testimony is stronger than that of Petero Waiswa and here suggests that it can only be overcome by that of another close kinsman.

merely assumed to exist by virtue of the common clan name and totem.

With respect to the problem of applicability—the problem of the meaning of "sister" in the law of adultery—*Nasani Beka v. Kibikyo* is a relatively plain case, which is why the problem of applicability is not explicitly argued. "Everybody knows" that a man cannot commit adultery with his sister in the patrilineal line. However, this does not fully dispose of the problem of the meaning of *bwenzi* as a concept of wrong, for not all persons who, in Soga terminology, call each other "sibling of the opposite sex" are related in the patrilineal line. Before proceeding to a case involving the possibility of adultery between other kinds of "siblings," however, it is worth pausing briefly to discuss the handling of the problem of fact in *Nasani Beka v. Kibikyo*. Here the case was not at all a plain one, which is of course the reason for the concentration of the arguments upon the fact problem and for the difference between the lower court's and the appeal court's decisions. The lower court clearly decided quite early in the proceedings that Kibikyo and Kafuko were a couple of unreliable characters and that Nabuti's testimony should be discounted as biased in support of his daughter. The lower court therefore chose to believe Nasani and his witness, Petero Waiswa, even though the crucial part of the latter's testimony ("I know about Kibikyo because I had a brother . . . with whom he used to converse at the home of Temusewo Kyeya . . . . But my brother and he are dead.") is admittedly hearsay. The appellate judges, perhaps in part because they lacked personal knowledge of the parties and in part because the passage of time had allowed passions to cool and the real merits of the arguments to emerge more clearly, decided that Kibikyo had the better case. His witness, Nabuti, was, after all, in a better position than Petero Waiswa to know that to which he testified. Furthermore, Nabuti's own personal interests in some respects ran counter to his testimony. He would naturally, perhaps, want to support his daughter's account of the affair, but by doing this he had to make himself more vulnerable to a charge of harboring if Nasani and Kafuko were, as Nasani claimed, still legally married. (This question was never litigated, at least during the following year.) Allowing Kibikyo to be convicted would have helped to take the "heat" off himself, since Kafuko's absence from Nasani's home could then be attributed to adultery instead of harboring. Kibikyo, furthermore, offered to bring a witness, Kyewalyanga, who would also be in a position to know the relevant kinship relations and who would be less influenced by the personal interests that might affect Nabuti one way or the other.

Genatio Magino v. *Yowasi Maliwa: the significance of step-sibling-ship*

For the present, however, my main concern is with the Soga courts' handling of concepts of applicability in determining the boundaries of concepts of wrong. I return, therefore, to the meaning of "sister" in the law of adultery. The case of *Genatio Magino* v. *Yowasi Maliwa* is of particular interest because in it the question of the reach of a concept of wrong is argued more explicitly than is usual in the Soga courts.

Yowasi comes before the court one day in January 1950, accused of "having been caught with the wife of G. Magino, who has been away from her husband since October 25, and of going to [Magino's] in-laws to negotiate bridewealth." Yowasi and the woman, Matama, defend their conduct:

Yowasi Maliwa: I will win because this woman Matama is my sister and she only stayed at my house for three days. . . . On January 9, 1950, I put her on my bicycle and took her to our father at Kyani, where this man Genatio found me and seized me and beat me so badly that I am still not well.

Q: Since you say that Matama is your sister, how many times did you visit Genatio's home while she was still there?

Again, the question about in-law visiting—a favorite of judges in such cases. Here the expected answer is forthcoming.

A: Yes, while Matama was still in that man's home, I used to visit there with our father and when they came to our home, I used to prepare the relish for the meal we cooked for them. . . .
Q: Do you have evidence to show that Matama is your sister?
A: Yes, there is Yose Toli—because he was the first husband of my mother—and Eryeza Kige. . . .
Q: What is your clan and what is Yose's clan?
A: I am Mwisemaganda; he is Mwisengobi.

Matama: We [she and Yowasi] are not from the same womb, but his father was married to my mother and that was where I grew up. When I went there, this Yowasi was a child.

Q: While you were still in Genatio's home, how many times did Yowasi visit there?
A: He visited there while he was still young, but after he was grown up, he no longer visited.
Q: Because you grew up in the house of Yowasi's father, you are therefore called his "sister"?
A: Yes, because I grew up in his father's house, I call Yowasi "brother" but we are not of the same clan; I have one father, he another.
Q: When Genatio found you at Yose's, where had Yowasi found you, so that he might take you there?

A: I was coming from Bugabula and night overtook me as I passed through Luuka. . . . I was tired and so I stopped at Yowasi's, though he wasn't at home when I arrived. The next morning, he put me on a bicycle to take me to the house of our father, Yose.

Q: From whose place in Bugabula were you coming?

A: I was coming from the house of Mukama Kiwande at Bulange.

Q: Is it true, as your husband says, . . . that you left his home in October?

A: Yes it is. I left him.

Here the assertion of kinship rests upon kinship ties quite different from those encountered in *Nasani Beka* v. *Kibikyo*. Yowasi and Matama do not claim agnatic kinship; they are "siblings of the opposite sex," they say, because their parents married. In English terminology, they are step-siblings, as shown in figure 5.

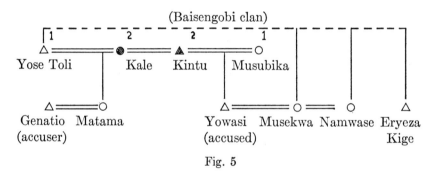

Fig. 5

Some names not yet given in testimony have been anticipated in the diagram so that Yowasi's defense may be followed more readily. Matama says that her mother, Kale, married Yowasi's father, Kintu. As will become apparent, this was a second marriage, following Kale's earlier marriage to Yose Toli, Matama's begetter. Thus, Yowasi says that Yose Toli "was the first husband of my mother," meaning Kale. The marriage of Kintu and Kale will also have followed Kintu's earlier marriage to Musubika, Yowasi's bearer. Yowasi and Matama say they were brought up together in the house of Kintu and Kale. In Soga kinship terminology, Yose Toli, Kale, Kintu, and Musubika are all "parents" to Matama and Yowasi and they are "siblings of the opposite sex" to each other. Later on, Yowasi will also claim that he is married to two other women, Musekwa and Namwase, who are "mothers" to Matama in the Baisengobi clan. For this reason, Yowasi calls Matama "daughter." This, too, is quite proper in Soga terminological usage. The question for the court, however, is whether or not such "sibling" and "parent-child" relationships as these have the same force in the law of adultery as those based upon common agnatic descent.

Apart from the assertion of these kinship ties, Yowasi's defense has consisted of building up a picture of his and Matama's behavior which would be consistent with a sibling or a parent-child relationship. Yes, he says, he and Genatio visited each other, like proper in-laws. Matama, however, is not very helpful. Yowasi no longer visited her and Genatio, she says, "after he was grown up." And she admits having left her husband three months earlier. Worst of all, she speaks of having traveled across the country, apparently unescorted, thereby displaying a certain contempt for the proprieties. The court, therefore, will have formed doubts and suspicions upon which Genatio can play as, under questioning, he builds his own case:

Q: Have you heard Yowasi say in his testimony that your wife Matama is his sister?
A: Yes, I have heard, but I don't know him and I don't know his father, of whom he speaks [meaning Kintu].
Q: When your wife, Matama, disappeared, did you report it to the headmen?
A: Yes, I reported it to the subvillage and village headman, but I didn't report it further [i.e., to the parish or subcounty chief].
Q: Did you visit Yowasi's home, as he says?
A: I never visited him. I don't know his home or his father.[16]
Q: This Yose Toli, of whom Yowasi speaks—did he marry [Yowasi's] mother, Musubika?[17]
A: My in-law [Yose] never married Musubika. The woman he married is Kale, the real mother of Matama who bore her.
Q: How did you know that it was Yowasi who took your wife and that on that day he was going to negotiate bridewealth?
A: I found out by discovering him at my in-laws, while I was walking along on my way to the shops.
Q: But if you just saw him there, how did you know that he had come to negotiate bridewealth?
A: No [I didn't actually know that]; I just saw him there.
Q: When your wife disappeared, did you go to your in-laws [i.e., Yose Toli] to tell them that your wife had disappeared?
A: Yes, I went there twice.
Q: Yowasi says that Matama is his sister and that he used to visit your home. How is that?
A: I don't know that and I call upon Yose Toli. If he knows that Yowasi is the brother of Matama, then I won't plead further.

16. Genatio does not mean to say that he literally does not know of their existence. He almost certainly does, but wishes to express his contempt for them and to reject their account of their kinship status.
17. The court (or the clerk) is apparently confused by Yowasi's rather complicated story. Yowasi has said that his begetter married Matama's bearer; the court is asking whether Matama's begetter married Yowasi's bearer. The effect would in either case be step-siblingship, but the mistake allows Genatio to avoid answering the relevant question.

An absolutely standard exchange in a case of this kind: the court
continues to probe for the kind of behavior to be expected if Yowasi
and Matama are siblings and if, consequently, Yowasi and Genatio are
in-laws. Genatio tries systematically to destroy this picture and to
construct another of himself as the deserted husband taking all the
proper steps to recover his runaway wife. Both sides, however, have
called upon Yose Toli for support. In examining his testimony, it is
important to remember that he himself is in a position of some danger.
His daughter has, by her own admission, been absent without leave
from her husband for some three months, thereby threatening Yose
with an accusation for harboring. Genatio has hinted at this, and
worse, in his opening assertion that Yowasi had gone to Yose's "to
negotiate bridewealth." If this were true, and if Genatio had not been
given back his bridewealth, Yose would be open to the charge of
"eating two hens." Yose, however, is in a difficult position. He does not,
for reasons that will emerge shortly, want to support Yowasi's defense
of siblingship, which would be one way of defending his own position.
He therefore chooses the other route—denying Yowasi's claim, but at
the same time denying having had any dealings with him:

Q: What do you know about these two people, Genatio and Yowasi?
A: I know that Genatio is my in-law and that Matama is my daughter, but
   that boy [Yowasi] I don't know.
Q: Yowasi says that Matama is his sister. How is that?
A: I know nothing of that; I didn't beget him!
Q: But your daughter Matama says that Yowasi is her brother. How is that?
A: I have a son, but I do not know that one.[18]
Q: Now, when Genatio says that Yowasi seduced his wife, Matama, is he
   right?
A: Yes, he is truthful.
Q: And Genatio says that he caught these two in your house. How is that?
A: Yes, it's true. I was at my home that morning, taking out my goats, when I
   saw this one [Matama] coming on a bicycle, together with this youth
   [Yowasi]. I was about to tell her that her husband was looking for her, but
   before I had a chance to speak to them,[19] I saw Genatio and his four
   friends seize the youth and the girl, Matama.
Q: Had Genatio come to report to you that his wife was missing?
A: Yes, he came twice and I told him to go and report it to the headmen.
Q: Genatio says that Yowasi came to your house to negotiate bridewealth.
   How is that?
A: I never saw him before [20] and he never came to negotiate.
Q: Yowasi says that you are his father and your daughter agrees that you are

18. Again, not a denial of actual knowledge, but rather a contemptuous refusal
to recognize a relationship.
19. Yose protects himself by denying any conversation at all.
20. Again, the words are not meant literally. He means: "I haven't had any
such dealings with him."

his father because the man Kintu married your wife and that therefore [Yowasi] calls [your wife] his "mother." How is that?

A: Kintu, the man they speak of [Yowasi's father], just stole my wife and the villagers know that he stole her.

Q: What do you know about Eryeza?[21]

A: Eryeza is of the Baisengobi [clan], brother of Kamu Mukama.

Q: When they seized Yowasi at your home, what did he say to you?

A: At my home, he told me nothing, except what he said in court—that is, [Matama] is his sister.

Thus Yose does not, in the end, really deny that which, on the factual side, is the heart of Yowasi's defense: the marriage between Yowasi's begetter and Matama's bearer. He does, to be sure, speak of Kintu's having "just stolen" Musubika, but this does not necessarily mean that no legitimate marriage took place; it may well mean no more than that the loss of his wife still rankles with Yose.[22] However, if this question were decisive, one would expect the court to seek further evidence. Instead, the judges simply ignore the point as they begin their final questioning of Yowasi:

Q: Have you heard your witness say that you are not his son and that you took another man's wife?

A: Yes, I have heard.

Q: Except for this witness, do you have other evidence?

A: Yes, I have Eryeza.

Q: Do you call upon him because he knows that both of you have the same female parent?

A: No, because we are not children of women of the same clan [*baiwa*].[23]

Q: . . . what do you call upon Eryeza for?

A: I call upon him because he knows that the mother of Matama brought me up.

Again, Yowasi returns to the same point, but the court ignores it and in a very brief decision, which makes no reference to the arguments, simply finds Yowasi guilty. Genatio is awarded 100 shillings compensation and Yowasi is to be imprisoned for four months and fined 50 shillings.

Thus, Yowasi has failed to draw either his accuser or his judges into a discussion of the question of applicability upon which his defense rests. He and Matama have argued more or less explicitly that step-siblingship is "true" siblingship for the purpose of the law of adultery.

21. Mentioned earlier by Yowasi as a potential witness.

22. Recall here the tendency of a bride's agnates to accuse her bridegroom of "just taking her by force," even when a marriage has been properly contracted and celebrated.

23. All children of the women of a patrilineal descent group are *baiwa*. See Appendix A.

There is little disagreement about the facts: Yowasi was, he admits, caught with the woman. Yose, for his part, admits (and Genatio has said he will accept Yose's testimony on the matter) that some sort of marriage took place between Yowasi's father and Matama's mother. There is some argument as to whether Yowasi behaved toward Genatio as a true in-law would, but this is peripheral. For the central argument is not about the facts, but rather about the reach of the relevant concept of wrong—*bwenzi*—with respect to the facts, and this argument turns on the reach of the subsidiary concept of siblingship. The court implicitly rejects Yowasi's claim that he and Matama are siblings under the law of *bwenzi* by simply ignoring this claim and by offering him the opportunity to claim other grounds for siblingship with Matama. ("What is your clan and what is Yose's clan?" "Do you call upon Eryeza because he knows that both of you have the same female parent?") But Yowasi's argument is never *explicitly* rejected.

Yowasi, however, remains undaunted. In the county prison, he composes a letter of appeal to the county chief, setting out his argument again. Such letters of appeal provide the closest approach to an explicitly argued brief known to the lawyerless courts of Busoga. In the preceding case, Kibikyo succeeded with such a document. Yowasi will fail, but in his effort to persuade the appeal court of the merits of his defense, he comes as close as a Musoga can to explicitly legal argument.

First, he asserts that Genatio, when he found him and Matama in Yose's courtyard, jumped to an unwarranted conclusion without stopping to consider other possible explanations of their presence there:

when he arrived at his in-law's house, he did not begin by asking him where his wife, who had left him long before, had been and why she was now seen [at Yose's]. Nor did he ask Yose about the man [Yowasi] he found in the house of his in-law. . . . Nor did he ask the reason that brought me to that courtyard, nor my relationship to it, nor my relationship to his wife Matama, my sister . . . nor the reason why I put her on my bicycle to bring her there. . . . He and his in-law admit this in their testimony. . . . He agrees that no one told him that . . . I had gone to negotiate bridewealth and be introduced.[24] And his witness, his in-law, agrees that I did not go to be introduced. . . . So when I say that he accuses me without reason, am I not right? I was a visitor. A person's relatives are many. How do you know when you find a person in the courtyard of your in-law whether or not he is related to that house? . . . There was nothing with which he caught me going to in-laws. There was no accompanying party, no goats, no shillings, no hens or salt or tobacco—things people give as presents. . . . When I say that it was anger with his wife . . . that caused him to act without thinking, am I not right?

24. The formal presentation of the bridegroom to the bride's people.

Next, Yowasi attacks the motives of his accuser and his accuser's witness:

Genatio knows me well, but in his testimony he denies [it] for these reasons: Both Kale and Kintu have died and he is therefore no longer interested in that courtyard. He wants to get money from me.[25] And he fears a case because he beat me and intended to spear me. . . . His in-law, Yose, it is the same with him . . . he wants money from me. I am not his child in his clan. He does not care if I am in danger . . . his evidence supports me. He does not say I went there to negotiate bridewealth, as Genatio claims. He only confuses the court by denying [that he knows] me and by saying that my father, Kintu, took his wife and didn't marry her in the right way. But it isn't so. The late D. Kidali was the first to marry her and the bridewealth was paid back to Yose. My father married her when she rejected the successors [of Kidali] and the bridewealth was paid to the brothers of the deceased.[26] . . . I go into this matter of Yose and my father to explain why, although his evidence supports me, he says my father spoiled his home.

Finally, Yowasi comes to the core of his argument about the meaning of "sister":

The [lower] court bases itself on the argument that the girl is not a relative to me, but it forgets the custom [*mpisa*] of the nation. It is well known that there is not just one kind of relationship and one kind of respect between people. And it is a mistake to think that because I am not of the same clan as a woman, or of the same maternal parentage, I can marry her. This is not true. It should not be forgotten that blood brothers become clansmen and call each other "real brothers." [27] Kale, who bore Matama, was married to my father, and her daughter grew up in the household. . . . Why shouldn't I call her "my sister"? [Furthermore], I am married to two princesses—Musekwa and . . . Namwase. Would I not fear to add a daughter to her mothers? They are truly of the same *ssiga*. . . .[28] So now I call Matama "my sister" and "my daughter." How can I make her my wife? . . . I wanted to bring my witness to show that my father, Kintu, married the mother of Matama and that he married her in the proper way and did not steal her, as Yose says. . . . But the court did not accept this.

When the case comes before the county court, on March 27, 1950, both litigants confirm the testimony given in the lower court. Then one of the judges questions Yowasi:

25. In compensation.
26. When a widow does not marry a member of her dead husband's lineage, her people must repay the bridewealth. This point arises in *Zakaliya Yande* v. *Amadi Simola,* to be discussed later in this chapter.
27. Blood brothers may not, for example marry women of each other's clans.
28. "Princesses" (*bambedha*) are in this case women of the Baisgengobi clan, the traditional rulers of Bulamogi. While sororal polygyny is common and approved, a man should not marry women of the same patrilineal descent group who are members of adjacent generations and hence call each other "mother" and "daughter." "*Ssiga*" is a Luganda term for the largest lineage within a clan.

Q: I have heard in your appeal that you called for a witness in the court of
   Musaale, but that this was not agreed to. Now, have you brought your
   witness?
A: I haven't brought him, because the evidence of Yose [is sufficient].

Perhaps Yowasi has by now lost heart; perhaps his witness is not
available. In any case, the county court confirms the lower court's
decision:

The appellant pleads that this woman Matama is his sister, but there is no
true evidence that Matama is a sister. For that reason, he is defeated.

It is significant that the court insists upon treating what is essentially a question of the reach of a concept as if it were a simple
question of fact, in spite of Yowasi's clear posing of the conceptual
issue in his appeal. ("It is well known that there is not just one kind of
relationship . . . between people.") What is quite apparent to the
outside investigator, to Yowasi, and probably in this case, at least, to
the judges themselves—that the court has ruled upon the meaning of
"sister" in the law of adultery—is left entirely implicit. It has not said
explicitly "persons who call each other 'sibling of the opposite sex' by
virtue of their parents' marriage alone are not immune from accusations of adultery," although only by inferring such a conclusion can
one understand the court's behavior. The court simply says: "Matama
is not Yowasi's sister," although if their parents were married and if
they grew up together in the same household—"facts" which are not
really denied by their accusers—Basoga would agree that they *are*
"siblings of the opposite sex" in everyday speech, even if not for
purposes of the law of adultery. There could be no better illustration
of the invincible implicitness with which Basoga reason with legal
concepts.

This decision is typical. While courts occasionally rise to conceptual
issues more explicitly than in this instance, especially, as will be seen,
in areas in which the law is changing, they seem to avoid doing so
whenever they can. Here the accused's argument in his appeal was
unusually explicit, but it was not a strong argument. Most people
would agree that step-siblingship is not a bar to *bwenzi*. Yowasi's
argument is therefore merely clever; it does not challenge the judges
intellectually.

WHAT IS A "WIFE"?

I have not explored all the legal boundaries of the word "sister" in
relation to adultery. It has been discovered that siblings by patrilineal
descent cannot, in the eyes of the A.L.G. courts, commit *bwenzi*, while

step-siblings can. As the discussion of Soga kinship terminology in Appendix A indicates, the word for "sibling of the opposite sex"—*mwanhina*—has another important referent: it also applies to all children of the opposite sex of women of one's mother's patrilineal descent group. It includes mother's sisters' children, mother's brothers' daughters' children, mother's brothers' sons' daughters' children, and of course, maternal half-siblings. Sexual relations with any of these is incest and hence, I suspect, persons so related are immune to charges of *bwenzi* in the official courts. This question, however, I shall have to leave unexplored; in any case, the essential point has been made: The legal concept of wrong *bwenzi* classifies kinsmen in a way different from that of the ordinary, everyday language of kinship.

The same point arises with respect to the word "wife." A man accused of *bwenzi* may argue in defense that the woman in question is his wife. But, like "sister," "wife" has many referents, some of which exclude adultery, while others do not. There are actually two words: *mukazi* and *mukyala.* Unmodified, the first means "woman," the second "lady." [29] *Mukyala* also means "Mrs." In the possessive, both also mean "wife" (e.g., *mukazi wange* or *mukyala wange:* "my wife"). In both of the cases to be discussed next, the men accused of adultery are quite correct, so far as everyday usage goes, in speaking of the women concerned as "wives." The legal consequences in the two cases are, however, quite different.

Mikairi Magino v. Sabani Kafuko: a valid marriage excludes adultery

The first case may be dealt with quite summarily, as, indeed, it was by the court. On February 15, 1951, Sabani Kafuko comes before the court accused of "marrying" a woman named Kiyigo, who has a husband, Mikairi Magino of Buwalira, Busiki. Sabani's defense is simple:

Sabani: I agree to contest the case and I expect to win. I paid 254 shillings, 6 hens, and 16 goats as bridewealth for her. I paid these to Ntumba, and he can confirm it.

Mikairi Magino's case is also straightforward:

Mikairi: I say that I will win because she is my wife and I paid 62 shillings, 1 cow, 17 goats, and 7 hens as bridewealth for her and it is now two years since the accused stole her from my home. The bridewealth was handed over to Ntumba, the one whom he has mentioned as his witness. My witnesses, who

---

29. As in the English distinction between "officers' ladies" and "enlisted men's wives."

can prove that she is my wife and that I paid those things as bridewealth, are Mukama, Federiko, Mutoto, Firikisi, and Wairumba.

Q: Were the witnesses you mentioned present on the day you paid Ntumba the bridewealth?
A: Yes, they were present.
Q: Apart from the witnesses, did you write anything?
A: Yes, we wrote agreements.

The next to be called is, of course, Ntumba:

Ntumba: I am a witness for Sabani because I refunded 104 shillings, 2 goats, and 1 hen to Mikairi . . . and when I called him to fetch the remainder, he refused. Then, after a time, someone came to tell me that Mikairi had found his wife in another man's home.

Q: You have said that you paid back a part of the bridewealth, but did you make a written agreement [about the repayment]?
A: He gave me an agreement, but it was destroyed when my house was burned.

The court has heard quite enough. Ntumba, the woman's father, does not deny that he contracted with Sabani for her, though he argues that he was justified in doing so because the earlier marriage had been dissolved by repayment of bridewealth. Whatever else may be true, therefore, Sabani is innocent of *bwenzi* because, in the words of the court's decision . . . "his in-law, Ntumba, has agreed that he was the one who allowed [him] to marry her." For Ntumba, this is not the end of the matter. The court adds: "The father of the woman will be accused of 'eating two hens.' See Case no. 42 of 1951." Ntumba's fate will be taken up later in connection with the discussion of "eating two hens" as a concept of wrong. For the present, *Mikairi Magino* v. *Sabani Kifuko* provides one clear boundary of the meaning of "wife" in the law of adultery. A man cannot commit adultery with a woman who is his "wife" as the result of a marriage validly contracted with her guardian. If a conflicting contract has been made, it is the guardian who is responsible.

Zakaliya Yande v. *Amadi Simola: widow inheritance*

Zakaliya Yande v. *Amadi Simola* raises more complex issues. Amadi is accused by Zakaliya of "seducing away my wife, Kalegere, with whom I caught him, having kept her for two months." There is really no disagreement about the "facts." It is common ground that Amadi and Kalegere have, indeed, been living together and there is uncontested evidence that Amadi properly calls Kalegere "my wife." It is also common ground that Zakaliya has earlier contracted a valid marriage for Kalegere with her father. How this tangled state of

affairs arose becomes clear as soon as Amadi and his witness come
before the court on October 27 to build his defense:

Amadi: I agree to plead and I will win because the woman with whom I was
seized is my wife. My brother Zefaniya married her and then died. When he
died I was made successor, but I was not present. I was far away in Luuka
and when I delayed returning, Zakaliya took my wife. I do not know him. He
is not of my clan. The sixty shillings and six hens were never paid back.

Q: After you succeeded your brother, did you at any time "marry" that
   woman?[30]
A: I didn't "marry" her because I was in Luuka from the time she left her
   husband's grave until Zakaliya married her. And she herself told me that
   the reason she married him was that I hadn't returned.
Q: Then you asked the woman and she told you she had been married?
A: Yes. . . .
Q: What did you do when she told you she was married?
A: I did nothing.
Q: That is to say, when Zakaliya seized you for the offense of stealing [his
   wife], he was right?
A: He was right.[31]
Q: When you returned and learned that your wife was married, did you go to
   your in-laws?
A: I didn't go.
Q: Do you have witnesses to testify that that woman was your brother's wife?
A: I have Walwalo and my in-law Eneriko Beka.

Walwalo: I agree to testify for Amadi whom I [as lineage head] placed as
successor to his deceased brother. But when his brother died, he did not come
because he was ill with the *kikedi* sickness,[32] so I gave another the task of
shaving.[33]

Q: When Amadi returned, did you introduce him to his in-law and did you
   show him his wife?
A: I didn't take him there.
Q: After you had completed the *kwabya olumbe* funeral ceremonies for your
   son, how long did the woman remain in your home?
A: I don't know how long she stayed because after I had installed the suc-
   cessor, I returned to my home, leaving her there.[34]
Q: Did you know that the girl had been married to Zakaliya?
A: I knew [it].

30. Here "to marry" means "to claim as a sexual partner."
31. Amadi is not admitting *bwenzi,* merely that he took the woman. He still
claims a right to do so.
32. Syphilis. Bukedi is the area to the northeast of Busoga. Like so many other
peoples, Basoga attribute syphilis to foreigners.
33. The significance of this will be explained below.
34. The court's question implies that the lineage head should have looked after
the widow until the successor claimed her. By his answers to this whole series of
questions, he admits to having been extremely negligent with respect to his
duties. His lineage mates might well proceed against him in a lineage tribunal
under these circumstances. I do not know whether or not this occurred.

Q: What did you do?
A: We did nothing.

Then the court questions Kalegere:

Q: Of these two, Zakaliya and Amadi, who is your husband?
A: My husband is Zakaliya Yande because when my husband Zefaniya died, Amadi Simola [did not come for me]. Bulu shaved me. Then I was married to Zakaliya for one cow. But the man who died gave twenty goats—ten young and ten mature ones.

The basis of Amadi's defense is the custom of widow inheritance, which in turn must be understood in the context of the corporateness and solidarity of the lineage. In this case, a lineage is defending its rights in a woman for whom one of its members has paid bridewealth (see fig. 6).

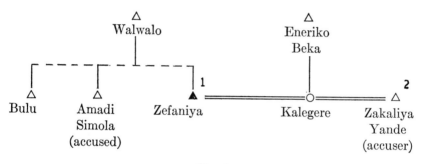

Fig. 6

The head of the succession lineage, Walwalo, testifies that he, on behalf of the lineage, installed Amadi as Zefaniya's successor. The testimony of a lineage head on such a matter carries much weight; in any case, the other side does not contest it. Now as successor, Amadi has, in custom, first claim on Kalegere. He would normally, as part of the kwabya olumbe ceremony, have spent a night with her and then they would have shaved each other's heads as a sign that the mourning for Zefaniya was finished. Since Amadi was away and incapacitated, Bulu served in his place—a perfectly acceptable procedure, since it is not simply Amadi as an individual, but rather the whole lineage group, that possesses rights in Kalegere by virtue of the payment of bridewealth for her. All members of the lineage of Zefaniya's generation, including Amadi and Bulu, have called her "my wife" ever since she and Zefaniya were married, in recognition of the fact that the wives of a man's brothers are, by the customs of succession and widow inheritance, potential wives to him. Again, the pattern is plain in the account of Soga kinship terminology given in Appendix A. The problem faced by the court, however, is that of deciding how much of this complex of custom is legally significant, and under what circumstances. In particular, does Amadi's succession to his brother make Kalegere his wife in the sense of placing his cohabitation with her beyond the reach of the concept *bwenzi*—even though a valid marriage has been contracted for her by a man outside the lineage? In pursuit of answers to these questions, the court calls Kalegere's father, Eneriko Beka:

Q: For whom do you agree to give evidence?
A: I give it for Zakaliya . . . because he married my daughter Kalegere.
Q: What did Zakaliya give you as bridewealth?
A: He gave me one cow and twenty shillings.[35]
Q: When Zakaliya married that girl, had she not been married before?
A: Yes, but the man she married before, Zefaniya Wadiba, died.
Q: Who succeeded your in-law?
A: No one succeeded [except that at] the *kwabya olumbe* it was Bulu.
Q: After the *kwabya olumbe* did they not shave?
A: They shaved; Bulu was the one who shaved.
Q: Amadi says that it was he who succeeded his brother Zefaniya. How do you answer that?
A: I don't know that Amadi; I've never seen him.[36]
Q: When you gave Zakaliya your daughter how long had she been in your home?
A: She had spent two years in my home and she had spent three years with Zakaliya.

Again the court, like that in *Genatio Magino* v. *Yowasi Maliwa*, has little difficulty with the facts, about which there is substantial agreement. As usual, the decision is terse and skeletal, but it does recognize that both arguments have some substance and it is perhaps for this reason that Amadi's punishment is less severe than that given to others convicted of *bwenzi* in previous cases:

The accused, Amadi Simola, has lost the case. It is true, as he claims, that he succeeded his brother, Zefaniya, but he did not marry her for five years after her husband died. However, Amadi did not receive his bridewealth. He will be imprisoned for two months and will pay twenty shillings compensation to the accuser.

35. Kalegere has said above that Zakaliya gave one cow for her. She has also said that Zefaniya paid twenty goats, whereas Amadi claims in his testimony that Zefaniya gave sixty shillings and six hens. Since the amount of the bridewealth is not under litigation, all this is unimportant. In part, at least, the differences are due to the Soga habit of expressing sums in equivalent value in different media. Basoga have not yet become accustomed to expressing all sums in terms of money. Part of the difference may also be due simply to Kalegere's ignorance. She is herself not a party to the bridewealth contract.
36. Again, not a literal denial of knowledge, but rather a rejection of a claim.

There is no need to follow the case to the county court on appeal. Amadi's letter of appeal simply repeats his arguments given in testimony and nothing new emerges from the arguments in the county court, which simply confirms the lower court's decision. Only the first trial, therefore, need be considered.

The court has concluded that at the time of Zefaniya's death Amadi did indeed have a right to claim Kalegere as a wife by virtue of widow inheritance properly carried out by the lineage.[37] It suggests that he still has a claim on the bridewealth which Zefaniya paid for her— though this would require a separate action for debt. But because both Amadi and his lineage mates failed to assert their claim upon Kalegere for several years and allowed her to marry again without taking action —this is the point of much of the court's questioning of both Amadi and the lineage head, Walwalo—Amadi's claim on Kalegere as a sexual partner, though not necessarily his claim on the bridewealth, has been extinguished. He has become subject to conviction for *bwenzi* by asserting his claim too late. Thus the meaning of "wife" in the law of *bwenzi* may be affected by the passage of time. This element in Soga legal reasoning will be encountered again in connection with claims to land.[38]

This chapter has been concerned primarily with the manner in which, in the application of a concept of wrong to particular sets of circumstances, the courts are required to take certain everyday kinship terms and give them specifically legal meanings, thereby making distinctions which everyday kinship language does not make. There are perfectly good reasons, in the logic of kinship, why step-siblings should be called "siblings": If one calls one's father's wife "mother," it is logical to call her children "siblings." Similarly, if all one's brother's wives are potentially one's own wives, it is logical to call them "wives." But kinship terminologies do not—perhaps cannot—recognize *all* the institutionalized similarities and differences in behavior among kinsmen.[39] Legal reasoning, with its necessity to reach simple "yes" or "no" decisions with respect to the applicability of concepts of wrong, must sometimes make distinctions that everyday kinship language can leave ambiguous. In the cases considered in this chapter, the courts

37. A certain vagueness remains here; it is not clear whether the substitution of Bulu for Amadi in the concluding phases of the *kwabya olumbe* affected the court's decision. Information given by informants suggests that this is a legitimate practice and the court, in its decision, emphasizes the passage of time as the decisive element.
38. See chapters 6 and 7.
39. See Appendix A.

have ruled that a man may freely associate with only certain kinds of "sisters" and certain kinds of "wives" without placing his actions within reach of the concept *bwenzi*. In the following chapters, the courts' application of other concepts of wrong will be seen to involve them in giving special legal meaning to other terms of everyday speech.

*It is always found that when someone's daughter
has disappeared she can be found in the father's home.*
—a father, accused of harboring

*How should one assess the loss of a wife—by the
month or the week or the day? He has the use of the
bridewealth, as well as her work in producing food.*
—a husband, accusing his father-in-law of harboring

5 In-laws at Odds:
Harboring, Eating Two Hens,
Divorce, Bridewealth Debt

Soga marriage is an ambiguous bond, easily loosened but
not so easily broken. Men and women begin their lives together with
divergent lineage loyalties and with a relationship which, by formal,
public definition, is extremely asymmetrical. For the woman, who
must trade the affection and respect of sister- and daughterhood for
wifely subordination in the forbidding environment of her husband's
community, discontent and rebelliousness come easily, especially during the early months or years before the compensations of motherhood
have strengthened and softened her ties with her husband's people. But
the mutual alienation which so often follows marriage is not readily
resolved by amicable separation. A contract, involving others, has been
entered into and a substantial payment has been given and must be
returned.

Like most aspects of Soga marriage, the opportunities for its dissolution are very asymmetrically distributed between husband and wife.
While her husband may simply dismiss her at will, a woman's ability
to escape from an unhappy union depends upon her husband's agreement to part with her and upon her father's willingness—and ability
—to repay. When escape is blocked, a common consequence is an

extramarital affair with a man who, just because he has not paid for her and because his authority over her is therefore not supported by the law, is perhaps a more congenial partner. It is precisely to cope with this possibility that the Soga courts have developed the concept *bwenzi,* whose application was analyzed in chapter 4.

Lovers, however, are not the only source of danger to the Musoga husband's legally extensive, but factually precarious, marital rights. Many an unhappy wife seeks the protection of her father or brother, and the affection and esteem with which they customarily regard her make them reluctant to withhold it. In this chapter I shall analyze the court's handling of concepts of wrong designed to regulate the husband's relations with his in-laws (*bako*).

The most frequently invoked of these concepts is "harboring a wife" (*kutuuza omukazi*), often qualified by the phrase "without sufficient reason" or "unreasonably" (*awatali nsonga*). Of all the concepts of wrong I shall discuss, I have for this one the best direct evidence of use in the precolonial Soga courts. In the book of "Native Court Cases" kept by the British district commissioner for the year 1904—only a decade after the establishment of British administration—there appear many cases in which wives are alleged to have "gone back to their fathers." [1] Since the volume was kept in English, the word *kutuuza* does not appear, but this is clearly what is meant. In the casebook of the subcounty court of Ssaabawaali, Kigulu, for 1923, many cases appear in which the concept is invoked in Luganda. [2] It seems quite certain, therefore, that this is a type of social conflict which is indigenous to Soga society and that the concept "harboring" is well established in Soga folk jurisprudence. Judges may be expected to apply it with skill and assurance.

The core meaning of the concept, already encountered in chapter 1 in *Yoweri Kibiri* v. *Yowabu Kabwire,* may be taken to be something like "the action of a father or guardian in allowing his married daughter or ward to remain away from her husband's home without the husband's consent and without sufficient reason." I shall not stop to cite the "plain cases," of which there are many, which make this core meaning clear, but instead will pass on at once to the more closely contested cases in which the courts are forced to clarify the margins of the concept. As in the case of the concept *bwenzi,* the courts, in testing the legality of particular persons' particular behavior against the concept of wrong, must take the various subsidiary concepts that go to make up the total concept *kutuuza omukazi awatali nsonga* and make

1. On file in the Central Offices, Jinja.
2. See table 4.

"yes" or "no" decisions concerning their applicability to the facts as determined. By virtue of the necessity for dichotomous choice, they must, at least implicitly, make precise what is left ambiguous by the everyday language in which the concept of wrong is invoked. In the application of the concept harboring, several subsidiary questions commonly arise: Who is "a father" or "a guardian" in the sense of being responsible under the bridewealth contract? Under what conditions may a woman be said to be "married," so that these responsibilities properly fall upon her father or guardian? And, assuming that the court has satisfied itself concerning the marital condition of the woman and the locus of responsibility, What kinds of behavior constitute "unreasonable" keeping? I shall begin with the question of the locus of responsibility.

HARBORING: THE QUESTION OF RESPONSIBILITY

In most of the cases in which the concept *kutuuza omukazi* is invoked, the problem of responsibility does not arise in the arguments because the runaway wife takes refuge in the home of her father—the person whom "everyone knows" is responsible to her husband under the bridewealth contract. This is then common ground and the litigation turns on other questions. The death of the wife's father (begetter), however, may complicate matters and force the question of responsibility upon the court's attention.

As long as the begetter remains alive, there is no question; it is he who enters into the bridewealth contract and he who is responsible for keeping its terms by seeing to it that the wife remains in her husband's home. My case materials and interviews reveal no exceptions to these generalizations. But with his death, either before or after his daughter's marriage has been contracted, his responsibilities with respect to the marriage are divided. In the widest sense, responsibility lies with his succession lineage—his near male agnates, who meet at his *kwabya olumbe* funeral ceremonies. Basoga express this corporate responsibility in their kinship terminology, described in Appendix A. To his daughter, all of a man's male agnates are "father" or "little father" (*lata* or *lata omuto*), "sibling of the opposite sex" (*mwanhina*), or "son" (*mutabani*), according to generation; to them, she is "daughter" (*mughala*), "sibling of the opposite sex" (*mwanhina*), or "father's sister" (*songa*). In corporate lineage contexts, they may speak of her as "our daughter" or "our sister." To her husband, all her male agnates will be "in-laws" (*bako*). They feel a strong sense of common moral responsibility for her welfare, but they do not continue to hold common legal responsibility for her marriage as an undivided corporate aggregate. Instead, they exercise their common responsibility, as a group assembled at her father's funeral ceremonies, by appointing an heir and a successor.

The heir (*musika*, or, more fully, *musika atwala ebintu:* "the heir who takes the property") is normally a male agnate of her own generation, usually a brother, if she has one. The successor (*musika ow'enkoba:* "successor of the belt"), also called the "guardian" (*mukuza*) of the children, is normally a male agnate of her father's generation, often not the father's brother by the same father, but rather the father's agnatic cousin, since it is felt that if brothers (in the English sense) succeed one another, the unity and solidarity of the succession lineage will tend to be reduced in favor of that of its constituent smaller lineages. These selections are, however, made at the discretion of the assembled succession lineage. The courts accept their decisions as binding.[3]

The man whose wife's father has died, therefore, is in a rather ambiguous position with respect to his marriage contract. The other party is no longer an individual, the wife's begetter, but rather an agnatic group whose members have designated certain of themselves to exercise the rights and responsibilities of the deceased. It *ought*, in principle, to be clear to everyone who is responsible for what, since the *kwabya olumbe* ceremonies are public and the husband (if the marriage has already taken place) ought to be among the mourners. Chiefs with whom I discussed the question insisted that, of course, everything would be well understood: so-and-so would be responsible to the husband for his wife's continued presence in his home and for repayment of the bridewealth if an agreed-upon separation should occur. Certainly at the *kwabya olumbe* ceremonies I observed it was clear who the designated heir and successor were. But all sorts of complexities are possible. How are the deceased's responsibilities divided between heir and successor under various sets of circumstances? What if the wife takes refuge with an agnate other than the successor?

These and other questions tend to be obfuscated by the highly passion-laden context in which charges of harboring arise. An accusation of *kutuuza omukazi*, like an accusation of *bwenzi*, is a criminal action in the sense that, if successful, it will result not merely in confirmation of the husband's rights in his wife but also in punishment of the accused. Before the matter comes to the sub-county court, a

---

3. When such a question comes before an A.L.G. court, the court's problem is simply to determine what, in fact, the lineage gathering decided. Sometimes, of course, there is conflicting evidence on this; then the court must inquire and makes its own decision.

whole series of authorities—sub-village and village headmen and parish and sub-county chiefs—will have tried to reconcile the parties or,
failing that, to effect an amicable separation by repayment of bridewealth. The marriage has long since failed as a conjugal enterprise and
the husband, full of self-righteousness and frustration, is simply, and
sometimes rather blindly, seeking revenge. (If he has given up his
emotional claims on his wife and simply seeks repayment of his
bridewealth, he sues for debt [*bbanja*], a type of action to be discussed
later.) In his anger, he may be careless of the facts of inheritance and
succession—if he knows them—and simply accuse the man in whose
house the wife is staying. Not uncommonly, of course, the marriage
will already have gone on the rocks before the father died, so that the
husband may not have been present at the *kwabya olumbe*. Or he may
have married her after her father's death. In any case, relations
between *bako* are, at best, not conducive to mutual understanding and
confidence. Meanwhile, the wife has probably been circulating among
the households of several male agnates in an effort to avoid him. She,
with their connivance, may add to the confusion—and to her husband's
anger—by deliberately taking refuge in the house of someone who is
neither heir nor successor, and it is this protector who tends to draw
her husband's anger and accusation.

Jabwire Itembe v. Mukama Kalungi: the lineage runaround; a kind of
    res judicata

The question of the locus of responsibility for harboring, then, is one
in which what ought to be plain is often obscure and in which passions
stimulate intransigent litigation. Much of this is well illustrated by
Jabwire Itembe v. Mukama Kalungi, in which Jabwire accuses Mukama on December 22, 1949, of "harboring my wife Igino for ten
months without reason." Mukama replies:

I've never harbored the wife of Jabwire. The woman he speaks of has her
father, Waitega of Bwayuyu. And the one who negotiated bridewealth with
him for that girl is Nsaju. And now [she] is staying in the home of Erukamu
of Namwiwa. The reason he accuses me is that I married her mother, but the
girl has a living father.

The genealogical situation is shown in figure 7.

Thus Mukama, in his defense, is arguing that, although he is indeed
a patrilineal kinsman to Igino, as well as husband to her mother, he is
not the one responsible for her. Jabwire, he says, has accused the
wrong man. The bench, however, continues questioning him:

Q: Do you have any testimony to show that you are not the one who harbored
    Jabwire's wife?

A: I have no testimony. The girl came to my home because of her mother, and she has been there recently. But just now she has gone to the home of her father, Erukamu, because he has been accused in the court of Mumyuka, Bulamogi, in a case concerning the same girl.

Q: Did Jabwire accuse you of this fault while the girl was in your home?

A: No, he accused me when she wasn't there—she was in the home of her father, Erukamu.

Q: Although you weren't the one who negotiated bridewealth with Jabwire, do you agree that you harbored that wife?

A: No, I didn't harbor her. She just came to visit.

Q: Is the girl of your clan?

A: Yes, she's of my clan. I call her "sister."

Mukama is here manipulating the ambiguities in the kinship terminology to his own advantage. Igino is quite clearly a generation junior

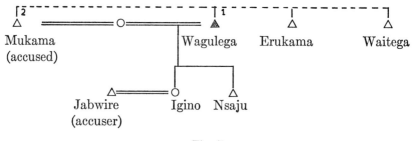

Fig. 7

to him in the lineage and the daughter of his wife. On both counts, she is his "daughter." But, in his anxiety to escape legal responsibility for her, he calls her "sister"—a term applicable, in the most extended sense, to all women of the lineage. Similarly, he says that she has a "living father," although her begetter is in fact dead and Mukama himself is as much her "living father" as any other member of the lineage of his generation.

Mukama having framed his defense—though he brings no witnesses in support of it—the case is adjourned and is not taken up again for several weeks. This often happens, for communications are often slow in rural Busoga and the courts are tolerant of delays resulting from other demands on litigants' and witnesses' time. When the case next comes before the court, on February 17, the previous record is read out and Jabwire, the accuser, is given an opportunity to answer Mukama's defense:

Q: You have heard the plea of the accused, Mukama. Do you accept it?

A: I have heard, but it is not true. That Mukama is the father of the girl. He, together with the girl's brother, Nsaju, negotiated bridewealth for her.

When I delivered the bridewealth, he was the one I gave it to. Nsaju, of whom he speaks, was not present. I married her with forty shillings, one female goat, and two hens. He didn't give me a written agreement. He said: "When you have finished paying the bridewealth, I will give you an agreement." If he knew he was not her father, he should have told me to take the things to her father.

Q: Have you testimony to show that Mukama has harbored your wife?

A: Yes, I have that of Zefaniya Mudali. I once took a case to him when he was village headman, and it went to the parish chief. For two months, the parish chief called him [Mukama] to come and litigate, but he didn't come. When the parish chief saw that he didn't come to his court, he sent me here to the subcounty court to make my accusation.

Q: Mukama himself says that he married the mother of your wife, but do you know that he actually begat that girl?

A: He begat her in terms of clanship. Her own father died, and I don't know the successor. But he [Mukama] was the one who negotiated the bridewealth and the one to whom I paid it. I call upon Nandiriko, my representative [mukwenda].

Thus, the issue is drawn on the question of who is responsible for Igino's presence in Jabwire's home. Jabwire argues that Mukama negotiated the bridewealth and thus is the one responsible. Mukama denies this and names others in the patrilineage as those responsible under the marriage contract. The "facts" concerning the girl's movements are not really in dispute. She has, Mukama admits, been in his home; but he asserts that this in itself does not make him a harborer.

During the seven weeks' delay, Mukama has had an opportunity to think about his case and, perhaps, to consult with his lineagemates. He now calls one of them, Erukamu, as a witness, and the bench proceeds to question him:

Q: Concerning the girl who is the subject of litigation: Among the three of you—Nsaju, Waitega, and yourself—who has authority over her?

A: Nsaju holds the authority because he is the heir of Wagulega. Next is Waitega, the successor. But Nsaju has authority over the girl.

Q: Where is the girl now?

A: I don't know where she went. I haven't seen her for some time.

Mukama has said earlier that the girl is staying with Eurkamu. Perhaps she has in the meantime gone elsewhere; perhaps one of them is lying. But the bench does not pursue this point, since it does not seem to bear on the central problem, that of responsibility:

Q: If you are all lineage mates, is Jabwire not right when he accuses Mukama?

A: He's not right, because Nsaju is her master.

Jabwire's witness, Zefaniya, the ex-village headman, is still to be heard from. As is the practice, Jabwire first took his case to the headman before going on to the sub-county court. The bench therefore hopes for further information.

Q: What do you know about these litigants who brought a dispute before you?

A: Jabwire brought a case to me, accusing Mukama of harboring his wife. At that time I told Jabwire to go to Mukama and said that I would join him there, but I didn't go. But I saw the girl staying in Mukama's house.

Q: Do you agree that Mukama is the father of that girl?

A: Yes, he is her father.

There is, however, no new information here; the court already knows that the girl has visited Mukama and the word "father" is a highly ambiguous term. Mukama has said he is Igino's "brother" in the lineage. As the husband of her mother and the brother of her father, he is her "father." But this says nothing about the question of responsibility. Meanwhile, the court hears of a decision by the court at nearby Namwiwa in the case referred to in Mukama's testimony. This seems to decide the matter at issue, so the decision is given:

> The case has gone against this accuser, Jabwire Itembe, because the accused is not the master of that girl Igino and he did not harbor his [Jabwire's] wife. The girl is in the home of her father, Waitega. And from case no. 18 of 1950 in the court of Nanwiwa, it appears that those who have authority over this wife are Nsaju, who inherited, and Waitega, the successor. The wife of Jabwire Itembe is with them. She just came to Mukama Kalungi's place to visit because her mother is Mukama's wife. The accuser is advised that if he wishes to appeal, he must do so within thirty days.

Jabwire no doubt feels that he has been given the runaround. Mukama, Erukamu, Waitega, and Nsaju are all "fathers" and "brothers" to his wife. All of them seem to have sheltered her at one time or another and at least two of them appear to have been involved in the bridewealth negotiations. But only one can be guilty of harboring—on this all my informants and case data agree—and Jabwire has thus far failed to locate that one. Here again, persons whom the kinship terminology classifies together must be legally distinguished. Jabwire can say, correctly, that Mukama is Igino's "father," on two counts: he is her father's brother and also her mother's husband. But Mukama can as correctly deny being her "father"—for purposes of the law of harboring. He is not the one legally responsible for her marriage—nor, apparently, is Erukamu, whom Jabwire unsuccessfully accused in the Namwiwa court.

But Jabwire appeals, fruitlessly, and the county court very quickly comes to an identical conclusion: ". . . Mukama Kalungi did not

harbor . . . Igino and he is not master of that girl . . . . Those who
have authority over her are Waitega, the successor, and Nsaju, the
heir."

Apart from what it says about the substantive question of responsibility for harboring, this case illustrates two general points about the
practice of the Soga courts. First, they operate with a concept of *res
judicata*—of a sort. These judges feel bound by the decision on the
same issue by the Namwiwa judges. The fact that their Namwiwa
colleagues found responsibility to lie with Waitega and Nsaju pre-
cludes any contrary decision here. However, as will be seen in cases to
be discussed later, *res judicata* is not a bar to *action*.[4] Even if the
Namwiwa decision had been known when Jabwire accused Mukama
(it was not; on the day this case first came to trial, Erukamu and
Igino were in Namwiwa to attend to the other case), Jabwire would
have been allowed to lodge his accusation. The only requirement for
action is a complaint which may plausibly be framed in terms of one
of the recognized concepts of wrong. Similarly, the courts are extremely free in granting leave to appeal. Leave must be obtained from
the chief presiding over the court from whose decision the appeal is
sought, but it seems never to be refused.[5] There is no scrutiny of
"grounds" of appeal. All this is, of course, appropriate to a system in
which the bases of decision are left so implicit. Since the courts do not
attempt to communicate their reasoning (as contrasted with their
conclusions) to each other or to the public, each hearing of a case tends
to represent a fresh start.

A second point that emerges nicely here is that the Soga courts are
not given to issuing *obiter dicta* ("an opinion upon a cause concerning
. . . a question suggested by the case at bar, but not . . . essential to
its determination"[6]). Here, for example, two sub-county courts and
their county court have declared that Waitega and Nsaju are the
persons responsible to Igino's husband, but none of them tells Jabwire
which of these two he should have accused. The question before these
judges is Mukama's guilt or innocence and they limit themselves to a
finding on this question. Of course the distinction between *obiter
dictum* and *ratio decidendi* ("the point in a case which determines the
judgment"[7]) can have no ethnographic, as contrasted with analytical,
significance in a system in which the reasoning behind decisions is so

4. See *Aminsi Waiswa v. Sajjabi Kibba.*
5. Even in such a transparently plain case as *Kunya Nyonyi v. Bulubutu.*
6. *Black's Law Dictionary*
7. Ibid.

little spelled out. But Soga courts can be said to share with Anglo-American ones the tendency to be satisfied with the minimum determination necessary to decide the case at hand.

With respect to the locus of responsibility in harboring, *Jabwire Itembe* v. *Mukama Kalungi* says rather clearly that when a wife's begetter is dead, his successor and heir are responsible. But which of these, and under what circumstances? There are hints in *Jabwire Itembe* v. *Mukama Kalungi* that the heir holds primary responsibility. Erukamu, Mukama's witness, says in response to questioning: "Nsaju [the heir] has authority over the girl"; and again: "Nasju is her master." And indeed, the consensus among judges with whom I discussed the question was that the heir would be responsible, provided he were an adult—at least eighteen years of age or married. If he were not, the successor, as guardian of both the heir and the girl, would hold responsibility. This of course makes functional sense: the heir has inherited his father's estate, including the bridewealth received for his sister; the obligations assumed under the bridewealth contract would

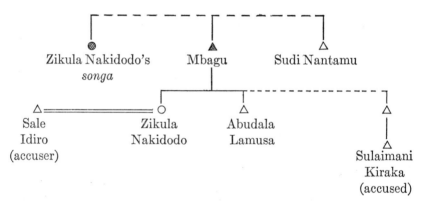

Fig. 8

naturally follow. But during his minority, the heir requires an adult administrator for these affairs.

This comes out quite clearly in two related cases heard at Ssaaba-waali, Kigulu, in 1950 and 1951. I shall take only brief note of these cases, for there is little new in them. They simply illustrate, again, that in this field much litigation is often required to establish what ought to have been plain from the start. The genealogical "facts," which are undisputed, are shown in figure 8.

Sale Idiro v. *Sulaimani Kiraka: a brother's son cannot harbor*

Again, a husband, Sale Idiro, is pitted against the agnates of his wife, Zikula Nakidodo. In the first case he accuses Sulaimani Kiraka, apparently on the ground that she had visited Sulaimani without Sale's permission. Sale argues:

I know that I will win, for my wife asked me for permission to visit Sulaimani because she had lost her father's sister (*songa*) and I refused her permission to go. Then she ran away and spent two and one-half months there. When I asked Sulaimani about my wife, he said she had returned to my place . . . the subcounty chief ordered him to bring my wife [to court], and he brought her.

Sale has a flimsy case, as becomes clear when the court questions him:

Q: You have said that Sulaimani harbored your wife for two and one-half months. How many times did it happen that you went to his home and found your wife and he refused to give her to you?
A: I went just once and he said my wife had returned to my place.
Q: Did Sulaimani write you a letter calling your wife to his place when her *songa* died?
A: He did not.
Q: If he didn't write to you, what evidence do you have that [it was he who called her and] kept her all that time?
A: Because when he was ordered by the court to produce her, he did so.
Q: When your wife first left, did you go to Sulaimani's to find out whether or not she had gone there?
A: I didn't go.

This line of questioning has been designed to bring out whether or not Sale has evidence that Sulaimani has acted as a man responsible for the woman would act. Sulaimani, questioning Sale, continues it with the familiar line about "visiting":

Q: How many times have I visited you since you married that woman?
A: Not once.
Q: How many times have you visited me since you married her?
A: I have never visited you.
Q: Since you say that we have never visited each other, what shows that I harbored your wife?
A: Because you brought her when ordered to do so.
Q: What . . . do I call your wife?
A: She is your *songa*.
Q: . . . did you come to my place and find her there?
A: I did not come.
Q: Did you go to the home of Abudala Lamusa, where I told you she was when we were at the [subcounty] headquarters?
A: No.

Q: If you did not, what evidence have you that I harbored her?
A: Because you brought her here.
Q: You say I brought her here; but why did you not just take her home with you?
A: I didn't want to take her. I wanted to accuse you!
Q: Does your wife agree that the person who had died when she asked permission to visit me was her relative?
A: She was her *songa*.
Q: Even if you did not see my letter calling her, still she asked permission and you refused. Who was in the wrong?
A: My wife was in the wrong.

Sulaimani is an unusually able self-advocate, while Sale is a poor one, with a weak case. Sulaimani has begun in his opening statement with the basic argument that he is not the person responsible: "She is neither my sister nor my daughter . . . she is my *songa*." And Sale has offered no counterargument. Sulaimani has now led Sale to admit that he had not acted as if he believed Sulaimani were the one responsible. ("How many times have you visited me . . . ?" ". . . did you come to my place and find her there?"); that he had not taken reasonable steps, steps suggested by Sulaimani, to recover his wife ("Did you go to the home of Abudala Lamusa . . . ?"); and that in any case he was not really interested in the wife, but only in punishing Sulaimani. Finally he has reproached Sale for refusing permission to visit. A woman certainly has a moral, if not a legal, right to visit her people when a close kinsman dies. Sale is reduced to the puny argument that Sulaimani produced the woman when ordered to do so, which proves nothing.

The court, finally, calls Sulaimani's witness, Ali Mukodo, and the wife, Zikula Nakidodo. Ali says that he and the other neighbors believe that the wife has been staying with Abudala Lamusa and that Sale has never been seen coming to Sulaimani's in search of his wife. Zikula Nakidodo testifies that she has been staying with Abudala, that Sale knows this, but that Sulaimani brought her to the court.

With this, the judges are ready to make a decision:

The case has gone against the accuser, S. Idiro, for he has failed to bring evidence to prove that the accused is the one who harbored his wife. And it has been found that he did not go to the home of the accused to find out whether his wife was there. Although the woman herself says that she was at the home of her brother, Abudala Lamusa, the accuser did not even go there to look for her. . . .

In this case, of course, the problem of the locus of responsibility is not squarely faced. The courts face issues only when forced to do so and here Sale has obviously struck out quite blindly. His wife has a brother—Abudala—with whom, Sale has repeatedly been told, she is staying. Sulaimani is her nephew and it is inherently improbable that he holds responsibility for her marriage. It is not impossible: Sulaimani *could* be the heir of Zikula's father, Mbagu, since the choice lies with the lineage, but Abudala is much the most likely candidate, as the court concludes.

Sale Idiro v. Abudala Lamusa: a minor cannot harbor

So Sale next accuses Abudala, who turns out to be a young boy. The judges question Sale:

Q: So now, if your wife refuses entirely to return to your home, who is required to pay back your bridewealth?

A: Abudala is the one responsible for paying back the bridewealth because he was the heir of Mbagu.

Q: Since Abudala is still a young boy, did you try to take the matter to the successor of the belt and did you inform him that Abudala was keeping your wife?

A: No, I didn't take the matter to him.

Q: Have you any witness who can prove that you once went to Abudala's place to fetch your wife and that he refused to give her to you?

A: I have no witness to prove that.

So the decision is given and Sale fails again:

The case has gone against the accuser, Sale Idiro, because . . . after he decided not to appeal [the first case], he did not try to see Abudala Lamusa to ask for his wife. . . . He did not go to see Sudi Nantamu, the successor of the belt [see the genealogical diagram above], about the matter, whereas he is the one who holds authority over Abudala and the wife. . . . The case has gone against him and he has been given his wife.

For a Soga court this is a relatively explicitly spelled-out decision. While two reasons are given for the decision—the responsibility of Sudi Nantamu and Sale's failure to take reasonable steps to recover his wife; and although it is impossible to determine the relative weight of the two reasons in bringing the court to its decisions, still, something relatively clear is said here about the locus of responsibility. If the heir is still young and under the control of the successor, the latter is responsible. The implication would seem to be that, if the heir is mature, it is *he* who is responsible.

Thus the courts have held that, among a woman's male agnates—the "fathers," "brothers," and "sons" in the lineage who, together, are customarily responsible for her in a general, moral sense—it is her begetter's heir or, during the latter's minority, her begetter's successor, who is responsible to her husband for her continued presence in his home and who, consequently, may be convicted of harboring. Other male agnates who may give her shelter are perhaps acting wickedly when they do so, but they are not guilty of harboring. Here again, the application of a concept of wrong cuts across the everyday categories of kinship terminology, this time with the aid of a concept of the locus of responsibility embodied in the terms *musika atwala ebintu* ("the heir who takes the things") and *musika ow'enkoba* ("the successor of the belt").

What Is "Sufficient Reason"?

In many of the cases in which *kutuuza omukazi awatali nsonga* is invoked, the locus of responsibility is clear and uncontested. The accused does not deny that he is in a position to harbor the woman in question, but rather asserts that his behavior does not amount to harboring. In such situations, the operative words in the customary formula are *"awatali nsonga"*: "without reason." The problem before the court is to determine whether or not the reasons for which the accused allowed his daughter or ward to remain away from her husband's home are such as to place him within reach of the concept.

Now before going further, it is important to stress again that too much weight should not be placed upon the structure of the verbal formula in which the concept is invoked—to the fact, for example, that the qualifier *awatali nsonga* is formally separable from the words *kutuuza omukazi*. In fact, in terms of the concept of wrong involved (as distinct from the words used to invoke it), it is not possible to "harbor" a woman for sufficient reason. If the reasons are sufficient, the behavior involved does not, in terms of the concept of wrong, constitute harboring at all. When a husband accuses his wife's father or guardian, he is invoking the concept of wrong: he always means *wrongful* keeping of the woman, just as, in English, "murder," in a courtroom context, always means "unlawful killing." When a man defends himself, he means (again, in terms of the concept of wrong) to say, "I did not harbor her because I had good reasons for what I did." Thus, no *legal* significance attaches to the addition of the qualifier in the formal charge which begins a case; it is, in legal terms, redundant.

But Basoga, in their courtroom dialogues, are not concerned to isolate and abstract the concept by means of a tightly and explicitly defined set of technical terms. The lawyers and judges who dominate the courtroom encounter in Anglo-American courts tend to do this much more. When they say "murder" in court they mean "unlawful killing" of a particular kind. In Soga courts, concepts of wrong are invoked and manipulated in language that remains very close to ordinary, extracourtroom language. They do not always invoke the concept "harboring" with the customary words *kutuuza omukazi;* and they will sometimes use the verb *kutuuza,* even in adjudicating a charge of harboring, in its extracourtroom sense. In ordinary speech, *kutuuza,* which is the causative form of *kutuula,* "to sit" or "to settle," means "to cause to sit" or "to cause to settle." (*Kutuuza omubbi,*" "harboring a thief," also expresses a concept of wrong.) In courtroom exchanges, judges and litigants cheerfully shift back and forth between the everyday use of the word, which does not necessarily imply the concept of wrong, and the technical legal use, which does. Thus, it is possible for an accused to say: "I kept [*kutuuza*] my daughter in my home for two weeks, but I did not harbor [*kutuuza*] her." Everyone present understands that he is using the word in its everyday sense in the first part of the sentence and that in the second part he is using it, in a culpable sense, as a technical legal term—a tag for the concept of wrong. Judges similarly shift back and forth between the two usages. Again, the concept harboring may be invoked without the word *kutuuza* being spoken at all. In one case in my collection, the husband accused the father of "losing" (*kubuza*) the wife, though it is perfectly clear, from the way the argument runs, that "harboring" has been invoked. Thus, the fact that a concept is often embodied in a customary verbal formula should not obscure the fact that this analysis is concerned with the concept, not the various particular words in which it may be expressed.

Let us return, then, to the problem of extracting from the case material the meaning of "sufficient reason" in relation to the concept "harboring." When the locus of responsibility is clear, the court may face the problem of deciding whether or not the accused father or guardian acted with "sufficient reason." In search of an understanding of this concept, it is useful to examine, first, a series of cases in which the defense was successful—in which the court was satisfied that the reasons were sufficient. I shall cite three cases from the 1923 casebook of the subcounty of Ssaabawaali, Kigulu. These cases are much less fully reported than those I have cited thus far, for at that time full transcripts were not taken. The records are, however, sufficiently complete to give the gist of the arguments.

Katengwa v. Yabinze: a two-week visit is not harboring

In the first case, Katengwa accuses Yabinze of "harboring his wife, Kadondo, for three months, without reason."

Yabinze: The woman Kadondo is my daughter. It has been two weeks since she came to my home. She came to charge her husband with a fault, saying that she had given him food and he had refused to eat it, and also that he had beaten her. I went into the matter and judged the case to go against him. But, to my surprise, before he had made any effort to fetch his wife, I heard that he had accused me.

Katengwa: I have accused my in-law because he always harbors my wife.

Q: Did you take a dispute before your in-law and did he judge the case to go against you?
A: Yes.
Q: How many weeks ago did your in-law judge the case?
A: Two weeks ago.

The court has found that the charge which Katengwa brought against Yabinze was not reasonable, and so it has been judged to go against Katengwa. He has been given back his wife.

The father here has acted quite reasonably. When friction arises between spouses, it is customary for them to appear before the woman's father and "plead their cases" like litigants in court, after which the father "gives judgment." For this purpose, the court decides, it is quite proper for a woman to return to her father's home, and two weeks is not an unreasonable time for her to spend there. The husband's claim that the wife had been away from him for three months is, he himself admits, greatly exaggerated.[8]

Muwanika v. Abudala Bujogo: visiting the sick is a legitimate reason

In the next case, another exaggerated complaint, lodged in anger, is rejected by the court. Muwanika accuses Abudala Bujogo of "harboring his wife, Kitasala, for whom he paid four female goats, one male goat, and eighteen shillings, for two months." The court questions Abudala:

Q: How long has the woman stayed in your home?
A: She has been there twelve days since she arrived and she came because she heard that I was sick. Moreover, when that in-law [Muwanika] came to my place to see about it, he stayed only a short time and went away without even seeing me.

The court then asks Muwanika:

Q: You have said that your in-law kept your wife for two months and he himself agrees that he kept her for twelve days. Now, of the two periods of time given, which shall we take as correct?
A: In my first statement I exaggerated. Twelve days is correct.

8. Such exaggeration is very common in accusations of harboring and is related to the tendency of husbands to react violently and somewhat irrationally to the infringement of what they see as their marital rights.

Therefore, the court has decided the case against the accuser, Muwanika. He has been given back his wife.

Again, a reasonable excuse; and Muwanika, having cooled down, realizes it. A woman may visit her father when he is ill and twelve days is not an unreasonable time for her to stay.

Esale v. Kyakumera: illness provides an excuse

Finally, there is the case in which Esale accuses Kyakumera of "harboring his wife, Sabawebwa, for two months without reason."

Kyakumera: I didn't harbor Esale's wife at all. Esale sent his wife to fetch two hens for a feast. So she came [to my home] and spent one day and went back. She stayed [at her husband's] for two weeks, during which time I didn't see her. The third week she came again and asked for more hens. The following day, she fell sick. I sent a message to her husband and he came and found her still sick. The sickness lasted three weeks.

Esale does not answer. The court has found that his charge is not correct and has judged the case to go against him. He has been given back his wife.

Again, the husband has been too impatient. He himself has sent Sabawebwa for the hens. When she fell sick, her father notified Esale. There is no evidence that she stayed away longer than her trips to fetch the hens and her subsequent illness required.

These three condensed case records reveal none of the subtleties of argument; indeed, all three appear to be quite plain cases of *innocence*, essentially trivial cases in which, one may suppose, there would be little subtlety of argument to reveal, even if one had verbatim records of the proceedings. They are useful, however, in establishing a kind of benchmark against which to view the more closely contested cases. They reveal that the courts recognize the continuing bond between a married woman and her own people. They recognize the strain between this bond and the radical transfer of authority over the woman that Soga marriage entails. They recognize the utility of the careful observation of mutual obligations between the two precariously linked kin groups—in the last case above, the provision of hens by the father for a feast held by the husband [9]—and of the father's efforts to adjudicate conjugal quarrels. If the affinal relationship is to be prevented by these means from degenerating into intransigent mutual hostility, the wife must be allowed some freedom to move back and forth between the two groups and the husband must be made to moderate his volatile suspicions. The concept "sufficient reason" applied by the courts to

9. These obligations are reciprocal. Husbands' and wives' people should contribute to each others' ceremonial feasts. Common occasions for this are *kwabya olumbe* funeral feasts and ceremonies to propitiate spirits.

accusations of harboring embodies a lively appreciation of all this.

It also, however, assumes that the father or guardian, in his dealings with the wife and her husband, will continually and conscientiously seek to settle their quarrels in good faith and in an even-handed manner. When he does not do so, or when his best efforts fail, the process of mutual alienation may continue to the point of irreconcilability. The husband tends increasingly to mistreat his wife and her father becomes increasingly committed to her defense. Then the dispute escalates, drawing in ever-higher levels of public authority until it comes before the official courts of record in a formal accusation of harboring. By this time, in most cases, all parties have, at one time or another, acted "unreasonably"—have done things that, in terms of conventional Soga moral standards, they ought to be ashamed of doing. In such cases, the courts must cut through an accumulated tangle of mutual recrimination and self-justification to define a *legal* standard of "reasonable" behavior.

To see these processes at work, it is necessary to turn to more fully documented recent cases. In examining these cases, it is well to be on guard against the temptation to read into them one's experience of marital disputes in the middle classes of contemporary Western societies. In all societies, of course, such disputes have a peculiarly sordid quality because, involving as they do the most fundamental and personal levels of emotion and self-definition, they tend to bring out behavior which, when aired in public court, is uncomfortably revealing for all concerned. But while Basoga men and women, like men and women elsewhere, make deep emotional investments in their relationships with each other, and while, consequently, the souring of these relationships can be a deeply humiliating experience, still the nature of the emotional investment and, hence, of the humiliation is rather different in Busoga from what it is in the modern West. The Soga relationship is more asymmetrical; and, since it involves a contract between two lineage groups, not merely an exchange of vows between two individuals, it is also less private. Basoga can therefore litigate about marriage with less of a sense that the whole proceeding reveals personal failure on everyone's part.[10]

Aminsi Kiregea v. Ali Mukodo: a husband's authority upheld

Aminsi Kiregea v. *Ali Mukodo* well illustrates the situation that may face the court when the relationship between the spouses, and

10. See Lloyd A. Fallers and Margaret C. Fallers, "Homicide and Suicide in Busoga"; and Lloyd A. Fallers, "Some Determinants of Marriage Stability in Busoga."

between their respective kin groups, has reached an advanced state of decay and when it is clear that the marriage can only be held together by coercive authority. On January 5, 1951, Aminsi comes before the court to accuse Ali of "harboring my wife, Samia Kadhaya, for whom I paid 130 shillings and 4 hens, for one month." Ali knows he has little hope of escaping conviction, but he defends his conduct:

Ali: I agree to contest [this charge] and I say that I will win because his wife came to my place having been beaten and since then her husband hasn't come for her. I didn't see him until he went to accuse me. I gave him his wife five times at my home after listening to their quarrels. The woman says that she is leaving Aminsi's home because he calls her a sorceress [*mulogo*]. I even gave her to him in court,[11] but even then he didn't stop beating her. She left Aminsi's home on November 5, 1950, and since then her husband hasn't taken the trouble to fetch her. Sulaimani Kiraka [12] is my witness; he can testify that I have never harbored the wife.

Q: You've said that you kept your neighbor's wife because her husband used to beat her, but did you ever try to take her before any chief to prove that this was true?
A: No.
Q: . . . [then] do you have any evidence to free you from the charge of harboring your neighbor's wife?
A: No, I have no evidence to free me. . . .
Q: Is there any need to bring your witness . . . ?
A: Yes, I still need him.

Aminsi: I say that I will win because he has harbored my wife seven times. The first time, I accused the wife [13] and I won the case. Her brother [Ali] said he would send her to me soon, but I waited for a long time without seeing her. Again I went to his place twice, but he didn't give her to me. Then I went a fourth time. This time he led her to the court and he gave her to me in the presence of the headman.[14] When I reached home with her, Ali came and asked whether I had beaten my wife. I said I had not—and they asked the wife and she said the same.[15] Then they left my home and my wife escorted them [16] and didn't return. I knew from that that they had arranged something [were deliberately keeping the wife], so I didn't bother to fetch her again. I accused him a second time. They asked him twice to attend court, but he

11. He means the "court" of the village headman, Sulaimani Kiraka, who will testify shortly.
12. In *Sale Idiro* v. *Sulaimani Kiraka,* Ali gave evidence for Sulaimani.
13. Before the headman.
14. All the "cases" mentioned by Aminsi were heard by the village headman in his "court." Aminsi may be exaggerating the number of such cases, but Sulaimani confirms below that there was at least one.
15. Not unnaturally! She knows that she probably will have to return to her husband.
16. It is good manners for a member of the household to escort a visitor a short distance along the path when he leaves. One does not simply say "goodbye" at the door.

didn't come. When he saw me coming to this court, he brought my wife and begged me not to accuse him. But I persisted. Sulaimani Kiraka is my witness, for I was taken to his place when they were giving me the wife.

Both have called upon Sulaimani, so, in spite of Ali's virtual confession of guilt, Sulaimani is called:

Q: What evidence can you give . . . and whose witness are you?
A: I am Ali's witness, because they brought the dispute about Aminsi's wife to my court. I found out, though, that it was all nonsense, for I failed to learn any good reason for her leaving Aminsi's home. So I gave her to her husband. When he reached home with his wife, he again punished her and took her clothes away from her.[17] Then Ali and Asumani went to see her in her husband's home, intending to accuse her husband for beating her. But she prevented them from doing so, so they returned home. . . . Aminsi's wife followed them. Then, after the woman had stayed three days in [Ali's] home, Aminsi accused him.
Q: When Ali brought Aminsi's wife to your court, how long did he say she had been staying with him?
A: Three days.
Q: Did Aminsi's wife return [to her husband] the same day you gave her to him? And did he beat her that same day?
A: Yes.
Q: After you judged Aminsi's case and after he went with his wife, was any case brought to prove that Ali did not harbor Aminsi's wife?[18]
A: No further case was brought to my court.
Q: Now, since you are a witness, how can you prove that the woman is not now in Ali Mukodo's home?
A: I know that the woman is still in Ali's home.
Q: . . . if she is still in Ali's home, is there anything to disprove the accusation that Ali harbored Aminsi's wife?
A: No.

The court loses no time in concluding that, since "he has told us frankly that he has no evidence to make him free from the charge," Ali is guilty and will be fined fifteen shillings or three weeks at hard labor.

Now it is clear that this is a marriage that has thus far failed to settle down and that the institutions designed to reconcile the couple have not yet succeeded. There is evidence that the wife has been beaten and otherwise mistreated—the witness, Sulaimani, who is testifying from the relatively neutral position of headman (though he is a lineage mate of Ali[19]), confirms it. The punishment is less than half that assessed in *Yoweri Kibiri* v. *Yowabu Kabwire* and no compensation is awarded to Aminsi. Basoga do not think it right for a man to

17. To punish her and to keep her from running away again.
18. That is, did Ali, having offered Aminsi his bridewealth, accuse him for refusing to take it?
19. From fieldwork data.

beat his wife severely; he may, in fact, be prosecuted for doing so, as table 1 shows. But the law, through the application of the concept "sufficient reason" comes down heavily on the side of the husband in such cases, placing the greater part of the burden of keeping the marriage intact on the wife and her guardian. The readiness, in this case, of the father to confess his guilt and the wife's reported reluctance to accuse her husband reflect this, and it is underscored by certain of the court's questions. Both Ali and the witness, Sulaimani, are asked whether Ali, on his own initiative, brought the beating to the attention of the authorities. The fact that he did not may mean that the beating did not actually take place or it may mean (this seems more likely, in view of Sulaimani's testimony) that the wife persuaded Ali not to press the matter. In either case, the court's questions clearly suggest that, if a wife's guardian thinks he has grounds for keeping her from her husband, he must take the initiative. If he does not do so, his grounds will not place him beyond the reach of a harboring charge. He is still responsible for seeing to it that the wife remains with her husband.

Tonda Nandabi v. Walwendo: the question of initiative; a cruel husband

Tonda Nandabi v. Walwendo provides some indication of how a father or guardian must proceed in such circumstances if he is to defend himself successfully. On November 21, 1950, Walwendo is accused by Tonda of "helping his wife, Ikesa, to escape for five months without sufficient reason." At the subcounty court, Walwendo's defense does not fare well; in fact, he hardly bothers to defend himself:

Walwendo: I agree to contest because I did not harbor his wife for five months, as his accusation says.

Q: In whose home did she stay during those months?

A: I know about only four months. I don't know about the rest. He is lying, because she left her husband's home and then, after two months, when she appeared, I took her to the chief's place.[20] It was [then] two months [that I kept her].

Q: Now do you agree that you are guilty of the charge of harboring your daughter for a period of four months?

A: Yes, I agree that I am guilty of the charge for the two months during which my daughter stayed in my home. And I myself took her to the chief. The other months I don't know about.

Walwendo's remarks are a bit difficult to follow; whether because he did not express himself clearly or because the clerk was careless in

20. The parish chief, as becomes clear below.

recording his words, one cannot tell. However, what he means is this. Two months after Ikesa left her husband's home, she appeared at Walwendo's and he took her to the chief. He then kept her in his home for two months. He disclaims responsibility for all but the two months spent in his home, but for these two months he offers no defense. The court then hears the woman Ikesa's version of the story:

Q: From where did you come to this court?
A: I came from the home of my father, Walwendo, because I have rejected my husband, Tonda. . . .
Q: How long did you stay at your father's?
A: I spent only one month there.
Q: But where did you spend the other four months?
A: For four months I stayed at our [her husband's] home. But when my husband returned from prison, he began to beat me, so I went back to my father's. When [Tonda] came, I told him I didn't want him, so he got ready to make an accusation of harboring. But I had already told him I didn't want him.
Q: Your father, Walwendo, says that you stayed in his home for two months, but you say one month. Now which of you is speaking the truth?
A: I am speaking the truth. It was one month. He is wrong.

Finally, Tonda is questioned:

Q: Do you have any testimony to prove that Walwendo harbored your wife for a period of five months, as your charge says?
A: I have the testimony of my wife Ikesa. She has spent five months away from my home and in the home of her father, Walwendo, who brought her here.
Q: Have you heard the witness, Ikesa, say she stayed with her father for one month, not five?
A: I have heard, but it is not true.

There remain large discrepancies among the three accounts with respect to just how long Ikesa spent away from her husband's home and in that of her father, but the court feels it unnecessary to probe further. There is sufficient common ground to conclude:

Because of the testimony of the wife, Ikesa, confirming that she stayed in the home of her father, Walwendo, for one month, and because he himself agrees that he harbored his daughter for two, but not five, months, the court concludes that he harbored a man's wife without reason for two months. . . . Therefore he will be punished with a fine of fifteen shillings and three weeks in the county prison. The woman Ikesa is given back to her husband, Tonda Nandabi.

The first trial at the subcounty court has been routine. The question of whether Walwendo acted with sufficient reason has not been considered because he himself has not raised it and the court has not offered him an opening. The questions and answers have been devoted entirely to trivial arguments about periods of time. However, it slowly dawns upon Walwendo that he may have a better case than he himself had realized, so he appeals. Perhaps he has had the advice of a more sophisticated kinsman or friend. In his letter of appeal and in the subsequent arguments in the county court, he gradually develops a defense based upon the concept of 'sufficient reason." Here, as in *Nasani Beka* v. *Kibikyo,* one can see the utility, in a system without specialist advocates and judges to draw out and clarify the issues, of the free granting of leave to appeal. For the modest sum of four shillings—the "accusation fee" [21]—the litigant gains an opportunity to consider the results of his first trial, to consult friends who may be more astute or more experienced in litigation and to reformulate his case. By the same token, the appeal court is given notice that there may be more to the case than the trial in the lower court revealed. In *Tonda Nandabi* v. *Walwendo,* in which the lower court has been content to take an apparently plain case at face value, the higher court, stimulated by Walwendo's appeal, takes more initiative in shaping the argument.

Walwendo writes: [22]

To the County Chief of Bulamogi:
Honoring you, I introduce myself to you, sir. I argued a case in which I was accused in the court of Mumyuka, Bulamogi. The accuser was Tonda Nandabi of Kiganda. He alleged that I harbored his wife, Ikesa, for four months. But I have never harbored her. The first thing that happened was that his wife disappeared from his home. I called him and gave him his wife, but the wife refused to go with him. So I set out and took her to the village headman and he took us to the parish chief and the parish chief turned us over to the subcounty chief. The subcounty chief gave me my daughter and said, "Go and give Tonda his bridewealth." So I called him in order to give him his bridewealth. But Tonda refused to fetch his bridewealth. Instead he went to court. Even though it was the court that ordered me to give him his bridewealth, it allowed him to accuse me of harboring his wife and I was defeated and fined fifteen shillings. Therefore I was not satisfied with the decision of the court of Mumyuka and I appeal.

Walwendo is a rather simple soul. It was not the subcounty *court* that suggested he give back Tonda's bridewealth, but rather the subcounty *chief,* trying to settle the matter out of court. He is an old man from the remote northern part of Bulamogi,[23] who does not thoroughly understand the present-day differentiation in roles, explained in chapter 2, between the chief as administrator and the chief as president of a

21. *Mpawabi;* literally: "that which accuses." At the subcounty level, the fee is two shillings.
22. Or rather, has written for him. It is clear that he is illiterate because, as is customary among unlettered Basoga, he signs with his inked thumb.
23. See map 2.

court. He also remains relatively inarticulate about his defense; as will appear shortly, he still has not made use of all the arguments available to him. But now he *has* located what will turn out to be the decisive point: when Ikesa left her husband, he, Walwendo, took the initiative in bringing the matter before the authorities. As he comes before the county court on December 11, this point is quickly taken up:

Q: Do you have anything new to add?
A: I want to call for testimony from two witnesses. Gampalanga and Omw. Sumei Magongo, the parish chief. . . .
Q: If those witnesses were not questioned at Mumyuka's court, for what do you call on them here?
A: I call on Gampalanga because he is my neighbor and he knows that I took my daughter back and gave her to her husband, and he knows I took her to the parish chief. I call on S. Magongo because I took my daughter and her husband to him five times when the girl refused to return to her husband. Finally he sent us to the subcounty chief.

The court now calls Tonda, the husband:

Q: Is it true that your in-law, Walwendo, took you and his daughter to the parish chief five times, and finally to the subcounty chief, because she rejected you?
A: It is not true. He didn't take me to the parish or subcounty chief.
Q: Do you have testimony . . . ?
A: I have. If the parish chief comes and agrees that Walwendo took [us], I will be defeated. And if the parish chief's letter sending us to the subcounty chief is presented . . . that will confirm it.

So the issue is drawn. Both sides have appealed to the same authoritative witness. Tonda, in addition, appeals to the documentary record. He knows now that the case turns on the question of who took the initiative and he clearly hopes that the evidence will at least be ambiguous on this point.

First, the relevant official correspondence is read into the record: a letter from the parish chief to the subcounty chief and a covering letter from the latter to the county chief, in answer to the court's request:

Mumyuka's Office
December 17, 1950

To County Chief, Bulamogi
Sir:
Honoring you, I am answering your letter ref. J/14/16 of 12/16/50. Sir, I send you the one letter of 10/11/50 which the Parish Chief wrote in sending Tonda to accuse Walwendo. I have searched this office for the other letter, but cannot find it.

I am, Sir, Y. B. Mukoba,
Your servant,
Mumyuka, Bulamogi

November 10, 1950

To Subcounty Chief Mumyuka

Sir:

Honoring you, I send you this man Tonda Nandabi who accuses Walwendo of harboring his wife, Ikesa, for five months without reason, because your authority exceeds ours.

I am S. Magongo
Parish Chief

A point for Tonda: the record of his accusation of Walwendo has been produced. But Walwendo claims that, before the matter came to the subcounty court in a formal accusation, he himself had been to the parish and subcounty chiefs on his own initiative. The county court has asked for a record of this, but the subcounty office cannot find it. Perhaps it has been lost; the clerks are by no means infallible. More likely, there was no letter on that occasion. The parish chief may have taken the disputants to the subcounty chief and conveyed his message orally. Tonda, knowing this, could confidently appeal to the files. But the parish chief, Sumei Magongo, is yet to be heard from:

Q: Did Walwendo and Tonda come to your place when Walwendo's daughter, Ikesa, rejected her husband?
A: Yes. . . .
Q: How many times . . . ?
A: Three times. I saw I couldn't handle it and sent them to the subcounty.
Q: Have you heard Tonda say that he was the accuser at your place?
A: First it was Walwendo who brought the matter to me three times, as he says. After I sent them to the subcounty, I don't know what happened. . . . But Tonda left while that was going on at the subcounty and came and accused his in-law in my court for harboring his wife. That was the case they are still litigating.

This is decisive, but before making a decision, the court again closely questions Tonda and Walwendo and also calls Ikesa, the wife. From this final round of questioning, it emerges that Tonda's time in the county prison—after which, it will be recalled, his wife says she first left him—was the result of a conviction for turning Ikesa out without her clothes; and that, on another occasion, the police had to be called in when Tonda threatened Ikesa with a knife. All this is sufficient to overturn the lower court's decision.

The appellant in this case, Walwendo, has won the case because of the testimony of the Parish Chief, S. Magongo; and also the explanation of the wife, Ikesa, that she rejects her husband, Tonda, . . . because he intended to kill her with a knife, . . . which Tonda admits. Therefore, this court sees that Walwendo was right in harboring his daughter.[24]

24. The court here uses the verb *kutuuza* in the everyday sense to embrace "lawful keeping" or "keeping with sufficient reason." Walwendo, in his appeal,

Taken together, *Aminsi Kiregea* v. *Ali Mukodo and Tonda Nandabi* v. *Walwendo* give meaning to the concept "sufficient reason" as applied to harboring. A husband's mistreatment of his wife is not sufficient reason for keeping her away from her husband. If her father is unable to settle the couple's disputes, he must take them before the proper authorities. Ali Mukodo, when asked by the authorities whether he had accused the husband of beating his wife—he had given this as an excuse for keeping her—had to admit that he had not, and was convicted. Walwendo, however, had taken the initiative; he and his daughter had accused her husband of mistreating her and had secured his conviction. When, after the husband had returned from prison, the couple still could not get along and the husband began to mistreat his wife again, Walwendo had patiently taken them to the parish chief several times. Thus, while the concept "sufficient reason" places most of the burden of keeping the marriage viable upon the wife and her father, it also provides them with a remedy when the husband proves utterly intractable.

WHAT CONSTITUTES A "MARRIAGE"?

In the two cases just considered, the central argument for the defense has been that the husband has mistreated his wife and that her father or guardian has acted with "sufficient reason" in keeping her. There is no claim that the husband's marital rights do not exist; rather, it is argued that there are circumstances under which a father's or guardian's right to protect the wife takes precedence over these. There is, however, still another possible basis for defense against a charge of harboring: the father or guardian may argue that no binding marriage exists. The court is then faced with the necessity of deciding what acts create a binding marriage. There are two logical possibilities here: the accused may argue that a marriage has not yet come into being or he may argue that a marriage which once existed has been dissolved.

Kayambya v. *Kakokola: partial payment is sufficient*

To throw light on the court's handling of the first possibility, I have only one briefly reported case from the 1923 casebook of subcounty Ssaabawaali, Kigulu. The question upon which the case turns is simple and is generally well understood, which is probably the reason why it is not often litigated. The question is: Is the full payment of the agreed-upon bridewealth necessary to the validity of a marriage for

---

had used it in the legal, concept-of-wrong sense, "keeping without reason"; "I have never harbored her."

purposes of the law of harboring? Since the record is brief, it may be cited in full without interruption. Kayambya is accusing Kakokola of "harboring my wife, Musubika, for three months without reason":

Kayambya: I was in my home when Kakokola came to fetch Musubika to attend a *kwabya olumbe* funeral ceremony. When the funeral was finished, I went to him and asked him to allow me to take my wife, but he refused to give her to me. So, seeing that there was nothing left for me to do but accuse him, I brought him to court.

Kakokola: I have nothing to say, but I do know that whenever he comes to fetch his wife I give her to him. I have never harbored her.

Q: How long has the woman been in your home?
A: For one month only.
Q: Is there any reason why she stayed in your home for one month?
A: Because he did not pay the part of the bridewealth that remained: 5 goats and 200 shillings.
Q: Do you not know that when an in-law fails to pay the bridewealth, the father of the girl should accuse him for it?
A: I didn't harbor her.

The court has found that Kakokola has harbored Kayambya's wife for one month only and so the case goes against the accused. He has been fined three shillings and Kayambya has taken his wife.

The clear implication is that, although the father or guardian may sue the husband for not fulfilling the terms of payment agreed to, he may not use this as an excuse for keeping the woman away from her husband. "Marriage" thus means different things in different legal contexts. In the context of the father's or guardian's responsibilities under the law of harboring, a marriage is complete when a marriage contract has been entered into; in the context of the husband's obligation to pay that to which he has agreed, it is complete only when he has paid in full. The latter obligation pertains to the law of bridewealth debt, which will be discussed later, not to that of harboring. The distinction is perhaps an obvious one, but it illustrates once more the way in which courts of law, in applying their issue-narrowing and morally simplifying legal concepts, must distinguish things which ordinary language lumps together.

Kayambya v. *Kakokola* turns on whether or not a marriage has come into being. More common are cases in which the accused argues that a once-binding marriage has come to an end for purposes of the law of harboring. Usually, when the relationship between husband and wife has deteriorated to the point of irreconcilability, repayment of the bridewealth will be arranged out of court, perhaps with the help of a headman or parish chief. But in the course of such divorce negotiations, while the wife is with her own people, tempers often flare; the husband may break off negotiations and accuse the father or guardian of harboring. The latter may then claim, in defense, that the husband has rejected his wife and agreed to take his bridewealth; but here again the burden of proof lies heavily upon the father or guardian. *Gabudieri Gukina* v. *Waibi Butanda* well illustrates this situation.

Gabudieri Gukina v. *Waibi Butanda: a father's duty to litigate*

Gabudieri accuses Waibi of "harboring my wife, Erivaida, for whom I paid 100 shillings and 1 goat, for four months." Waibi defends himself with a long and complex account of marital conflict and of divorce negotiations in progress:

Waibi Butanda: . . . in 1949, when peanuts were being planted, I saw my in-law bringing my daughter, saying he did not want her and that he wanted his bridewealth back. I gave him forty shillings, but he said he did not want half his bridewealth. So I gave him back his wife, but she refused to go with him. I took them to the subvillage headman and then to the parish chief, until finally she went with him. She stayed with him four months and then came back. Gukina came and I gave him his wife and she refused to go with him. I again took them to the subvillage headman and the parish chief. The parish chief ordered me to give him his wife, so I did. But she refused to go. So I took them to the subcounty chief and she agreed to go with him. She stayed for one month. Then Gabudieri came and told me that she had escaped from his home and that I should give him a letter so that he might go look for her. I refused, saying he should go look for her and I would do the same.[25] Right after he left, I saw his wife coming. I asked her where she had been and she said she had been in Ikonia, Luuka, where her mother lives. Again I took her to the subvillage headman and the parish chief. The parish chief ordered me to write to my in-law telling him to come for his wife. I did . . . and he came. I gave him his wife, but she refused to go. Then they fought.[26] So again I took them to the subvillage headman and the parish chief. The parish chief asked Gukina: "Why don't you compromise with your in-law so he can give you back your bridewealth?" He replied, "I want my bridewealth back, but my in-law wants to give me only half of it." I wanted to send my daughter to her brother, who knows about the other twenty shillings and one goat,[27] but Gukina said: "Since I have a bicycle, let me go for him. I will bring my agreement[28] as well." Since then, he hasn't come back. I just saw him going to accuse me. My witnesses are the parish chief and the subvillage headman. They know that I did not harbor his wife, because I took her to him whenever she returned to me.

25. A father still on reasonably good terms with his son-in-law would give such a letter to indicate his recognition and support of the son-in-law's marital rights. The refusal suggests that at this point Waibi had given up trying to reconcile the couple.
26. Not just verbally, but physically.
27. These may have been given to the brother for his own bridewealth payment. See *Tomasi Wanume* v. *Magino.*
28. The written agreement containing the terms of the marriage contract.

Gabudieri Gukina's account is, of course, quite different. He does not admit that divorce has ever been discussed:

Q: You have heard the accused say that he did not harbor your wife, but that you came and asked for your bridewealth. What do you say to that?

A: . . . I never went there for my bridewealth, but rather for my wife. To show that I want the wife and not the bridewealth, I have accused him of harboring.[29] And he has never accused me of asking for my bridewealth and then refusing to take it. Also, my wife has never accused me of refusing to take back my bridewealth and wanting to keep her. . . .

Q: The accused says that whenever you went to his home he took you to the subvillage and parish courts, and that the last time [this happened], you left him with your wife at the court, saying you would fetch the brother who knew about the twenty shillings . . . and your agreement.

A: Except for the first time, when I went there to accuse him of harboring my wife, I have never gone to his place.

Taking up what it considers the central point in Gabudieri's argument in prosecution, the court turns back to Waibi:

Q: If your in-law brought your daughter to you, wanting his bridewealth, why did you repeatedly give him your daughter instead of the bridewealth?

A: Because he wanted the whole amount and I had only half of it.

Q: You have said that you went to the courts three times. Did you ever try to get the amount you were short and offer it to him, and did he then refuse to take it . . . ?

A: Yes, I got the whole amount and he refused to take it.

Q: Have you heard the accuser say that you never accused him for refusing to take his bridewealth . . . ?

A: I didn't know that when an in-law refused to take his bridewealth he should be accused for that reason.

After this ingenuous statement, there is no need to follow the remainder of the proceedings in detail. The subvillage headman and the parish chief, as witnesses for Waibi, confirm his account of his many appearances before them with his daughter and son-in-law. No witness is called on Gabudieri's side in support of his contention that none of this took place. But the court decides that this is not relevant and, in an unusually expansive decision, concludes:

The case in which G. Gukina accused W. Butanda has been judged with great care. It has been found that the accused harbored his daughter, Erivaida, for four months, though he says he did not. The accused says that the accuser brought his wife to the accused and asked for his bridewealth; that he gave him forty shillings and he refused to take it; that he tried to get the whole amount, and got it, but still the accuser refused to take it. But he has failed to tell us why he did not accuse the accuser, Gukina, for having

29. Gabudieri cannot now admit that he once agreed to accept his bridewealth, even if he did so, which is not unlikely. To admit this would prejudice his case, as will be seen in the case following.

refused to take his bridewealth, though he had asked for it. The evidence of
the village headman and parish chief has not been relied upon because they
have not told us whether or not the accused had accused his in-law for having
refused to take the bridewealth for which he had asked. . . . he has been fined
twenty shillings or one month's imprisonment in the county prison at hard
labor.

The court's questions and decision in *Gabudieri Gukina* v. *Waibi
Butanda* suggest that if a father or guardian is to protect himself from
a charge of harboring on the ground that the husband has brought the
marriage to an end, it is not sufficient to offer return of the bridewealth; his most prudent course is to force the issue himself—to press
the bridewealth upon the husband and, if the latter refuses it, to accuse
him for refusal in a divorce action. I shall shortly examine an action of
this sort.

First, however, it is worth taking note here of the notion that if a
man has a claim he ought to litigate it, and that if he does not do so he
forfeits his claim. With respect to the law of harboring, the idea that a
father must press a divorce action in order to protect himself may well
be related to the special strains that beset affinal relations: if marriages are to be prevented from being even more unstable than they
are, the burden must rest heavily upon the wife's father or guardian to
prevent her returning to her own people except in the most rigidly
controlled conditions. But a similar notion of the duty to litigate appears, as will be seen, in the field of landholding, in situations in which
no such "functional" explanation seems warranted. I shall therefore
suggest in chapter 8 that there is at work here, in addition, a general
feature of Soga legal culture.

Of course negotiations for divorce out of court may break down at
any point. Just as a husband may accuse the father or guardian of
harboring when the bridewealth has been only partly paid, he may
also do so when it has been partly repaid. *Kayambya* v. *Kakokola*
showed that failure of the husband to pay in full is no defense against
harboring. *Mikairi Magino* v. *Ntumba* turns on the question of whether
a husband may successfully accuse a father or guardian when the
bridewealth has been partially repaid.

EATING TWO HENS

The charge in this case is actually not harboring, but rather "eating
two hens"; that is, the father is accused not just of keeping his daughter from her husband, but also of contracting marriage for her with
another man. However, cases in which eating two hens is alleged may
be treated along with those in which the charge is harboring, for the

legal concepts involved are mostly the same, even though eating two hens is a more serious charge and the punishments imposed upon conviction tend to be more severe. In both cases, the father's possible arguments in defense include denial of responsibility and denial that the marriage with the accuser is still valid. The position with respect to the other subsidiary concept I have considered—that of sufficient reason—is unclear. Where, as in *Tonda Nandabi* v. *Walwendo*, the father succeeds in establishing sufficient reason for keeping the wife, the husband may still sue for return of his bridewealth. Although I have no case law on the point, judges assured me that this is so. Indeed, judges say flatly that any sort of termination of marriage except the death of the wife involves a legal obligation to return the bridewealth, though the husband may waive his right to it.[30] But whether, in a case like *Tonda Nandabi* v. *Walwendo*, where there was "sufficient reason," the husband retains any rights other than that to his bridewealth—whether, for example, he can successfully prosecute for eating two hens if the wife remarries before his bridewealth has been repaid—I do not know. With respect to the problem of the existence of a valid marriage, however, accusations of harboring and of eating two hens are on the same footing. The problem of what acts bring a marriage to an end has the same bearing on both kinds of case.

Mikairi Magino v. *Ntumba: partial repayment frees a wife*

Mikairi Magino accuses Ntumba of "eating two hens by giving his daughter, Kiyigo, to Sabani Kafuko, whereas she already has a husband, Mikairi Magino." [31] Ntumba argues that the marriage between Kiyigo and Mikairi has been dissolved:

I know that I will win because I gave back some of the bridewealth which Mikairi had paid for my daughter, Kiyigo—104 shillings, 2 goats, and 1 hen. The remaining part was 13 goats, 1 cow, and 6 hens. When I got them, I called him to come for them, but he refused. . . . I told the village headman about it and he understood it. That's why I allowed Kiyigo to marry another man. My village headman, Gasita, is my witness.

Q: Was the village headman actually present when you were giving Mikairi part of his bridewealth?
A: Yes, he was present. . . .
Q: In addition to the village headman, do you have an agreement given you by Mikairi to show that he was given part of his bridewealth?
A: He gave me an agreement, but it was burned when my house was burned.

30. See *Mutizo* v. *Bulukani Bamubayaki*.
31. This same Mikairi Magino earlier accused Sabani Kafuko of adultery, without success.

Mikairi challenges Ntumba's evidence concerning the return of the bridewealth and tries to construct an image of Ntumba as a persistent harborer.

I know that I will win because I have never been given back any part of [my] bridewealth. His daughter disappeared for two years and he gave me a letter to look for her. I have the agreement which he gave me when I paid the bridewealth. . . . I have the agent [*mukwenda*] who took the bridewealth to him and have brought him here to the court to give evidence. I once accused [Ntumba] of harboring my wife and the case went against him. I was given back my wife and the cotton she cultivated at his place was given to me. . . .

Next the court hears the two witnesses: the village headman, Gasita, and Ezera, Mikairi's agent:

Gasita: I am Ntumba's witness. I know that he paid back part of Mikairi's bridewealth—104 shillings, 2 goats, and 1 hen, which had been paid for his daughter, Kiyigo.

Q: How did you happen to know this?
A: I was called by Mikairi and Ntumba to be present.
Q: When did this happen?
A: In June 1950.

Ezera: I am Mikairi's witness. I was the agent who took the bridewealth to Ntumba's house. . . . First I gave the bridewealth to Muwanika, Ntumba's agent, and he gave it to Ntumba.

Q: In addition to your taking the bridewealth, do you know anything else about Ntumba and Mikairi?
A: The wife of Mikairi disappeared and Mikairi caught her with another man. And Mikairi has never been given his bridewealth back.
Q: Since you are Mikairi's agent, whose responsibility is it to call you when he is given back his bridewealth?
A: It is Mikairi's responsibility.
Q: If Mikairi doesn't call you . . . can he take it himself?
A: He can take it, but it's not right.

Very carefully put! Mikairi should, according to custom, call his agent to witness the repayment of bridewealth, but the fact that he has not called him does not show conclusively that nothing has been repaid. The case seems relatively clear, then, but the court returns to the principals to tie up a few remaining points. First Ntumba:

Q: Did you give Mikairi the letter, which he says you gave him to go look for his wife, before giving him part of his bridewealth?
A: I didn't give him a letter. . . .
Q: When did you give him part of his bridewealth?
A: When Kafuko was county chief of Busiki.[32]

32. A traditional method of dating, still sometimes used. Lacking a fixed reference point for counting the years, Basoga used to date by reference to famines, epidemics, and the incumbencies of rulers and chiefs. Yoweri Kafuko was county chief of Busiki from 1946 to 1950.

Then Mikairi:

Q: When did you accuse him of harboring your wife and what was the number of the case?
A: It was in 1949. I didn't actually accuse him. I just told the chief's assistant about the matter.
Q: Who gave you the letter . . . to look for your wife? Who wrote it? The accused cannot write.[33]
A: Sitanule Ngobi wrote it.
Q: . . . have you brought Sitanule as your witness?
A: No. . . .
Q: If you have never been given part of your bridewealth, did you ever go to the village headman, Gasita, to accuse Ntumba for harboring . . . ?
A: I went there in December 1950.
Q: What did [he] do?
A: He did nothing.
Q: If your witness knows only about your paying the bridewealth, and if the letter you show us was not written by the accused, have you any evidence to show that you were never given back part of your bridewealth? The accused has brought the village headman, who was present. . . .
A: I have no other evidence.

So the court concludes:

The accused, Ntumba, has been freed of the charge. . . . From the evidence given by the village headman, Gasita, it has been found that Magino . . . has long ago taken back part of his bridewealth . . . and that he himself allowed his wife to marry another man.

The court has given Mikairi every opportunity to show that the marriage is still binding—by inviting him to show that he had been given a "search" letter, presumably since the time when Ntumba claims to have partially repaid; or by calling the headman to say that, again since the alleged repayment, he had lodged a complaint for harboring. But Mikairi's case dissolves under the court's questioning and the decision is clear: acceptance of even partial repayment dissolves a prior marriage and makes an accused immune to charges of "eating two hens."

It is worth taking passing note of the court's and litigants' use in *Mikairi Magino* v. *Ntumba* of a conception of how Mikairi might have been expected to act if the facts had been as he claims—if two years had passed after his wife left him without his receiving, or agreeing to receive, repayment. The court considers, and Mikairi knows this and anticipates it, that a husband truly wronged in this way would have pursued his rights more vigorously. He cannot, however, convince the court that he did this.

33. He will have had to sign with his thumbprint after giving his opening statement.

The court's decision in this case is ambiguous on one point. The decision says that Mikairi's accusation failed because he had accepted partial repayment *and* because he agreed to set his wife free. But which of these acts is the decisive one? Presumably, accepting repayment indicates that a man has renounced his claims, but is acceptance of repayment the *only* decisive evidence that he has done so? The most instructive case would be one in which a father or guardian was successful in defending himself against a charge of harboring or eating two hens on showing that the husband had renounced his claim without repayment. I have no such case, and data collected on all separations in five villages indicates that repayment occurs in the great majority of instances.[34] There are, however, exceptions, and I have a case—not one in which either harboring or eating two hens was invoked—which suggests that a husband may legally renounce his claim without repayment.

Muzito v. Bulukani Bamubayaki divorce by renunciation

In *Muzito* v. *Bulukani Bamubayaki*, the charge is extortion. Muzito accuses Bulukani Bamubayaki of "coming to the house [of Muzito] and getting thirty-seven shillings from him, even though previously [Bulukani] had sent his wife away with a letter saying he would not claim his bridewealth back and that his wife could marry anyone she pleased. She married Muzito." Bulukani, it is charged, has reacted to an unsatisfactory marriage by simply setting his wife free without obligation—an uncommon, but quite plausible, response to the difficulties that beset Soga marriages. He has then thought better of his self-denial and has extorted money from Muzito on threat of an adultery charge. He now admits his guilt, is given one month at hard labor, and is ordered to repay the thirty-seven shillings. The case does not, of course, prove that a man who agrees in writing to relinquish his marital claims without repayment necessarily forfeits his ability to accuse successfully in court for harboring or eating two hens, for the continuing validity of the bridewealth contract is not at stake here. This conclusion is merely suggested by the language of the accusation.

Speculating further, there is some evidence to suggest—nothing more—that just as a marriage may be brought to an end by a husband's consent, so one may be *brought into being* by a father or guardian's consent and that the payment of bridewealth is not legally necessary,[35] though again it occurs in the overwhelming majority of cases.

34. Fallers, "Some Determinants of Marriage Stability."
35. *Kayambya* v. *Kakokola* showed that a father's or guardian's obligations to the husband were established by partial payment.

Luketa v. Mongoi: "marriage" without father's permission is fornication

In a briefly reported case from 1923, *Luketa* v. *Mongoi*, Luketa accuses Mongoi of "marrying my daughter Kauma without first *consulting* me." After a very brief argument, in which Mongoi offers only his and Kauma's mutual devotion as an excuse, Mongoi is found guilty and fined for not *"inform[ing]"* Luketa when marrying his daughter." Here the relevance would be clearer if Mongoi had claimed verbal permission, even though he had not paid bridewealth. Again, the language merely suggests what the reasoning in such a case might be.

This is as far as my cases will carry me with respect to the problem of the acts which create or dissolve a marriage. Judges assured me that a father's consent is sufficient to make a marriage and that a husband's consent is sufficient to dissolve it. The point seems likely to receive greater attention from courts in the future, for there is now a small, but growing, group of young men and women who feel that the payment of bridewealth is degrading for the woman. Of course youthful idealism does not in most cases survive the social pressures of adult society, particularly in a matter like marriage in which kinsmen play so prominent a role. Still, as women's education spreads, the demand for consent marriage and divorce seems sure to increase. What constitutes such consent will, of course, be for the courts to decide and, since in both cases payment is the customary pattern, one has the impression that the burden of proof will lie heavily upon the party who would benefit from the waiver of payment—the husband in the case of marriage, the father or guardian in the case of divorce.

DIVORCE BY COURT ACTION

Thus far I have considered the establishment and dissolution of marriage as a subsidiary problem in connection with the concepts of wrong "harboring" and "eating two hens." That is to say, I have considered those situations in which a father or guardian is accused in terms of one of these two concepts of wrong and have analyzed the manner in which the litigants and judges have used the subsidiary concept of valid marriage in determining whether or not the facts of particular cases, as found, place them within or without the reach of these concepts of wrong. It is most often in this way—as a subsidiary problem—that marriage and divorce come before the Soga courts, and the reason, of course, is that in Busoga marriage and divorce are private arrangements, to which the state is not a party. Customary Soga marriage thus bears more resemblance to Western "common law" mar-

riage than to Western "civil" or "religious" marriage, in which an officer or agent of the state must "solemnize" the union and in which, consequently, a court must dissolve it.[36] Of course in Busoga, marriage by
private agreement is the normative form, not the semilegitimate sort
of thing it is in the West. Also, today many Soga marriages *are* "solemnized" by "marriage officers"—usually Christian or Muslim religious functionaries—but, as will be seen, the British protectorate administration has acted to make certain that this will have no practical
legal consequences for Soga marriage. Customary marriage, viewed according to customary conceptions, is what matters to the Soga courts.
When the courts consider marriage, therefore, it is usually to decide
whether, by their own actions, the parties themselves have created or
dissolved a marriage and this determination is usually subsidiary to a
decision about the reach of some concept of wrong upon which the existence of a marriage depends.

It is, however, possible for a wife and her father or guardian to sue
in court for divorce. A husband does not need to do this: he may
simply send his wife away. If he wishes his bridewealth returned, he
may sue for it, but I heard of no case in which a wife and her father
contested a husband's right to dissolve a marriage at his pleasure. It is
consistent with the general asymmetry of Soga marriage that it is the
wife and her father who must sue for divorce. And it is consistent with
the private nature of the contract that the concept of wrong relevant
in such circumstances is not invoked in words easily translatable as
"suing for divorce." There is a word, *kugatulula*, which means "to
separate" or "to divorce," but the wife and her father do not ask the
court to "grant a divorce"; rather, they appeal to the judges to order
the husband to grant it, usually by the device of ordering him to accept repayment of his bridewealth.

The concept of wrong involved is therefore best described as "refusal
to grant a divorce" and, since bridewealth has normally been paid, it is
usually with some such words as "refusing to accept repayment" (*ku-
gaana okuweebwa ebintu bye*, literally: "refusing to accept his things")
that the husband is accused and hailed into court. In two cases already
discussed judges have asked fathers accused of harboring why they had
not taken the initiative and accused the husband in these terms,[37] the
suggestion being that if there were good reasons for the woman to be

---

36. *"Divorce suit:* . . . a civil proceeding . . . wherein the married parties are
plaintiff and defendant and the government, or public, occupies, without being
mentioned in the pleadings, the position of a third party." *Black's Law Dictionary.*
37. *Aminsi Kiregeya* v. *Ali Mukodo; Gabudieri Gukina* v. *Waibi Butanda.*

absent from her husband's home, such an action would be the best way of establishing this. As tables 1 through 4 indicate, however, this type of action is relatively infrequent, perhaps because husbands rarely refuse to accept their bridewealth when it is actually offered to them. By the time a father or guardian has managed to assemble the goods and money—often a difficult and painful process—the marriage has probably deteriorated to the point where even the most tenaciously possessive husband can see the futility of trying to maintain it. Thus, I have only two full case transcripts on the basis of which to analyze the court's handling of the concept. These reveal something about the conceptions the courts seem to apply in determining the conditions under which a husband must agree to divorce. As one would expect from everything that has been said thus far about Soga marriage, these conditions are relatively restricted; an action for refusal to grant a divorce is difficult to win.

Samasoni Ntuyo v. Mubakali Kiwomero: a flimsy case

In the first case, the guardian of the wife claims that bridewealth has never been paid. He therefore accuses the husband of "forcing my daughter, Amina Mpiya, to stay married to him against her will and of not paying bridewealth for her." The suit turns out to be a rather futile and foolish one, but the arguments are nonetheless of interest for present purposes. The accuser is Samasoni Ntuyo; the accused, Mubakali Kiwomero. Mubakali denies both the failure to pay bridewealth and his wife's dissatisfaction:

Mubakali: I agree to contest. His statement that I did not pay bridewealth for her is untrue. I became attached to her when she was at Juma's home at Bumila. She "married" me.[38] I went to Juma and reported that I had taken her to my home. Juma raised no objections, but said that the girl had a brother, Mukama, and that if Mukama would agree, she could be my wife. When Mukama came, he did not object, but "fined" me 10 shillings for not telling him before I took his sister. . . . Then Juma died . . . , but Mukama had not yet asked for bridewealth for his sister. Then Samasoni came and said his clan had fined him a bicycle because he had not yet collected bridewealth for the wife. I gave Yoweri 10 shillings and 2 goats to be given to Samasoni and he gave them to him. Afterward, he came and said the mother of my wife wanted a goat, and I gave him one worth 30 shillings.[39] Again, she asked for 20 shillings and I gave it to her. . . . Later her [the wife's] brother came to me in need of money to get a wife. I gave 100 shillings and 3 goats to Yoweri, who gave them to him. Then I asked Mukama for an agreement, for by now my bridewealth had become very large. He gave me one. When Samasoni says I

---

38. Again a euphemism; they were at this point merely cohabiting.
39. This payment of a goat to the bride's mother is a customary one, not considered part of the bridewealth.

want to keep his daughter and that she doesn't love me, it is not true. Samasoni called my wife to come for some beans, and since then she hasn't come back, though she said she would return. . . . So I went there and asked why she had not come back, but he said he didn't want to see me. So I went and accused him [of harboring] before the court of Mumyuka of Bugweri and he was fined 20 shillings and I was given my wife. But on our way back, she said she wanted to stop at her father's to fetch her child's clothes. So when she reached there, Samasoni prevented her from returning to my home. Again I took the matter to Mumyuka and he advised me to wait a few days before accusing him again.

The apparent genealogical situation is shown in figure 9.

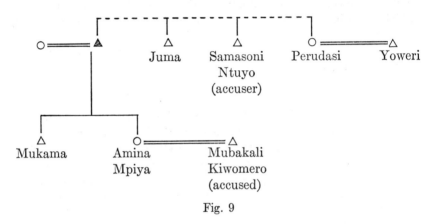

Fig. 9

It appears, from the role allegedly played by Amina's brother, Mukama, that Juma was the successor, and Mukama the heir, of Amina's begetter, whose name is not given. Only if the begetter had died would the brother, as heir, have a voice in the marriage and a claim on the bridewealth.[40] Juma then seems to have died and to have been succeeded by Samasoni. Yoweri acted as Mubakali's *mukwenda*, or agent. His marriage to Samasoni's sister comes up in later testimony.

Mubakali has pictured himself as generous and patient to the point of irresponsibility in the matter of paying the bridewealth. Indeed, he has paid it, he says; he has paid far too much! And Samasoni has been a persistent harborer; even now Mukabali has been on the point of accusing him again for harboring. The suggestion is that Samasoni has brought this suit simply to forestall the harboring charge. Samasoni, of course, gives a somewhat different account:

40. See *Sale Idiro* v. *Abudala Lamusa*.

Samasoni: . . . what he says is a lie. He wants to keep her against her will and she has not wanted him since 1949. He took her to Mumyuka's court and she was given to him unwillingly. . . . He accused me for harboring his wife and the case went against me. He was given his wife and she escaped while they were on their way home. Mubakali came with the village headman, Semeyi Byansi, but he did not see his wife. . . . The headman asked her why she did not go to her husband. She said it was because she did not love him and because he stinks and is a thief—he had stolen a box of wire and some nails, and a bicycle. Then I, as the father, said he was lying when he claimed to have paid bridewealth for my daughter . . . that he had never given it to me. In his statement [he says] he gave Yoweri [the bridewealth], but he never gave it to me. Yoweri himself paid twenty shillings for my sister, Perudasi, and [after they were separated] I paid him back his money. But I never made an agreement . . . with them for my daughter, Amina.

Mubakali does not, of course, claim to have made an agreement with Samasoni and the court quickly turns to Mubakali to confirm this:

Q: Did you make your agreement with Samasoni or Mukama?
A: I made it with Mukama. . . .

Then back to Samasoni:

Q: How long has your daughter been married to her husband?
A: This is the ninth year since she married him.
Q: During those nine years, have you ever accused him for not paying bridewealth?
A: No, because I called him and he refused to come.
Q: Have you any other evidence, besides the fact that you were twice in Mumyuka's court . . . to prove that she does not love him and that he wants to keep her against her will?
A: I have no other evidence.
Q: Have you any evidence to support your statement that he has never given bridewealth for your daughter?
A: I have no evidence, but I accuse him for keeping her unwillingly. . . .
Q: You say he never paid bridewealth, but he says he paid and that your son Mukama took the bridewealth and gave him an agreement. What about that?
A: He is lying; he has no agreement.
Q: Why did you interfere in the accusing of Mubakali and not leave the woman herself to accuse him for keeping her unwillingly?
A: The chief . . . prevented her from doing it herself and said that I, the father, should do it.

This last exchange should be kept in mind, for it becomes significant in the light of the next case to be discussed. Otherwise, it is clear that Samasoni's argument is so riddled with weaknesses that the court has no difficulty in rejecting it. He claims that Mubakali has not paid bridewealth, but the decisive element is the consent of the father or guardian, and Samasoni does not really dispute that this was given.

Samasoni admits to being a convicted harborer, which shows that he is
the person responsible. This, together with the fact that he has allowed
nine years to pass without accusing Mubakali for bridewealth shows
that he has accepted the marriage as valid—again, the principle that if
a man has not litigated his claim, he forfeits it. Finally, he brings no
supporting testimony—from Amina or anyone else—to show that she
has substantive reasons for wanting a divorce. This, as will be seen, is
the central problem in the handling of "refusal to grant a divorce" as a
concept of wrong. The court touches upon all these points in its decision:

> Samasoni Ntuyo has lost the case because it has been found that the accused
> did not keep his daughter without her consent, but rather that her father has
> persuaded her to reject her husband, to whom he had given her, and from
> whom he got bridewealth of 100 shillings and 3 goats.[41] He was fined twenty
> shillings in Mumyuka's court in case no. 64 of 1950 for having harbored his
> daughter. Though he said at first that the accused had not paid bridewealth
> . . . , afterward he agreed that he was not accusing him for bridewealth, but
> for keeping his daughter against her will. Finally, he has failed to produce a
> witness to help him. . . . He has been ordered to tell his daughter to go to her
> husband.

Such a weak case tells little about the reach of the concept of wrong
under consideration. Because Samasoni has complicated matters with
his claim that bridewealth has not been paid, the court does not have
before it the typical accusation that bridewealth has been offered and
has been refused. And Samasoni offers only trivial and unsupported
reasons for Amina's wanting to be free from her husband. One therefore learns only that a guardian's *assertion* that the wife wishes to be
free, supported by evidence that she stayed away from her husband
long enough to convict her guardian of harboring, is insufficient to
satisfy the court that the "facts" fall within the reach of the relevant
concept. But the last exchange between the court and Samasoni (". . .
why did you interfere . . . ?") is interesting. At least one member of
the bench thinks that Amina herself should have made the accusation.
Samasoni replies that "the chief"—this may be either the subcounty
chief, who is chairman of the court, or his deputy, who may have been
minding the subcounty headquarters when Samasoni came to lodge
his accusation—told him that he himself must do it. In the next case,
the wife herself makes the accusation; and she offers, and the court
seriously considers, the *grounds* upon which she wishes to be free of her
husband.

41. The court here accepts Mubakali's argument in defense concerning the
bridewealth without substantiating testimony because Samasoni has offered no
such testimony in accusation.

Maliyamu Kyazike v. *Samwiri Wakoli: a child bride frees herself*

Because the accused husband, Samwiri Wakoli, is a senior chief and a man of great eminence—he is county chief of Bulamogi and heir to the rulership of the old kingdom of Bukoli, now Bukoli county—the case is originally tried in the Busoga district court.[42] On April 2, 1950, Omw. Wakoli is accused by his wife, Maliyamu Kyazike, of "not accepting his bridewealth, eighty shillings and two goats, which has been offered to him by my father, Isifu Sabakaki." Omw. Wakoli defends himself by denying that Maliyamu has any grounds for dissatisfaction:

Omw. Wakoli: I do not agree that the case goes against me because when my wife ran away from my home we had never had any difficulty—we had never had a dispute before my in-law. His daughter never gave him any information which could cause him to want to separate us and repay my bridewealth. When I went to fetch her, her brother Aminsi asked the father if there was any trouble that was causing my wife to refuse to come back.[43] The last time I went, Isifu told me that he had no daughter to give me.[44] I returned home and a short time later I was called to court by my wife.

Maliyamu then gives the grounds for the accusation:

Maliyamu: My father gave me to Omw. Wakoli while I was very young. When I became old enough, I "married" him.[45] Then I became tired of him. I went back to my father's home and told him how tired I was of the man to whom he had given me. When my father asked the reason, I said I simply didn't love the man. My husband came for me, but I refused to go back with him because I dislike being in his home. When they continued to press me, I said I didn't have any particular reason, but that I was simply tired of him. After two years had passed, with my husband coming for me and I refusing to go, my father told Omw. Wakoli that, since I refused to return to him, it would be better to repay the bridewealth. He said he couldn't tie me to him. But the master refused, saying that if he took back his bridewealth he would be unable to kill [46] me for separating from him while he still wanted me. All that is the reason I came and accused him.

Q: How long have you been in Omw. Wakoli's home?
A: Eight years. . . .
Q: Why did you want to separate from Omw. Wakoli?

42. If the case were to be tried in subcounty or county court, the bench would be made up of the accused's own subordinates. Only by moving it to the district court can he be tried by his "peers."
43. Suggesting that even her brother could not see any reason why Maliyamu should be dissatisfied.
44. A formula for: "she won't go."
45. Again a euphemism: "began to have sexual intercourse."
46. Spoken in frustration and anger. There is no evidence of actual mistreatment.

A: I was tired of him—that's all, as I have already said.

Q: Why did you and not your father accuse Omw. Wakoli?

A: My father was sick, and I was feeling desperate—that's why I came and accused him.

Q: What does Omw. Wakoli give you to do that makes you tired of him?

A: I simply don't love him—I hate him.

Q: Your husband still wants you and you say you have no reason for separating. . . .

A: I simply don't love him.

Much that is left unsaid here, despite the court's probing, is understood when one adds that Omw. Wakoli is nearly sixty years of age. Maliyamu is a young woman of perhaps twenty-two, who was given in marriage before puberty. More on this theme is forthcoming when her father, Isifu, is heard from:

Q: Why does your daughter refuse to go with her husband?

A: I can't really say, because when I asked them what the trouble was, no one told me. The third time they came . . . the wife told him she didn't love him, because I gave her to him while she was so young, and that now she wanted to select [a husband] for herself and that I must repay the bridewealth. I asked my in-law to take back what he had given me, but he refused. Once my daughter disappeared and we found her in Bukedi.[47]. . . I gave her to him, but she came back. That is why I told him to take his bridewealth, but he refused, saying he still loved his wife.

Q: Do you agree that you gave her to the accused when she was still young?

A: Yes, when she was about thirteen or fourteen years old, when her sister Kantono separated from Omw. Wakoli. I gave her to him to look after the child Mwonja, whom Kantono had left there.

The court now returns to Omw. Wakoli, apparently convinced that a separation is desirable:

Q: When you go to your in-law for your wife and she tells you frankly that she doesn't love you, why don't you agree to accept your bridewealth?

A: I still love my wife and there has been no trouble that would cause her to leave my home. Also, she says she was given to me while she was very young, but when she was introduced to me by her father, we discussed it with her.

Q: You suggest that she accepted you . . . , but she says that she hates you. Why can't you agree to take your things?

A: I don't see any reason why she should leave my home.

Q: Did your in-law offer you your things and did you refuse to take them?

A: I received a letter calling me to fetch my bridewealth, but I didn't go because I still love my wife.

Q: Have you heard her say she doesn't love you?

A: Yes, but I still love her. I am not tired of her. In the custom [*mpisa*] of Busoga, a wife must give a reason for separating from her husband. . . .

47. A neighboring district.

Q: If we give her to you, how will you take her?
A: I will take her by force.

So the court concludes:

The accused, Samwiri Wakoli, is defeated because the accuser was given to [him] while she was very young. She did not choose him herself. The accused agrees that she followed her sister . . . and that if the court gives her to him, he will take her by force. But it is not the custom [*mpisa*] of the court to do this. He agrees that he went twice to his in-law . . . and that she refused [to go with him] and that his in-law asked him to take his bridewealth. The wife's father agrees that she was given to S. Wakoli while she was very young because he first married her older sister Kantono, who separated from him and left a young baby. . . . Maliyamu was given to him to look after the son.

But the court splits, four to two. This has been a difficult decision, and one must ask why. The central problem, at least in this case, in determining the reach of the concept of wrong "refusal to grant a divorce," is that of determining whether the accuser has adequate grounds or "reasons." There is no significant disagreement about the "facts," and no other subsidiary problem is raised. But the striking thing, as one looks back over the record, is what appears at times to be a total lack of common understanding about what adequate reasons might be. This simply cannot, in this case, be attributed to any lack of skill or experience in handling the relevant legal concepts. The accused is himself a senior chief of several decades' experience on the bench. And the court is the highest in the land, manned by experienced judges. Here, for the first time, a case reveals one of those frontiers of the law where differences in values produce differences in the meaning of a concept of wrong. What is an adequate reason to the naïve accuser and to a majority of the bench is not an adequate reason—indeed is not comprehensible as a reason at all—to the legally experienced accused and to a minority of the bench.

Maliyamu says, and her father and the accused confirm, that she was given in marriage as a child to a much older man, that she herself did not choose her husband, and that she does not love him. She is uncertain whether or not these are "reasons" for the court ("I said I didn't have any particular reason."), but they are *her* reasons. Omw. Wakoli simply does not understand what she is talking about. After hearing her argument—surely not for the first time—he says, "In the custom [*mpisa*] of Busoga, a wife must give a reason." There has been no allegation of mistreatment, for example, no suggestion that Maliyamu has been deprived in any material way. As Omw. Wakoli's wife, she has probably lived at the most affluent level Soga society can provide. Her father is puzzled. He sympathizes with her discontent, but admits that "when I asked them what the trouble was, no one told me." He, too, cannot have been unfamiliar with what Maliyamu thought her reasons were; indeed, he repeats them. But he seems doubtful whether or not they are significant reasons. Some members of the bench, at least, also have doubts; after hearing Maliyamu's argument, they continue to press her for "reasons."

These doubts and failures of communication are of course the result of a shift in values concerning the position of women in marriage, a shift dramatically personified here in the encounter between the two leading figures in the case: Omw. Wakoli, the accused; and the chairman of the court, Omw. Zefaniya Nabikamba, county chief of Kigulu,[48] who will have dominated the bench, though the clear majority will have made it unnecessary for him to exercise his deciding vote. Both are men of modern Busoga, products of the period of mission schools and British administration, who accept the legitimacy of the many Western influences in Soga life; they have served together in the government of Busoga for almost half a century. But within this common social and cultural setting, they represent quite distinct emphases. Extracts from my interviews with them, undertaken for quite a different purpose,[49] provide useful data for interpreting their roles in this case—Omw. Wakoli's conduct of his defense and Omw. Nabikamba's decision for the majority:

Omw. Wakoli: I am descended from a line of thirty-eight rulers. . . . From the start, when my father was made ruler in 1902, I was automatically given a subvillage to rule. . . . When I was fifteen, I was made a village headman by my father. I was introduced to Mr. Grant, who was then officer in charge of Busoga. From my village, I was appointed *mukungu* [50] chief of Bugobi, in the present subcounty of Bulange. Then the Provincial Commissioner told the hereditary rulers that they would have to send their sons to school if they wanted them to be chiefs. I was taken to school in Jinja, and later to Namirembe School in Kampala. After three years, I took the examination for King's College Budo,[51] but I failed in English because I was by that time a grown man with a family. In 1911, I was sent home, because my father refused to pay my fees. He was accused for this by the district commissioner but told him, "If I give you a son to serve you, why should I pay for it?". . . So the D.C. gave me a job in the office and I did good work. In 1912, I was appointed subcounty chief of Ssaabaddu in Bukoli. After five years, I was transferred to Kigulu. In 1920, on my father's recommendation, I was made county chief of

48. The chairman of the district court is the Kyabazinga, but a county chief often acts for him.

49. The study of chiefs reported in Lloyd A. Fallers, *Bantu Bureaucracy*, pp. 189–96. I did not know of this case at the time of the interview.

50. *Mukungu:* an appointed chief. Though Omw. Wakoli is a prince (*mulangira*) with claims to the rulership, which he later assumed, this was an appointive post that might have been held by a commoner.

51. An elite boarding school in Buganda.

Bukoli, after my father retired. In 1940 I was transferred to Luuka County and in 1948 was transferred here. The people are angry because they can't have their hereditary rulers. They don't like all this transferring around. Maybe one day the hereditary chiefs will return. . . .

Omw. Wakoli proudly showed me his robes of office, his livestock, and his wives, complaining, by the way, of the Christian rule of monogamy. He is a Christian, but his polygyny—five wives were at that time in residence—made him a noncommunicant.

Omw. Wakoli is a conservative with a strong sense of lineage and an appreciation of authority. He—and his father—accepted the Europeans as superior rulers. For Omw. Nabikamba, on the other hand, they were primarily teachers of a superior moral order:

Omw. Nabikamba: My father, Nua, was *katikkiro* [deputy] to Tabingwa, ruler of Luuka; and later became the first nonhereditary county chief in Busoga. . . . We did well because we were friends of the missionaries. Nua was so pleased with them that he was baptized in 1906 by Archdeacon Buckley. In 1896, I learned to read. A Muganda, Paulo Kiwanuka, was sent to teach the children and he stayed in the *katikkiro's* house at Kiyunga, my father's house. . . . In 1904, I was baptized. In 1905, I went to Kamuli to communion. I met Archdeacon Mathers, who asked me to be a houseboy at the Kaliro mission. I helped with teaching children. . . . In 1906, District Commissioner Boyle noticed me and made me *katikkiro* to my father, who had been made chief of Bugweri. In 1907 I was sent to Mengo High School . . . then I went to King's College, Budo, for three years. In 1913 I returned and in 1917 I was made a subcounty chief in Bulamogi. In 1924, I became acting county chief . . . and in 1925 county chief of Luuka. . . . In 1940 I became chief of Bugweri and Bukoli combined and in 1950 came here. . . .

The hereditary rulers were very cruel. My mother was the daughter of a prince in Bugabula and she told me how the ruler impaled his wives for infidelity and cut off people's ears for disobedience. Chiefs should be chosen on merit. . . . To be a friend of _____ [a senior chief of princely lineage], you must give him bribes. I am too poor to do that. I have too many children to educate. . . . People are jealous of us because for a while we [his family] had more chiefs than the royal clans.

For Omw. Nabikamba, with his mission upbringing, Maliyamu has perfectly adequate reasons for a divorce. He considers it quite wrong to give preadolescent girls in marriage and feels that such a marriage should not be binding because it cannot have been maturely consented to. The whole process, he feels, constitutes a violation of the girl's rights. Omw. Wakoli, on the other hand, clearly has custom on his side. Child marriage is said to have been common in precolonial Busoga. It is consistent with the whole institutional structure surrounding Soga marriage that it should be primarily a matter for agreement between the bridegroom and the father, supported by their respective lineages. a virtuous father will take his daughter's wishes into account and will take steps to protect her from mistreatment by her husband, but this is only one of many responsibilities he must weigh, including the advantages to his descent group of an affinal tie to a princely dynasty.[52] In this instance, Maliyamu's father acted to maintain such a link after the earlier marriage to her sister had failed; instead of leaving Kantono's infant son to be reared by another wife or removing him from Wakoli's home,[53] Isifu sent Maliyamu to fill Kantono's role. In terms of traditional Soga morality, Maliyamu's case is incomprehensible. If she has been well treated—and there is no evidence that she has not—she should be happy to bear and rear princely children who will be *baiwa* (sister's children [54]) to her own agnatic descent group.

The trend in present-day Busoga is clearly toward Omw. Nabikamba's view.[55] My concern here is not, however, with changes in attitudes toward women as such, but rather with the consequences of such changes for the courts' handling of legal concepts. Legal thought *uses* moral sentiments and transforms them into legal concepts. Such concepts are tools for thinking about moral problems—more particularly for making "yes" or "no" decisions about particular moral situations. I have argued that legal culture is not coextensive with everyday moral culture—that the necessity to categorize involves moral oversimplification and that to the extent to which legal culture is institutionalized in a distinct adjudicatory structure, it may run ahead of, or lag behind, everyday morality. But the reach of legal concepts is clearly influenced by the moral ideas held by judges—and by those of litigants, too, since they, by their arguments, help to shape the issues. In present-day Busoga, certain moral ideas are changing, and with them the reach of certain concepts of wrong. Relatively little of this has appeared in the field of marriage and sexual relations.[56] Only in this case does it become strikingly clear. For some of the participants, including a majority of the court, morality has shifted sufficiently that child marriage has become a reason for placing a set of circumstances within reach of the concept "refusal to grant a divorce." For others, it

52. See chapters 2 and 6.
53. The child belongs to its begetter, but customarily a mother separated from the begetter keeps the child until it nears puberty.
54. See Appendix A.
55. H. F. Morris, "Marriage and Divorce in Uganda"; A. W. Southall, "On Chastity in Africa."
56. It is quite possible that Walwendo's defense against the accusation of harboring in *Tonda Nandabi* v. *Walwendo* would not have been accepted fifty or one hundred years ago. One would expect a drift toward wider grounds for defense in such cases. The difference between the decision of the court of first instance and that of the appeal court in that case might be interpreted as evidence of such a drift.

clearly has not. It is perhaps significant that here, too, for almost the first time,[57] there is explicit talk of "custom" (*mpisa*), in the sense of "rule." Explicitness seems to increase as consensus about the law declines. The conceptual gap is striking because the difference is a substantial one and because it is articulated by prominent and legally experienced men.

Accompanying the difference concerning the reach of the concept of wrong is a difference of view on procedure, apparent in this case and in the preceding one, *Samasoni Ntuyo* v. *Mubakali Kiwomero*. In the latter case, Samasoni was asked why he "interfered" and did not allow the wife herself to accuse. In *Maliyamu Kyazike* v. *Samwiri Wakoli*, Maliyamu was asked why she, and not her father, accused Omw. Wakoli. At issue is the legal competence of women in marital and sexual disputes. The traditional view, still held by most judges, is that women are not competent to accuse or be accused.[58] I have no cases in which women are accused of adultery or of wrongfully leaving their husbands. In one of these divorce cases, a woman was allowed to accuse; in the other, reportedly, she was not, although in both the judges were uncertain enough about the point to raise it. Clearly, the handling of a concept of wrong will be influenced in some degree by the interests of the person who handles it. Allowing a woman to plead for herself constitutes a recognition that her interests may diverge from those of her father.

I shall not further pursue here the problem of the uncertainty in the application of legal concepts created by changes in values. The problem will arise again in the field of land tenure and I shall want to consider it at greater length in that context. For the moment, I return to a final category of disputes involving marriage—one which changes in morality seem not yet to have greatly affected.

BRIDEWEALTH DEBT

The order in which I have considered the various concepts of wrong that may be invoked in the field of sexual relations and marriage has followed, more or less, the natural history of an unsuccessful marriage. I began by analyzing cases of adultery and harboring, in which husbands accused alleged lovers and fathers or guardians of violating their rights under still-extant marriages; I then moved on to cases of eating two hens, in which fathers or guardians were alleged to have

---

57. See also Yowasi's appeal in *Genatio Magino* v. *Yowasi Maliwa*.

58. In cases involving sexual relations and marriage. Women may, however, accuse and be accused in cases involving debts other than bridewealth and offenses against persons and the state.

contracted a second marriage without arranging to have the first dissolved; and finally I have considered a concept of wrong under which wives and their fathers or guardians may take the initiative in dissolving marriages. There remains the final possibility of a marriage which has been dissolved by mutual consent but in which the husband claims that his bridewealth has not yet been repaid, or not repaid in full. His recourse, then, is to invoke the concept of wrong generally expressed by the word *bbanja,* which I shall translate "debt." The word *bbanja,* with its related verbal form *kubanja,* "to dun," applies to any kind of debt. My concern here is with the special conceptual problems involved in its application to the repayment of bridewealth.

The general understanding among Basoga is that when a marriage is terminated by any means other than the wife's death, the wife's people —which of them will be discussed in a moment—owe the husband or his successor the full amount of the bridewealth. There is no evidence that the Basoga, like some African peoples, have ever held the wife's people responsible for replacing her or repaying the bridewealth in the event of her death.[59] If the husband dies, however, as has been noted, the wife's people must repay if she does not marry the successor or another member of the lineage. Neither is the amount of the bridewealth to be repaid dependent upon the wife's fertility, as in some parts of Africa.[60] A husband may dismiss his wife for infertility, as for any number of other reasons, but the bridewealth must always be repaid in full if the husband insists. Given this general situation, a number of subsidiary questions may arise: the existence of a valid contract, the locus of responsibility, evidence of amounts paid and repaid, evidence of a husband's renunciation of the debt, and perhaps others. Since these questions are similar to those that arose in connection with other concepts of wrong I have discussed, for the obvious reason that they pertain to the same institutional complex, I shall cite only two cases: one which illustrates the similarity of the concept of the locus of responsibility in bridewealth debt to that in harboring; and one in which a father argued, unsuccessfully, that the solemnization of the marriage by a clergyman has a bearing on bridewealth debt.

Tomasi Wanume v. Magino: heir and successor are responsible; the most reliable witness

Tomasi Wanume v. Magino involves the inheritance of the bridewealth debt upon the death of the wife's begetter. On September 1, 1950, Tomasi Wanume accuses Magino of "refusing to repay bride-

59. L. P. Mair, "African Marriage and Social Change," pp. 15–16.
60. I. Schapera, *A Handbook of Tswana Law and Custom,* p. 145.

wealth—one cow, three goats, four chickens, and forty shillings—with which I married his daughter, Gambo, who left me in 1947." Magino simply denies any involvement in the matter:

Magino: I will win because I did not take bridewealth from him and I have never begotten a child called "Gambo." . . . If he brings testimony confirming that I have bridewealth from him, I will lose the case. I shall have nothing with which to argue.

Q: Do you have testimony confirming that Tomasi did not marry your daughter and that you didn't take bridewealth from him?
A: Yes, I have that of Daudi Kyangwa and Alipakusadi Kayanga—they are the ones who know.
Q: But the girl Gambo who married Tomasi—don't you know her at all?
A: Oh, I know her, but she married the late Yekoniya, brother of Tomasi. Gambo lived with that brother . . . for nine years.
Q: But the late Yekoniya, brother of Tomasi, didn't he marry your daughter? [61] And what about the bridewealth?
A: He married her, but I don't know about the bridewealth, since I was [then] a small child. I think I heard my father . . . say he married her with forty shillings, three goats, one cow, and three hens.
Q: But wasn't this Tomasi paid back the things with which his late brother married Gambo?
A: No. . . .
Q: So, if he was not paid back . . . . , is he not justified now in accusing you? . . .
A: No, because the one who succeeded our father is Kapere . . .
Q: But can you bring the one who succeeded your father to testify?
A: I can't bring him.
Q: If you can't bring Kapere, who succeeded your father, then what evidence is there to remove the charge from you . . . ?
A: All right, I can bring Kapere. . . .
Q: Is Kapere, who succeeded your father, the one who gave the girl to the person she's married to now?
A: Since her husband died, she hasn't remarried. She's living alone.
Q: When will you bring your father Kapere to court?
A: I'll bring him on September 8.
Q: If you don't bring him on that day, will you agree that you lose the case?
A: Yes, I will lose it.

Magino is a sullen and defiant young man, in contrast with Tomasi, his accuser, who appears much more reasonable:

Tomasi: . . . I know I will win. My brother, Yekoniya, who died, married Gambo, and Kapere took his bridewealth. When Yekoniya died, I succeeded him, but the wife rejected me. So then I went to Kapere to ask for the bridewealth. But he answered me by saying, "Magino, whom they left in my care, refused to pay you the bridewealth. Go accuse Magino. . . ." So I came here to accuse him.

61. She turns out to be his sister, but the court does not yet know this.

Q: Do you have testimony to show that your brother Yekoniya married Gambo?

A: Yes, I have that of Firipo, the agent [*mubaka*] who delivered the bridewealth.

The fact of the marriage has not been contested, but, in order to confirm it, the court hears Firipo:

Q: Do you agree to give testimony for these two people . . . ?

A: Yes, . . . and I will give it for Tomasi, concerning the bridewealth with which Tomasi's brother Yekoniya married Gambo . . . one pregnant cow; three goats, of which one was a nanny, one a billy, and one a female kid; forty shillings; and four chickens. I was the agent who handed those things over to Kapere. . . .

Q: If you handed those things over to Kapere . . . . , why does he accuse Magino?

A: He accuses him because Kapere . . . says that the bridewealth belongs to this boy, Magino.

A no-nonsense witness, as an agent should be. The case is now adjourned and is taken up a week later on September 8, the day on which Magino promised to bring Kapere. The court questions Magino:

Q: Have you brought Kapere, whom you called upon?

A: I haven't brought him because he is ill with an abscess.

Q: Since you haven't brought him, do you agree that you lose?

A: I don't lose! My witness is sick!

The court decides that Magino has been bluffing, since he cannot produce the witness who, he himself has agreed, is the key one. The decision, therefore, goes against him and he is ordered to repay the bridewealth, otherwise ". . . some of his property will be seized to pay the accuser."

A somewhat chastened Magino decides to appeal, but before hearing his plea to the county court, it will be useful to review the proceedings to date, with the aid of a genealogical diagram (see fig. 10).

Yekoniya married Gambo, and, since Gambo refused to marry Tomasi when Yekoniya died, some member of Gambo's patrilineage owes Tomasi forty shillings, three goats, one cow, and three hens. This much is common ground. It also seems to be common ground that Kapere succeeded Gabangulwa, who, it soon comes out, was the begetter of Gambo and Magino. Now Kapere, who is allegedly too sick to testify, is quoted by Tomasi and his witness, Firipo, as having referred to Magino as "having the bridewealth" and "refusing to pay." The suggestion is, clearly, that Magino is Gabangulwa's heir. The court believes this, thinking that Magino has not brought Kapere because he fears that Kapere would confirm it. In Magino's appeal, however, he denies this and claims, inter alia, that the heir is Sirivesiteri Jabuliwo, a brother of his and Gambo's. He also again calls upon his witnesses, Daudi Kyangwa and Alipakusadi Kayanga, whose identities are never made clear. "If he brings testimony," Magino concludes, "to firmly prove that I am the heir of my father and that I received [62] the bridewealth, then . . . the accusation [is correct]."

When the county court takes up the case on November 3, both

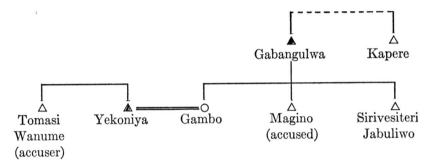

Fig. 10

parties stand on their previous arguments. The court, however, closely questions Magino:

Q: Who was it who took Gambo from Tomasi's home? [63]
A: I don't know. . . .
Q: . . . in whose house does she stay now?
A: She stays in Kapere's house.
Q: Now do you agree to bring as your witness Kapere, the successor who is in charge of Gambo, who received bridewealth for her, and in whose house she now stays?
A: I can't bring him because Tomasi said in Musaale's court that he was the one who told Tomasi to accuse me.

This will be crucial; Magino does not bring Kapere, he suggests, not because he is sick, but because he is somehow prejudiced against Magino. If this is correct, Magino is in a bad spot; a person's guardian, successor to his begetter, should be a reliable witness for his interests. The courts tend to assume this, as did the lower court in this case. The appeal court, however, takes up the suggestion and probes for alternative testimony:

Q: If you won't bring your father Kapere, . . . then what testimony is there that is better than your father's?
A: Daudi Kyangwa and Alipakusadi Kayanga—they know that I was not the

62. He means "received by inheritance."
63. After the funeral feast. That is to say, when she rejected Tomasi, to whom, among her agnates, did she return?

heir of Gabangulwa, but that his heir is Sirivesiteri Jabuliwo, and that he ought to pay the bridewealth.

For whatever reasons, the court, like the lower court, is supremely uninterested in these two characters. One guesses that they are young friends of Magino's, who are in no position to testify with authority. The court has its own ideas about witnesses:

Q: This Sirivesiteri Jabuliwo, do you agree to bring him . . . to say that he is the heir and ought to pay the bridewealth?
A: I would bring him, but I don't know where he is.
Q: If you don't know [his] whereabouts . . . now is Tomasi right when he says that you are the heir of your father?
A: He's not right!

The court seems impressed by the tenacity of Magino, who until now has been given all the difficult questions, and so it turns to Tomasi with a question that turns out to be decisive:

Q: Have you heard the argument of Magino that he isn't the heir of his father? Do you call upon the head of the clan [64] to say that Magino is the heir of Gabangulwa?
A: I don't call upon him. This Magino isn't the heir, but the reason I accuse him is that the things with which my brother married Gambo were given to him to buy a wife. That's why I accused him, but the heir was someone else.
Q: Now do you accept the argument of Magino that he isn't the heir?
A: I accept that.

This is decisive, and the court concludes:

. . . in his own testimony, Tomasi agrees that Magino is not the heir of his father. Therefore he . . . should go and accuse the successor and heir of his in-law Gabangulwa, who ought to repay the bridewealth, and not this Magino, whom he has until now been accusing.

This case clearly takes place in the conceptual world encountered in the discussion of the locus of responsibility in harboring. The problem is: Among the wife's male agnates, who, precisely, may be accused of harboring when the marriage is still intact or of bridewealth debt when it has been dissolved? Just as, in *Jabwire Itembe* v. *Mukama Kalungi*, the court found that the persons responsible for harboring are the heir and successor, and not necessarily the person in whose home the wife has been sheltered, so in *Tomasi Wanume* v. *Magino* the court finds that the debt belongs to the heir and successor, and not necessarily to the person who was allotted the use of the bridewealth. With respect to both allotment of bridewealth received and the residence of a married daughter/sister, a descent group may make internal arrangements of

64. Clan here means "succession lineage." See chapter 2.

which the court will not take cognizance. It is, of course, morally wrong, in Soga eyes, for a male agnate who is not the wife's begetter, or his heir or successor, to shelter her without adequate reason. It is likewise morally wrong of Magino, if he was given the bridewealth for his own marriage (and he does not deny this), not to help reassemble it so that the debt to the successor to Gambo's late husband may be discharged. But the courts, through their concept of locus of responsibility, make only the heir or successor, as appointed by the lineage, *legally* accountable.

The question of credibility is interesting here. Given the above concept of the locus of responsibility, the evidential problem is that of determining the identity of the heir and successor. Accusers in cases like these, in which the locus of responsibility is at issue, may bring evidence to suggest that the accused behaved as a person responsible would. Jabwire (in *Jabwire Itembe* v. *Mukama Kalungi*) argued that the fact—which was common ground—that Mukama had sheltered the woman indicated that he was the guardian. Similarly here, Tomasi brought uncontested evidence that Magino had been allotted the bridewealth and that he had refused to repay it, suggesting that he was the heir. These arguments are, of course, based upon probabilities of Soga social behavior. One might well, as a Musoga, expect persons responsible to behave in these ways. Such behavior is evidence, but not the only or, in the court's view, the best evidence. More direct, and better, evidence is that which indicates who was chosen as heir or successor by the lineage. In *Jabwire Itembe* v. *Mukama Kalungi*, this turned out to be *res judicata;* another court had already decided. Here, in *Tomasi Wanume* v. *Magino*, when confronted by the possibility of testimony from one who would surely know what the decisions of the lineage had been, the accuser conceded. Evidence of what the lineage had decided is also, of course, a matter of probability. One reason the courts in *Tomasi Wanume* v. *Magino* took so long to reach their final decision was that the accused seemed reluctant to call upon another witness, Kapere, who would have had authoritative knowledge of the decisions of the lineage. Kapere, the successor, would surely know, but Magino seemed to stall when asked to bring him. This, the courts thought, could only mean that Kapere's testimony would run against Magino's argument in defense. One can only conclude, after hearing others' reports of Kapere's behavior and statements, that this would indeed have been the case—that for some reason there was bad blood between Kapere and Magino, perhaps just because Magino refused to help repay the bridewealth. Kapere clearly seems to have tried to shift legal responsibility onto Magino. The normal expectation that a per-

son in Kapere's position would give true testimony therefore proved
unreliable. The courts only accepted this when Tomasi, faced with the
possibility of testimony from an even more authoritative witness,
conceded.

Asa Nzalambi v. *Erinesti Lwondo: the consequences of Christian marriage*

The final case I shall consider carries the discussion beyond the field
of customary Soga legal concepts to the boundary between that field
and the national marriage legislation introduced by the British authorities. I have said that the British protectorate administration has been
careful to preserve the integrity of customary family law, even in the
case of Christians whose marriages have been solemnized under the
terms of the Marriage Ordinance.[65] *Asa Nzalambi* v. *Erinesti Lwondo*
illustrates one way in which this has been achieved. Asa accuses
Erinesti of "failing to repay my eighteen goats . . . and seventy
shillings given for his daughter, who left my home in 1946." On
October 29, 1950, when the case comes to trial, Erinesti responds with
a plea that the couple, having been married in church, must first be
divorced by the church:

Erinesti: I don't agree that I lose because I didn't take his wife from him, as
he charges. She is a ring wife,[66] and I want him to go to the clergyman and get
him to separate them before I can pay him his things. The things I know are
forty shillings, twelve goats, and two chickens. . . . The county chief of
Bulamogi gave me a letter to this subcounty directing us to go to a clergyman
to separate them before I should repay his things.
Q: Do you have evidence to show that Asa gave you only forty shillings,
   twelve goats, and two chickens?
A: Yes, I have that of . . . Enoka Muliro.

Asa, in his opening statement, seems to wish to avoid the matter of
the church marriage and instead dwells on the shortcomings of Erinesti
and his daughter:

Asa: I have heard [what he says], but it is not true. He himself caught his
daughter staying with a man in his [the man's] home. As a result of that, his
daughter left my home and went to Mbale, and when I caught her there she
went to Kakira. I caught her there and took her to Erinesti's so he might give
back my things, because she spoiled my home. That woman has spent four
years away from my home and she continues to say that they will pay back
my things. . . .
Q: Is it true that your wife is a ring wife?
A: I won't answer that.
Q: Now Erinesti says that if you will go and get a divorce . . . from a
clergyman, he will give you your things. How is that?

---

65. Chapter 2.
66. *Mukyala ow'empeta*, the common term for "wife by Christian marriage."

A: The woman isn't accusing me now about the ring [suing for divorce], but instead I am litigating about the bridewealth. If the woman accuses me concerning the ring, we will go to court [67] to be separated.

Q: Erinesti says the woman should accuse you before the clergyman. How is that?

A: Erinesti took his daughter to the clergyman, saying that I drove her away, and the clergyman directed him to return with me so that I might have an opportunity to refute her in front of him.

Asa thus argues that his claim for bridewealth is a matter quite independent of the church marriage. So the court returns to Erinesti:

Q: Asa says you took your daughter to the clergyman so she could say he had rejected her. When the clergyman questioned her, did she reject him?

A: I never took my daughter to the clergyman. . . .

Q: What is it that prevents you from paying his bridewealth?

A: Because they have not been divorced, and do not have a letter to say they are divorced—only that.

Q: Where is your daughter now?

A: In my home.

Q: Apart from the ring marriage, does the church have any authority over the bridewealth?

A: I'm not certain about that.

There is some additional testimony concerning the amount of the bridewealth, after which the court gives its decision:

The accused, Erinesti Lwondo . . . , loses the case for not paying Asa Nzalambi his things with which he married his wife . . . , seventy shillings and eighteen goats. The accused argues that he bases his refusal to repay the things to his in-law . . . on their not having been separated. He wants the church authorities who married them to separate them before he pays back the things. But this court did not go into the matter of the ring, only that of the bridewealth, which the accused received and which he knows about. Further, the wife left the home of Asa Nzalambi and stays in the home of her father. The church, on which he relies, never ordered him to take his daughter from her husband's home. . . .[68] Punishment: to pay back the things of the accuser, seventy shillings and eighteen goats.

Now this case actually turns on the provisions of the Native Courts Ordinance to the effect that "a claim arising only in regard to bride-price or adultery and founded only on native law and custom" is adjudicable in the local courts.[69] Erinesti is quite wrong and Asa and the court quite right; Asa's suit for return of his bridewealth is not affected by the fact that there had been a church marriage. It is characteristic, however, that neither Asa nor the court refers explicitly to the relevant national legislation. Chiefs are quite unaccustomed to looking up the legislation relevant to their work in the law books—if

67. The British magistrate's court.
68. A nice rejoinder!
69. Section 10 (b).

indeed there are copies of these in their offices, which often there are not. They simply *know* (or think they know) that such-and-such is the law. Section 10(*b*) of the Native Courts Ordinance has been absorbed into the conceptual apparatus of the Soga courts in the form of the notion that the A.L.G. courts deal with questions involving the bride-wealth, the national courts with those involving the "ring."

In this case, Erinesti appealed, repeating all his previous arguments. The county court trial brought out nothing new, but the county chief now took the precaution of consulting the district commissioner who, in a letter, assured him that the lower court's decision was correct. Erinesti's testimony that the county chief had earlier agreed with him that church action was necessary may have been truthful, in which case the county chief was less well informed than Asa and the lower court judges.

However, it is quite understandable that Erinesti and the county chief, both of whom I knew well, should have been confused. For, although national legislation firmly establishes the jurisdiction of the local courts and customary law over disputes of the sort I have discussed in this chapter and the last, there are also in the national law provisions which in a broader sense seem quite incompatible with this jurisdiction. Many Basoga nowadays, including Asa and Erinesti's daughter, are married by clergymen and have their marriages regis-tered under the national Marriage Ordinance, which, together with the Divorce Ordinance, establishes a regime of marriage law similar to that in force in Great Britain around the turn of the century.[70] Basoga and other Africans who undertake such marriages are in theory subject to this regime *as well as* to the provisions of customary law. Thus Erinesti is right in thinking that his daughter, having been married under the Marriage Ordinance, can only be divorced (in the English sense) under the Divorce Ordinance by a magistrate of the national court system (not, of course, by "the church," as he puts it). Further-more, the Marriage Ordinance provides that anyone who marries under the Ordinance, having previously contracted a customary mar-riage, or who contracts such a marriage after marrying under the Ordinance, is guilty of bigamy and punishable by the national courts (there is separate legislation for Muslims). As Morris notes, with a large measure of understatement, if these provisions were to be en-forced, the prisons of Uganda would be "full to overflowing."[71]

The turn-of-the-century framers of this legislation, in addition to providing for Europeans resident in Uganda, seem to have envisaged a growing group of African "*évolués*," who would choose to live under a

70. Morris, "Marriage and Divorce in Uganda," pp. 197–98.
71. Ibid., p. 198.

fully Western form of marriage. In fact, as I have noted, the pattern has instead been a syncretistic one; a preference for the rites of Christian marriage has spread to a very large part of the population, while a commitment to monogamy and other supposed concomitants of such rites has remained limited to a few. The provisions of the Marriage Ordinance have simply not been enforced with respect to Africans; and the Native Courts Ordinance of 1941, which placed the customary contract of marriage with bridewealth firmly within the customary jurisdictions, was a belated recognition of this. But the anomaly remains: Erinesti must repay Asa's bridewealth under customary law in order to dissolve the customary union, but if either Asa or his ex-wife were to remarry, whether by customary contract or under the Ordinance, he or she would in theory be subject to prosecution. In fact this does not happen and few Basoga are even aware of the possibility, but Erinesti and the county chief are aware of it, and their reasoning about what logically should follow has led them astray.

Further confusion has resulted from the fact that in Buganda, to which Basoga tend to look for models of thought and action, the position is different. Under the leadership of a deeply Christian group of chiefs,[72] the Buganda courts, on their own authority, decided early in the century not to recognize customary marriage. (Because of its position of greater autonomy within Uganda, legislation such as the Native Courts Ordinance of 1941 does not apply in Buganda.) Claims for the return of bridewealth are not entertained, with the result that, while customary marriage seems to have been very similar in precolonial Buganda and Busoga,[73] the payment of bridewealth has declined in Buganda. Erinesti and the county chief are aware of this Ganda pattern and consider it more virtuous, though it must be said that Erinesti's emulation of the Baganda has been one-sided: he was ready enough to *accept* bridewealth, but doesn't like having to return it.

Thus the legal position of Soga marriage is potentially an unstable one. While all this has as yet had little or no effect upon the vast majority of Basoga, it was clear at the time of my observations that change was in the air. An organized force for change had appeared in the form of the Uganda Council of Women, a group of educated women who were agitating for reform of national marriage and family law. Meanwhile, the fact that the overwhelming majority of village-dwelling Basoga continued to accept unquestioningly the customary regime in marriage and related institutional fields is an indication of the continued vitality and legitimacy of the A.L.G. courts and their law.

72. Southall, "On Chastity in Africa," pp. 212–13.
73. L. P. Mair, *An African People in the Twentieth Century*, chapter 4.

A chief does not rule land; he rules people.
—Luganda proverb

For the village headman, land is like a cow that never goes dry.
—A subcounty chief

6 Land in Litigation:
Law in a Changing Institutional Setting

The field of landholding, like that of marriage and sexual relations, is governed by "customary law" in the sense that the Soga courts, in deciding disputes in this field, draw upon their own fund of ideas and experience rather than upon statutory provisions laid down for them by the Uganda government. The ordinances which direct the African Local Government courts to "administer and enforce . . . native law and custom" insofar as it is not "repugnant to natural justice or morality" or "in conflict with the provisions of any [national] law in force" have buttressed this free use of indigenous ideas and experience with the authority of the national government, and no other legislation has encroached upon it. Land law in Busoga is free of any of the (largely theoretical) conflicts between local and national law found in some aspects of marriage law.[1] The small area of land in Busoga, held by Basoga, which has been surveyed and registered under national land legislation is firmly and unequivocally under the jurisdiction of the national courts. Its Basoga holders are on exactly the same footing with respect to it as are European and Asian

1. See *Asa Nzalambi* v. *Erinesti Lwondo.*

holders of similar titles.[2] The remainder of the land is equally unambiguously under customary jurisdiction. Thus, from the standpoint of
the national legal system, land law is perhaps the most "purely customary" of all the fields which fall under the jurisdiction of the Soga
courts.

This does not mean, of course, that in deciding disputes over land
the judges apply in a mechanical way the same body of ideas that
their predecessors applied to such disputes before the British administrators appeared upon the scene. Here, as elsewhere in this study,
"customary law" means simply the part of Soga law that is unencumbered by superordinate judicial and legislative authority—the part
that emerges from the judges' application to disputes of ideas drawn
from their experience of Soga life, both ancient and contemporary.
"Customary law" does not connote something fixed in the mold of the
past.[3] Indeed, in these chapters on litigation over land the *changing*
character of Soga law will be a major focus of concern. In the field of
sexual relations and marriage the law appears, on the whole, to have
remained relatively settled, so that the courts are able to apply their
received body of concepts with a good deal of assurance and certainty.
It is the occasional ambiguities and uncertainties stemming from quite
recent tendencies toward change in the social position of women that
stand out. In the field of landholding, major changes in the institutional context began much earlier and have been much more far-reach-
ing. Despite its purely "customary" character (in the above sense),
therefore, Soga land law is in major respects unsettled and uncertain
—more unsettled and uncertain than Soga marriage law. The writer of
the annual administrative report for 1955 who attributed the large
number of land cases to ". . . the varying land tenure system or lack
of system in Busoga"[4] was perhaps guilty of exaggeration (for there *is*
a system), but the difficulty he experienced in discerning a pattern will
be appreciated (and its sources, I hope, better understood) as the
efforts of the Basoga judges themselves to impose legal order in a
changing and disordered area of life are analyzed.

The quotations that precede the title of this chapter point to a major
source of the court's difficulties. Land, which was once thought of as

2. The very small amounts of land involved are held under the Registration of
Titles Ordinance of 1924.
3. The notion of customary law as something which has continued unchanged
since "time immemorial" is inconsistent with my view of what law—any kind of
law—is, or can be.
4. Uganda Protectorate, *Annual Report on the Eastern Province, Western
Province, Northern Province and the Kingdom of Buganda for the Year Ended
31st December, 1955,* p. 15.

the territorial and economic basis of political relations, has in the twentieth century increasingly come to be viewed as a source of wealth quite apart from political relations. In part this is a result of the growth of cash-crop agriculture and of a market for its products which is external to the political hierarchy. In part, also, it has resulted from changes within the political hierarchy itself—from the conversion of the old kingdom states, organized on the basis of kinship and patron-client relations, into an institution for modern local government. In the past, such of the villager's produce as was not consumed by himself and his household, or exchanged with other villagers, was given in tribute to his personal political superiors, who ruled and protected him; today it is sold in an impersonal market for cash with which to purchase goods and services in equally impersonal exchanges. That part of it which still goes to support the polity is paid in taxes to the A.L.G. and the national government, which in turn pay out fixed salaries to their servants and purchase the means for the provision of social services. The connection between rights in land and personal political rights and duties has not, to be sure, been dissolved entirely. The village or subvillage headman remains more (or less) than a landlord pure and simple, and the villager has become neither a freeholder nor a rent-paying tenant. But both villager and headman, who together with their descent-groups share most of the rights in land, increasingly view these rights as sources of money income rather than as incidents to a network of personal political ties. The difference between the view of land suggested by the anonymous author of the proverb and that conveyed by the contemporary subcounty chief's figure of the perpetually yielding cow is a measure of the economic and political change which the Basoga judges have been asked to bridge in administering the "customary law" of land tenure.

Land on the Docket: Statistical Evidence of Uncertainty and Change

There is evidence of uncertainty of a "harder" sort in the statistics of cases of various kinds which come before the courts. In chapter 3 it was suggested, on the basis of a "vertical sample section" of dockets at each level of the court system, that land cases are, of all the types that come before the courts, the most difficult to settle. Data secured from a court not covered by tables 1 through 4 in chapter 3 confirm this suggestion and provide a basis for comparing in greater detail the relative difficulty experienced by the courts in settling land cases as compared with those arising from marriage and sexual relations.

Table 5 shows the appellate history and disposition of all the land and sex-and-marriage cases heard on appeal in 1950 by the county court of Bugabula. All these cases had been appealed from the various subcounty courts in Bugabula; and before that, it is fair to assume, village and subvillage headmen and parish chiefs had tried, unsuccessfully, to settle them. All the cases in table 5 are therefore difficult, recalcitrant ones. Of all the cases, of all types, appealed to this county court in 1950, 33 percent involved claims to land, while 10 percent involved breaches of marital or sexual norms.

Table 5 provides three measures of "difficulty of settlement." Land cases are, first of all, more frequently reversed on appeal. Forty-four percent of the land cases were reversed at least once above the sub-

TABLE 5

DISPOSITION OF LAND AND MARRIAGE CASES HEARD ON APPEAL BY THE COUNTY COURT OF BUGABULA IN 1950.

	Land Rights	Breaches of Marital and Sexual Norms
Number of cases	62	18
Reversed on appeal	27	5
Reversed more than once	3	—
Court of appeal reached:		
County	32	16
District	21	1
District Commissioner	8	1
High Court	1	—

NOTE: The total number of appeal cases heard by the court during 1950 was 189.

county level, while this is true of only 28 percent of the sex-and-marriage cases. Land cases are also more frequently reversed more than once. Finally, litigants in land cases are more tenacious, appealing more readily to higher courts. Of these cases, almost half of those concerned with rights in land were carried beyond the county court, while only 11 percent of the cases involving sexual relations and marriage went beyond this level. As in tables 1 through 4, the sample is a small one; but the differences are striking, and they help to explain, even if they do not fully validate, the observation of the annual administrative report for 1950 that ". . . where land is involved it can now be taken as a general rule that the unsuccessful party will go on appealing and petitioning, as a matter of course, until he has had his case dealt with by the High Court." [5]

There is also evidence that the sheer frequency of land cases has increased greatly over the decades of this century. It is not, unfortu-

5. Uganda Protectorate, *Annual Report on the Eastern Province, Western Province, Northern Province and the Kingdom of Buganda for the Year Ended 31st December, 1950*, p. 46.

nately, possible to trace in detail change in the frequency of various types of litigation for the Soga courts as a whole over the whole period of British administration, for the published reports of the Uganda Government classify cases only under very broad headings. Recent annual reports, for example, give only consolidated figures for all "civil" cases and classify "criminal" cases under these headings: "criminal force," "theft," "disobedience of local laws," "adultery," "tax default," and "other." It seems significant, however, that remarks in administrative officers' reports about the growing burden of land litigation of the sort quoted earlier do not become common until the 1940s and 1950s. *Something* seems to have occurred during the fifteen years prior to my observations in 1950–52 to increase greatly the traffic of cases involving individual landholdings.

This does not, of course, show that disputes of this nature did not occur at earlier periods. It does, however, suggest that whatever disputes arose among villagers and between villagers and their headmen with respect to landholding did not, until recently, begin to appear in significant numbers on the dockets of the A.L.G. courts, and that only recently has the application of customary law to their settlement become a major concern of the courts. One reason for the high rates of appeal, and of reversal of judgment on appeal, may be that the field is in some sense a novel one for the judges; their concepts for framing issues for decision may be less well developed, less efficient as a result of constant use, in this field than in the field of sexual relations and marriage. Before examining current cases for evidence of such a state of affairs, however, it will be useful to consider in somewhat greater detail the institutional context out of which the cases arise. In this field, as in that of sexual relations and marriage, it will be helpful to look for the institutional "trouble spots" from which litigation springs —particularly those which may have resulted from recent social changes.

Land Use and Landholding: The Contemporary Pattern

In Busoga, land tenure, like marriage, is compounded of individual-contractual and corporate-hereditary principles. It is a matter of corporate descent in that both headmen and peasant cultivators hold rights in land which may be passed on to their heirs, chosen by their succession lineages. In both cases, it is the *musika atwala ebintu* ("the heir who takes the things") who inherits.[6] But land tenure also in-

---

6. As the earlier discussion of inheritance in chapter 2 has indicated, there are two heirs or successors: the "heir who takes the things"—usually a son or brother's son—and the "successor of the belt"—usually a brother or patrilineal cousin—who becomes guardian of the deceased's children.

volves an individual-contractual element in that a lineage's hereditary rights originate in an agreement between one of its members and some higher authority. In the case of the peasant cultivator, either he or his ancestor will have contracted with the headman or his ancestor. In the case of the headman, either he or his ancestor will have received the position, and with it the accompanying rights in land, from a ruler or chief under the old political system. Today these latter authorities have of course been replaced, in their higher governmental functions, by the official A.L.G. parish, subcounty, and county chiefs. Their rights in the land, however, continue to receive a certain recognition in the customary law, as will be seen.

Basoga use two words to express, respectively, the individual-contractual and the corporate-hereditary dimensions of land rights. Rights which have been passed to an heir through the corporate action of his lineage are expressed by the word *butaka,* a word made up of the root *-taka,* "land" or "soil," and the abstract class-prefix *bu-.* An alternative expression is *busika*—"patrimony"—compounded of the abstract *bu-* and the root *-sika,* which also appears in the noun *musika* —"heir" or "successor"—and in the verb *kusika*—"to succeed" or "inherit." A cultivator who claims rights in a holding by lineage-mediated succession speaks of it as "my *butaka.*" A headman who claims to hold his village or subvillage on the same basis will similarly speak of the village or subvillage as "my *butaka*" or "my *busika.*" Each will support his claim by pointing to the graves of his ancestors within the relevant area. Holdings and headmanships which have not passed to an heir through lineage action are spoken of as *kyerere* ("empty") or *-tongole,* a root whose most general meaning is "delegated" or "allocated." In the language of the A.L.G. administration, it has the meaning of "official" or "departmental." Thus an official of the A.L.G. may be spoken of as a *mutongole,* one of its departments as a *kitongole.* As applied to land tenure, it means land allocated, or available for allocation, by higher authority—land in which no lineage has acquired corporate rights by passing it to an heir. Thus a holding (*kibanja*) or a subvillage (*kisoko*) whose holder has himself received it from a higher authority or which is available for allocation is spoken of as *kitongole.* The corporate-hereditary principle, however, affects only the hereditary *transfer* of rights, not their day-to-day exercise. A headman administers his village or subvillage as an individual and a cultivator works his holding in the same way. Until one of them dies, they confront one another as individuals.

The words *butaka* (or *busika*) and *kitongole* will be encountered frequently in the examination of cases which come before the courts, for much litigation turns on the precise application of these concepts to rights in particular holdings and headmanships. It is the present lack of consensus about their application that makes land cases so common and so difficult to settle. These concepts themselves, however, are common to all Basoga in their thought and discourse concerning land.

The basic unit of landholding, to which these notions are applied, is the *kibanja*, typically a tract of some seven to nine acres, cultivated with the short-handled hoe and made up of a banana garden, usually adjacent to the dwelling houses and outbuildings, an area in annual crops, and an area under fallow. For convenience, the cultivator prefers to combine all this in a single compact holding, and sometimes this is possible. It will be recalled from the description of the Soga countryside given in chapter 2 that the village typically occupies a low hill—an area of high land surrounded by swamps. Apart from the granite outcroppings which sometimes crown the village area, the higher parts normally have the deep, rich red soil which is most suitable for bananas. As one descends toward the swamp, one crosses the thinner, poorer soils which are best devoted to the cultivation of annual crops. Finally, the margins of the swamps, which are subject to seasonal inundation, varying with the wetness of the year, consist of thick, black soils suitable only for sweet potato cultivation and grazing. A holding running down from the high part of the village land, combining areas of all these types of soil, is regarded as ideal; but where the high land between swamps is broad and flat, not all holdings can be so arranged. In such cases the core of the *kibanja*, consisting of the homestead and banana garden, may be separated from some or all of its fields by land belonging to others. In a largish village, much of the black soil on the margins of the swamps tends to consist of isolated fields belonging to persons whose homesteads are located on higher ground. The lowest and most frequently inundated land is uncultivable and remains unappropriated into *kibanja* holdings; this is used for seasonal common grazing.

The group which occupies the homestead and which is supported by its holding typically numbers 4 or 5 persons and includes only one married couple and their children.[7] In a total census-survey which I carried out in five villages, 506 households were found to contain a total population of 2,251 persons, of whom 83 percent were male household heads and their wives and children. Young married Basoga thus prefer to establish independent households, regarding such domestic independence as an inherent part of their new adult status. As they grow older, there is some tendency for their households to grow larger, but only slightly larger. In the villages surveyed, the households of

7. The statistics on household structure given here are reported in greater detail in Lloyd A. Fallers, *Bantu Bureaucracy,* chapter 4.

men under forty-five contained an average of 4 persons, while those of men over forty-five contained an average of 5. Larger households, when they do occur, are usually the result of either polygyny or the addition of patrilineal kin. In the villages surveyed, 18 percent of the adult males currently had more than one wife. And of the members of households who were not household heads' wives and children, 68 percent were patrilineal kin or widowed or divorced mothers of household heads. As the earlier discussion of marriage and the status of women generally would suggest, women seldom live alone. Among the 506 households, only 14 were headed by women, 5 of whom had dependents living with them. Much more commonly, and normatively, a widowed, divorced, or single woman lives with her father, brother, son, or brother's son. Where she does not, the land she cultivates is not, in law, hers, but rather that of her male guardian. The few cases of multiple family households are usually those of headmen or lineage heads, but such households are rare; of the total household population surveyed, only 6 percent represented married son's families and married brothers and their families.

The *kibanja*, then, typically supports a domestic unit of four or five persons whose core is a nuclear family. The *lusuku*, the banana garden adjacent to the homestead, is the province of the women and girls, who painstakingly cultivate it and harvest and prepare the fruit, which forms by far the largest part of the daily diet. Women also help in the cultivation of annual crops, but the fields (*nnimiro*) devoted to them are managed by the men, who do the clearing and planting and plan the rotations that maintain the fertility of the soil. Grain crops (principally millet) and cotton (the leading cash crop) are rotated with peanuts (grown for both consumption and sale) and other legumes, and with periods of fallowing, which vary with soil depth and fertility. Apart from food and cash, the holding also supplies most of the materials for building the thatched (or occasionally sheet-iron roofed) dwelling houses and food stores, whose walls are wattle-and-daub on a framework of posts. Usually there is a house for each married pair and their young children. Additional wives or attached adults usually have dwellings of their own, for domestic privacy is much valued. The whole homestead cluster, with its bare earth courtyard, is tucked away behind the bright green screen of its own banana garden, out of sight of neighbors whose own homesteads may be only a few dozen yards away.

This typical small domestic unit on its own holding is not, however, a social isolate. Although the bridegroom usually establishes his own independent household, he normally does this, if he can, on land in the subvillage in which he was born. As a result, many of his neighbors are also his patrilineal kinsmen, his classificatory "fathers" and "brothers." While the local group of patrilineal kinsmen do not cultivate their holdings in common—each holds and manages his *kibanja* independently—they do commonly assist each other, especially with the heavier tasks, such as clearing. They also tend, through the natural process of lineage growth, to form, together with other close patrilineal kinsmen in neighboring subvillages and villages, the local succession lineage, which has been described as the effective corporate unilineal descent group.[8] It is this group that exercises hereditary rights in land by choosing an heir when one of its members dies. Provided there is an heir and a succession lineage to install him, the headman's right to dispose of the land lies dormant, for his is a reversionary right which comes into effect only when the land is *kyerere* or *kitongole*—without an heir and available for reallocation. When there is an heir, he need only be presented to the headman by the succession lineage to assume full use rights in the land, without further obligation to the headman. So long as lineage continuity is maintained, the headman's rights are limited to restraining the holder from disposing of it by means other than lineage-mediated testation.

The ability of a bridegroom to establish himself in his native subvillage—or, to look at the matter from the point of view of the group, the ability of the lineage to retain its young men—depends upon a number of factors. It of course rarely happens that a man dies just when his son is ready to marry and set up his own household. If he dies while his son is young, a brother or patrilineal cousin—normally the successor of the belt—may hold it in trust. If the son matures and marries before the father dies, he may for a time remain in the father's household, waiting to inherit—although the desire for independence works against this. If he wishes immediately to establish his own household on his own holding, there remain two possibilities short of emigration. If there is vacant land in the subvillage, he may apply to the headman for it. But if his lineage is a large one—one with many members in the subvillage—he may inherit from someone other than his own father. The larger the local lineage, the greater the likelihood that he will be chosen as heir to one of his father's brothers—perhaps one without a son. The larger the local lineage, then, the greater its chances of maintaining local continuity.[9]

8. See chapter 2.

9. Of course the larger the local lineage, the more competitors for the land the young man will have; but while, *ceteris paribus,* the number of holdings held by a lineage's members rises in direct proportion to its membership, the likelihood that one of its members will die *at about the time* another of its members comes to maturity increases with the size of the group.

Succession lineages vary widely in size, both within any one local area and throughout Busoga as a whole, as the five villages surveyed demonstrate. Three are neighboring villages in Busambira, one of the smallest of the old kingdoms, now a part of the subcounty of Ssaaba-waali, Kigulu County. This area was severely affected by an epidemic of *trypanasomiasis* (sleeping sickness), which ravaged much of south-ern Busoga in 1902–5, at which time much of the population died or migrated elsewhere. When the area was resettled, many newcomers from others parts of Busoga joined the native returnees, with the result that local lineage groups are typically very small. The other two, also neighboring villages, are located in subcounty Ssaabawaali, Bulamogi, which was largely unaffected by the epidemic. Here the average local lineage group is much larger. This phenomenon is difficult to quantify by census-survey methods, but table 6 provides a crude measure of the difference.[10]

TABLE 6
SIZE OF THE LOCAL CLAN GROUP

NUMBER OF CLANMATES	PERCENT OF MARRIED MEN	
	Busambira villages *	Bulamogi villages **
1–5	63	29
6–10	9	14
11–15	5	19
More than 15	23	38
Total	100	100

* n = 233 men
** n = 262 men

The table compares two groups of married men of roughly equal size (one group is in fact 12 percent larger than the other) in terms of the number of clanmates members have in their respective groups. The groups comprise all married men within the two adjacent Bulamogi villages and the three adjacent Busambira villages respectively. These data do not, of course, show the actual size of succession lineages, for two reasons. First, some persons' effective succession lineages will contain men who live in other neighboring villages not surveyed. Second, clan membership has been used instead of lineage membership because, while the clan is a fixed group, marked by a clan name which every member knows, "lineage" (*nda*) is a relative term.[11] In one

10. These and the following data on community structure are reported in greater detail in Fallers, *Bantu Bureaucracy*, chapter 5, and in idem, "Some Determinants of Marriage Stability in Busoga."
11. Recall the discussion of the use of these terms, chapter 2.

context, a man may speak of himself as belonging to the lineage of his father, while in another he may use the term to refer to descent from a quite remote ancestor. Eliciting from informants the lineage which is effective for the control of inheritance (a unit which Basoga, in every-day contexts, tend to speak of as "the clan") is far too complex a procedure to be used in a census-survey. Counting clans instead of succession lineages will have had the effect of understating the difference between the two areas in table 6. In Bulamogi, where population has been much more stable, most clanmates within the neighborhood will be quite closely related—will tend to be succession lineage mates. In Busambira, where there are many immigrants from other areas, two members of, say, the Baisemagumba clan may be very distantly related indeed. This factor perhaps compensates for the difference in the size of the two samples, which tends to exaggerate the difference.

TABLE 7

BIRTHPLACES OF HUSBANDS IN CURRENT MARRIAGES

BIRTHPLACE	BUSAMBIRA VILLAGES		BULAMOGI VILLAGES	
	Number	%	Number	%
Same subvillage	84	27	247	77
Same village	32	10	5	2
Same county	113	36	53	17
Another county	86	27	15	5
Total	315	100	320	100

NOTE: Since each marriage is counted separately, polygynous men are counted more than once.

What table 6 measures, then, is not the actual size of the succession lineage in the two areas, but rather the *difference* between them. While more than half of the married men in the Bulamogi sample have more than ten clan mates within the two villages, only 28 percent of the Busambira men have that many, in a neighborhood group of roughly the same size. At the other end of the scale, almost two-thirds of the Busambira men have fewer than six clan mates in the group, while only 29 percent of the Bulamogi men are so isolated.

In part, at least, this difference is the result of Busambira's depopulation and resettlement, the impact of which is shown in another way in table 7. Where in the Bulamogi villages more than three-quarters of the married men are living in their native subvillages, in the Busambira villages almost three-quarters were born outside the subvillages in which they now reside, while more than one-quarter have immigrated from outside the county.

Figures 11 and 12 illustrate the difference in the density of kinship

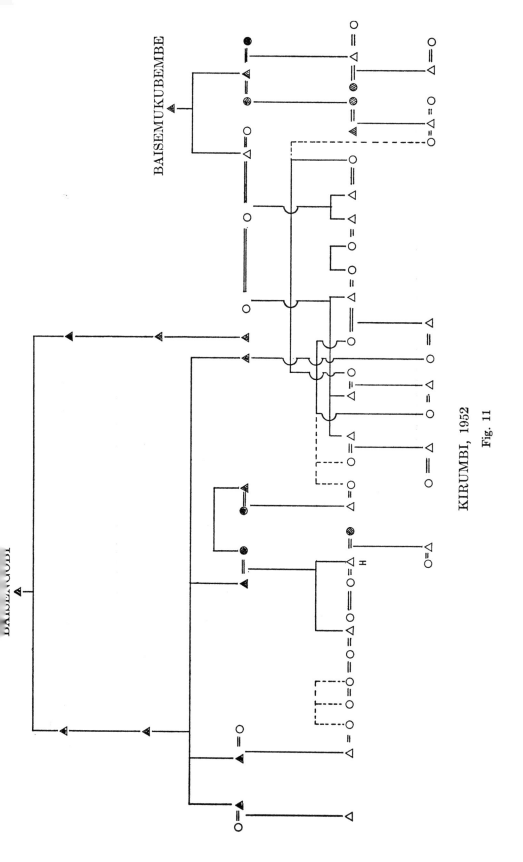

BAISEMUKUBEMBE

BAISENGUDI

KIRUMBI, 1952

Fig. 11

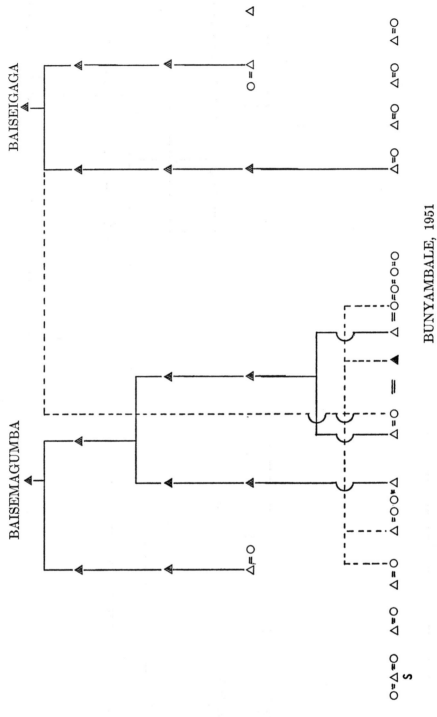

BAISEIGAGA

BAISEMAGUMBA

BUNYAMBALE, 1951

Fig. 12

ties that results from this difference in population stability. Figure 11 shows the genealogical structure of Kirumbi, a subvillage within the area surveyed in Bulamogi. Here every married male member of the community is related in some way to every other and to the headman, whose lineage is the second largest. In Bunyambale, a Busambira subvillage shown in figure 12, half the married men have no kinship ties within the community. The headman, a member of the Baiseigaga clan, does not live in the community; he is represented there by a steward (*musigire*), who is related to no one.

The lineage fragmentation characteristic of Busambira and the other areas of Busoga affected by the sleeping-sickness epidemic tends to be perpetuated by the land tenure system. The sons of the men of Bunyambale who have no lineage mates in the neighborhood will have little chance to inherit within the subvillage if they mature and marry while their fathers are still alive and active. Of course inheritance is not limited to subvillage or village members. A lineage isolate in a subvillage like Bunyambale may inherit elsewhere, perhaps in the area from which he migrated. But this does nothing to decrease the lineage fragmentation of Bunyambale. Most of such a community's sons will not be able to inherit there and thus will have to seek land by allocation from a headman, either within the subvillage or elsewhere.

The subvillage headman may allocate to anyone he likes, in exchange for an entry fee, any land within his subvillage not held by inheritance. The land may be uncultivated bush—uncommon, but present in some areas—or it may have been left without an heir or simply abandoned. Basoga not uncommonly simply pick up and leave, perhaps in search of better land or a job or to escape from conflicts with neighbors and kinsmen, which sometimes eventuate in accusations of sorcery. A common difficulty of this latter sort involves brothers, for the lack of a clear succession rule, which leaves the choice of an heir to the senior members of the lineage, often turns brothers into rivals.[12] When a man's in-laws live nearby, the kinds of conflict described in chapter 5 may also drive him out of the community. For whatever reason, vacant land is often available and hence headmen often have the opportunity to exercise their reversionary right to allocate.

Beyond the rights of the subvillage headman, there are those of his descent-group and of his superior, the village headman. To the latter, he owes a portion of each entry fee he collects from peasant allottees.

---

12. Sibling rivalry is an explicitly recognized pattern. When a woman becomes pregnant, her older child often becomes fretful and sickly because, it is said, of *eryuse*—a term also applied to rivalry between adult brothers.

The former selects his heir, when he dies, just as does the descent group of the peasant cultivator. If the subvillage headman should die without leaving an heir, or if he should abandon his headmanship, the position would be *kitongole,* and would revert to the village headman or some higher authority for reallocation in exchange for a fee, again just as an individual holding reverts to the subvillage headman. But such vacancies are rare, for two reasons. First, a headman need not physically occupy his post to maintain his rights. He may appoint a *musigire* (steward) to "do his work," as Basoga say, paying him a salary or a portion of the entry fees. Second, since a headmanship is much more valuable than an individual holding, a descent-group is much less likely to allow the line to die out. Furthermore, the head-man's descent-group is much more likely than that of the peasant to be well represented locally. The descent-group's possession of the office will itself have helped to hold the succession lineage in place and to maintain its numbers. A headman's office, therefore, seldom reverts— seldom becomes *kitongole* or *kyerere* ("empty") through abandonment.

Rights in headmanships originate in arrangements made under the old political system, when the present-day counties and some of their subdivisions were independent kingdoms, each ruled by a dynasty within a royal clan. The headman represented the lowest level of a hierarchy whose members held office either by descent or by appointment as personal clients of the ruler. Some headmanships were held by princely lineages—junior lineages within the royal clans—while others were filled by the appointed clients of rulers, princes, or senior commoner chiefs, the latter themselves clients of rulers. Some were held as *butaka* by commoner descent groups, though in principle both princely and commoner *butaka* seem to have been held at the pleasure of the rulers.

Today each village headman holds reversionary rights in the subvillages within his village and the heirs to rulership hold such rights in the villages within the boundaries of their ancestors' kingdoms.

SOURCES OF CONFLICT: ECONOMIC AND POLITICAL TRANSFORMATIONS

This, then, is the pattern of land use and landholding as it appears to a contemporary observer. The pattern seems clear and consistent enough; nevertheless there is a great deal of litigation where there appears to have been little before. If the various parties' rights in land are in principle clear, they become sufficiently unclear or unrecognized in practice so that headmen frequently—and increasingly—find themselves in conflict with their superiors and their people, and peasant cultivators at odds with one another. The reasons appear to lie in a series of changes in the headman's role. Where formerly his place in the land tenure system and his position in the political life of the society reinforced each other, today the various aspects of his role seem to be out of joint. All this has been analyzed in some detail, from the point of view of the political system, in *Bantu Bureaucracy*. What was there termed "the headman's dilemma," and the processes that have led to it, need here only be summarized briefly, therefore, as background to the more strictly legal concerns of this study.

The seeds of change in the relationship between the headman and his people were sown—in a quite literal sense—during the first decade of this century with the introduction of cotton cultivation for export. Within the decade following 1905, when the first seed was issued, production grew to more than one thousand tons, unginned; by the end of the following decade, it had exceeded seventeen thousand tons and there was more than an acre of land under cotton for every Soga household.[13] The economic transformation which this involved is evident in the reports of administrative officers. In 1901 the officer in charge of Busoga reported that the first effort to impose a money tax—a tax on guns, owned mostly by chiefs—had failed because there was insufficient money in the country. "All except a few chiefs," he reported, had turned in their guns because they could not pay. Such revenue as was collected was assessed in ivory.[14] In 1909, a five-shilling hut tax still proved difficult to collect and encountered organized opposition.[15] By 1913, however, with ". . . high prices for cotton and good wages to be had on every side, much money [had] come into [Soga] hands and the result of this [was seen in] the demand for European goods—especially bicycles." [16] A money economy had come into being and tax collection was no longer a serious problem. In 1923, Basoga cotton growers were paid 4,614,400 shillings for their crop, or some 80 shillings per taxpayer (that is, per able-bodied adult male). From this source, and to a lesser extent from the wages earned by working for ginners, for the few European planters, and on government public works, 939,933 shillings were paid in poll taxes.[17] The average

13. An acreage of 87,333 for a population estimated at 290,000. These figures are taken from administrative officers' annual reports on file in the Central Offices, Jinja.

14. E. A., Busoga, 1900–1901, Uganda Archives.

15. Provincial Commissioner's Report for September, 1909, Central Offices, Jinja.

16. District Commissioner's Report for the year ended March 31st, 1913, Central Offices, Jinja.

17. Provincial Commissioner's Report for the year ended March 31st, 1923, Central Offices, Jinja.

Musoga villager was far from rich, but his labor and his family's were now producing, in addition to their subsistence, substantial money income for the district as a whole. The question was: How would this be distributed?

Prior to these developments, when production consisted entirely of subsistence goods and craft products, the villager's "surplus" goods and services were distributed in two ways. At periodic local markets, producers traded agricultural produce, fish, livestock, iron implements, pots, and barkcloth with each other; they also rendered tribute in labor and in all these commodities to their headmen, chiefs, and rulers, as well as serving in the militia units which made up the rulers' armed forces. Labor tribute built and maintained the dwellings of rulers, chiefs, and headmen, and the network of paths that connected them and tribute in goods supported them and their households; but relatively little could actually be consumed in this way and there seems to have been little opportunity for external trade until late in the nineteenth century.[18] Most of the produce and craft goods collected, as well as the booty from successful wars, were therefore "invested" in political authority by redistribution. Members of the hierarchy at each level rewarded faithful subordinates by practicing lavish hospitality and gift-giving. At the base of the system, the headman offered continuous hospitality to the men of his village or subvillage, numbers of whom would gather each evening at his house to eat, drink, and discuss political affairs. The produce of the land was thus used to knit together political relations at all levels.

There appears to have been no shortage of land for cultivation. This is of course difficult to establish with certainty, since no population density data are available for periods before the first census in 1911. Population estimates are made even more difficult by the depopulation of southern Busoga which resulted from the sleeping-sickness epidemic at the turn of the century. Censuses carried out in 1911, 1931, and 1948 found the African population of the district to be 243,403, 378,394, and

18. In the 1870s and 1880s, a substantial, though brief, trade with the East African coast developed, in which slaves and ivory were exchanged for guns and cloth. See D. A. Low, "The Northern Interior 1840–84." There was apparently a similar trade to the north toward Khartoum. On June 17, 1895, the officer in charge of Busoga reported a "slave market" in Bugabula, the northwesternmost kingdom, in which Nyoro hoes were exchanged for slaves, presumably for transport to the Sudan. See East Africa, Staff and Miscellaneous, 1895–1, Uganda Archives, Entebbe. Busoga, however, did not lie directly on either of these trade routes. Bunyoro was the terminus of the northern route, while the southern one ran along the southern shores of Lake Victoria and terminated in Buganda. The impact of both was felt by Basoga principally in Ganda and Nyoro raids and demands for tribute.

505,998 respectively.[19] The depopulated area, which late nineteenth-century travelers describe as rich and thickly populated—the "garden of Uganda," one called it [20]—is estimated by contemporary observers to have suffered something of the order of 100,000 deaths during the great epidemic.[21] Thus it seems very unlikely that the nineteenth-century population was greater than the present one; most likely the 1949 figure represents, roughly, a recovery to the preepidemic level. In any case, in the early 1950s, with a substantial strip along the shore of Lake Victoria still closed to settlement by *tsetse* fly infestation, the district was able to carry more than half a million people without overpopulation.[22] Furthermore, this population was undoubtedly cultivating more land per head than the pre-1900 population had done, since cash-crop cultivation had been added. It seems almost certain, therefore, that in nineteenth-century Busoga land was plentiful and that the peasant cultivator was not tied to his headman by sheer economic need. Then, as now—as genealogies strongly suggest—he was ready, despite the high value placed upon patrilineal continuity, to leave an unsatisfactory situation and take up land elsewhere, even crossing the boundaries of the old kingdoms.[23] And this, of course, would have given point to the redistributive economy: the people of an oppressive or ungenerous headman would simply drift away, leaving him to rule over empty bush.[24] Viewing the situation in economic terms, from the point of view of the headman as "entrepreneur," the scarce factor was people, not land.[25] And this has remained the case; the recent increase in land litigation is not in any substantial degree the simple result of general land shortage.

19. A discussion of population, with references, is given in Margaret C. Fallers, *The Eastern Lacustrine Bantu,* pp. 20–21.

20. G. Wilson, in Hesketh Bell, *Correspondence Relating to the Famine in the Busoga District of Uganda,* p. 11.

21. H. B. Thomas and Robert Scott, *Uganda,* p. 300.

22. My own observations are supported here by the *Report of the Agricultural Productivity Committee,* which dismissed the problem of the availability of land in Uganda with the statement: "The general conclusion[s] we draw . . . are that, except in one or two localities, there is land to spare for expansion of the human population, and that while there is over-stocking in certain areas, this is due to maldistribution. . . ." (p. 13). The report makes it clear that neither qualification was made with Busoga in mind.

23. See Fallers, *Bantu Bureaucracy,* pp. 36, 107–14.

24. See Christopher Wrigley's analysis of the situation in Buganda, where similar conditions prevailed: "The Changing Economic Structure of Buganda," in L. A. Fallers, ed., *The King's Men,* pp. 20–24.

25. See my general discussion of such situations, common in Africa: "Social Stratification and Economic Processes," in *Economic Transition in Africa* ed. M. J. Herskovits and M. Harwitz (Evanston: Northwestern University Press, 1964), pp. 113–30.

The man-land ratio was not changed significantly by the introduction of cotton, since there was more than enough land to absorb the added acreage under cultivation, but other aspects of the relationship between peasant villagers and their rulers were deeply affected. The establishment of external trade and a money economy made available a new range of consumer's goods. The establishment of schools, which charged fees, and from among whose graduates, it soon became clear, chiefs would now be recruited, provided a further new field for expenditure. At the same time, the network of political relations was now underwritten by the colonial government. Whereas formerly there had been something like free political competition, with the peasant villager being able to offer his labor and military support, if not to the highest bidder, at least to alternative headmen and chiefs if his own proved intolerable, now a common regime of dues and services could be applied throughout Busoga—and indeed throughout much of Uganda. The balance of power tipped significantly in favor of the political hierarchy, which, having formerly consisted of a series of autonomous local dynasties and their retainers, now tended to become something more closely approaching a districtwide ruling class with rising economic expectations and a new style of life incorporating new goods and services.

The agents of much of this organizational change were the Baganda "advisers," headed by Semei Kakunguru, who were brought in by the British in 1906. Under their regime, the larger kingdoms became "counties," their subdivisions and the smaller kingdoms "subcounties." Clusters of villages within the subcounties became "parishes." Each county was now divided into *butongole* ("official") and *bwesengeze* ("personal profit") areas. The ruler, now "county chief," administered the former part on behalf of the Protectorate Government, collecting only the official tax, from which he received a rebate; from the latter he collected personal tribute in money and labor (which could now be used on his own cotton fields). In 1922, these obligations were regularized at ten shillings or one month's labor each year from each able-bodied adult male. The system was repeated at the subcounty level and the proceeds were allocated according to a set schedule among the chiefs of various grades and the village and subvillage headmen.

This arrangement represented an attempt on the part of Basoga chiefs and their Baganda advisors to emulate the system of landholding established in Buganda under its 1900 agreement with Britain. There, in an effort to enlist the support of the chiefly hierarchy, the colonial government had arranged for the distribution of something in excess of half the cultivable land in freehold estates among the Kabaka and the chiefs and headmen than in power.[26] Baganda peasants became rent-paying tenants. The *bwesengeze* areas were clearly modeled on the Ganda *"mailo"* freeholds (named for the "square miles" in which they were calculated). The British administration, however, soon had second thoughts about the Buganda scheme on the ground that it invited exploitation of the peasants, and it was never extended to other areas.[27] It is an essential element in the politics of Soga land tenure that Basoga chiefs and headmen have always deeply resented what they felt as unfair treatment in comparison with their Baganda counterparts, with whom they strongly identified themselves.

Beginning in the 1920s, the administration moved in quite a different direction in Busoga. Instead of landlords, dependent for income upon peasants' rents, dues, and services, chiefs were to become salaried civil servants of the Busoga African Local Government. In 1926 *bwesengeze* was abolished; all areas were now governed and taxed in the same way. Four shillings "tribute" (in addition to the tax) were still collected from each adult male and distributed according to a set schedule; of each ten men in a subvillage, four paid tribute to the subvillage headman, three to the village headman, and one each to the parish, subcounty, and county chiefs. The chiefs, in addition, received salaries. While these changes were resisted—in the case of some county chiefs, particularly, the salaries represented only a fraction of their income from *bwesengeze* dues and services—they were ultimately accepted, in part because the former rulers still hoped to receive freehold estates on the Ganda pattern. In the mid-twenties these men and their kinsmen and clients still dominated the chiefly hierarchy.

During the decade of the 1930s, their dominance was much diminished and their aspirations to landlord status finally disappointed. In 1930, the protectorate government offered to allot eighty-five square miles among the ruling dynasties; the offer was rejected as inadequate.[28] Shortly thereafter, no doubt partly as a result of the mutual alienation that had resulted from these unsatisfactory negotiations over "The land question," [29] the administration began to appoint and transfer chiefs about more freely without regard to hereditary claims.

---

26. H. B. Thomas and A. E. Spencer, *A History of Uganda Land and Surveys,* chap. 13; D. A. Low and R. C. Pratt, *Buganda and British Over Rule,* pp. 25–105.

27. Much smaller grants were offered to rulers and chiefs in other districts, including Busoga. In Buganda itself, the effects of the system were later moderated by statutory limitations upon the rents and dues that could be charged.

28. Report of the Provincial Commissioner for the Year Ended 31st December, 1930, Central Offices, Jinja.

29. All during the 'thirties, administrative officers' reports speak of the preoccupation of the chiefs with the "land question."

The last appointment made in recognition of hereditary status occurred in 1930. Although the last man so appointed was not retired until 1952, it became clear during the thirties and forties that hereditary claims no longer counted and that education and administrative ability were the keys to success in the A.L.G. service. And as education expanded and money wealth became more evenly distributed, these qualifications were no longer so concentrated in the families of former rulers and their retainers.

During the same period, these policies fell with particular force upon the headmen. The abolition of *bwesengeze* in 1926 had affected them relatively little, for they were the main beneficiaries of the tribute payments which remained. In the mid-thirties, however, the administration attempted to complete the bureaucratization of the political hierarchy by abolishing tribute and turning the headmen into salaried civil servants, as had been done earlier with the chiefs. At this point, the headmen rebelled. With a unanimity which reveals the degree to which Busoga had, as a result of administrative unification and improved communications, become a single political community, they unanimously rejected the change. Their stand was supported by a substantial element among the senior chiefs. In 1937, the provincial commissioner reported:

An attempt has been made, not without some success, to create a more tranquil atmosphere in Busoga, a district of long-standing discontent with respect to land tenure and concomitant matters. The D.C. reports that . . . some . . . of the leading chiefs are becoming more and more appreciative of the fact that measures which bring privileges for only one class follow the road that leads to the eventual downfall of that class. In this connection it should be explained that all [30] county and *ggombolola* [subcounty] chiefs are also village chiefs [headmen] in their own right and it can therefore be realized how difficult it is to persuade [them] that the policy we propose to adopt is in the best interests of the tribe. Throughout the year the [village and subvillage headmen] maintained their opposition to the insistence by Government that they personally could no longer collect tribute for themselves from the peasants. Payment of salaries should have afforded sufficient compensation for any financial loss incurred, but none agreed to accept this offer, contending that, if they did so, they would become salaried officials liable to appointment and dismissal. . . . In further explanation of their attitude [they] stated that they would sooner lose financially and be allowed to collect one shilling a year from every taxpaying peasant as personal tribute than to be paid a salary equivalent to twice that value.[31]

30. "All" is an exaggeration, but many chiefs did hold such rights.
31. Report of the Provincial Commissioner for the Year Ended 31st December, 1937, Central Offices, Jinja.

Further issues between the headmen and the administration developed in the late 1930s and 1940s. Areas of southern Busoga long empty of population as a result of *tsetse* fly infestation were being cleared and made available for resettlement. Headmen who had survived the earlier exodus from the sleeping-sickness zone, or their heirs, planned to return to preside over the allotment of holdings, but the administration had hoped to seize the opportunity presented by a large tract of rich and empty land to initiate what it regarded as a more efficient and modern regime under the guidance of agricultural experts. Again, when land was being condemned for the building of roads and railways and for the expansion of townships, headmen felt that they, as well as the holders of individual plots, were entitled to compensation. The administration, however, took the line that only the actual cultivators of the holdings appropriated suffered "material loss" requiring compensation; the headmen's reversionary and allocation rights, it was argued, should be viewed as an administrative service, not a source of personal gain. These and other controversies preoccupied the district council, in which headmen were well represented, in its correspondence with the administration, and served to further politicize the headman's role in relation to land.[32]

No doubt unwisely, the administration thus forced the headmen into a position of ambivalence, not to say alienation, vis-à-vis the A.L.G. organization. On the one hand, to protect what they felt to be the essence of their status—their hereditary roots in their communities— they had had to give up the remuneration which had helped them, in a money economy, to maintain the pattern of life of a hospitable village squire. At the same time, the A.L.G. could not operate without them. In 1935 an agricultural officer, obviously in response to a proposal by the administration to abolish the headmen entirely, wrote:

So far as this parish is concerned [he was reporting on land use in one local area] it is undoubtedly true that the brunt of the work is done by the *kisoko* [subvillage] headmen. They decide who has the right to cultivate any specified piece of land. . . . Neither the *muluka* [parish] chief nor the *mutala* chief [village headman] can be relied upon to know. . . . There will either have to be a very large increase in the number of *miruka* [parish] chiefs, or a corresponding increase in the amount of work done by them, if the office of *kisoko* headman is ever abolished.[33]

32. Minutes of the Busoga District Council for December 17, 1937; March 7, 1938; September 19–30, 1944; November 3–22, 1945; June 18, 1946; May 31–June 11, 1949; October 24–November 2, 1950; on file at the A.L.G. Headquarters, Bugembe.

33. Annual Report of the Department of Agriculture for the Year Ended 31st December, 1935, p. 30.

As previous chapters will have made evident, the headmen are in fact the agents in their communities of local government in all its aspects. In addition to their functions with respect to land, they help maintain law and order, assist in tax collection and in agricultural, veterinary, and health administration, and attempt to adjudicate disputes before they reach the A.L.G. courts. Parish chiefs, who are subject to frequent transfer and hence know their people much less well, would, even if they were more numerous, have great difficulty carrying out these tasks. Indeed, a centrally appointed bureaucratic official at this primary group level (subvillages in the areas surveyed averaged sixteen households, villages one hundred households) is a practical absurdity, since precisely what is needed is a locally rooted figure able to mediate between the community and the bureaucracy. Thus, a central position in the land tenure system is held by men of whom the larger political system asks a great deal, but to whom it denies any material reward.

This, it may be suggested, is the key to an understanding of the great increase in land litigation in recent decades. In the nineteenth century, the chief or headman, as the proverb has it, did not rule land; he ruled people. Such land disputes as occurred were probably settled relatively easily by headmen, whose authority was intact and whose interests lay in securing their people's loyalty. Some land disputes there doubtless were, despite the fact that land was plentiful. The perennial plantain garden and the attachment to land as the burial-place of ancestors must have made villagers as tenacious of their rights as they are today. Neighbors must occasionally have encroached upon one another's holdings, giving rise to boundary cases of the sort that still occur, though they now form only a small portion of all land litigation. But headmen must have been in a position to act as relatively impartial adjudicators, since they had no interest in questioning villagers' rights as such. With the introduction of cotton, land rights acquired a money value and the reinforcement of chiefs' and headmen's authority by the colonial government seems to have increased their ability to exploit their people's labor. But until the late 1930s, it was as political head of his community that the headman shared in the new productivity, receiving regular annual tribute from each villager. His villagers' security of tenure still ran parallel with his own interest.

When tribute was abolished, however, this common interest was destroyed and headmen turned to what they saw as their only alternative source of income. The administration would not allow them to collect rent, but they could, following ancient custom, collect an entry fee. What apparently had been a token payment in recognition of the headman's authority over the village now grew to a substantial sum of money. Furthermore, a headman might increase his income by increasing the turnover among his villagers. He now had an incentive to assert his reversionary right as often as he could—to assert, whenever possible, that land had become *kitongole* and available for reallocation. It was to his advantage to squeeze in additional villagers at the expense of existing villagers' holdings. As he was no longer a disinterested party, his authority to settle disputes himself, even in cases in which his own interests were not involved or in which he had acted honorably, was eroded. Villagers, now less likely to recognize even his legitimate rights, were more likely to try to treat their own rights as amounting to something approaching freehold, exchanging rights in land among themselves for consideration without reference to the headman. Cases resulting from all these kinds of illegal or extralegal action are common on today's dockets.

The development of the Soga political order from a cluster of autonomous kingdoms to a unified, bureaucratically administered, districtwide polity has also stimulated litigation over headmanships. Such litigation is nothing new, for while land has always been plentiful, headmanships have always, of course, been limited—tenaciously held by those who possessed them and eagerly sought by those who did not. But the political developments of recent decades have provided new sources of dispute.[34] In the nineteenth century, informants say, headmanships were held, ultimately, at the pleasure of rulers. In practice, as local histories and genealogies show, they often—perhaps usually —became hereditary in princely or commoner lineages so long as the ruler, who was then the final authority in such matters (unless, as sometimes happened, the Kabaka of Buganda was able to exercise suzerainty), was satisfied with the incumbent's loyalty and performance, especially in the frequent wars with neighboring kingdoms and the struggles with rival princes for rulership. Since the peasant militia was the sole source of armed strength, the loyalty of its leaders, the headmen, was crucial. During the first two decades of this century, when most chiefs were still rulers, princes, or their commoner clients, broadly the same situation seems to have prevailed. Headmen were still the personal links between their communities and the chiefs, though with the elimination of the recourse to arms by the *pax britannica* political rivalry was now confined to peaceful intrigue. But the headman's tenure now became subject also to satisfactory performance of his new duties for the Busoga-wide administration. Thus,

34. Administrative officers' reports from the late 1890s contain many references to such conflicts.

he might be deposed for corruption or for failure to carry out administrative duties.[35]

However, as traditional status ceased to be recognized as a basis for chiefly office, and as rulers, princes, and their clients were, in consequence, retired from the A.L.G. service, there developed a growing body of men, outside the official hierarchy, who could claim traditional residual rights over the allotment of headmanships. Many have acted to assert these rights, much as headmen have done with respect to individual holdings. In an effort to replace their lost salaries and to recapture their status honor (*kitiibwa*), they have sought to take headmanships back into their own hands or to claim them as *kitongole* —available for allotment to others in exchange for a fee. All this occurred with greater frequency during the 1930s and 1940s—the very period when headmen were becoming increasingly assertive of *their* rights in land and hence were increasingly claiming that, since they were not members of the official hierarchy (they had been denied tribute and had rejected salaries), these rights must be recognized as strictly hereditary. As land questions became increasingly politicized, cultivators of individual holdings, too, became increasingly self-conscious about their own hereditary rights, while asserting at the same time the right to dispose of them in any way they saw fit.

Today, with the increasing disengagement of land from its former connection with office in the official hierarchy, and with the growing interest in land as an economic resource, each person in the system tends to assert his own *butaka* (hereditary) right against the *kitongole* (allotment) right of his superior, but also to assert his own *kitongole* right—the right to dispose freely of what the holds. To further complicate matters, since "inheritance" is in Busoga a property of descent groups, not individual blood lines, the rights of these groups also become involved in the melee of claims and counterclaims. Disputes over succession to rulership, chieftainship, and headmanship which in the past had been resolved by recourse to arms or by superior authority cannot now be resolved in these ways, because the offices involved have been detached from the going political hierarchy. They therefore come before the courts in increasing numbers.

These contradictions, it might be thought, would, logically, divide Soga society into contending political camps: ex-rulers and ex-chiefs against headmen and headmen against their people. Individual disputes do, indeed, involve such conflicts, as the cases that come before the courts show. But Soga society, knit together as it is by ramifying

35. See *Zibairi Muwanika* v. *Azedi Bwami.*

ties of kinship and clientship, does not easily divide into self-consciously politicoeconomic classes. Despite their frequent conflicts, headmen and the scions of the former ruling dynasties are linked by ties of kinship and clientship established by their ancestors. Indeed, the two groups substantially overlap. Some headmen are princes—descendants of rulers—while some are rulers themselves, or would be if rulership were still recognized. Commoner headmen derive their positions from grants by former rulers or their subordinates, to whom they are often related affinally or matrilaterally as a result of marriages of political convenience. Consequently, far from dividing into opposing groups, headmen and ex-rulers and ex-chiefs tend to respond to their common feelings of deprivation by uniting to form a kind of parallel, or even counter, political system alongside the A.L.G. In several areas, including most notably the county (and former kingdom) of Bulamogi, heirs to rulership head what purport to be reconstituted royal governments. In Bulamogi, the pretender appoints his own subcounty chiefs, some of whom, following the traditional pattern, are princes, while others are commoners. These hold "subcounty courts," while the pretender himself holds a "county appeal court." Headmen, and people in Bulamogi generally, recognize the legitimacy of this shadow government, especially in matters pertaining to rights in land.

Again, although particular disputes often find headmen in conflict with individual villagers, headmen and their people are often related to each other by ties of kinship and clientship, as figures 11 and 12 show, just as headmen are related to their own traditional superiors. Furthermore, their anxieties about land, though different and even sometimes contradictory in content, tend to further unite them in opposition to "the government." This tendency has been reinforced by the fear of large-scale alienation of land to European settlers. Although such alienation has been contrary to stated protectorate government policy for some decades, Basoga are keenly aware of the political influence of the settler community in neighboring Kenya and occasional official suggestions that the two territories might be joined have served to keep such fears alive.[36] Thus, during the decade and a half following World War II, disaffected headmen and chiefs were able to act as the natural leaders of nascent "nationalist" movements,

36. The depth of these anxieties was demonstrated in 1953 when the then Colonial Secretary, Oliver Lyttleton, spoke casually at a dinner in Nairobi of the possibility of "still larger measures of unification . . . of the East African territories" (*Withdrawal of Recognition from Kabaka Mutesa II of Buganda*, Cmd. 9028, London, 1953, p. 7). In Buganda, the speech precipitated the so-called Kabaka Crisis of 1953–55. In Busoga, it produced a wave of antigovernment sentiment and a surge of identification with Buganda.

attracting a popular following through a combination of traditionalist and anticolonialist appeals. A "County Chiefs' Hereditary Society" was formed to promote the restoration of hereditary rulership, while a number of headmen and ex-chiefs were active in such political organizations as the Young Basoga Association, the *Bataka* ("Elders") of Busoga, and the Uganda National Congress, as well as a number of cooperative farmers' organizations, many of which were more political than economic in orientation.[37]

Again, however, not even the emergence of the politics of nationalism has fundamentally destroyed the integral quality of Soga society. Just as ex-chiefs, headmen, and people do not divide neatly against one another, so they do not unite monolithically against the A.L.G. The headmen and ex-chiefs are far from forming a sociopolitical group distinct from the A.L.G. They should not be visualized as quite different sets of persons of different sorts, one representing the old order, the other the new, pitted against one another. As was noted earlier, many present-day A.L.G. chiefs are descendants of nineteenth-cetury rulers, chiefs, and headmen. Though they cannot today claim A.L.G. office by virtue of descent, princely or chiefly birth has given them superior education and added "pull" in the politics of A.L.G. recruitment. By the same token, many serving chiefs still hold villages and subvillages looked after for them by stewards. Headmen, while they resent their loss of tribute, nevertheless value the local authority and status that their position gives them and gain satisfaction from the realization that the effective functioning of the A.L.G. depends heavily upon their cooperation.

The A.L.G. and the royal governments in the counties are thus recruited from the same social sources and even, to a substantial degree, the same persons. The headmen are in practice members of both. At the higher levels, the serving chiefs and the pretenders are simply the "in" and "out" members, respectively, of the same sociopolitical establishment, a fact which comes out most clearly with respect to the office of the Kyabazinga, the elected head of the A.L.G. organization. Since it was established, the office has been held in turns by the heirs to the rulership of the two most prestigious dynasties, those of Bulamogi and Bugabula. During the period of my fieldwork, when the Bugabula pretender held the office, he naturally attracted the allegiance of the serving chiefs, some of whom he had been instrumental in appointing or promoting. He also toured the country, making speeches on behalf of the programs of the A.L.G. and the Protectorate Govern-

---

37. David Apter discusses these organizations in the wider context of Uganda politics in *The Political Kingdom in Uganda,* chap. 14.

ment. During this period, the heir to the Bulamogi rulership gained a
following from among the "outs" and lent his support to movements
critical of "the government." As everyone was aware, however, the
position had been reversed only a few years before when the Bulamogi
pretender had been Kyabazinga and the present incumbent had been
the leader of the "outs," the darling of aggrieved headmen and land-
anxious people, and the principal proponent of the legitimacy of the
royal governments in the counties. It is precisely the essentially uni-
tary nature of the Basoga elite and their dual legitimacy as represent-
atives of both continuity with the past and achievement and competence in the new political order that has enabled them to lead Busoga
relatively undivided through a period of rapid and radical change.

While change in the political and economic context of land rights
has not—or at any rate not yet—resulted in structured political conflict within Soga society, it has produced conflicts of interest and
normative uncertainties which manifest themselves in litigation. Perhaps just because these conflicts and uncertainties have not crystal-
lized into clearly defined policy alternatives, no legislative remedy for
them has emerged. All parties agree that something is wrong, but there
is no consensus—or even structured dissensus—about the nature of the
problem or its proper solution. As is perhaps inevitable in a terminal
period of colonial rule, Soga feelings in the matter, expressed in
frequent but inconclusive debates in the district council, tend to lay
the problem at the door of the government. The protectorate administration, despite its anxiety over the growing burden of land litigation,
has not felt it appropriate to intervene, for it is heavily committed to
a regime of "customary law" in land matters. Thus on July 4, 1946, the
district commissioner wrote to the district council, commenting upon
one of its perennial debates on "the land question":

> Government has left the old system of land tenure and succession in the
> hands of the hereditary and traditional power. . . . Should any party to a land
> dispute be dissatisfied with the decision, he may take a case in the Sub-County
> Court, but this case is for one purpose and one purpose only: to ascertain
> whether tradition and custom have been followed.[38]

The administration senses, correctly if rather vaguely, that "tradition" and "custom" are not what they once were—that the profound
political and economic changes of recent decades have created conflicts
and ambiguities in customary law. But since "customary law" is in
practice defined as the law administered by the A.L.G. courts, there is
little administrative officers can do about this beyond complaining, as

38. Minutes of the Busoga District Council.

they often do, that all parties—ex-chiefs, headmen, and people—increasingly engage in "illegal" land transactions. The resolution of the resulting disputes, and of the normative ambiguities that underlie them, is thus left to the courts.

This is not to say that all is chaos in Soga land law. As the outline of land use and landholding given earlier in this chapter indicates, conflict in this field occurs within limits defined by certain widely shared ideas and mutual expectations. All Soga discourse concerning land tends to begin with the two fundamental notions: *butaka* and *kitongole*—"inheritance" and "allotment." Cases involving either headmanships or individual holdings commonly begin with one of two kinds of charges: "he is accused of taking (or 'eating' or 'stealing') my holding (or village or subvillage) which was allotted to me by so-and-so"; or: "he is accused of taking (etc.) my holding (etc.) which I inherited from my father (or ancestor)." Sometimes the charge is "falsely claiming" (*kwewayira*), for the accuser need not allege actual dispossession; he may bring suit simply to disprove another's claim. Even when the circumstances are similar, verbal formulas may differ, since Soga legal ideas are expressed in everyday language, not in specialized terminology. However, except in the few cases of what may be termed "pure" boundary disputes, in which a man accuses his neighbor simply of "jumping the boundary" (*kubuuka ensalo*), there is invariably some reference in either the accusation or the opening arguments to inheritance or allocation. The two notions may, of course, be combined, for Soga pleading does not value parsimony. A man may trace his claim back through several generations of inheritance to an original allotment. Whether invoked singly or in combination, however, the central concepts of wrong in Soga land law are violations, by word or by deed, of rights founded upon *butaka* and *kitongole*.

These are, without doubt, concepts indigenous to Soga legal thought. Both are rooted in institutions fundamental to Soga life: the first in the continuity of the unilineal descent group, the second in the authority of the ruler or chief. Throughout the period with which this study is concerned, these institutions have existed in some form and hence the legal ideas associated with them have remained meaningful. Their actual working, however, has changed profoundly during the lifetime of living men, and they have worked in different ways in different parts of Busoga at the same time. Thus, while the basic concepts of wrong have remained constant and universal—Busoga is essentially and increasingly a single sociocultural community and a single legal jurisdiction, with a common corps of judges freely transferred about the country—the subsidiary conceptual structure for relating these basic notions to particular sets of circumstances has been uncertain. The arguments that come before the courts in different cases—or even in the same case—may come from quite distinct moral worlds in which *butaka* and *kitongole* have different contextual meanings. Courts may be faced with claims originating from any of these contexts and supported by arguments appropriate to whichever of them the litigant feels will best support his case. It is almost as if the history of English landholding and land use from the preconquest period to the nineteenth century had been compressed into a single lifetime; as if this history had run its course much more completely in some areas than in others; and as if the courts were then asked to apply a single "customary law" to this whole universe without the guidance of either legislation or an organized system of precedent. That the result is a less-than-nicely-integrated body of legal concepts is less surprising than that the courts *are* making *some* progress in legally ordering the kaleidoscopic jumble of claims and counterclaims.

Since the institutional variations that underlie legal ambiguity manifest themselves rather differently in disputes over headmanships and individual holdings, the two fields are best dealt with separately.

RIGHTS IN HEADMANSHIP: THE LEGAL HANDLING OF POLITICAL
HISTORY

The most profound ambiguities in the law of headmanship are associated with spatial and temporal variations in the place of the royal governments in Soga political and legal life. A subcounty chief in Bulamogi who had had substantial judicial experience elsewhere in Busoga told me:

> There are few land cases of any kind here. I've gone six months without one. . . . What cases there are are decided by the chiefs of the hereditary ruler. If those people decide a case in Bulamogi, no more is heard of it. In Kigulu, on the other hand, there is competition between the chiefs of the hereditary ruler and the A.L.G. courts. This is because there are three claimants to the rulership. . . . Cases concerning villages and subvillages present especially difficult problems. You must decide them on the basis of who gave the village or subvillage. In the old days, villages and subvillages were given by the rulers. They had the power to depose a headman and put in another. Now they [the headmen] all want to be hereditary. If a man claims for a subvillage that was taken away from him many years ago, he is usually unsuccessful because he has not worked in it for many years. If the ruler wants to take away a village or subvillage now, he may succeed by just saying that the headman has been working as a steward. But such cases don't come before the A.L.G. courts here because people accept the ruler's power.

This perceptive statement contains a number of very interesting implications with respect to the application of legal concepts to rights

TABLE 8

PROVENIENCE OF LAND CASES APPEALED TO THE BUSOGA DISTRICT COURT DURING 1950

	Bulamogi	Kigulu	Bugabula	Butembe-Bunya	Busiki	Bugweri	Bukoli	Luuka
Individual holdings	4	25	20	17	12	11	2	15
Subvillage	—	3	8	2	1	2	2	2
Village	—	—	2	6	2	1	—	2
Total	4	28	30	25	15	14	4	19
Population in 1949	48,790	61,476	148,663	66,213	63,776	35,854	35,180	44,833

in land, and particularly to rights in headmanships. There is the suggestion, first of all, that in areas in which the authority of the ex-rulers and their chiefs is recognized, this process is largely in their hands. Land cases of all kinds are submitted to them for decision, and litigants, though free to do so, do not appeal beyond them to the A.L.G. courts. In other areas, where there is no commonly recognized royal government, land cases come to the A.L.G. courts in larger numbers, presumably either because pretenders and their chiefs do not hear them or because their decisions are not respected.

The evidence of A.L.G. court dockets is consistent with these observations. Table 8 shows the number of land cases of various kinds appealed to the Busoga district court from the several counties during 1950. One year's cases, of course, constitute a very limited sample, but the differences among counties are substantial and in the expected direction. Kigulu, where the royal government is said to be weak because of a disputed succession, sent twenty-eight cases, three of them concerned with headmanships, to the district court; while Bulamogi, with its strong royal government, sent only four, all of them involving individual holdings. For Bulamogi, I also have the numbers of land cases appealed to the county court from the subcounty courts over a three-year period—May 1948 to July 1951. The total for this period is twenty-six, of which two involved headmanships. Thus more cases were appealed *from* the Kigulu county court in one year than came *to* the county court of Bulamogi in the course of three years. My informant somewhat overstated the case; *some* land litigation, including some litigation over headmanships, *does* appear on A.L.G. court dockets in Bulamogi, but the traffic is substantially less than in Kigulu and well below the national average. The heaviest traffic, as table 8 shows, comes from Butembe-Bunya, the county which was most severely afflicted by sleeping sickness and famine at the beginning of this century. This area, which represents a consolidation of several former kingdoms, each with its own royal dynasty, was largely depopulated and has only recently and partially been resettled. There is much dispute concerning succession to the various rulerships, and the boundaries of their territories. In Bukoli, on the other hand, where there was also much depopulation and resettlement, very few land cases came to the A.L.G. courts. But there the boundaries of the modern county essentially correspond with those of a single former kingdom; the pretender is universally recognized as the legitimate heir and is greatly respected.

Thus the pretenders and their chiefs seem to exercise vis-à-vis the law of headmanship a kind of concurrent jurisdiction whose effectiveness in competition with the A.L.G. courts varies with their popular legitimacy. But they are more than simply judges of others' causes; they themselves claim certain rights in headmanships. My informant says that when disputes involving headmanship do come before the A.L.G. courts they are often difficult to decide because there is disagreement about the rights of various parties, including rulers. Claims originate, ultimately, in grants made by rulers. In the past, they had the right to "give" and "take away," and some pretenders claim this right today, though headmen like to claim that their own positions are hereditary. These claims are of course incompatible. In general terms, the concepts *butaka* and *kitongole* are contradictory. Since both clearly have some standing in the law of headmanships, judges must have some subsidiary conceptual equipment for deciding under what circumstances each applies. Of course, where the pretender's right to give and take away is universally recognized, there is no problem from the A.L.G. judges' point of view, for no cases will result. But if a dispossessed headman takes his case to court, what then? And this is only the beginning of the problem. Apart from deciding whether, or how far, present-day "customary law" sustains the pretender's right to withdraw and allocate or the headman's right to hereditary succession, the courts must still adjudicate claims based upon events which occurred at various periods in the past. Is a hereditary claim superior to rights acquired by allocation in 1930? Or 1920? Or 1910? And under what conditions? The whole political history of landholding becomes potential material for judicial decision.

From the A.L.G. courts' standpoint, the application of the concepts *butaka* and *kitongole* to the facts of particular cases is problematical in a sense in which the application of the concepts of wrong employed in the sex-and-marriage field is not. Adjudication in the latter field— or indeed, as I have argued, in any social field subject to adjudicatory proceedings—always involves the resolution of ambiguity with respect to the applicability of generally accepted concepts to particular sets of facts-as-found. It involves the simplification of the full moral complexity of a situation, first by forcing its consideration in terms of one out of a limited repertory of concepts of wrong, and then by requiring a "yes or no" answer, determined by the use of subsidiary concepts. In the law of headmanship, there is a historical ambiguity as well. Since the system has been changing, and changing at different rates in different areas, the courts require concepts that will enable them to cut through not only the variability of individual sets of circumstances within a given institutional frame but also the continuity and variable velocity of institutional change.

To see the full range of these problems as they present themselves to the courts, it is therefore necessary to view cases in their local contexts. As my informant's remarks have suggested, Bulamogi and Kigulu present an enlightening contrast. The former exemplifies the situation in which royal government is able to handle rights in land to a great extent on its own terms, and within its own organizational structure; the latter illustrates the legal consequences of the disintegration of royal authority. In juxtaposition, they reveal a good deal about the interaction between political history and the growth of law.

The heir to the rulership of Bulamogi, the Zibondo, is a commanding figure who combines all the qualities that give a man *kitüibwa*, "status honor." In 1908, while still a young boy, he was chosen by the princes and senior chiefs in the traditional manner to succeed his father and his right to the office is unchallenged. In the manner of the time, he was trained for office by being sent to mission schools and then to the prestigious King's College at Budo, near Kampala. Upon returning to take up his position as Zibondo, he impressed British administrators:

> The Basoga of this county are among the most primitive of the tribe, but the county has recently made good progress due to the personality of the county chief, Ezekeri Zibondo. He is young, has a good education . . . keen, energetic, and pro-government.[39]

In 1918, following the retirement of the Muganda paramount, Kakunguru, the Zibondo was chosen by the county chiefs, with the concurrence of the administration, to succeed him as Kyabazinga, or "President," and in 1920, the provincial commissioner reported his pleasure at the results:

> The remarkable improvement in this District . . . has not only been maintained but further progress has been made. . . . This state of affairs has been greatly due to the very able work of the President, Ezekeri Zibondo. . . . He is courteous and manly and studiously works for the people's interests. The District Commissioner reports that he practically filled the post of a second Assistant District Commissioner.[40]

This euphoric rapport with the Protectorate government, which earned the Zibondo the King's Silver Medal in 1921, did not, of course, last. In the eyes of the administration, his work declined from "good" in 1930 [41] to "adequate" in 1932.[42] By 1934,

39. Provincial Commissioner's Report for the Year Ended March 31st, 1918, Central Offices, Jinja.
40. Ibid., 1920.
41. Ibid., 1930.
42. Ibid., 1932.

It was necessary to impress upon [him] that his appointment [as Kyabazinga] was a government appointment and not one sanctioned by tribal custom, that the appointment was made as a form of liaison between the government and the tribe and not to form a focus to foment discontent among the chiefs.[43]

The subject of this discontent was rights in land. Throughout the 1920s and 1930s, administrative officers reported chiefly "anxiety" and "dissatisfaction" over the government's failure to allot freehold estates to chiefs on the Buganda model. The same period saw the growth of discontent among headmen over their loss of tribute, and the rise of popular anxiety over possible alienation of land to European settlers. The Zibondo made himself the spokesman for these interests, so that as his favor with the administration declined, his popular support grew. By 1949, when he retired as Kyabazinga, he had become the symbol and the organizational focus of a traditional order in the administration of land. In Busoga at large, this was reflected in his leadership of the "County Chiefs Hereditary Society"; in Bulamogi, to which he now returned to hold court in an impressive house with an adjacent meeting hall, he invested his energy and prestige in the revivification of his royal government. At the time of my fieldwork, one felt that he was the real power in the county. The county chief, a man of considerable talent and personal popularity, but born in another county and possessing no traditional claims to high office, told me that he found the post a very difficult one. When he was first appointed, people wrote letters to the district commissioner complaining and accusing him of "spoiling the country." He found evidence of the activities of the Zibondo's royal government "everywhere."

The central organization of this government consists, in addition to the Zibondo himself, of a *katikkiro* (prime minister), a man whose father served as *katikkiro* to the Zibondo's father, though the office is not considered hereditary; and a *ssaabalangira* ("chief of the princes"), whose position is hereditary in a junior line of the royal clan. The latter office represents a self-conscious borrowing from Buganda, whose inclusion in a government that purports to be "traditional" testifies to the high regard in which Ganda institutions are held, though its functions are rather different from those of the Muganda *ssabalangira*.[44] In addition to these central officials, there are

43. Ibid., 1934.
44. In Buganda, the ruler is clanless and princes are generally excluded from administrative office. The *ssaabalangira* represents their interests to a great extent *against* the ruler. In Busoga, where there is a royal clan and princes are included in the government, he becomes a kind of hereditary assistant to the ruler.

seventeen chiefs in charge of "subcounties," ten of whom are princes of the royal clan (*balangira*), while seven are commoners (*bakungu*). Three of the princes are hereditary—heirs of lines within the royal clan that in the nineteenth century had established a degree of hereditary autonomy vis-à-vis the Zibondos. There is no parish level within the Zibondo's government, as there is in the A.L.G. hierarchy, but the Zibondo's subcounties are much smaller and more numerous. The A.L.G. subcounties number only five. In those matters considered to fall within their purview, the Zibondo's chiefs deal directly with the headmen.

The raison d'être of the Zibondo's government is the administration and adjudication of land rights. Each subcounty chief holds a "court" within his own area and the Zibondo holds a "county court," presided over in his absence by the *katikkiro* or the *ssaabalangira*. The practice of these courts closely follows that of the A.L.G. courts—a tribute to the legitimacy of the latter and also a reflection of the Zibondo's long and deep involvement in its affairs. Most of his chiefs, as well, have been A.L.G. servants. In the Zibondo's appeal court, for example, the bench is made up, in addition to the chairman, of three princes and three commoner subcounty chiefs, sitting in rotation, just as in the A.L.G. courts the bench consists of equal numbers of chiefs and elected members. The principle of selection is different—more particularistic in the case of the Zibondo's courts—but the method of representing what are regarded as the main elements in the population is similar. From the point of view of the A.L.G. and the Protectorate Government, these are the appointed chiefs and the people; from the Zibondo's (and his chiefs') point of view, they are the princes and the commoners. A.L.G. practice is also reflected in a set schedule of court fees, which in the case of the Zibondo's courts go to the judges, and in court procedure. The cases I saw argued in the Zibondo's court hall followed essentially the procedure prevalent in A.L.G. courts. Much of this similarity is doubtless due to the fact that the two institutions draw upon the same precolonial political-legal tradition, but it also suggests that such changes as were introduced by the early administrators have now become fused with this tradition. No one questions the general legitimacy of the A.L.G. courts or the quality of the justice they administer in other fields. I never heard the slightest suggestion, for example, that the Zibondo's courts should adjudicate cases in the field of sexual relations and marriage. It is only with respect to land disputes that superior legitimacy is claimed for them.

According to the case register of the Zibondo's county court, which records cases in the A.L.G. manner, though in much less detail, the court heard eight land cases in 1949, five in 1950, and six in 1951. Two of these concerned subvillage headmanships and all but one of the others involved individual peasants' holdings. The only case during this period not concerned with land was a trial of the *ssaabalangira* on a charge of misappropriating court funds. In previous years—the case register has been kept intermittently since 1926—one finds a few cases of other kinds, principally concerned with alleged wrongs against clan norms. In 1926, for example, one prince accused another of not sharing with him the bridewealth received for their sisters. In 1927, two men were accused of falsely claiming to be members of the royal clan. In 1934, an accused was charged with failing to fulfill the responsibilities devolving upon him as his deceased brother's successor, and in the following year a prince was tried for incest. The Zibondo's courts thus function also as a clan court for princes analogous to those held by other clans, adjudicating disputes and accusations beyond the jurisdiction of the A.L.G. courts.[45] It is only in land cases that the Zibondo's courts assert, and are granted by popular opinion, a jurisdiction concurrent with that of the A.L.G. courts. Occasionally litigants appeal from one system to another. Doubtless some of the cases in table 8 were heard by the Zibondo and his chiefs before coming to the A.L.G. courts (though I was able to verify only one instance of this), but the opposite also occurs. One of the two headmanship cases heard by the Zibondo's county court in 1949 had previously passed through the entire A.L.G. system. All courts in both systems, incidentally, concurred.

The Zibondo also claims the right to give and take away headmanships. Much is made in the mythology of the Bulamogi monarchy of the Zibondo's ultimate sovereignty over land. A royal chronicle, reduced to writing out of oral tradition by the present *ssaabalangira* as propaganda for a restoration, asserts:

> The Zibondo distributed land, from banana gardens to villages and subvillages, and chieftainship of every kind was in his power. This power descends undiminished to the present Zibondo. . . . From the founding of Bulamogi to the present, no Mulamogi rebelled against the power of the Zibondo. . . . In Bulamogi everyone was free to use the place he had been given by Zibondo and chiefs subordinate to Zibondo, to whom he had given the power to rule those under him, had the power to give out land in their areas. Until today Zibondo has the power to rule all the land and people of Bulamogi as a patrimony.

The stress on "land" as such doubtless reflects recent economic trends. Also, there is in these statements the sort of hyperbole usual in

45. See chapter 3.

the language of monarchy and monarchists. More candid discussions with the present Zibondo and others make it clear that the political reality of nineteenth-century Bulamogi was rather different. At any given moment, some chieftainships and headmanships would be considered hereditary, while others were direct appointees of the ruler, but there was constant flux; a generation later the situation might be radically changed. Rulers constantly attempted to treat all subordinates as personal appointees, but the universal ruler's dilemma of *quis custodiet, ipsos custodes?* (who guards the guards?), exacerbated by the pervasive influence of descent groups in Soga kinship, made this impossible. Appointed chiefs and headmen tended to put down local roots and to develop hereditary aspirations. This tendency could only be checked by further royal appointments, whose beneficiaries, however, soon developed the same tendencies. The ruler's sovereignty, therefore, was precarious and could be maintained only by a sedulous playing-off of one subordinate against another. Princely chiefs were particularly dangerous as potential secessionists and usurpers. Rulers sought to "watch them," as one informant put it, by appointing commoner clients in neighboring areas. Similarly, an entrenched princely or commoner line might be balanced by the appointment of a ruler's son. This, however, meant storing up potent trouble for the future, for such sons would become the potential rebel princes of the next generation. Monarchical mythology to the contrary, it is well known in Bulamogi that in the late nineteenth century three rebel princes attempted to assert their independence of the Zibondo and almost succeeded. The Zibondo was able to expunge one of these princely lines, but the other two survived to form part of the hereditary element in the present Zibondo's royal government.

Conditions have, of course, changed. Civil war is extinct and ultimate power is now in the hands of the A.L.G. and the protectorate government. The Zibondo's "sovereignty" over the land of Bulamogi now rests entirely upon his ability to maintain his legitimacy through the shrewd use of the limited resources left to him. These include: a modest fortune acquired during his A.L.G. service and maintained by his A.L.G. pension; a network of kinsmen and clients in the A.L.G. organization, again built up during his long tenure of office; unchallenged succession to the charisma of the Bulamogi rulership; and, perhaps most importantly, a fine skill in the art of creating power by using it. If he can no longer field militia armies, as his ancestors did, or mediate relations with the protectorate government, as he himself once did, he can "give and take" chieftainship and headmanship in a manner which strikes his people as truly royal. This means recognizing the legitimate claims of various groups among his people while at the same time balancing them so that his own supremacy is maintained. Thus, although "objective conditions" have greatly changed, the pattern, the style, remains for the time being effective.

Let me illustrate. I traced the recent history of chieftainship and headmanship in the area of southern Bulamogi in which I carried out my village surveys (fig. 13). In the time of Zibondo Kisira, the sons of his brother Kiige—Bwoye, Tajuba, and Muyodi—were in possession of the villages of Budini, Kasokwe, and Buyodi respectively. These princes, however, involved themselves in the revolt mentioned earlier, and Kisira deposed them. Budini was given to a commoner, Bamutaze, and Buyodi to another commoner, whose name I did not learn. Ka-

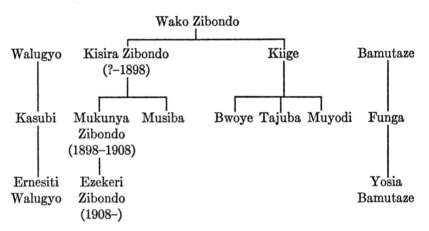

Fig. 13

sokwe was given to Kisira's son, Musiba. The present Zibondo, no longer threatened by princely revolt, felt able to recognize the claims of the descendants of Kiige. Muyodi's descendants were restored to Buyodi and Bwoye's to Budini, though Bamutaze's descendants retained one subvillage. In a further adjustment, Kasokwe was just recently divided into two villages, Musiba's grandson retaining one while the other was given to Tajuba's grandson. But the trend is not entirely toward princely oligarchy. Throughout this whole period, another neighboring village, Butongole, was held by a commoner line and the present headman, Ernesti Walugyo, was recently made "subcounty chief" of the area in the royal government. The Zibondo's minute book, which records the proceedings of his council of chiefs sitting as an administrative body, contains many other recent examples.

To the extent to which the Zibondo's right to "give and take" headmanships is recognized as legitimate, the concepts *butaka* and *kitongole* do not come into play as legal concepts in litigation. They rather remain political concepts, denoting elements in the dynamics of royal government. *Kitongole* represents sovereign power, *butaka* the claim to hereditary headmanship against royal sovereignty. In Bulamogi, this, for the most part, remains the situation: most claimants to headmanship are content to accept the consequences of monarchical politics; few appeal against the Zibondo's acts of sovereignty to the A.L.G. courts. As I noted earlier, two headmanship cases have been taken to the A.L.G. county court in recent years, but unfortunately I failed to obtain the case records and so do not know the circumstances. Two cases are also recorded in the Zibondo's county court register— one a dispute over succession in which both litigants argued from *butaka* rights, the other an appeal by a litigant claiming *butaka* rights against the assertion of the right to allocate by one of the Zibondo's chiefs. These records, however, are too sketchy to be of much use in the analysis of legal reasoning. In any case, the point about Bulamogi is that there the concepts *butaka* and *kitongole* seldom come before the courts in headmanship disputes. To see what happens when they become the tools for litigation, and the institutional circumstances under which this occurs, it is more profitable to turn to other areas of Busoga.

The county of Kigulu, in whose A.L.G. courts actions of this sort are much more common, has had a political history very different from that of Bulamogi. Whereas the Zibondo is universally acknowledged to be the rightful ruler, there are at least three pretenders to the office of the Ngobi, the Baisengobi ruler of Kigulu—a situation which is the result of two generations of disputed succession. Ngobi Miro, the last precolonial ruler, died in 1906 and for ten years the area was governed by a Muganda chief, one of Kakunguru's men. In 1906, Miro's son Gideoni, who like the Zibondo belonged to the first generation of rulers' and chiefs' sons to be educated at King's College, Budo, returned from school to take office. Today some say that he owed his succession to the British administration and that another prince was the choice of the royal clan and chiefs. Gideoni, the dissidents say, "did not spear the bull at his father's grave," as a rightly chosen successor would have done. However that may be (I did not go into the matter deeply enough to form an opinion of my own as to the historical facts), he did not retain official favor for long. Within two years, the district commissioner reported that Gideoni "was found entirely unsatisfactory, unpopular with his people and immersed in trade rather than administration." [46] In 1922, he was dismissed "for bad work, incompetence, and drinking," [47] to be replaced by a prince from another part of Busoga. From 1938 to 1946 yet another member of the Kigulu royal line—Gideoni's father's brother's son—served as county chief. Again, some recognized him as the legitimate Ngobi, while others rejected him as the "Ngobi of the Europeans." He, Gideoni's son, and Gideoni's rival all have partisans today.

Thus the combination of official recognition and traditional legitimacy which sustained royal government in Bulamogi has been absent in Kigulu. The difference is a rather subtle but decisive one. The Zibondo also succeeded with the approval of the administration, but he subsequently had a long and successful career in the A.L.G. system, building there a political base which made him substantially independent of administration support. "Hereditary" legitimacy in Busoga has always, I think, depended to a substantial degree upon political success. In precolonial times succession was often disputed, for there was no clear-cut succession rule; it was the prince who, through personality and ability, could win the support of the major political forces in the kingdom who commanded legitimacy. In the twentieth century, the administration has been recognized as one among these forces—a crucial one. I suspect that it was Gideoni's failure to *retain* administration support that, in part at least, cast doubt upon his legitimacy, and, in retrospect, made official sponsorship of his succession a matter of reproach.[48] In any case, none of the claimants to the rulership of Kigulu commands anything like the Zibondo's authority and prestige. None has been able to maintain a hierarchy of chiefs and a system of courts with generally recognized authority in land matters. Traditional government above the village level has been decapitated and the A.L.G. reigns essentially unchallenged.

To make matters more complex, the boundaries of the present county of Kigulu do not, as in Bulamogi, correspond neatly with those of the nineteenth-century kingdom. In the south, an area corresponding roughly with the present subcounty of Ssaabawaali was formerly occupied by the petty kingdom of Busambira, whose ruler, the Kisambira of the Baiseigaga clan, denied the overlordship of the Ngobi. (fig. 14). I suspect that in fact the Kisambira was, in the late nineteenth

46. District Commissioner's Report for February, 1918, Central Offices, Jinja.
47. Provincial Commissioner's Report for the Year Ended December 31st, 1922.
48. Perhaps, conversely, his lack of legitimacy contributed to his lack of authority, and hence undermined administration support for him. All this may sound overly intricate, but such is the nature of the politics of "indirect rule," by which a colonial regime seeks to both preserve and control the authority of its native agent.

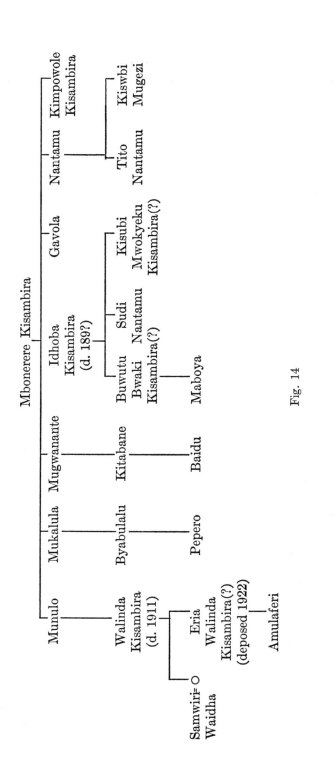

Fig. 14

century, in the process of being "mediatized," as historians of medieval Europe put it. Present-day Basambira like to say that the Ngobi often "sought the Kisambira's help" in wars against neighboring kindgoms, but given the great disparity in size between the two kingdoms the relationship can hardly have been one of even reciprocity. At any rate, British administration, in its efforts to unify and rationalize Busoga's administration, soon completed the process of mediatization. The Kisambira became a subcounty chief in the Kigulu A.L.G. hierarchy.

The kingdom of Busambira survives as an ideal in the sentiments of its people, but the processes that militated against the survival of a strong royal government in Kigulu as a whole were repeated in Busambira and were compounded by its subordination to Kigulu. The succession dispute which divides the loyalties of Basambira today dates from the last decade of the nineteenth century, when Miro was Ngobi and when the first British officer was organizing the administration. In the version of history accepted by most present-day headmen, Kisambira Kimpowole died and his brother, Idhoba, was chosen by the princes and chiefs to succeed him, with the support of Ngobi Miro. The British officer, however, together with the Baganda, instead recognized Walinda, the son of a brother of Kimpowole and Idhoba. Walinda died in 1911 and, after a six-year regency under Walinda's commoner *katikkiro*, was succeeded by his mission-educated grandson, Eria Wambi. The latter suffered the same fate as Ngobi Gideoni and in the same year. In 1922 he was dismissed for incompetence and thereafter the area was governed by a succession of subcounty chiefs with no claims to rulership. Today most of Busambira recognizes Kisubi Mwokyeku, son of Idhoba, as Kisambira, but Eria retains a substantial following.

The Baiseigaga of Busambira cherish a myth of monarchy similar in form to that of the Baisengobi princes of Bulamogi. Everything was on a smaller scale, of course; Busambira in 1949 had a population of only some seven thousand, compared with Bulamogi's nearly fifty thousand. There seem to have been no territorial chiefs between the Kisambira and the headmen. But the structures were similar: the Kisambira had his commoner *katikkiro* and he "cut the land" into villages and subvillages, which he "gave out" in a manner designed to strengthen his sovereign authority. "Each Kisambira had many sons," I was told, "and he divided the land among them"; but he also gave villages to commoners "so that his brothers might not steal them." He aimed "to please the commoners so that when war broke out they would fight bravely." "It was for the Kisambira to do as he liked with the land."

Inspired by this image of the past, the Baiseigaga of Busambira attempt to maintain a royal government. They succeed in holding tribunals to adjudicate conflicts of the sort defined in Busoga as "internal clan matters" lying outside the purview of the A.L.G. I witnessed one such tribunal, at which a young man was tried, convicted, and fined one goat for burying his deceased father and claiming his estate without calling together the succession lineage. 1 was also told of incest cases that had been dealt with in this way. In theory, land disputes involving succession within the clan are also "internal" matters and the Baiseigaga, as well as other clans in Busambira, attempt to adjudicate them for their own members. But such disputes can be carried to the A.L.G. courts and often are. Again, in theory, the A.L.G. court's role in such cases is merely to determine and enforce the decision of the succession lineage.[49] But when something as important as headmanship is at stake, and when the events in question have taken place in the distant past, there may be little consensus among present-day lineage members concerning the nature of the decision. The A.L.G. courts are therefore ineluctably drawn into the task of interpreting and applying the concept *butaka*. The Kisambira is even less successful in asserting jurisdiction over land disputes involving non-Baiseigaga, and his sovereign power to give and take away headmanships has lapsed completely. The unresolved dispute over succession to the rulership and Busambira's long subordination to other powers have destroyed the fabric of monarchical legitimacy. Sovereignty, the source of the power to allot headmanship as *kitongole*, has become a purely historical source of rights, to be interpreted by the A.L.G. courts, along with hereditary claims.

Court v. *Eria Wambi; Eria Wambi* v. *Samwiri Waidha: the end of sovereignty; contempt*

It is possible in Busambira to trace these processes in the records of litigation. Litigation is of course an active agent in the dissolution of royal government, and not merely a result of it, for once headmanship disputes have come before the A.L.G. courts, the new superordinate judicial power has claimed them for its own. This effect is well illustrated by *Court* v. *Eria Wambi*, which came up for hearing on November 20, 1950, while I was in Busambira. Eria is the son of Walinda and one of the pretenders to the rulership—the one dismissed as subcounty chief in 1922. On this occasion, he attempted to assert his sovereignty over the subvillage of Waitambogwe in the village of Buluza and to allot it to his son Amulaferi. In possession was Samwiri

49. See chapter 3.

Waidha, a commoner who claimed to have been allotted the subvillage by Walinda while he was serving as Walinda's *katikkiro*. Eria, as it turned out, chose a singularly unfortunate subvillage on which to test his authority. Not only was his claim rejected, Waidha could point to a case in 1923 in which the same principals had litigated for the same subvillage. And the records had survived to prove the matter *res judicata*. In *Eria Wambi* v. *Samwiri Waidha* of that year, the court had heard witnesses for both and decided in Waidha's favor, declaring, "The court has found that the subvillage was given to Waidha a long time ago." The implicit meaning is clear: by 1923, in Busambira, the sovereign power was already dead; a ruler could not take back that which his predecessor had given. And since this had been decided in 1923 with respect to this very headmanship, Eria was, in 1950, in contempt of court in trying again to assert his sovereignty, which is why the 1950 case was brought by the Court (*"Court* v. *Eria Wambi"*) and not by Waidha, and why the court fined him ten shillings (or fourteen days) instead of merely confirming Waidha in possession. Also, the judge in 1950 was more explicit: ". . . it was [Eria's] mistake to give the subvillage to another man when *it had been taken out of his hands long ago by the court,* as recorded in the court book." The concept of *kitongole*, once a term of royal government, as it still is in Bulamogi, had become a legal concept denoting past powers no longer exercisable. Eria's sortie may have represented the last gasp of royal government in Busambira. It is generally agreed that the headmanship of Waitambogwe will now be hereditary in Waidha's lineage.

Court v. *Eria Wambi* marks only one boundary of the concept *kitongole*, and that only vaguely. It implies that a ruler cannot today take away a headmanship as a sovereign act of will, but nothing is said about circumstances. Eria evidently simply wanted to give Waitambogwe to someone else for political reasons, as a ruler could do in the past, but he made no effort to justify himself in legal terms. Informants say that the *kitongole* power is still active today in one circumstance: when the headmanship falls vacant through abandonment or depletion of the incumbent's line. Then, it is said, it reverts to the ruler, just as a deserted peasant's holding reverts to the headman for reallotment. Deliberate abandonment must be rare almost to the point of nonoccurrence, for headmanships are prized and one cannot easily take one up elsewhere as one can a peasant's holding. Depletion of the line would also, in fact, amount to abandonment, for the Soga succession lineage is subject to expansion to the limits of the clan itself in the search for an heir. But there is room for argument—and litigation—over what *legally* constitutes abandonment, and the indefatigable Eria tested this ground as well. In 1951, he attempted to reclaim another subvillage on the ground that the incumbent, Salimu Waiswa, had not maintained a residence in it and had, therefore, abandoned it.

Salimu Waiswa v. Eria Wambi: an absentee headman upheld

Here I have only the subcounty court's judgment. The case had been appealed and consequently the transcript had been forwarded to the county court. I had no opportunity to obtain it or to determine the ultimate disposition of the case. The subcounty judgment, however, is interesting because its reasoning is more than usually explicit. Eria was again pitted against Samwiri Waidha, this time as a witness. Waidha testified that as *katikkiro* to Eria's father, Kisambira Walinda, he had been directed to dismiss the previous headman and to install Salimu's father, Bumali. A commission sent by the court to investigate on the spot—a common practice in land cases—reported that the graves of Bumali and his father and mother were clearly to be seen in the subvillage, but that Salimu had indeed not maintained a residence there. After reviewing all this, the court concluded:

> The fact that [Salimu] has no house or banana garden in the subvillage does not prove it is not his. In Busoga a person may own three or four villages or subvillages without having a house in any of them. For example, [Eria] has no house or banana garden in the village of Kiboyo, in which the subvillage for which they are litigating is located, but still he is regarded as its owner.

There may be other conditions which a headman must fulfill in order to maintain his rights, but the tendency is clearly toward limiting almost to the point of extinction the circumstances under which a ruler may assert the right to withdraw and reallocate. As *kitongole* is eliminated, *butaka* is left in command of the field; headmanships tend to become uniformly hereditary.

This does not, of course, dispose of *kitongole* as a basis for claims, for while the courts reject the exercise of such power today, they clearly, as the cases just discussed indicate, accept *past* withdrawals and allocations as valid. But "the past" is not one period. The grants of headmanship to Waidha and Bumali were made by Walinda during the last decade of the nineteenth century, when British control was only just being established and when, as present-day Basoga see it, rulers still ruled in the old way. The period between that time and 1923, when Eria's claim to sovereign powers was rejected by the court, was one of great political changes in Busoga. In Busambira and other areas of the south, it was also a period of catastrophic epidemics and famines which decimated or displaced large populations and disrupted existing social arrangements. Throughout the southern area, headmanships changed hands in circumstances which have provided fertile sources for subsequent disputes.

Tito Nantamu v. Kisubi Mwokyeku: waiting too long

One such dispute was litigated in *Tito Nantamu* v. *Kisubi Mwokyeku* in November, 1949. Tito had accused Kisubi, who is recognized by most Baiseigaga today—including Tito—as the rightful Kisambira, of ". . . taking my subvillage, Nawandala, and calling it his, whereas it is mine and I inherited it from my father Nantamu." Figure 14 shows the genealogical relations among the principals and main witnesses in the case, which develops, as so often happens in such affairs, as a contest between *butaka* and *kitongole* claims.

Kisubi asserts that "in the first place" the subvillage belonged to Idhoba Kisambira; when he died (around the turn of the century), both the rulership and subvillage Nawandala passed to his son, Buwutu Bwaki. At the latter's death a few years later, Kisubi became Kisambira and Nawandala was held in trust, under a steward, for Buwutu Bwaki's young son, Maboya. The latter also died and the steward either emigrated or was dismissed. At this point, Kisubi says, "I took it and it has been in my hands ever since." Under questioning, he adds that Idhoba had inherited Nawandala from his brother, Gavola; and that recently, "after the meeting and agreement of the clan," he has allotted it to another Mwiseigaga, Baidu, "who came to the clan to beg for it."

Tito's story is that Idhoba, upon inheriting Nawandala from Gavola, "left it to be run by Nantamu." Afterward, Nantamu was given "another subvillage of his own" and was "chased out of Nawandala," but Buwutu Bwaki subsequently "called Nantamu back and gave him the subvillage again after he had paid one cow and three goats for it." After Nantamu's death, Tito argues, "the subvillage remained in my hands, for it was a subvillage of inheritance," but "when Kisubi saw that my father had died, he took it from me, saying that my father didn't possess a subvillage at all."

Both parties bring witnesses. Pepero, Sudi Nantamu, Tenywa Wakada, and Fenekansi Kiwumwe, all elders of the subvillage, simply support Kisubi's story: Kisubi has authority over Nawandala as the Kisambira; he allotted it to Baidu; Tito "has never ruled it." Samwiri Waidha, the old *katikkiro* of Walinda who is considered by all the most authoritative expert on Busambira's political history, supports Tito: Nawandala belonged to Nantamu and Tito is Nantamu's heir; Kisubi is claiming it because he wants to give it to others. But upon being asked how long Tito ruled the subvillage before Kisubi took it away, he adds: "He worked in it for three years and then left it in the hands of Kisubi Mugezi when he was going to Buwuma." Kisubi Mugezi, also testifying for Tito, elaborates: "After [Nantamu's] death, Tito went to Buwuma and I stayed in Nawandala and kept it until Kisubi Mwokyeku came and told me to pay something so that I might be empowered to rule it." He reported this to Tito in Buwuma, he says, and Tito gave him two goats and a sheep to be handed over to Kisubi, who then "gave the subvillage to me." He adds that he can't remember exactly when this happened.

So the court has before it two incompatible stories and a number of lines of investigation appear to be open to it. It might, first of all, press the question of Tito's succession to Nantamu and Nantamu's succession to Gavola, who, all agree, once held Nawandala. Samwiri Waidha, a knowledgeable and disinterested witness, has supported this story. Second, it might inquire further into Kisubi's claim to succession and into the various accounts of his acts as Kisambira. Which of these actually took place? Were they justified? But the court's questioning follows neither of these paths. Ignoring the conflicting accounts of earlier events, it fastens upon the fact that Tito is only now asserting rights which he claims to have possessed for several decades:

Q: How long did you work in the subvillage?
A: I have not worked in it yet because I left it when the country was attacked by sleeping sickness and went to Buwuma and I have only just returned for the first time.
Q: How long . . . since your return from Buwuma?
A: Only fifteen years.
Q: Did you ask Kisubi to give the subvillage back to you when you returned?
A: I took it to him several times, but each time he told me to wait a bit. He was just tricking me. He had already given it to Baidu.
Q: Are the statements of your witnesses correct?
A: Waidha's testimony is right, but Kisubi Mugezi's isn't.

Tito, of course, dislikes Kisubi Mugezi's claim to have paid for, and received, the subvillage, for this might complicate his case by requiring him to show that this was done on Tito's behalf. But this, too, the court ignores. It is interested in Tito's own actions:

Q: If Waidha's statement is true, is it correct, now, to say that you worked in Nawandala for three years?
A: Yes.

Tito has now contradicted himself, and the court presses him harder:

Q: You have said that you inherited the subvillage and that Kisubi took it from you. This is stated by your witnesses also. But when did he take it? . . ."

A: . . . during the famine of Bukaala [1902].
Q: . . . did you accuse him?
A: No, I didn't.
Q: You said at first that when you went to Buwuma you left the subvillage in the hands of Kisubi Mugezi. Now, you say it was taken from you during the famine of Bukaala. . . .
A: The truth is that he took it from me during the famine of Bukaala.

In the judges' view, Tito has destroyed his own case. They conclude that "he has never ruled the subvillage for which they are litigating." This conclusion is justified because his testimony concerning the circumstances of the alleged dispossession by Kisubi has been inconsistent, but above all his case falls to the ground because ". . . he has failed to give reasons why he did not accuse Kisubi immediately after he took it away." The court has applied a subsidiary concept of temporal limitation: nearly fifty years have passed since the events of which Tito complains and it has been fifteen years since he himself returned from Buwuma. He has had ample opportunity to sue. If his claim were sound, he would have asserted it earlier.

Temporal limitation is a potent conceptual tool for simplifying the historical complexities that so often confront the courts in headmanship disputes and it may be applied equally to claims based upon *butaka* and *kitongole*. It is sometimes said that, as Allott has put it in reference to Ghana, "there was [in African customary law] no such thing as a stale claim." [50] I do not wish to argue that the Soga concept corresponds precisely with any of the various devices of Anglo-American law ("estoppel," "limitation of actions," "prescription," "laches," etc.) by which stale claims are voided. All of these are the products of specialist jurists—technical terms of a sort unknown to Soga law. Perhaps the Anglo-American concept closest to the Soga one, just because it is most general in its reach, is that of estoppel: "a man's own act or acceptance closes his mouth to allege or plead the truth." [51] In any case, the reasoning of Soga judges in these matters was made clear to me in discussion with the subcounty chief who presided in the above case: "If a man waits a long time before bringing his case to court," he remarked, "it shows that he was just waiting for important witnesses to die."

Nevertheless, the mere passage of time does not, by itself, destroy an otherwise valid claim. Particular sets of circumstances must still be taken into account, and for this purpose other concepts are required.

50. Anthony Allott, *Essays in African Law, with Special Reference to the Law of Ghana*, p. 297.
51. *Black's Law Dictionary*, pp. 648–51.

Two cases from the county of Bugabula are particularly interesting because in each of them temporal limitation is considered and ultimately rejected as a solution because the ancient claims of litigants are found to be solidly based. Both are difficult cases, involving split decisions or reversals upon appeal.

Yekoniya Kirya v. Matayo Kapere: historical relativity

Yekoniya Kirya v. Matayo Kapere turns upon the court's assessment of the present-day significance of events said to have occurred in or about the year 1920. The essential facts are not in dispute. There is

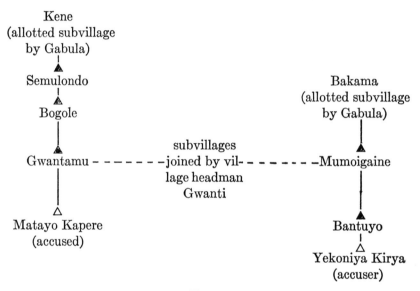

Fig. 15

some initial sparring, in which the litigants and their witnesses argue about details and overstate their cases, as is common; but it is shortly agreed by all parties, as well as by the commission sent by the court to investigate, that the ancestors of the principals were alloted neighboring subvillages in the village of Naminage by the Gabula, the ruler of Bugabula. It is also agreed that "when Daudi Mutekanga was county chief and Bulasio Nume was subcounty chief"—this would be around 1920, according to my inquiries—the then village headman, Gwanti, joined the two subvillages under the headmanship of Gwantamu, Matayo's father, thereby dispossessing Yekoniya's grandfather, Mumoigaine (See fig. 15).

The reason for the amalgamation was administrative rationalization. This was the period of the *bwesengeze* system, under which the officials of the political hierarchy were supported by ten shillings or one month's labor collected each year from every able-bodied male. The tribute from every ten men was divided among headmen and chiefs according to a fixed schedule. Apparently to facilitate this division, subvillages containing less than ten tribute-payers were combined with others. Mumoigaine's subvillage, it is said, contained only six.

Yekoniya now argues that since the area presently contains more than thirty adult males it should revert to its former status as a separate subvillage. And, since he is the heir of Bantuyo, who in turn was the heir of Mumoigaine—all this, too, is uncontested—he should be recognized as headman. Matayo denies this, arguing that Yekoniya's father, Bantuyo, "never ruled a subvillage." The subcounty court, in its decision, agrees and adds, as further grounds for leaving things as they are, that "Matayo has ruled that subvillage for a long time." The administrative taking and giving, apparently, has irrevocably destroyed Yekoniya's claim to *butaka* rights, even though the circumstances which justified it at the time no longer obtain; and in any case, Yekoniya seems to have waited too long. At one point, in answer to the court's question, Yekoniya admits that by 1940 there were already more than twenty ablebodied men in the area he claims.

But Yekoniya refuses to accept the decision and in his letter of appeal to the county court he argues, first, that his hereditary claim is still good: "Bakama was the father of Bantuyo, who was my father." Second, although the lower court "said that I was too late in bringing my case, this is not true . . . when the subvillage was joined there were few people in it, but now there are many." The time he has waited before acting upon this change of circumstances has not been unreasonably long. With so much common ground as to the facts, the hearing at the county court, not surprisingly, consists of little more than a restatement of old arguments. But the county judges evaluate them differently:

> It is clear that Yekoniya owns the subvillage, which was amalgamated when it had only a few people. The accused himself [Matayo] also agrees that the subvillage once belonged to Y. Kirya's grandfather, and was added to his. Since the subvillage now has more than thirty people, the accuser wants it to be separated. . . . Therefore, following to the evidence given in this court . . . the decision of the subcounty court has been altered.

The implicitness so common in Soga legal reasoning is particularly striking here because of the agreement as to the facts. Matayo Kapere and the subcounty court state these facts and conclude that "therefore" the subvillage belongs to Matayo. Yekoniya Kirya and the county court restate them, but say that "therefore" Yekoniya must have his subvillage returned to him. The county court's implicit reasoning must be (1) that the concept of temporal limitation does not apply—the time involved is, incidentally, a good deal shorter than in *Tito Nantamu* v. *Kisubi Mwokyeku;* (2) that the fact that Yekoniya's father never acted as headman is no bar to his succession to rights that would have passed to him had the administrative reorganization of the *bwesengeze* period never taken place; and (3) that the institutional standards of the past must be taken into account. When the reasons for the amalgamation—depopulation—no longer obtain, the *status quo ante* must be restored.

Taken together, points (2) and (3) amount to a concept of historical relativity—a notion that the concept *butaka*, and doubtless *kitongole* as well, must be applied in the light of political history. The courts seem in this connection to distinguish two general periods prior to the present one: that of the sovereign kingdoms, before British administration; and that of roughly the first three decades of the present century, when headmen were considered members of the A.L.G. hierarchy and subject to its administrative control. Withdrawals and allotments of headmanships which took place during the period of kingdom sovereignty are not, so far as I could discover, considered subject to challenge.

Lameka Waiswa v. *Anderea Mpendo: acts of a sovereign ruler stand*

The courts of Bugabula County came close to stating this explicitly in *Lameka Waiswa* v. *Anderea Mpendo*, litigated in 1950. The circumstances are similar to those of *Yekoniya Kirya* v. *Matayo Kapere:* a subvillage held by Lameka's ancestor was joined to one held by Anderea's ancestor. Lameka wants it restored to him. But this joining occurred in the time of Kagoda Gabula, before British administration, and the county court, concurring with the subcounty judgment, concludes:

> The accused [Anderea] has brought a witness, the village headman, Y. Kiyuba, who supports him completely. According to his testimony, it is true that Mutyambigo, the grandfather of the accuser [Lameka] was the owner of that subvillage, but it was given away by Kagoda Gabula. Therefore there is no evidence that the subvillage is his.

Lameka fails where Yekoniya succeeds, before the same county court in the same year, because during the period of kingdom sovereignty rulers' allotments and withdrawals of headmanship were political acts, not justiceable in the courts. It would not be reasonable to

review them judicially today. Later, when headmen were members of
the new administrative structure established by the British, headmanships could be taken, and perhaps given,[52] for administrative reasons.
These reasons become material for litigation and adjudication in cases
arising from events occurring during that period. Today, when headmen are not formally a part of the A.L.G., but still perform some
important functions for it, the A.L.G. may seek their dismissal for
cause by court action, but since the position has become an almost
entirely hereditary one, the choice of a replacement is in the hands of
the lineage.[53]

Erukana Mawerere v. *Yona Kirya: time does not make a headman of
a steward*

The other case in which the concept of temporal limitation is considered as a solution, and ultimately rejected, is *Erukana Mawerere* v.
Yona Kirya, which was fought through the Bugabula courts to the
district court in 1950. This is a marginal case indeed. All agree that
Erukana has acted as subvillage headman of Kasozi, unchallenged, for
forty years. For all this time his name has appeared at the head of the
poll-tax register for Kasozi. Now Yona comes and claims *butaka*
rights, though he admits to not having asserted them since he left for
school as a small boy in 1910. He has already been to the "county
court" of the royal government of Bugabula and his claim has been
sustained. But in Bugabula royal government is less substantial than
in Bulamogi, and Erukana goes straight to the A.L.G. courts to accuse
Yona of "falsely claiming." At first he prevails easily on the ground
that Yona has allowed his case to grow stale. "Although [Yona]
claims that it was given him in 1906," the subcounty decision runs, "he
did nothing about it." And, "in the subvillage register, Erukana is
confirmed as headman." The county court concurs: for too long, Yona
"did nothing." But the district court disagrees:

52. There are suggestions in early administrative officers' reports that during
the first two decades of this century headmen were sometimes appointed by them
or by chiefs acting upon their orders. In the "Safari Book for Bugabula County,"
I found the following entry for February 27, 1920: "I explained the changes in
chieftainship and said that chiefs, on their part, must evict and replace useless
village headmen and parish chiefs."

53. On September 1, 1943, the district council resolved: "A village headman
who neglects his work, after being warned by the county chief, may be dismissed
and replaced by another appointed by the clan." This never became a formal
bylaw and thus has no legislative effect, but it expresses the common understanding of the position today. In all recent cases which came to my attention, the
"dismissal" took place through a court-initiated action for "neglect of duties."

Although a long time passed during which [Yona] didn't work in it, the people's testimony confirms that the subvillage is his. . . . Erukana Mawerere, although he spent a long time working in it . . . has no one at all who confirms that he was given it to be his own. And no fault has been reported which takes it away from Yona Kirya. . . . The decisions of the subcounty and county courts have been altered.

But the judges divide, four to three, with the chairman, as rarely happens, exercising his vote to break a tie. The concept of temporal limitation very nearly reaches to include the facts of *Erukana Mawerere* v. *Yona Kirya,* but not quite. For Yona's claim, dilatory as he has been in asserting it, has proved unassailable.

A portent of ultimate failure appears in Erukana's initial exchange with the subcounty court:

Q: You have heard the accused, Yona Kirya, say that he has not falsely claimed the subvillage, but that it is his. . . . Do you have any testimony to disprove his argument?
A: I have heard, but I do not have testimony, because all the people who knew that the subvillage was mine have died. The only testimony is from my own mouth.
Q: If you say that you have no testimony at all in this case, then is that to say that . . . Yona Kirya . . . is truthful?
A: He is not truthful. The subvillage is mine. I have been listed in the poll-tax register as subvillage headman from 1910 to 1950.

This is really all he has to say. From first to last, he brings no witnesses.

Yona's case is that he was given Kasozi in 1906 by his father, Muwaluka, who was then headman of the village, Kakoge, in which Kasozi is located. Yona was then at school and Muwaluka chose one Kalibakatya to act as steward. In 1910, Kalibakatya was dismissed for administrative inefficiency and peculation and Erukana was made steward. Yona says: "He was our scribe"—a position common at the time when few headmen were literate and when the new British administration was instituting the keeping of records—"and this gave him an opportunity to enter his own name in the register as headman." In 1943, Muwaluka died and was succeeded as village headman by his son, Erugenensi Kolobe, Yona's brother. All this time, Erukana continued to act as headman. Yona meanwhile remained away, working in the neighboring district of Teso. He did not return until 1949, and even failed to appear at his father's funeral feast to have his rights confirmed, as he certainly should have done. This story runs consistently through Yona's testimony, his letters of appeal, and the testimony of his three witnesses: his brothers, Erugenensi Kolobe and Semei Bibi, and his father's old *katikkiro*, Seperiya Kabola.

Yona, by his own admission, has been exceedingly careless of his rights, but these rights, based squarely upon unchallenged evidence of inheritance, cannot be overturned by a mere steward, even one with forty years of undisputed possession. In *Tito Nantamu* v. *Kisubi Mwokyeku*, both parties could bring witnesses in support of plausible claims. The concept of temporal limitation was brought in to decide between them. Erukana Mawerere, however, can bring no evidence that he is more than a steward, serving at the pleasure of the real headman. Temporal limitation alone is no basis for rights in headmanship.

Before leaving the sphere of headmanship I should like to say a final word about the significance of the royal governments in Soga legal development. I suggest that the varying authority of these governments, as manifested in their varying ability to compete with the A.L.G. courts for jurisdiction over rights in land, may be viewed as an index of the differentiation of rights in land from political authority— an index of the "legalization," in the sense of rendering more subject to law, of a field of Soga life which was formerly governed to a greater extent by political considerations. The royal governments represent an attempt, more or less successful depending upon their popular legitimacy, to maintain the old link between land rights and general political authority—to assert that, in the language of feudal Europe, *dominium* over land and *dominium* over its inhabitants are one.[54]

There is irony here: the ex-rulers and their chiefs are not the ruling power in the land, nor even, in a sense, do they claim to be. They recognize the general authority of the A.L.G., claiming only that they, and not the present incumbents, are its rightful servants. Their courts do not compete with those of the A.L.G. for jurisdiction over cases other than those involving land rights. Thus, they themselves are in a sense the vehicles for a separation of land administration and jurisdiction from government at large. The way in which they administer land and adjudicate land disputes, in the areas in which they are strong, is modeled upon the political order of the past, in which rulers, chiefs, and headmen ruled land and people together. Thus, the rulers claim to exercise the sovereign's right to appoint and dismiss chiefs and headmen, as well as to adjudicate disputes arising from their subordinates' acts. But the existence of the A.L.G. court system, to which litigants may always resort, is a constant threat to this sovereignty—a constant

54. F. W. Maitland, *Domesday Book and Beyond*, p. 268.

invitation to treat *legally,* within the logic of litigation and adjudication, ideas which were formerly political.

The position of the royal governments is obviously an unstable one, but their decline has been in progress for many decades and has not yet been completed. It began, perhaps, before the arrival of the British, when lesser rulers fell under the suzerainty of greater ones and the latter, in some cases, under that of the Kabaka of Buganda. It was hastened by the establishment of British administration. In each case, mediatization—suzerainty—has tended to destroy sovereignty by providing a higher court of appeal, before which the former sovereign becomes merely another litigant or judge whose actions, through the logic of litigation and adjudication, are brought under the sway of legal concepts. The persistence of sovereignty in Bulamogi, however, testifies to the tenacity with which political values in capable hands may resist this logic, even when it is backed by "a monopoly of the legitimate use of force."

The monkey does not decide cases pertaining to the forest.
—Luganda proverb

Concepts, once . . . they have entered into thought processes, tend to take on an appearance of solidity, reality and inherent value which has no foundation in experience.
—Karl Llewellyn

7 Headman and Peasant: *The Growth of a Law of Tenancy*

In discussing the law of headmanship, I have tried to trace the processes through which *butaka* and *kitongole* have increasingly become legal concepts through subjection to the logic of litigation and adjudication. What at one time was more in the nature of a political office has evolved in the direction of a bundle of rights in land as an economic resource. As this evolution progresses, *butaka* and *kitongole* change from vehicles for the assertion of power in the political arena to categorizing concepts used to frame claims justiciable in the A.L.G. courts. Subsidiary concepts are developed to facilitate the adjudication of these claims in a changing institutional setting.

The legal application of *butaka* and *kitongole* is probably not entirely modern. When a nineteenth-century ruler himself withdrew and allocated headmanships or chieftainships in his capacity as sovereign, he was acting politically. Then *butaka* and *kitongole* might enter as terms of political consideration—as assertions, respectively, of the moral primacy of lineage continuity and solidarity, or of the prudential value of individual talent and loyalty. But headmanships were also allocated by ruler's subordinates; and sometimes, one is told, disappointed contenders appealed from these subordinate acts of authority to the ruler. Then the proceedings might take on a more legal coloring, the ruler sitting with his chiefs to adjudicate contending claims. No doubt the line between the exercise of sovereign authority and the exercise of appellate jurisdiction was indistinct. The word *lukiiko* ("court," "council," "meeting"), when used without a qualifier, still applies indifferently to judicial, administrative, and legislative bodies and proceedings. But there is distinct language for talking about litigation and adjudication, as contrasted with order-giving and rule-making, and these distinctions are not, I think, new. The language of legal proceedings is used to describe the pleading (*kuwoza*) that took place "before the face of" the ruler: there was an accused, an accuser, and witnesses; there was a cause (or "case" or "fault": *musango* means all of these); there was a decision—a "cutting (*nsala*) when, as Basoga say, the cause was "cut." Given the centrality of both corporate unilineal descent and dyadic relations of authority in Soga society, such events must inevitably have involved the invocation of *butaka* and *kitongole* ideas and their legal manipulation. A body of subsidiary concepts must have been developed in this context.

The reception accorded British administrators, once Busoga had been "pacified" and it had become clear where ultimate power lay, strongly suggests that the legal treatment of authority over land and people was a familiar thing. There was little hesitation in conferring the role of "cutter of cases" in this field upon the British officers who produced the first written records of litigation. And the cases they heard were couched in terms reminiscent of present-day disputes. In 1905, for example, one Ngugwe appealed to the administrative officer, sitting as a judge, invoking the *butaka* concept against the action of the ruler of Luuka, the Tabingwa: "My father was allotted land—two villages—by the Tabingwa years ago. When my father died, only a small piece [a holding? a subvillage?] was given me. I want my villages." In reply, the Tabingwa's *katikkiro* asserted that Ngugwe's father was a usurper and that Ngugwe's claims to *butaka* were excessive, if not wholly unfounded: "The Tabingwa merely sent him [the father] as an emissary to collect cattle from the villagers. He stayed and took more cattle for himself. Then the villagers killed him and the Tabingwa put another man in that place. This Ngugwe, who was only a boy, was left in the true *butaka* of his father." [1] Ngugwe's claim, the officer found, was unsound; the sovereign had never given the father that which the son now claimed. The point here, however, is simply

1. Volume entitled "Native Court Cases, 1904," on file in the Central Offices, Jinja.

that the *"Bwana* D.C." quite naturally became an appellate judge, deciding issues already framed for him by Soga society and culture.

Wherever there was general superordinate authority, then, whether of the ruler over his chiefs or of the British officer or a more powerful neighbor over the ruler, there was appellate jurisdiction—the authority to hear pleadings and to adjudicate. While there remain to this day places like Bulamogi where sovereignty persists, and with it the political use of the notions *butaka* and *kitongole,* the mediatization of formerly sovereign powers must always have brought with it some legalization of these concepts—often, perhaps, only temporarily, for in Busoga, and the larger interlacustrine Bantu world of which it was part, conquest and secession were continuous. Thus, while the political history of the past half-century has presented many new problems in the adjudication of disputes over headmanship, the judges have come to these problems equipped with basic conceptual tools whose legal use runs backward in time as far as written records and elders' memories penetrate.

Today these basic concepts are also fundamental to the flood of litigation over individual holdings that threatens to inundate the A.L.G. courts. Examining these cases, one is immediately struck by their conceptual continuity with the headmanship cases. Clearly, the litigants in their pleadings and the judges in their decisions are drawing upon the same fund of legal ideas. In general terms, the village or subvillage is viewed as the kingdom in microcosm: the headman is a little "ruler," seeking always to obtain a free hand in "taking and giving"; the peasant householder is a petty "chief," struggling to put down hereditary roots and thus to place his rights in his tiny domain beyond his master's reach. But if there is conceptual continuity, there is also a rather puzzling historical difference: many headmanship cases appear in the earliest records, suggesting that the A.L.G. courts simply inherited an existing field of litigation from the tribunals of the old kingdoms; down through the 1920s, however, disputes over individual holdings seem to have been almost absent from court dockets. The past twenty years have seen a tremendous increase in such litigation. Thus the social fabric surrounding rights in individual holdings seems to have been affected in a particularly radical way by recent economic and political change.

The evidence of a dramatic increase in litigation is quite clear. Tables 1–6 show how common disputes over holdings have become today and how difficult they are to settle. (In table 5, in which all land cases appealed to the county court of Bugabula in 1950 are lumped together, such cases account for forty-six of a total of sixty-two—the remainder being headmanship cases.) In earlier periods, in contrast, land litigation of which there is any record seems to have been almost exclusively concerned with headmanships.

There is, first of all, the correspondence between the British officer in Busoga and his superiors in Kampala during the first decade of British administration—the years 1893–1902.[2] In the letter cited in chapter 2, the officer in Busoga was urged, in April 1893, to "try to settle land cases locally" instead of sending them on to the Kabaka of Buganda.[3] (The British were of course endeavoring to substitute their own suzerainty—and appellate jurisdiction—for that of the Kabaka.) There are many references to "land cases" in this correspondence, but in all instances in which particulars are given, these appear to have been headmanship disputes. All the litigants are rulers, chiefs, or headmen. The same letter of April, 1893, for example, speaks of a dispute over a number of "shambas" allotted by the late ruler of Bukoli to his sons. Now "shamba" is a Kiswahili word which in various parts of East Africa may denote a land holding of almost any size, from an individual family holding to a large plantation.[4] It is quite clear, however, that in these documents it refers to a subvillage or village, which the British officers thought of as a "plantation," cultivated by villagers for the headman's benefit, just as, today, Basoga tend to use it only when speaking of European- or Asian-owned plantations. On March 20, 1894, for example, the officer in Busoga reported that "Mutambada [5] is still a chief, but one shamba has been taken and given to his brother, Kibali. . . . His four uncles formerly had fifteen soko [bisoko: subvillages], or small parts. They were reinstated." Again, on February 15, 1896, the officer in Busoga reported that "Lugula, a subchief of Makoba," had been "chasing people out of Makoba's shambas."

During the decade of the 1890s, while British administration was still tenuous, European officers did not hold regular courts to hear cases on appeal. But by the first decade of this century, a regular district administrator's appeal court had been established and cases were recorded in the register of "native court cases" mentioned earlier. Again the word shamba is used in a context which clearly suggests that it meant a village or subvillage. On June 27, 1904, for example, one

2. Uganda Government Archives, Staff and Miscellaneous, 1893–1902.

3. E. J. L. Berkeley to Officer-in-charge, Busoga, April 24, 1893, Uganda Government Archives, Staff and Miscellaneous, 1893.

4. Frederick Johnson, A Standard Swahili-English Dictionary. The word, from the French champ, seems to have been introduced to East Africa, along with the plantation cultivation of cloves, from Mauritius.

5. W. T. Grant to Captain Gibb, March 20, 1894, Uganda Government Archives, Staff and Miscellaneous, 1894.

Bangiri litigated with Menya, ruler of Bugweri, for the *"shamba"* Wirima, claiming that he had given four cattle and twenty goats in payment. The British officer, after hearing the arguments, concluded that "for this amount a *mutala* [village] would have been obtained. . . . I therefore give judgment for the plaintiff." He and other administrative officers are using *"shamba"* as an inclusive term for villages and subvillages. The casebooks contain many such cases, but none involving individual holdings. In these records the contrast between the apparent stability of patterns of litigation arising out of marriage and the change in patterns of land litigation emerges quite clearly. The 1904 casebook contains many adultery cases and accusations of "harboring" by husbands against their wives' fathers or guardians, just as do present-day dockets.

Finally, the casebook of subcounty Ssaabawaali, Kigulu, for 1923 (table 4) provides data for comparison with the contemporary dockets. Again there are seven headmanship cases and none involving individual holdings—in a subcounty in which, in 1950, there were five cases of the latter type. In contrast, again, patterns of litigation arising out of sexual relations and marriage in this subcounty seem to have changed little over more than a quarter of a century.[6]

The upshot of the evidence, then, is that cases involving individual holdings, which today make up such a large proportion of the "civil" litigation in Soga courts, particularly at appellate levels, apparently are a quite recent phenomenon in these courts. Just how recent, it is unfortunately impossible to judge, for I failed to collect dockets from the 1930s and 1940s. However, administrative officers' reports indicate that the really dramatic increase occurred only during the 1940s and 1950s.

It is very difficult to believe that disputes over individual holdings simply did not occur in the past. Even though land seems never to have been really scarce, Basoga today exhibit an attachment to their particular holdings which can hardly be new, focusing as it does particularly upon the perennial banana gardens which provide subsistence (the primary word for "food"—*mmere*—means *matooke*—"banana mash"—unless otherwise specified) and which shelter the ancestors' graves (thus *butaka*, too, means particularly the banana garden), rather than upon the cash-producing fields of annual crops. About the banana garden cluster some of the most powerful sentiments in Soga life: patrilineal continuity, symbolized by the graves; maternal nur-

6. All the kinds of sex-and-marriage cases enumerated in table 4 are found in the 1950 casebook and in both years "harboring" cases are the most common.

turance, symbolized by the almost total delegation of responsibility for the garden and its produce to women; male fertility, symbolized by the pendant banana flower, which Busoga quite explicitly view as the most phallic of everyday phenomena. It seems quite unlikely that rights in such a value-laden object were not occasionally—even frequently—contested.

A much more likely hypothesis is that such conflicts did, indeed, occur, but that their appearance in greater numbers on the dockets of higher tribunals is the result of the changes in the role of the headman which have been traced in chapter 6. I have suggested that until roughly the 1930s headmen had little interest in disturbing their people's security of tenure. Quite the contrary: the headman's power, wealth, and honor all depended upon his ability to attract and hold the allegiance of his people, in a situation in which people were scarcer than land. From this posture, he must have been able to adjudicate disputes between neighbors in a relatively disinterested manner, and thus to maintain a reputation for justice. No doubt his authority was sometimes insufficient. He was not always disinterested with respect to conflicting claims. Headmen, it is said, following the pattern of kingdom-level politics, liked to maintain a certain balance within the community between members of their own clans and others in order to maximize their own authority. This sort of political manipulation of *butaka* and *kitongole* elements must occasionally have resulted in appeals to higher authority, just as it did at upper levels in the political system. In general, however, until headmen opted out—or were pushed out—of the A.L.G. organization after losing their right to tribute, their interests ran with those of their people in maintaining stable, productive communities.

It was, I think, when they turned to the maximization of income from entry fees to replace their lost tribute that this community of interest was destroyed. This last statement may seem to place too much weight on a single form of interest-calculation on the part of headmen; it is, of course, true that this pattern of behavior developed in the context of a general shift toward a more narrowly economic view of land rights by all parties. Up to this point, however, the headmen had been able to participate in the more general movement without upsetting their peoples' security. Under the *bwesengeze* system and the tribute system that survived it into the thirties, headmen shared in the new money wealth derived from cotton. While the tribute was not graduated, and hence provided no incentive for headmen to encourage increased production, still they received it from every able-bodied adult male every year. When this source of income was cut off, the maximization of entry fees presented the logical alternative *given the existing framework of custom.*

The entry fee—*nkoko* or *nsibuzi*[7]—had a traditional precedent in the symbolic payment made in recognition of the headman's authority —to show, as Basoga put it, that the peasant "wanted to be the headman's man"—"wanted to be ruled by him." It could not, therefore, be viewed as "illegal." But now it became a substantial sum of money or livestock and headmen increasingly sought to collect still more in fees by stimulating turnover in their communities' populations —by asserting the *kitongole* right to reclaim and reallocate whenever possible. "Headmen especially like to allocate to foreigners," one subcounty chief told me, "because they shift about more frequently and bring in more *nsibuzi* fees. Even my father [a subvillage headman] does this." More blatantly fraudulent are the frequent attempts to squeeze in additional peasants by cutting off bits of existing holdings. Such practices are notorious and frequently are deplored as constituting a national problem: I once heard the Kyabazinga bitterly upbraid the county council of Kigulu, whose membership includes many headmen, for not doing more to put a stop to them. But headmen, of course, feel that the logic of their situation justifies their actions, especially since their people also frequently seek to realize profit from land rights in ways that violate traditional morality. The chief who complained to me about headmen's manipulations as a source of litigation also spoke of shady practices by villagers: the creation of subtenancies, the selling of land without reference to headmen or, more subtly, agreeing to vacate in exchange for money while encouraging the headman, in exchange for part of the money paid, to allocate to the payer.

All this, of course, tends to destroy the fabric of personal allegiance between headman and people and to undermine the headman's ability to justly adjudicate in land disputes among villagers, as he still does much more effectively, for example, in sex-and-marriage disputes; for the headman now becomes a party to the increasingly cold-eyed struggle to turn land rights into a marketable commodity. Like the monkey among his fellow-animals in the forest, whom Basoga regard as unendowed with human civility, the headman ceases to be an effective arbiter. The whole burden of adjudicating cases concerning land rights—and, since no legislative solution has been forthcoming, of developing out of received legal ideas and present experience a law of tenancy adequate to the new situation—thus falls upon the A.L.G. courts.

---

7. *Nkoko* means "hen"; I am uncertain about the literal meaning of *nsibuzi.*

In the minds of those who most of all must bear this burden—the county and subcounty chiefs who chair the courts—there is a proper way of doing things which, if followed, will prevent litigation. A man who wishes to take up land presents himself to the headman as a *musenze*. The term is coming to mean "new tenant," but it also still carries definite overtones of personal allegiance: "one who joins a new master." (The verbal form, *kusenga*, means "to attend upon" or "to pay homage to" a superior.) The prospective *musenze* approaches the subvillage headman or, particularly if he is a stranger, asks a friend or kinsman to make the approach on his behalf. In the ensuing negotiations, he should be represented by a *mukwenda*, an "agent," whose office is similar to that of the agent in bridewealth negotiations.[8] The land he seeks to take up will most likely once have been *butaka* which has now become *kitongole*—available for allocation as a result of abandonment. After the amount of the entry fee, which may vary from a few shillings to several hundred in cash, livestock, or other goods, has been agreed upon, and also the time or times of payment (installments are common), the contract will often be embodied in a written agreement. When payment is made, the *mukwenda* should make it, either to the headman or, more properly, to a *mukwenda* selected by the headman. The two *bakwenda* may then serve as witnesses to the contract and to the payment if a dispute should subsequently arise.[9] The headman then, either himself or through a *mubaka*, an "emissary," accompanies the new tenant in beating the bounds of the holding in the presence of the *bataka:* "elders" of the community who hold descent-group rights there and hence, presumably, know that the land to be allocated is free of descent-group claims. The *bataka*, too, will be important witnesses in any subsequent dispute. The headman or his *mubaka* should mark by planting saplings any section of the boundary not marked by prominent natural features.

Having paid the entry fee, the new tenant owes no further obligation —no rent or due or service—to the headman in connection with the land. So long as he remains in effective occupation by tilling it or maintaining a house on it he is secure, though he may not alienate it to anyone else. His lineage may pass it on to his heir on similar terms, without further obligation. While the heir should be presented to the headman and should indicate that he recognizes his authority, no new entry fee is payable. With the installation of the heir and the burial of

---

8. See chapter 4.
9. Indeed, the *mukwenda* is legally *obliged* to testify on behalf of his principal. In *Samwiri Waibiyo* v. *Yoswa Kibwika* (Ssaabawaali, Kigulu, 1951), the accused was successfully sued for the amount he had caused his principal to lose by not appearing to testify as *mukwenda* in a bridewealth case.

his predecessor in the banana garden, the process has gone full circle: the land has passed from *butaka* to *kitongole* and back to *butaka*.

Litigation occurs because persons seek to profit by contravening or circumventing this correct way of proceeding; or because its requirements are in some respects ambiguous, so that even the well meaning may find themselves in court. As in the case of the law of marriage and sexual relations and the law of headmanship, I shall begin the examination of cases with the areas in which the law is relatively clear and firm and work toward its more ambiguous margins.

A PLAIN CASE AND SOME BENCHMARKS

Aminsi Waiswa v. Sajjabi Kibba: an avaricious headman; res judicata

Aminsi Waiswa v. Sajjabi Kibba, which was tried in the subcounty court of Mutuba VII, Bugabula, in 1950, is a useful case with which to begin because it illustrates particularly clearly the difficulties that arise when headmen, upon whose proper behavior an orderly regime of land rights depends, become avaricious. Aminsi and Sajjabi are neighbors and Yonasani Kisuwa is their subvillage headman. Aminsi accuses Sajjabi of "jumping the boundary we were given [by the headman] and taking [part of my banana garden] seventy-nine yards long and the width of the garden." What happened is really quite clear to the court from the beginning. Sajjabi occupies *butaka*—a holding inherited from his father, Kibba. The headman, Yonasani, in allotting a neighboring holding to Aminsi, has tried to include in it, no doubt in exchange for a suitably large fee, part of Sajjabi's banana garden. The outcome—restoration to Sajjabi of the disputed portion—is never in doubt, but to achieve this result in the face of the headman's persistent attempts to prevent it requires much time and effort on the part of a conscientious court system.

As is the case whenever a boundary is at issue, it is necessary for the court to send a commission of inquiry, chosen from among its members, to investigate on the spot. There they examine the boundary and interview elders of the community, brought by the litigants. Their written report, which is read out in court and incorporated into the record, gives a good account of "the facts":

Sir:
    As your commissioners, we humbly present the conclusion of our commission on which we were sent to the part of a banana garden [claimed by] A. Waiswa and Sajjabi Kibba. A. Waiswa brought two elders, Waluga and Mawerere. Sajjabi brought three elders, Kalaja, Maiga, and Kabi.
    Sir, Waluga, the accuser A. Waiswa's elder, said that the contested part is A.

Waiswa's. [He said that] on the boundary there are three *mituba* trees and at the top of the rise a *mukomakoma* tree and a dead *kibere* tree. This part of the boundary was marked by the headman when [the land] had been abandoned by Kaswabuli and another Mugisu (man from Bugisu district). Mawerere, however, dissociated himself from Waluga, saying that he was familiar with the banana garden but was not certain about the disputed part of the boundary.

Sajjabi's elder, Kalaja, said that the part in question belonged to Sajjabi and was inherited by him from his late father, Kibba. He said that he [Kalaja] had planted the boundary for Sajjabi's father. It is marked by two *mituba* trees, one of which is dead. He said that this is the part of the garden won by Sajjabi from Yonasani at the county court. The two other elders, Maiga and Kabi, did not dispute Kalaja.

My lord, the three trees shown us by Waluga were measured and in my view, they are only one and a half years old. The boundary shown us by Kalaja is as he says. . . . From this we see that the garden in question belongs to Sajjabi, son of Kibba.

Sir, we are respectfully,

> A. B. Waiswa, Parish Chief, Musale
> E. M. K. Mugweri, Court Member

This is really quite damning from the standpoint of Yonasani Kisuwa, the headman. He appears to be the sort of headman who allots to transient foreigners ("when the land had been abandoned by Kaswabuli and another Mugisu"). And it turns out that the whole thing has been through the courts before, when Sajjabi accused Yonasani ("the part of the garden won by Sajjabi from Yonasani at the county court"). Sajjabi refers to this previous case in his opening statement:

I shall win because I have not jumped the boundary . . . there is a definite boundary between us . . . when I litigated at the county court with the subvillage headman, Y. Kisuwa, I won. Then the emissary of the county court went around the boundary planting trees to mark it. I call upon Swaliki Mafali, because he was there.

Swaliki, a neighbor, agrees:

The old boundary was marked by *mituba* trees. In the past, there were also *birowa* trees, but these were cut down and now the boundary is marked by new trees planted by the county court. When the county emissary came in 1949, he found the [boundary] but later [the new trees] were cut down by Yonasani Kisuwa, after the emissary had gone.

Nor does Aminsi contest these facts:

He [Sajjabi] crossed the boundary which was marked by the subvillage headman, Yonasani Kisuwa when he was handing me the garden.

Q: Now, about the boundary that you consider the right one, doesn't he [Sajjabi] reject it because it was annulled [*yamenyebwa*: "broken"] by the county court?

A: I agree, it was annulled, but Y. Kisuwa didn't appeal to the district court.

In other words, Aminsi feels that the headman has not been zealous enough in defending their mutually advantageous transaction. He wants to litigate the matter himself. Hearing the headman's testimony, as Aminsi's only witness, one understands his anxiety:

I know that the seventy-nine yards in question belong to Aminsi, for I gave him the garden, including those seventy-nine yards, and I planted trees to mark the boundary. . . . When Sajjabi came with the emissary of the county court to be given the garden over which we had litigated, he indicated the seventy-nine yards of Aminsi's garden as his [Sajjabi's]. When I spoke about this, they rejected my complaint [saying] that Sajjabi had beaten me.

There is no attempt here to justify the transaction—nothing but a reiteration of what has become abundantly clear: it has already been determined in a previous case that Yonasani wrongfully gave Aminsi part of Sajjabi's garden. The court, therefore, can only conclude that:

The accused, Sajjabi Kibba, has won the case because he has already [in the previous case] accused the subvillage headman, Yonasani Kisuwa, of taking this garden of his and giving it to Aminsi. And Y. Kisuwa did not appeal [against the adverse judgment] but simply tried again to return the garden to the accuser.

But this is still not the end! Aminsi appeals, simply saying that he is "dissatisfied with the subcounty decision" and urging the county court to "reexamine the case carefully." So another commission of inquiry is sent out and all the testimony is heard again, with precisely the same result.

As a source of data on the Soga law of land, this case is supremely uninteresting. The headman and the new allottee have been caught in an act of illegality so obvious and of such a common sort that the arguments tell us nothing not perfectly patent: they indicate only that a headman cannot without cause seize and reallot his tenant's *butaka*. Here no cause at all has been given. However, I have cited the case for two reasons. First, it illustrates the manner in which the Soga courts handle some common procedural problems. Apart from his obvious weakness on the substantial question involved—rights in the contested piece of garden—Aminsi's case is flawed from the start by the circumstance that the substance has already been decided in the same courts before, when Sajjabi accused the headman. Sajjabi was right to first accuse the headman and not Aminsi, because it is the headman who holds the residual right to allot. The matter is thus *res judicata*. This does not mean, in Busoga, that it cannot again come before the courts, but it does seem to mean that the courts will not alter a previous decision on the same issue. In the present case, the court's questions and judgment clearly indicate that the earlier decision is considered decisive. I found no case in which a previous decision on the substance was not so considered. Allott's statement, again in reference to Ghana, that "Native law and the native courts . . . did not recognize *res judicata* . . . and any claim might be re-opened" [10] applies in Busoga only in this sense: Aminsi can reopen the case, but he cannot reopen it without prejudice. It is perhaps consistent with the semiamateur character of the bench and its lack of specialized, technical concepts that it is quite permissive with respect to causes of action. Provided a litigant can even remotely relate his accusation to one of the recognized concepts of wrong, he can get a hearing; and he can appeal on the vaguest grounds, as Aminsi's appeal in the present case shows. Notions related to the Anglo-American *res judicata, estoppel,* etc., enter into the *arguing* of a case rather than into its acceptance for argument. It is, however, surprising that the headman, Yonasani, was not charged with contempt of court on the evidence that he cut down the boundary trees planted following the earlier decision, as happened in similar circumstances in *Eria Wambi* v. *Samwiri Waidha.*

Second, I have cited this case because it shows how focal is the headman's position and how much litigation may arise when he abuses it. The mischief wrought by Yonasani has been great. Four hearings in court (two each at the subcounty and county levels), two commissions of inquiry and two visits by court emissaries to plant boundary trees (a second will be necessary, since Yonasani seems to have destroyed the work of the first) have been required to dispose of a perfectly plain case. What makes all this possible—what, for example, encourages Aminsi to fight the case again—is the large residue of respect which still attaches to the headman's position and authority, despite the public awareness of widespread abuse. Drawing upon this respect, which derives from their traditional position as "rulers" (*bafuzi*) of their communities' land and people, headmen can sometimes (often?) get away with that which Yonasani failed to get away with. One does not lightly litigate with one's "master" (*mukama*); and if one does litigate with him, his word is apt to carry great weight with the court.

Court v. *Nikodemu Balizalinya; Court* v. *Yahya Magobi: "giving the power" to steal*

The continuing potency of the headman's authority in his community and the dilemmas with which this may confront a legal system

---

10. Anthony Allott, *Essays in African Law,* p. 297.

moving toward greater individualization are nicely illustrated by a theft case heard by the subcounty court of Ssaabawaali, Kigulu, in February, 1951. The affair originated in a dispute over the boundary between two neighbors' banana gardens. The headman, Yahya Magobi, indicated a boundary in favor of one of them, Nikodemu Balizalinya, and when Nikodemu proceeded to cut bananas within the disputed area he [Nikodemu] was charged with theft. In its decision, written by the chairman, the court divided three to two:

> The accused has brought the headman who allowed him to cut the bananas, and he [the headman] agrees that he allowed him to do it. Three members of the court have found that the accused stole, but I and another member have seen that the headman is the one who should be found guilty. Since [the accused] has only two members to support him . . . he will be imprisoned for one month at hard labor and has been ordered to pay thirty-five shillings for the bananas. The headman will be charged for having hidden the bananas, which were an exhibit of the court, and for making a disturbance in the community by giving Balizalinya power to cut bananas in Y. Waiswa's garden.

So charged in a separate action, the headman was convicted by a unanimous court and given three months at hard labor plus forty shillings or an additional two months. Contrast the disagreement concerning the guilt of the one who took that which was not his with the consensus on the guilt of the one who "gave him the power" to take it, and also the relative severity of the sentences. What the headman should have done, of course, if there was doubt about the boundary, was to hold a tribunal on that question. If either party remained dissatisfied, the headman should have directed him to take the matter on to the A.L.G. courts for formal litigation. It is considered especially shocking that the headman, who is supposed to be the keystone of law and order in the community, should instead condone direct action. He possesses great authority. Members of the community are inclined to do as he directs them. It is particularly incumbent upon him, therefore, to use his authority justly. That he often does not, but nevertheless remains in a central position in the land tenure system, is indicative of the crisis presently afflicting the law of land rights in Busoga.

When there is widespread feeling in a community that the law is unjust—that it denies persons' legitimate interests—then the stage is set for much litigation on points on which the law is quite clear. At the root of much of the present-day litigation over land in Busoga lie attempts by headmen—usually more subtle than that which came to light in *Aminsi Waiswa* v. *Sajjabi Kibba*—to utilize their authority to traffic in land rights in ways that their people and the courts consider illegitimate, but that they themselves justify as compensation for their loss of official status and income. Or, of course, it may be the tenant who, viewing the headman as a mercenary gouger and hence fair game, seeks to evade his responsibilities or to go beyond his rights. The outlines of what the courts regard as the basic rights and responsibilities of headmen and tenants toward each other are best seen in run-of-the-mill litigation in which no interesting legal problems arise —in which disputes are attributable to attempts to evade the law rather than to its ambiguity. *Aminsi Waiswa* v. *Sajjabi Kibba* was clearly a case of this sort. A further series of such relatively plain cases may serve as benchmarks for the later analysis of more problematical areas of the law.

I have said that the rights of a tenant and his descent-group originate in a "contract" entered into by tenant and headman. There has recently been some controversy about the appropriateness of using the word "contract" in analyzing African legal systems.[11] The argument seems to turn on the Anglo-American distinction between "contract" and "tort"—between obligations specifically agreed upon by the parties and those inherent in the status relationship between them. Without at this juncture entering into the intricacies of this argument, I use the term "contract" in connection with the headman-tenant relationship, as I used it earlier in speaking of the relationship between a bridegroom and his in-laws, because in both cases there is, in the Soga view of things, "an agreement, upon sufficient consideration, to do or not to do a particular thing."[12] In both cases there is an *ndagaano*— a "bargain," "covenant," or "agreement"[13]—which creates specific obligations on both sides. However, it is also true enough that the specific element in these contracts is rather limited and undifferentiated, so that most of the obligations owed by headmen and tenants to each other are perhaps best compared with those arising from the law of tort. Violations of them are "independent of contract"—violations of duties "imposed by general law . . . upon all persons occupying the relation to each other which is involved in a given transaction."[14]

For the present, I shall assume that there is only one sort of tenure and that the only variable elements in the headman-tenant relationship are the entry fee and the particular piece of land to be exchanged. Thus, under the contract the headman is obliged to turn over to the tenant a particular piece of land and the tenant is obliged to pay the

11. Max Gluckman, *The Ideas of Barotse Jurisprudence* (New Haven, 1965), chapter 6.
12. *Black's Law Dictionary*, s.v. "contract."
13. E. M. K. Mulira and E. G. M. Ndawula, *A Luganda-English and English-Luganda Dictionary*, s.v. "ndagaano."
14. *Black's Law Dictionary*, s.v. "tort."

headman a particular price. Once these contractually specific obligations have been fulfilled I shall assume tht the two parties, together
with their descent-groups, enter into a relationship which is always
governed by the same general law—the "general law of tenancy," I
shall call it. I shall assume that no special obligations may be contracted for. Today, with the increasing commercialization of land
rights, certain variant forms of tenure seem to be emerging, but their
legal status is problematical. The courts are grappling with them—attempting, where possible, to force them into existing legal categories
or, where this is not possible, to develop new categories for dealing
with them.

Thus, the distinction between contract and tort is not irrelevant to
the Soga situation, provided it is regarded as an analytic, and not a
classificatory, distinction. The headman-tenant relationship involves
elements of both tort and contract. If the parties to this relationship
simply agreed henceforth to regard each other as "ruler" and "man," if
the headman's obligation to provide the tenant with adequate land and
the tenant's obligation to pay something to the headman were simply
fixed incidents of the status relationship between them, then any
breach of obligation between them would be "tortious." This may have
been the case at some time in the past when the relationship was more
political than economic, but it is not so today. Now a definite contractual element is involved; the relationship is only entered into for
consideration. And the new forms of tenure which seem to be emerging
tend to increase the contractual element—an instance of Main's famous movement "from status to contract." However, all this will be
discussed later. The "plain cases" which I shall take up first concern
the general law of tenancy, involving both contractual and status
elements, about which the courts are relatively clear.

Sitanule Gowa v. *Kisubi Mwokyeku: a holding not paid for reverts*

First of all, the entry fee contracted for is clearly a legal obligation,
default of which permits the headman to assert his *kitongole* right to
repossess the land. In *Sitanule Gowa* v. *Kisubi Mwokyeku,* heard in
the subcounty court of Ssaabawaali, Kigulu, in 1951, Sitanule accused
Kisubi, the headman, of wrongfully taking back a holding belonging to
Waibi, child of his late brother, Balaba, for whom he (Sitanule) was
acting as guardian and trustee. Kisubi agrees that he has reclaimed the
holding, but defends himself on the ground that Balaba, from whom
the child Waibi claims, through Sitanule, to have inherited, failed to
pay the agreed-upon entry fee. In answer to a question from the court
designed to reconcile the parties, Kisubi says that no, he won't allow

Waibi to keep the holding even if the fee is now paid: "He has taken too long to pay. Now I don't want the fee." The crucial exchange comes quickly as the court questions Sitanule:

Q: What does your witness know about the matter?
A: He was present when they were allotting the holding to my brother, and I have the things which were written by Balaba before he died [his testament].

But it is not the original allotment or the inheritance that is in question:

Q: Is there any written evidence that your brother had paid the fee demanded by Kisubi?
A: There is nothing.
Q: Have you any other proof that Kisubi took away a holding that had already been paid for?
A: Because he didn't accuse me.

The decision, quickly arrived at, is that "the late Balaba . . . died before paying the necessary fee and therefore the accused took back the land. . . . The holding remains with its owner [Kisubi]."

Sitanule's last argument ("because he didn't accuse me") is significant. He is trying to argue that Kisubi has waited too long—has acquiesced in Waibi's inheritance. As will be seen, this can be a potent argument; *kitongole* may become *butaka,* and vice versa, through the passage of time. But here it appears that Balaba has died within the year. Kisubi has in fact asserted his claim at the best time: Balaba has died, and hence it cannot be claimed that he will still pay; but Balaba has died *recently,* so neither can it be claimed that Kisubi has acquiesced in Waibi's inheritance. The conclusion to be drawn from the case is that failure to pay the agreed-upon fee within a reasonable time causes the holding to revert to *kitongole.*

This case is interesting in another respect. The chairman of the court explained to me that the accused and the accuser were close agnates—lineage "brothers." The entry fee charged was unusually low—a *kkanzu* (white muslin gown) worth only a few shillings—because "one can't charge one's brother a high fee." But the fee is still a legal obligation, arising from the contract. Even in a case like this, where there was some obligation—moral if not legal—to supply the allottee with land on grounds of status, the court views the contractual obligation as essential. Why did Balaba default on such a minimal fee? "Because," the chairman told me, "he felt sibling jealousy against Kisubi. He thought to himself: 'Kisubi thinks himself better than I, so I won't pay.'" The contractual relationship between superior and subordinate which raises the headman above his brothers (and the ruler above his fellow princes) as "ruler of all the people" without distinction is clearly one of the roots (or manifestations) of the particular Soga form of sibling rivalry.

Maliko Okere v. *Yenusu Mutoto: the headman's obligation; literal estoppel*

The corollary to the tenant's obligation to pay is, of course, the headman's obligation to supply the land contracted for and, lacking sufficient reason for repossessing it, to leave the tenant in peaceful possession. If the headman defaults, he must repay the fee. *Maliko Okere* v. *Yenusu Mutoto*, again from the 1950 docket of Ssaabawaali, Kigulu, illustrates this in a rather entertaining way. Yenusu, who is accused by Maliko of "chasing me out of my holding, which I bought from him for thirty-five shillings, without returning the money," is the prickly sort of headman who feels that present-day tenants lack a proper respect for their masters:

I expect to win [the case] because when Maliko came to beg for the holding I warned him not to despise me as the other man whom I had chased away from the holding used to do. One day I gave him two shillings to dig a piece of ground for me, but he refused. When I asked him the reason, he just took up his stick to beat me. I said nothing more to him. I just walked away. The next day he came to my place and carried on about the incident, asking why I had asked him to dig for me, etc. As it was nightfall, I told him to go away and return the next day. The next morning . . . we went into the matter and Maliko agreed in the presence of Yakobo that he wanted to beat me. So . . . I handed the money to Musa and Musa handed it to Yakobo and Yakobo handed it to Maliko. [Musa and Yakobo would be acting as *bakwenda* (agents) here.] Then . . . I asked him for the two shillings I had given him to dig for me. After a short time, I heard that he had accused me for not refunding the thirty-five shillings he had paid for the holding.

The accuser, Maliko, describes a quite different chain of events:

He is telling lies! He didn't refund the money. But one day I was away from home and when I returned my wife said that Yenusu had ordered us off the land. . . . As I had had no trouble with him before, I carried on with my digging, but when he saw me he stopped me at once. When I asked him why, he said that he had power over me and that I should obey his orders. . . . So I took the matter to the village headman . . . and then to the parish chief . . . and he allowed me to accuse him here. After registering my accusation, I went home. On the following morning, Yenusu and his wife went into their garden and I went into mine. As I was digging, he raised an alarm and many people gathered. He said, "I am preventing this man from cultivating my land, but he is refusing to stop." . . . I replied that he had not refunded the money . . . and I produced our contract and gave it to Jemusi to read. But as he was reading it, Yenusu snatched it away from him and put it into his mouth and chewed it up and swallowed it.

There follows a long parade of witnesses—most of the population of the subvillage seem to have heard or seen something of this very public dispute—but in the court's view "from the evidence of Jemusi, from whom the contract was snatched and swallowed, it has been proved that Yenusu swallowed the agreement before refunding Maliko the thirty-five shillings and so the court has decided the case against him. . . ." The accused has "closed his mouth to plead" with the very evidence itself—a most literal instance of estoppel.

Difasi Genga v. Eria Kisambira: eviction without "reason" is illegal.

From the phrasing of the charge in *Maliko Okere v. Yenusu Mutoto* ("chasing me . . . without returning the money") one might think that a headman may evict a tenant at will, provided he refunds the fee. But he cannot, as *Difasi Genga v. Eria Kisambira* shows. Eria is the pretender to the office of Kisambira whose persistent efforts to dispossess one of his headmen were recounted in chapter 6. He himself is headman of two villages, and in this capacity has tried to evict one of his tenants. In Difasi's words:

They tried to find a way to chase me out of the holding. . . . Kisambira tried to give the fee back to the *mukwenda* ("agent") . . . but he refused to take it. So . . . he just threw the money at the *mukwenda*. . . . The following morning, I found people building a house in my holding, though he had said that he would never evict me. So that's why I accused him.

Eria tries almost every courtroom tactic known to Soga pleading. First he claims that he "does not know" the accuser—that his contract is with the man who turns out to be the accuser's *mukwenda*. Then he tries to put the blame on the subvillage headman, since "he is the one responsible for that holding." He flatly denies having ordered the house built on the land in question and he gives an elaborate account of his own efforts to have the affair arbitrated by the parish chief, claiming that Difasi repeatedly failed to turn up when summoned. But all this merely extends the hearing by requiring Difasi to call witnesses to support every element in his own very different account of "the facts." This he is able to do and at the end of a tedious day the court concludes:

He [Eria] agrees that on June 25, 1950, he went to the house of . . . the accuser's *mukwenda* and threw down the forty-shilling fee, telling him to take it to the accuser. In doing this, he intended to evict the accuser from the holding. And that is also the reason he ordered people to build a house in the accuser's holding. . . . Therefore the court has decided the case to go against him.

The position of the headman under the contract of tenancy is thus similar to that of the bride's guardian under the marriage contract: the "seller" cannot reclaim that which he has "sold" merely by returning the consideration; he must also give "sufficient reason." [15]

Asumani Wagubi v. *Musa Kafero: criteria for abandonment*

Under the "general law of tenancy"—some of the novel forms of tenure now appearing raise special problems to be considered later— "sufficient reason" essentially comes down to failure on the part of the tenant to maintain effective occupation, so that the holding reverts to *kitongole* status. In *Asumani Wagubi* v. *Musa Kafero* (Ssaabawaali, Kigulu, 1951), Asumani accused his subvillage headman, Musa, of "sending me away from my holding, which was given to me by Sowobi (the village headman)." The case turns on the significance of the fact, upon which all agree, that in 1938 Asumani took up a holding in another subvillage and moved his household there, though he claims that he continued to cultivate the land in Musa's subvillage. The question is: Does this constitute abandonment?

Musa argues that it does: "He left my subvillage and joined [another]. . . . When I saw that, I gave parts of that land to some people to plant cassava. That's why Asumani [accuses me]." Musa's two witnesses agree, saying in almost the same words (the phrasing is important): "I am Musa's witness, because the holding for which they are litigating is Musa's. Asumani left it in 1938 and joined another subvillage"; and "I am Musa's witness because Asumani left that holding and joined another subvillage." Asumani puts it differently: "I have never left my holding, as the accused says. But because it wasn't giving good yields, I decided to take up another in another subvillage." And his witness says: "When Asumani got another holding in [another] subvillage, Musa sent him away from the first one." Thus Asumani and his witnesses speak in terms of rights in, and use of, *holdings*, while Musa and his witnesses stress *membership in communities*. The court, implicitly accepting Asumani's way of putting the question, ignores the matter of "leaving" and "joining" and simply concludes: "The holding which [he] claims from Musa is his. It was allotted to him by Sowobi." The chairman of the court commented to me that *either* continued cultivation *or* maintenance of a household on a holding constitutes effective occupation (the word used is *kukozesa:*

15. See chapter 5.

"to use"). Unless a tenant fails to do either, the headman cannot reclaim the holding as *kitongole*.

Thus the courts today recognize a differentiation between land rights and political status. In the nineteenth century, when the headman "ruled land and people together," such differentiation was probably not recognized. Or perhaps it is better to say that such a situation would not have arisen. A man "joining a new master" would expect to find land with him as an incident of their relationship; as he could not "serve two masters" loyally, he would not expect to hold land in two communities. The argument of Musa and his witnesses seems to hark back to such a state of affairs; they speak as if it were self-evident that a man who "joins a new subvillage" must give up his land in the community he leaves. "Effective occupation" is probably a twentieth-century legal concept—a device by which the courts recognize the present differentiation between rights in land and authority over men. Actually, there is an added complication in this case: Asumani does not claim that he continues to cultivate the old holding in Musa's subvillage with his own hands. He says he "lends it out" to others to cultivate. The court in this case simply accepts this without argument as constituting continued "use" by Asumani, though it is in fact an instance of a still more recent tendency toward special contractual arrangements which cannot yet be said to have found a settled place in the general law of tenancy. This side of the case will therefore be discussed later.

Everything I have said thus far about the obligations of tenants and headmen toward each other also applies to their respective successors through lineage-mediated inheritance. We have seen that the obligation to pay the entry fee contracted for passes to the tenant's heir; so also does the obligation to maintain effective occupation. Default on either of these obligations places the holding within reach of *kitongole*. Provided these obligations are met, the tenant's rights pass undiminished to his heir. Similarly, the headman's rights and obligations pass to *his* heir. To round out this account of the general law of tenancy, then, it is necessary to say something about the courts' handling of inheritance—*busika*—by which rights in land become *butaka*—beyond the reach of *kitongole*.

Actually although the term *butaka* is not used until rights have descended through lineage-mediate inheritance, land allotted to a tenant is already beyond the reach of *kitongole*, provided the obligations already discussed are fulfilled. But with proper succession, the rights of the tenant's line are, so to speak, doubly validated: by the initial allotment and by unchallenged succession. The latter itself becomes *prima facie* evidence of rights. This is why, in *Sitanule Gowa* v. *Kisubi Mwokyeku,* the headman was careful not to let the succession go unchallenged when the deceased tenant had not paid the entry fee. Had he done so and then later claimed *kitongole* rights on the ground of default of payment, the court's first question to him would have been: "Why did you not assert your claim earlier?"

So succession is crucial, but the A.L.G. courts do not themselves apply a law of succession. The choice of an heir lies with the succession lineage, meeting at the funeral feast. The court's role is to determine, as a matter of fact, what was decided there, should the succession be challenged. Normally, as I have said, the heir is a son, or at least a close agnate, of the deceased. The deceased may have left a written or oral testament and this has some moral force, but the succession lineage is free to arrive at its own decision and the courts will accept and enforce it. Nor do the courts inquire much into the process by which the decision was arrived at—whether, for example, the right people were present at the funeral gathering and whether proper procedures were followed. These are *ebyo mu kika*—"internal clan matters." One can think of all sorts of problems that might arise—conflicts which the courts might be asked to adjudicate—but the judges' inclination is to stand aloof wherever possible and to regard the gathering at the funeral feast as a kind of constituent assembly, sovereign within its sphere.

Sabasitiano Gavamukulya v. *Bumali Mawa: a fictitious clan*

This comes out most strikingly in *Sabasitiano Gavamukulya* v. *Bumali Mawa* (Ssaabawaali, Kigulu, 1950). Both claim to be "brothers" of the late Yoweri Bikaba and to have inherited his holding. Bumali argues:

Sabasitiano wasn't a brother of the late Bikaba. I am his brother because he left his holding in my hands. The widow, Naudo, stood up before the clan on the funeral feast day and said that her husband had no brother. But I stood up and said that I was his brother. So we held a tribunal and the head of the clan of Baisekantu appointed Amiri Kisambira to be chairman. I brought the letter written by the late Bikaba and after reading it the clan found that the holding was left in my hands. So the chairman decided in my favor.

Sabasitiano and his witnesses, including the widow Naudo (who is hardly a disinterested witness, since she will be inherited along with the holding), do not actually deny that the clan gathering decided in Bumali's favor, but they report conversations with Bikaba during his last days suggesting that he had intended "his brother" Sabasitiano to succeed him. The decisive testimony, however, comes from Amiri Kisambira, chairman of the clan tribunal:

When I arrived [at the funeral gathering] I found the widow saying that her husband had no brother and that he left no will. The head of the Baisekantu clan appointed people to settle the matter. We found that the widow was wrong, so the holding was given to Bumali. Also I heard that the late Bikaba had said that he had a friend [Sabasitiano] with whom he was working and that when the friend returns Bumali should allow him to continue to use the workplace where they worked together as smiths. Bumali showed us the written will. Then the tribunal appointed Yakaya as emissary to install Bumali in the holding.

Q: What sort of will was it?
A: He [Bumali] showed us a piece of paper on which the late Bikaba had written: "I have no brother, but Bumali Mawa is the one who will take my holding."

Another member of the tribunal, Yusufu Waiswa, testifies to the same effect. So the court "relies on the testimony of Amiri Kisambira, the one chosen as chairman by the gathering of the village, and that of Y. Waiswa, a member of the tribunal which sat to hear the dispute on the day of the funeral feast. For this reason, B. Mawa has won the case and the holding remains in his hands."

On one level, the decision is commonplace. As usual, the court has ascertained the clan gathering's decision and has enforced it. But certain puzzling statements are made. Bumali says that "I am Bikaba's brother *because* he left his holding in my hands." Sabasitiano's witnesses speak of him [Sabasitiano] as "Bikaba's brother," but the widow and the will say that Bikaba had no brothers. The decision refers to the gathering at the funeral feast as the "gathering of the village," not the clan. Discussing all this with the chairman of the court, I learned that the "clan of Baisekantu" was a legal fiction. The area had been largely depopulated by sleeping sickness and now was peopled in the main by recent immigrants with no local kinship ties. Bumali was a parish chief, transferred to the community from another area. He had been a friend of Bikaba, as also had Sabasitiano, Bikaba's partner in the smithing craft. "Baisekantu" means, roughly, "clan of human beings." Faced with the problem of disposing of the estate of a man with no actual descent-group in the vicinity, the community had constituted itself, for legal purposes, as a descent group and had treated Bikaba's closest associates as if they were his agnates. In this sense, both Bumali and Sabasitiano were his "brothers" and a choice between them was arrived at, taking into account evidence of Bikaba's wishes. Thus, Bumali can say: "I am his brother *because* he left his holding in my hands." And the court has accepted this without explicit discussion. The only evidence in the record that a legal fiction has been brought into play is the argument about "brothers" and the court's reference to the "gathering of the village."

Kalenzi v. *Okawa: trusteeship*

The descent-group, then, "real" or "fictional," [16] exercises the authority to name an heir which makes land rights *butaka*. It can also, for a period, hold land in trust for a minor heir. *Kalenzi* v. *Okawa* (Ssaabawaali, Kigulu, 1949) concerns a holding left by the late Kiribaki, who was survived by two sons (see fig. 16). Kalenzi is the subvillage headman, Okawa the brother of Kiribaki—his *musika ow'enkoba* ("successor of the belt") and *mukuza* ("guardian") of the children. The oldest of the children, Kigenyi, has grown to adulthood ("he pays poll tax"); he held the land for a period, but has now gone elsewhere to work as a teacher. Kalenzi, arguing that this constitutes abandonment, claims it as *kitongole:*

Kigenyi succeeded and he was in that holding for three years and then left it. But after he left it, I found Okawa in it, digging and planting. . . . That's why I gave part of it to another man.

Q: . . . which of you, yourself or Okawa, gave it to Kigenyi?
A: Okawa, head of that lineage, gave it to him.
Q: If you know that Okawa had the power to give it . . . why do you call it yours?
A: Because Kigenyi left it.

The court, however, holds that Okawa may keep the holding in trust for Kiribaki's other son, Yowabu, who is still a minor:

The accuser agrees that the children are there and that Okawa has the responsibility of looking after the children—for whom he is going to keep the holding.

The concept *butaka,* then, protects the rights of an agnatic group. So long as one of its members—a legitimate heir or his trustee—maintains effective occupation, its land lies beyond the grasp of *kitongole*-wielding headmen.

Acquiescence: The Passage of Time and the Sequence of Events

The account of the general law of tenancy given to this point has treated it as essentially ahistorical—as lacking a sense of the passage of time. This distortion must now be corrected.

---

16. See Appendix B for a discussion of "fictions."

In order to bring out as clearly and simply as possible the basic rights and obligations of headmen and tenants, I have thus far discussed cases in which litigation has followed more or less immediately upon the behavior complained of and defended—cases whose histories have been relatively short and simple. But not all cases are of this sort. For one reason or another, rights based upon either *butaka* or *kitongole* may not be asserted at once; then the courts may face the task of evaluating the legal significance of the passage of time and the sequence of events, and for this purpose they require appropriate concepts —concepts of a historical sort. In the law of headmanship, the notions of temporal limitation and historical relativity were found to enter into the arguments in cases of this kind.[17] If, as I have suggested, the law of headmanship and that of individual holdings are closely congruent conceptually, then similar notions should be encountered in the

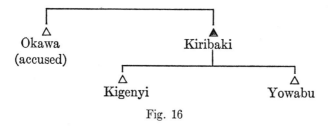

Fig. 16

latter field. In each of the cases to be discussed next, temporal limitation enters as an important concept.

It would, of course, be misleading to suggest that some cases have a historical dimension while others do not. "Objectively," all human action, including that which results in land disputes, takes place in time. And while time may be variously treated by different systems of thought, I would not wish to suggest that *in the minds of Basoga judges and litigants* some disputes have a historical dimension while others do not. All the rights and obligations of headmen and tenants are, I believe, subject to the qualification "within a reasonable time." With sufficient case material and a sufficiently patient audience, one could, I think, demonstrate this with respect to fulfillment of the terms of the contract of allocation, maintenance of effective occupation, and the other rights and duties already outlined.

But cases do differ in the degree to which historical questions become central to the courtroom encounter—the degree to which, in the minds of litigants and judges, they come to turn upon such ques-

17. *Yekoniya Kirya* v. *Matayo Kapere; Lameka Waiswa* v. *Andereya Mpendo.*

tions. In most of the cases discussed so far, such issues were not raised or, if raised, were dismissed as peripheral. In *Sitanule Gowa* v. *Kisubi Mwokyeku,* for example, the issue of whether or not Kisubi had allowed too much time to pass before reclaiming the holding in dispute arose only momentarily and marginally, for Kisubi had, it seems, been quite prompt. In general, rights in individual holdings, like rights in headmanships, tend to wither legally as they are left unasserted; conversely, rights enjoyed tend to become ever more secure. A litigant who has allowed more than a year or two to elapse before asserting or defending his rights invites being asked: "Why have you waited so long?"

There is not, of course, a direct and automatic relationship between the "objective facts" and the way in which the legal process deals with them. A concept enters into that process effectually only when it is taken up and invoked in argument by judge or litigant. Popular and unprofessionalized as Soga jurisprudence is, one cannot assume that all judges and litigants are equally knowledgeable and skilled in handling the common legal culture and hence that the concept of temporal limitation (or any other) is invoked in every case in which it might be relevant. If neither the bench nor his opponent thinks to ask a litigant "Why have you waited so long?" then naturally he need not answer the question and the outcome may be quite different than if he had been required to do so. The notion is, however, a sufficiently common one so that the intelligent litigant whose circumstances make him vulnerable from this direction will anticipate and try to forestall it.

Alamanzani Zirabamuzale v. *Magola Kinyaga: temporal limitation: a concept of credibility*

This is nicely illustrated by *Alamanzani Zirabamuzale* v. *Magola Kinyaga* (Ssaabawaali, Kigulu, 1949), a case in which temporal limitation clearly becomes the crucial issue. Magola has been going around claiming a certain holding in the village of Nyenga as his *butaka,* inherited from his father, Kinyaga. Alamanzani, who now holds it, says it was allotted to him by the headman, Musa Kafero; although Alamanzani is in possession, it is he who sues, in order to get his rights clarified, accusing Magola of "wanting to take. . . ." In his opening statement, Magola is eager to show that he has zealously pursued his *butaka* rights:

I know that I will win because the holding is mine by inheritance. My father died and left it [to me]. He was given it by Sowobi [the village headman]. But Musa [the subvillage headman] stole it from me and gave it to Alamanzani. I accused Musa . . . to the village headman, but he [Musa] refused to come [to litigate], so I beat him "by law." [18] I was given my holding. I don't know Alamanzani, only Musa. I'll litigate with him; I won't litigate with Alamanzani.

This, as it turns out, is very pertinent pleading but, as also shortly becomes evident, it comes too late and constitutes a very selective account of what happened. Alamanzani replies with his own version:

> The holding is mine. It was given me by Musa in 1934. When he says he won't contest with me, he is just trying to find a clever way of taking my holding. That it is not his is shown by the fact that it has been held by six people [since his father died]: Asaka, Mbalabigo, Kawafu, Alamanzani Bin Sowedi, Ali Mugweri, and myself. Once Kinyaga [Magola's father] accused me to the parish chief and the case went against him. The parish chief gave me some emissaries to come and confirm me in my holding.

Then comes the parade of witnesses: three for Magola, two for Alamanzani. They support their principals' stories, but one of Magola's witnesses, under questioning, admits that Magola's father was not buried in the holding and asserts that it has been "two years" (not sixteen) since Musa "stole" it. The commissioners sent by the court to investigate on the spot themselves question various residents of the area and conclude that:

> From the evidence given . . . and from what we have seen, we find that the holding belongs to [Alamanzani]. He has brought people who were the owners before him, to whom the subvillage headman gave it before it was given to him and . . . while the late father of [Magola] was still alive.

With all this in hand, the court produces a decision that marches along almost in *ratio decidendi* fashion:

> It has been found that the holding belongs to the accuser, Alamanzani Zirabamuzale, and that it was given to him by the subvillage headman in 1934. It has been found that it was taken from the hands of Magola's father some time before he died. It was left empty (*kyerere* [19]). It was given to five people. The accused [Magola] has failed to show that he has been using it since his father died. . . . The accused was wrong to go to the accuser and tell him the holding was his; he should have gone directly to the one [Musa] who gave it to the accuser.

Magola has seen that he is open to the argument that he has "waited too long," but neither his claim to have brought the matter before the village headman nor Alamanzani's admission that Magola's father took it to the parish chief is sufficient to meet the point. Clearly, neither father nor son thought enough of his rights to press for a definitive decision in the official A.L.G. courts. Magola's argument that

18. That is, by default. See chapter 2.
19. Or *kitongole*.

he wants to litigate with Musa, not Alamanzani, comes too late. He has pressed his claim upon Alamanzani and now stands accused for this; he no longer has a choice of adversary. His witness tries to save him from the argument that he has waited too long by saying that only two years have passed since Musa "stole" the holding, but the court is satisfied that in fact the elapsed time has been sixteen years (1934 to 1950). Most likely the claim was actually lost long before, when Magola's father died without asserting his rights—if, indeed, he possessed rights. At the conclusion of the case, the chairman remarked to me that the father "must have known that Musa had good reason to reclaim the holding; otherwise he would have taken him to court before he died."

This recalls the comment of the chairman in *Tito Nantamu* v. *Kisubi Mwokyeku*, discussed in chapter 6. In "cutting" that ancient and complex dispute over a headmanship, the court concluded, setting aside a mass of detailed historical testimony, that fifty-odd years was simply too long to wait. Whatever may have been the situation in the past, Tito no longer had a claim. In that case, the chairman explained the decision by saying that Tito "was just waiting for important witnesses to die." These out-of-court judicial remarks say something interesting about the meaning of temporal limitation in Soga land law. Many—perhaps most—legal systems contain some principle of limitation of actions.[20] Generally, however, these notions, whether statutory or customary, are interpreted as resting upon substantive norms of public policy to the effect that ". . . persons should not be vexed by stale claims." [21] With respect to land law specifically, limitation of actions" has for its object the security of titles, which would be jeopardized if ownership could be questioned at any time." [22] Now again, like *res judicata*, temporal limitation is in Busoga no bar to *action,* for the courts are highly permissive in this respect. In *Tito Nantamu* v. *Kisubi Mwokyeku*, the concept was no bar to Tito's bringing suit; it merely stood in the way of his doing so successfully. So also in *Alamanzani Zirabamuzale* v. *Magola Kinyaga:* Magola, the one who waited too long, did not bring suit, though he might easily have done so. But, having been sued, temporal limitation destroyed his defense.

But more than this, the Soga notion, unlike most others apparently, does not relate to any substantive concern for security of tenure; it is rather, in Soga minds, a criterion for assessing *evidence.* The fact that

20. Charles Sumner Lobingier, "Limitation of Actions," pp. 474–80.
21. Allott, *Essays in African Law,* pp. 296–97.
22. Lobingier, "Limitation of Actions."

Tito and Magola waited so long, the judges say, shows that their claims were *never* well founded—shows that their accounts of the *facts* are *implausible*. To revert to the language I adopted in chapter 4, temporal limitation is, in Soga law, a major concept of *credibility*. In that earlier discussion, I suggested a threefold working classification of legal concepts: concepts of wrong, defining a cause for which one man may take another to court; concepts of applicability, by means of which the courts decide whether or not a given set of facts-as-found fall within the reach of the concept of wrong; and concepts of credibility, for ascertaining the facts to be so measured. In the land law, notions concerning, for example, the events constituting legitimate inheritance (proceedings of lineage gatherings, etc.) and allotment (conclusion of valid contracts, etc.) and the conditions for legitimate reversion (failure to maintain effective occupation, etc.) are used to establish the application of *butaka* and *kitongole,* and hence the existence or violation of rights based upon them. Determining whether or not these events have occurred is often a matter of reconstructing the chain of events in some detail, with the aid, of course, of appropriate concepts of credibility. In cases already discussed, courts have applied concepts of bias ("how are you related to the accuser?") [23] and of the lesser value of hearsay ("were you present?") [24] to the testimony of third parties. They have applied biological concepts to determine the probable age of boundary trees.[25] In general, of course, the longer the history of the dispute, the more complex this task of historical reconstruction becomes; but the elaboration of historical argument is checked by the notion that the older the claim, the less plausible, and the more insistent the question: "Why have you waited so long?" I have, however, found no suggestion in any of the cases that it would be *wrong* for a possessor to be "vexed by stale claims," nor did any of the judges with whom I discussed the question see it in this light. The passage of time does not undermine established rights and create new ones; rather it lessens the likelihood that alleged dormant rights have ever existed. (In chapter 8 I shall consider more generally the significance of this tendency in Soga law to treat as questions of fact what in some other legal systems are viewed as matters of substantive law.)

"Temporal limitation" is actually not the best name for the concept under discussion, for it is not concerned with the sheer passage of absolute time. While collecting cases in the field, I was puzzled by my inability to discover anything like a fixed time limit upon the assertion

23. *Nasani Beka* v. *Kibikyo.*
24. *Nasani Beka* v. *Kibikyo.*
25. *Aminsi Waiswa* v. *Sajjabi Kibba.*

of claims to rights in land. Under the influence of the idea of a strictly temporal limitation of actions which appears to be ancient and general in Western legal systems,[26] I was searching for a fixed period of years; but I searched in vain. The reason is this. When the judges ask: "Why have you waited so long?" they have in mind not only the passage of time but also the sequence of events. They want especially to know why the litigant has waited until certain events have taken place before pressing his claim. In *Alamanzani Zirabamuzale* v. *Magola Kinyaga* the difference between two years (Magola's witness) and sixteen (Alamanzani) is doubtless significant, but perhaps even more significant is the fact that since Musa, the headman, reclaimed and reallotted the holding, Magola's father has died and four other persons have been allotted the holding—all this is uncontested—without Magola's asserting his claim. The father should have sued when the land was taken; Magola should have sued when his father died and when he himself inherited the alleged *butaka* rights; again, Magola had additional opportunities to sue each time the land was allotted to a new tenant. It is these acts of *acquiescence* that the court stresses in its judgment, and "acquiescence," I think, is the best name for the concept employed. Acquiescence in events incompatible with the rights claimed acknowledges the factual unsoundness of the claim.

Ezekeri Lyavala v. *Bwiso Isisa: acquiescence; the irrelevance of absolute time*

That the sequence of events is more significant than the passage of absolute time comes out very clearly in *Ezekeri Lyavala* v. *Bwiso Isisa* (Bulamogi county court, 1950), in which rights in a piece of land, presently fallow, are at issue. Ezekeri is acting headman of the village, the steward of the proper headman, who happens to be Ezekeri Wako, pretender to the Zibondoship. Ezekeri Lyavala claims to have been allotted the land "as a place from which to rule" when he was appointed by the Zibondo. At that time, he says, the land in question was "empty," the previous holders having abandoned it or died without leaving heirs. Bwiso's case is that at least part of the land now occupied by Ezekeri is his—Bwiso's—by *butaka* right, having previously belonged to his father, Isisa, and his brothers. As in *Alamanzani Zirabamuzale* v. *Magola Kinyaga*, just discussed, the possessor is the accuser; Ezekeri takes Bwiso to court for "falsely claiming" the land.

26. Lobingier, "Limitation of Actions."

In his opening statement, Ezekeri confronts Bwiso with his own (Bwiso's) acquiescence:

I have heard, but I don't accept Bwiso's argument because I have spent sixteen years in the land, which I was allotted by the subvillage headman, Amosi Muwaya, together with the emissary of Ezekeri Wako (the Zibondo), Erukana Wako [the parish chief].[27] And when I was given the land I still occupy, Bwiso had his own, which he now occupies. So, if he says the land in dispute was his all the time, what has he been doing about accusing me? Has he been away?

The classical question, and it proves to be decisive. First the subcounty, and then the county court (Bwiso appeals) find that not only has Bwiso failed to accuse Ezekeri, but that at least two others have also held the land without interference, after Bwiso's father and before Ezekeri. All this comes out clearly in rather lengthy testimony by the subvillage headman and the Zibondo's emissary and in the reports of the investigating commissions sent out by the subcounty and county courts. However, to follow the full course of the arguments would be redundant and uninteresting. The point I wish to draw from the case is simply that the courts are much more interested in the fact that a series of persons have used the land undisturbed than they are in the period of time involved. In their questioning, both courts are careful to establish that at least two other tenants, Gamutunduka and Kalimongo, have held the land since Bwiso's father ("Those people . . . have they held that land?") and that Bwiso himself has acquiesced in the allotment to Ezekeri ("Were you there?" the judges ask Bwiso; "What did you do?" "Did you complain?"). And both courts repeat both points in their judgments.

The subcounty court:

That land belonged to two other men . . . and this accuser [Ezekeri] was given it when he was given the village of Kaliro in 1945. This other man [Bwiso] had nothing to say.

And the county court:

The case has gone against the appellant Bwiso because . . . he himself agrees that the fallow in question had been occupied by three people.

Yet it is not possible from the case record to date within eleven years the single most important event in the case: the allotment of the land to Ezekeri! The Zibondo's emissary, who ought to know and who

27. Erukana Wako, the parish chief, and Ezekeri Wako, the Zibondo, are both members of the royal clan of Bulamogi, but the agnatic relationship between them is not close.

is under some obligation to tell the truth,[28] says it happened in 1945. He even remembers the day: October 15. Ezekeri himself claims to have held the land for sixteen years, which would place the allotment in 1934. Bwiso, under questioning, puts Ezekeri's tenure at ten years —since 1940. But the courts are utterly careless of the conflict of testimony on dates. The lower court seems to accept 1945, while the county court, in its judgment, speaks of "sixteen years." No attempt is made, in the questioning of litigants and witnesses, to reconcile the testimony and to arrive at the "actual" date. One should not, I think, conclude from this that Basoga are in general indifferent to time or to history. The conclusion to be drawn is rather than in the concept of acquiescence the passage of absolute time is only one element, and not always the most important. A man should claim his rights within a reasonable time after an event that seems to cast doubt upon them. The court in *Ezekeri Lyavala* v. *Bwiso Isisa*, I think, considers that Bwiso has acquiesced several times over. The more precise dating of the allotment to Ezekeri is therefore simply superfluous.

Acquiescence does not always operate to the benefit of the headman in his effort to maximize opportunities to allot. In both the cases just discussed, persons claiming *butaka* rights have failed on the ground that they have acquiesced in the assertion of the *kitongole* power of headmen, but the reverse situation may also arise; a headman who acquiesces may lose his opportunity to reclaim and reallocate. Or rather, as Basoga judges seem to prefer to see it, a headman who claims *kitongole* rights after having acquiesced in events incompatible with these rights will generally not be believed.

Gwampiya Kire v. *Erifazi Birobere: acquiescence; a headman's step-son*

Gwampiya Kire v. *Erifazi Birobere* (Bugabula county court, 1950) illustrates this and at the same time provides some excellent samples of Soga-style close argument. Gwampiya accuses Erifazi, the subvillage headman, of "removing me without reason from my garden, in which I have lived for twenty-four years and which was given me by Balugambire in 1927." The cast of characters here is large enough to warrant a diagram showing their genealogical relations (see fig. 17).

This much is common ground. Gwampiya has indeed occupied the garden since the 1920s, when his mother, a widow named Mudola, married Balugambire, whose brother, Mulyabwire, was then subvillage headman. Mulyabwire allotted the garden to Balugambire to provide

---

28. The emissary (*mubaka*), like the agent (*mukwenda*), has an official status vis-à-vis any litigation arising from the transaction.

for his new wife and her son, then a young boy. Some time later, Mulyabwire died and Balugambire succeeded to the headmanship. Now, within the past three years, first Balugambire and then Mudola have died. Erifazi, grandson of Mulyabwire, has succeeded to the headmanship and also, he claims, to the garden occupied by Gwampiya. "I told him to leave," Erifazi says in his opening statement, "but he refused. So I accused him to the village headman, who decided against him. Then he brought the case here."

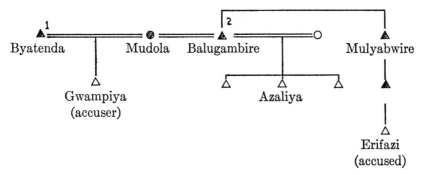

Fig. 17

The back-and-forth succession between two lines within a lineage is fairly common—a recognized means of "holding the clan together." [29] Thus the following exchange between the county bench and Erifazi:

Q: Why were you the successor of Balugambire and not one of his sons?
A: He had sons, and they were given gardens, but the clan gave me the subvillage.
Q: Which son was the heir [30] of Balugambire? Did he agree to your taking the subvillage?
A: It was Azaliya; he joined with [other members of] the clan in giving me the subvillage. . . .
Q: Have you brought Azaliya and the head of the clan [to testify]?
A: I haven't, but I am willing to bring them to court.

They never appear to testify. As often happens, the court accepts willingness to call upon a witness as corroborating evidence on the point in question. In any case, Erifazi's story is plausible; descent-group solidarity is highly valued and the group that can contain its inevitable internal rivalries is admired. Erifazi appears to have his agnatic kinsmen behind him.

But can he evict Gwampiya from the garden he and his mother have

29. See chapter 6.
30. He means: Which son inherited the greater part of Balugambire's land?

occupied for so long? Erifazi asserts that when Balugambire died in 1947 he, Erifazi, inherited that garden along with the headmanship. That the succession lineage intended he *should* inherit it seems clear; at any rate the court accepts it without further discussion. It is also clear that Gwampiya cannot claim *butaka* rights as Balugambire's heir, for he is merely a stepson. In Soga law, widows and stepchildren have no rights whatever in a husband's estate.[31] This is so well known that no one would think of mentioning it. Therefore, although Gwampiya at one point speaks of Balugambire as "my father" (*kitange*),[32] his argument is rather that Balugambire, in his capacity as headman, *allotted* the garden to him as a new tenant. Since it was Balugambire's to give, and since he gave it, Gwampiya argues, Erifazi cannot have inherited it. Balugambire had, so to speak, made it *kitongole*, thus erasing his descent group's *butaka* rights in it, by reclaiming it from himself and allotting it to someone not a member of the group—someone who happened to be his stepson. Furthermore, this has been acquiesced in for more than twenty years.

This argument finally prevails, but not before the bench closely questions both principals and their witnesses. First Gwampiya:

Q: Have you witnesses who can confirm that Balugambire gave you that garden?
A: I have three: Sepiriya Kabola, the village headman, Kirabe and Aminsi Kire, who showed me around the holding [when it was allotted]. . . .
Q: The accused [Erifazi] says that you just went [to that garden] with your mother, but you say that you went as a tenant. Who is right . . . ?
A: The accused is right, but I was quite grown up when I was given the holding.

He came, that is, as a dependent stepchild, but later became a tenant in his own right. One of his witnesses, Aminsi Kire, supports this, somewhat ambiguously:

The garden in question belonged to Balugambire until he died.

Q: And how did Gwampiya come to have it?
A: He came to me and I went to Balugambire on his behalf to ask for it.
Q: . . . first you said it belonged to Balugambire until his death and now you say you took Gwampiya to him to ask for it. Which is correct?
A: That Gwampiya was using it.

The evidence of a real contract of allotment is rather thin here! Nor does the village headman, Sepiriya Kabola, do much to advance Gwampiya's cause:

31. Compare *Genatio Magino* v. *Yowasi Maliwa,* in which a defense against adultery on grounds of step-siblingship failed.
32. See the discussion of Soga kinship terminology in Appendix B.

I was familiar with the late Balugambire's home until he died, but I don't know how the accuser was given that garden.

Q: Is it lawful in your village for a new tenant to be given a garden by the subvillage headman without being introduced to the village headman? [33]
A: It's true that the subvillage headman should introduce him.

The upshot of the testimony by Gwampiya's third witness is much the same. Thus, he has little in the way of a positive case to support the allotment by Balugambire. There is no *mukwenda* (agent), no one who will stand before the court and say: "I was present when Balugambire allotted Gwampiya that garden." And the village headman's denial of knowledge is damaging. But Erifazi's case turns out to have even more fundamental flaws as the bench turns to question him:

Q: Gwampiya says that he has spent twenty-four years in the garden, but you say he just went to visit his mother. Which is correct? [The two statements are not, of course, literally contradictory, but the first tends to affirm Gwampiya's rights, the second to deny them.]
A: My statement is right.
Q: Do you agree that the accuser grew up there and first paid taxes there?
A: I am sure of it.
Q: Did the accuser have another place, which he left?
A: He has nothing else. . . .
Q: Are there any witnesses to testify that the accuser has not used that holding for twenty-four years?
A: Mpango and Waibi; I appeal to them because they know that the accuser was never given that garden, but that it is mine.

Mpango and Waibi are called, but both say, noncommittally, that the land was once Balugambire's, that Gwampiya has occupied it since his mother married Balugambire. "I don't know who gave it to him," Mpango says, and Waibi says the same. All this evades the issue upon which the court is now concentrating: the issue of acquiescence. The court has given Erifazi the opportunity to claim that Gwampiya really belongs somewhere else, but his admission that Gwampiya has occupied the land unchallenged and that he has always paid his poll tax there proves decisive. An adult man does not pay taxes in a community in which he holds no land. By collecting from him, the headmen have affirmed that he is a landholder and citizen. Although there is little *direct* evidence of an allotment by Balugambire, the judges are therefore satisfied. One of them, pointing to Gwampiya, demands of Erifazi:

Q: Is this your man? How long has he lived in your subvillage?
A: [no reply]

33. This is meant ironically to mean something like: "Do you really do things in such a slipshod way in your village?"

And so the decision is arrived at:

> The accuser has won the case. It is true that he owns the garden, which was given him by Balugambire, who had married his mother, Mudola. During the twenty-four years which the accuser has spent in the garden, the accused should have initiated the case. . . .

Erifazi has of course been headman for only three years, since Balugambire's death, but here his name stands for all the headmen— Balugambire and Mulyabwire as well as himself—who have acquiesced in Gwampiya's occupation. Both elements of acquiescence— passage of a substantial period of time (twenty-four years) and the occurrence of relevant events (payment and collection of taxes)—are present and they show, the court reasons, that Gwampiya "owns the garden which was given him by Balugambire." Erifazi's appeal to the county court arguing, correctly enough, that the direct evidence of Balugambire's allotment to Gwampiya is poor ("Did Balugambire give him the garden in secret? He doesn't even call the neighbors to give evidence!") has little success. After desultory questioning of the principals, "the judgment of Mumyuka's court is confirmed."

The Challenge of Change: The Treatment of Novel Tenures

In the account of the law of headmanship given in chapter 6, it was shown that the courts work with another historical concept besides acquiescence: namely, historical relativity. In the cases cited there, the courts took account of the changes through which the institutional framework of headmanship has passed and applied to the events comprising the "facts" of these cases the norms appropriate to the period in which they had occurred. Changes in the institutional environment have also been recognized by the courts in their handling of the law of individual holdings. During the period of my fieldwork, there was a spate of cases in which tenants who had served in the British armed forces during World War II accused headmen of reclaiming and reallotting their holdings during their absence on duty. For these accusers, the courts of course generally relaxed their application of the concepts of acquiescence and maintenance of occupation. A man who returned after three or four years with the King's African Rifles was not considered to have abandoned his land or to have acquiesced in his headman's seizure of it. In general, however, tenancy has been less directly affected by changes in the formal structure of society than has headmanship. The protectorate government and the A.L.G. have not intervened directly in the relationship between tenant and headman as they have in that between the headman and his superiors, and hence, with the exception of the two periods of wartime, one does not find in tenancy cases evidence of concepts of periodization of the sort that came out in litigation over headmanships. In the law of tenancy, change has been more in the nature of a gradual drift toward recognition of greater individualization, contractualization, and commercialization.

An instance of this has already been encountered in *Asumani Wagubi* v. *Musa Kafero*. In that case, though the issue was never made very explicit, some of the participants seemed to assume that land rights were an incident of political status—community membership—while others treated these as independent of each other. The court, again without explicit statement, accepted the latter view; Asumani, it was held, had maintained effective occupation, even though he had moved his residence to another village, because he had continued to "use" the land. Today most Basoga judges would, I believe, agree; hence my use of the case in illustration of the present-day "general law of tenancy." But there is also present in *Asumani Wagubi* v. *Musa Kafero* an element which, in the minds of many judges, should have defeated Asumani: after removing his residence to another community, Asumani had not continued to cultivate the land with his own hands and for his own household's sustenance and income. He himself said that he "lent" it (*kwazika*) to others to use. Although the court accepted this without comment as constituting continued "use," in fact the legal status of "lending" is highly problematical. It is today the vehicle for novel forms of tenure concerning whose legitimacy the courts are by no means agreed. In considering these, one enters that area of the land law which is most unsettled—which is productive of litigation not only because persons, knowing the law, attempt to evade it to their own benefit, but because there is reasonable doubt about what the law is.

I shall therefore conclude this account of the growth of a law of tenancy with a series of cases which, I believe, might easily have been decided differently had they come before other judges. There is much evidence of uncertainty: split decisions, appeals, reversals upon appeal, and seeming contradictions among final dispositions. One finds it difficult to account, on the basis of differences between sets of facts-as-found, for some of the differences between decisions. No doubt this is partly a product of inadequate data and insufficient analytic penetration. Nor, presumably, is any body of law ever entirely settled and certain; a certain measure of variance is "natural." But the existence of a real and marked legal uncertainty with respect to just those forms of tenancy with which these cases are concerned does, I suggest, make sense in the light of some of the changes at work in Soga society today. In these cases, judges encounter disputes which they find it difficult to resolve because they arise out of tenure arrangements not foreseen by their received body of concepts, arrangements involving greater individualization and commercialization. In some cases—I am tempted to say "wherever possible"—novel findings of "facts" seem to be pressed and pared to make them amenable to older modes of conceptualization. Only in cases in which the new wine very obviously overflows the old bottles do judges seem to break with the received conceptual structure.

New forms of tenure, as I have said, often involve the notion of "lending." Now the lending of land on short term in exchange for a fee or a portion of the crop is in fact not uncommon today, and perhaps has always occurred. For example, a young man, recently married, may be lent a plot by a neighbor or kinsman with more land than he presently cares to cultivate in order to maintain himself and his wife until such time as he can find a proper holding. Some headmen keep aside a bit of *kitongole* for this purpose. Often enough, such arrangements are entered into, and subsequently dissolved, quite amicably. But this presupposes a mutual understanding and consensus among lender, lendee, and headman, for transactions of this kind are not well protected by the general law of tenancy as understood by most judges.

This law, to repeat, knows only two categories of land: *butaka*, in which members of a descent-group possess hereditary rights; and *kitongole*, which is free of such rights (except, of course, for the hereditary rights of the headman's descent-group in the headmanship itself), and hence is available for allotment. The contract of allotment transforms *kitongole* into *butaka;* abandonment or depletion of the tenant descent-group transforms *butaka* into *kitongole*. This conceptual scheme envisages a community of peasant descent-groups engaged in subsistence agriculture and bound in political loyalty to a headman. The "purpose" of land (for people do moralize along these lines) is to support this political community—this institutional structure. One might say that the *meaning* of *kitongole* is "land available for allotment in order to establish new headman-tenant ties"; and that *butaka means* "land entailed for the support of a continuing descent-group." Lending violates this scheme. A headman who, for consideration, lends his *kitongole* instead of creating new political ties with it is misusing it; so also is a tenant who does the same with his *butaka* instead of cultivating it for the support of his household. While lending *may* be carried out in all innocence and charity, the law does not know how to distinguish the generous headman or the good neighbor from the profiteer. One may perhaps say that in that case the judges are suffering under a tyranny of concepts—that they have become prisoners of their own tools. I shall argue presently that such "rigidity" is an understandable concomitant of legal change. It will, however, be best to defer this argument until the case material which provides the data for it has been presented.

Lending is poorly protected by the law in the sense that a person who attempts to repossess land that he claims to have "just lent" will rarely succeed. It will be very difficult for him to convince the court that the land has not passed completely into the hands of the borrower to become the *butaka* of his descent group. Frequently the concept of acquiescence becomes the vehicle for this presumption, as in *Kaluna Mukungu* v. *Musa Bin Juma* (Ssaabawaali, Kigulu, 1950).

Kaluna Mukungu v. *Musa Bin Juma: the rigidity of categories; "lending" rejected.*

It is agreed by all parties that the land in question here had belonged to one Abudala Byayi, father of Musa. However, nine years earlier, in 1941, Abudala had moved to another village, and from this point the accounts of "the facts" diverge. Kaluna claims that, before leaving, Abudala "sold" him the land. Musa counters with the assertion that the land was merely "lent" to Kaluna so that he might build a shop on it. Musa was then away at school, he says, and the village headman, Kibiwe, was instructed by Abudala to turn it over to Musa when he returned to set up a household. Accordingly, "in 1945, when I left school, it was given to me. Then I started to cultivate and Kaluna said nothing. But when he saw me cultivating this year . . . he started to abuse me." Kaluna now accuses Musa of "cultivating my land and cutting my *nsambya* trees and yams." Abudala cannot, of course, have "sold" or allotted the land to Kaluna by himself, for only a headman has that authority. Kaluna's case, as one of his witnesses testifies, is that he (Kaluna) paid Abudala twenty shillings for the land and that the headman, Kibiwe, was present and gave his consent. In other words, Abudala vacated the land, leaving it *kitongole*, and Kibiwe allotted to Kaluna. The witness, Sabani Kisubi, claims to have been present and to have written a "contract" of sale, though no such document is presented to the court.

The key witness would seem to be Kibiwe, the headman. He stands before the court and supports Musa completely:

I know that the land which Musa claims is his because when Abudala was leaving the place he came to me and said: "The land which I have left will be given to Musa after he leaves school." And I'm surprised to hear that Kaluna is claiming land that doesn't belong to him.

The judges also believe that Kibiwe is the key witness, but they have not yet heard all they want to hear from him:

Q: When did you give the boy the land that Abudala asked you to keep?
A: In 1945.
Q: What do you know about Kaluna's being lent the plot?
A: I know that he was just lent it for the purpose of building a shop.

Notice now how the noose tightens:

Q: For how long did you keep the land for Musa?
A: For three years.
Q: Did the accused plant his bananas while you were still keeping it?

(To this point we have heard nothing about bananas.)

A: No, he planted them after I had given it to Musa.
Q: Did Musa bring a case against Kaluna after seeing him plant the bananas?
A: No, he didn't bring a case.

Then Musa's father, Abudala, is called to testify and he also corroborates Musa's story. He is questioned:

Q: Kaluna states that you sold him the land and made a contract with him and also that he planted bananas. How is that?

(Actually it was the headman who, led on by the court, had spoken of bananas.)

A: I have never sold him the land or made an agreement with him. He just went ahead and planted the bananas on his own.
Q: . . . when did you know that Kaluna had planted bananas. . . . ?
A: I knew it in 1947 [three years earlier].
Q: What did you do then? Did you bring a case against him?
A: No, I didn't. . . .
Q: As you didn't accuse him when he planted bananas, is he right, now, to say that you sold him the land?
A: No, he is wrong to say so, for I have no power to sell land by myself without the headman.

The investigating commissioners then report, *inter alia*, that "in the land for which they are contesting, we found graves where Kaluna had buried his people." It is clear, then, what the decision will be:

From the evidence . . . , it has been seen that the land *belongs* to Kaluna, the accuser, for he has a banana garden in it and also potatoes and cotton. He planted all these things . . . in full view of Byayi and Kibiwe and they had the power to prevent him if it was not *his land* and they never sold it to him, as they claim.

One does not know, of course, what "really" happened, but there is hardly overwhelming direct evidence to support Kaluna's story that he was "sold" (or allotted) the land. The testimony on this is conflicting, with the headman supporting Musa. But the court, significantly, takes no interest in the notion of "lending." There is no consideration of what the respective rights of lender and borrower might be, for the court never accepts the possibility of such a transaction. The land is either Musa's or Kaluna's, in the full sense of land entailed for the use of a descent group. (This is the meaning of "belongs to Kaluna" and "his land" in the decision.) Since Musa, Abudala, and Kibiwe acquiesced in Kaluna's planting of bananas—a long-term investment [34] —and his burying of kinsmen (the decision doesn't mention this, but it will have been an important consideration; an ancestor's grave is perhaps the firmest circumstantial evidence in support of a claim to land), they must have intended to transfer full rights in the land to him. The case makes apparent the nature of the problem faced by the litigant who claims to have lent and wishes to repossess. The general law of tenancy knows only *butaka* and *kitongole* and only one sort of land acquisition, apart from lineage-mediated inheritance: namely, the contract of allotment, in which the only variable terms are the amount of the consideration and the identity of the land. The major subsidiary concept employed—acquiescence—tends to push land into either the *butaka* or the *kitongole* category. For "lending" to acquire legal protection, the notion of contract for a period of time or for specified use must be developed.

Asupasa Kibalya v. Kaligya Nume: a chairman's dissent; criteria for "lending"

Asupasa Kibalya v. *Kaligya Nume* (Bugabula county court, 1950) shows some movement in this direction. I shall cite the case only very briefly, for the circumstances are very similar to those in *Kaluna Mukungu* v. *Musa Bin Juma*. Before he died, one Kibalya left his garden in the hands of the headman (who also happened to be head of the succession lineage), in trust for his son, Asupasa. The headman claims to have lent it to Kaligya during Asupasa's minority. Now Asupasa claims it, with the support of the headman. In the subcounty court, Asupasa wins on the ground that "his witness, the headman, has given evidence that the garden belongs to him." But in an interesting dissent, the chairman adds:

---

34. Properly tended, a banana garden will bear for many decades. Each stem bears only one bunch, but new stems come up from the root.

All the [other] members agree with this decision, but in my opinion the garden belongs to the accused, Kaligya. He must have been given [not lent] it because . . . he has no other garden such as the headman would have given him if he had lent him that one.

Here the chairman is trying to work into the body of legal ideas criteria for one legitimate form of lending. A headman lends to a prospective tenant while looking for a holding to allot to him in the regular way. Since, it comes out, seventeen years have passed, the headman cannot have tried very hard to find such a plot. The land lent (if it was lent) thus becomes a regular holding. On appeal, the county judges reverse the decision. Siding with the subcounty chairman against his colleagues, they add a further criterion: "The headman says that he entrusted the garden to Kaligya, but he does not indicate the period of time for which he intended him to hold it." Thus, the possibility of a contract for a term of years is recognized.

In *Kaluna Mukungu* v. *Musa Bin Juma* and *Asupasa Kibalya* v. *Kaligya Nume,* lending has eventuated in the borrowers' acquiring full rights in the land; it has become the *butaka* of their descent-groups. But of course the other possibility, in terms of the received conceptual scheme, is that the land may become *kitongole.* In the above two cases, the headman has, by his own admission, been a party to the lending, and has also joined in the acquiescence.

Yasoni Salamuka v. *Mutono Wangaiza: an attempted sub-tenancy*

In *Yasoni Salamuka* v. *Mutono Wangaiza* (Bulamogi county, 1950), the headman, Yasoni, dissociates himself from the transaction and argues, successfully, that since he was not consulted, the land returns to him as *kitongole;* Mutono, the lender, has established an illegal subtenancy. So Yasoni accuses Mutono of "falsely claiming" and Mutono responds:

I don't agree that the case goes against me because there is someone who allotted the land to me—Yowasi Nyiro—and the emissary who installed me was Gideoni Gwolwo. Later I brought my in-law, Tigatola, and lent him that part. He died in 1949 and the heirs did not want to stay there. But one of them, Tibigaitwa, returned without my knowledge and [later] I saw that he had marked off a piece with *birowa* saplings and sold it to another person, Magino. But I had taken it back into my hands when the heirs all left it, so I went and told my master, [Yasoni] Salamuka, and he told me to [return later]. But whenever I went to the headman, Tibigaitwa failed to appear. It seemed that he had joined with the headman in selling that land. . . . Then Yasoni called me and said: "You gave away land that wasn't yours."

The excellent report of the subcounty commission of inquiry contains a sketch-map showing the layout of the land in dispute (see fig. 18).

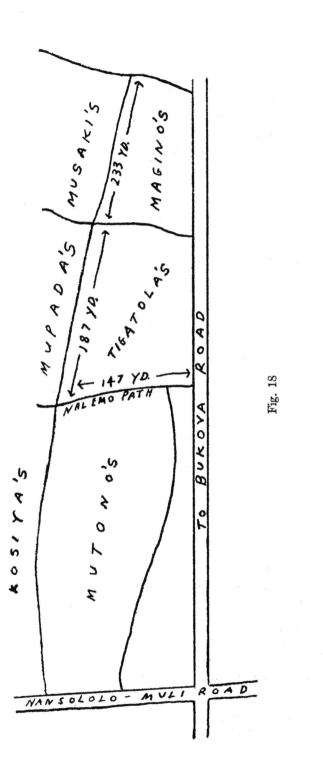

Fig. 18

There are actually, by Mutono's account, two levels of subtenancy here: Mutono "lent" part of his holding to Tigatola and the latter's heir in turn "sold" a part of the lent portion to Magino. Both Mutono and the headman, Yasoni, now claim the parts marked "Tigatola's" and "Magino's."

The case-file is a thick one, for much evidence is presented in both subcounty and county courts (Mutono loses and appeals). Many witnesses testify on both sides and lengthy reports are received from two commissions of inquiry. Much of the evidence is concerned with the original allotment to Mutono, which Yasoni contests. There is also much testimony concerning a notorious local scandal. At one point, it seems, part of the land in question was briefly used by three young servants of the subcounty chief, who molested Mutono's daughter and were driven away at his insistence. Yasoni and his witnesses argue that Mutono's acquiescence in this brief occupation (until the incident with the daughter) makes the land *kitongole*. The subcounty court mentions both these arguments in deciding against Mutono. For present purposes, however, a third element in the case is more interesting. It appears first in the questions addressed to Mutono by the subcounty judges:

Q: When you found out that Tibigaitwa had cut off and sold a part, why did you accuse him to the headman? You agree that he is the heir [of Tigatola]. Did he do wrong to sell the land he had inherited?
A: He did wrong in selling it without telling me. As *kitongole* it would escape me; I would no longer control it; it would go out of my hands.

Mutono recognizes clearly enough what the issue is from his own standpoint. If his subtenant successfully transfers his interest to another, the residual rights Mutono claims will be extinguished. But he seems not to see that, by the same reasoning, his own earlier "lending" to Tigatola endangers the headman's residual interest. The judges' concern about this comes out clearly when Mutono is questioned in the county court:

Q: When you gave that land to your in-law, Tigatola, were you a headman?
A: No, I was only a peasant. I just lent that land. . . .
Q: When you lent that land to Tigatola, did you agree to a time for which he would use it?
A: We didn't agree to a time because he was my in-law.

(As chapters 4 and 5 will have made clear, affinal relationships in Busoga are such that men usually hope to have friendly dealings with their in-laws and are usually disappointed.)

Q: When you lent Tigatola that holding, did you take him to the village or subvillage headman?

A: I didn't take him.
Q: Why didn't you take him?
A: Because I was just lending my own land.
Q: When the headman says he didn't know that you lent to Tigatola, then, is he correct?
A: Yes.

So the county decision, too, goes against him:

> When he was lending Tigatola that land, no one was present at all. Neither subvillage nor village headman knew. . . . The decision of subcounty Ssaabagabo is confirmed. The disputed land is not his, but rather *kitongole,* to be allotted . . . by headmen.

Mutono seems naïve, both about in-laws and about the implications of his own arguments, but his naïvete helps to bring out some of the legal uncertainties of "lending." Again, since "lent" is not an accepted category for land to occupy, the judges' inclination is to treat it as either *butaka* or *kitongole.* Mutono has relinquished his own claim by transfering the land to Tigatola and, not being a headman, he cannot retain residual rights on behalf of his descent-group and himself. Were a tenant able to do this, he would be making himself a headman— which is what the subcounty judges are charging him with when they ask: "were you a headman?" The only remaining possibility, then, in terms of the received categories, is that the land has become *kitongole.* In fact, things have, in the courts' view, gone a stage further: Yasoni, the headman, seems to have accepted the transfer from Tigatola's heir, Tibigaitwa, to Magino, and most likely has participated in it by collecting an allotment fee from Magino. The court is thus recognizing what has already taken place: The headman has exercised his *kitongole* right to reclaim, since Mutono has relinquished his holding, and has reallotted it to Magino.

Thus far, then, the courts have rejected lending as a legal concept applying to land in the sense that they have in each case denied the lender a residual interest on the basis of which he might reclaim. Either the land has been found to have become the *butaka* of the borrower's descent-group, through the acquiescence of the lender and the headman, or it has been declared to have become *kitongole* on the ground that the lender has relinquished his rights. There have been suggestions that the courts might recognize and enforce a contract of lending for a definite period, which presumably means that such contracts are sometimes entered into; judges, in fact, told me they had heard of such. Unfortunately, however, I was unable to find a case in which the question had been litigated. One can only guess that, with the increasing commercialization of land rights and the growing use of

written contracts, an increase in such practices and their legitimation
by the courts is in the offing, despite the hostility with which many
Basoga continue to regard them. I did, however, find two cases in
which the residual rights of a lender had been recognized. The first is
interesting because the change in judicial reasoning involved is subtle
and very implicit, the second because it involves an explicit acceptance
of contractual specificity, although the terms specified pertain to the
use to which the land might be put rather than to the period of the
lending.

Mpaulo Wakaze v. *Malagala Musenero: injustice or change?*

The first case, *Mpaulo Wakaze* v. *Malagala Musenero* (Bugabula
county court, 1950), looks, upon first inspection, very much like
Kaluna Mukungu v. *Musa Bin Juma* and *Asupasa Kibalya* v. *Kaligya
Nume,* except that, unaccountably, the decision goes the other way.
The lender is allowed to repossess. The "facts" agreed to by all parties
are these. Malagala, a young man without land, had been living with
his father, Febiano Kibi, and lacked money with which to pay his poll
tax. Mpaulo needed help with his cultivation and so, in 1948, he agreed
to pay Malagala's tax in exchange for labor. Malagala asserts that
Mpaulo also "gave" him a plot in which to cultivate his food and build
his hut. Mpaulo says he only "lent" the garden, and now he accuses
Malagala for refusing to vacate.

In the subcounty court, Mpaulo's account of the affair is supported
by his son and by a neighbor, both of whom say they were present at
the lending. Malagala's father, Febiano, supports Malagala's story,
but admits to not having been present when the arrangement was
made. Yoweri Kamya, the acting subvillage headman, also says he was
not present, but testifies that, in his official capacity, he later collected
tax from Malagala as a resident of the subvillage. The court decides in
favor of Mpaulo: "Mpaulo just lent [Malagala] the land as his
laborer." This decision, the court adds, has been arrived at because
Mpaulo's witnesses speak from direct personal knowledge of the transaction, while Malagala's do not. The latter "do not help him."

At this stage, it is difficult to put one's finger on the difference,
whether of "facts" or of judicial reasoning, that allows Mpaulo to
succeed where Musa Bin Juma and Asupasa Kibalya failed. The
element of acquiescence that defeated the latter seems to be present
here, too. The acting headman, at any rate, clearly knew that Malagala was occupying and using the land, for he collected tax from him.
But the court ignores this and seems to take its stand on the narrow
ground of the relative value of direct, as against indirect, evidence.

Perhaps the time has been too short (only two years) for acquiescence to apply. With direct, and fresh, evidence that only lending was intended, the judges are willing to return the land to the lender.

But in his appeal to the county court, Malagala raises the acquiescence issue so compellingly that it seems difficult to ignore:

> If he says he just lent to me, did he prevent me from planting bananas? The [subcounty court] says that I have no [direct] evidence, but what about the banana plants and the *birowa* [boundary saplings] . . . aren't they enough evidence [of allotment]? He . . . said that I just went there as a laborer, but can a laborer plant bananas or can *birowa* be planted from him [as a boundary]? I ask the court to choose commissioners to . . . question my neighbors. The *birowa* and the bananas which I planted, are my contract.

The argument for the application of the concept of acquiescence could hardly have been put more eloquently. Mpaulo and the acting headman have allowed him to make the long-term investment of planting a banana garden; they have planted boundary saplings, as is done when a regular allotment is made. Other courts have accepted such "facts" as indicators of acquiescence, but here that notion is not even alluded to when the case comes before the county court. Essentially the same evidence is given by the same witnesses. This time the headman, as well as the acting headman, appears. Both deny direct knowledge of the transaction between Mpaulo and Malagala, though again the acting headman speaks of having collected tax from him, and the headman says he believes that the acting headman allotted to him.[35] And again, after observing that Mpaulo's witnesses were present, while Malagala's were not, the court decides for Mpaulo, concluding:

> It has been found that Malagala is falsely claiming a garden which was just lent him to [grow his] food while he was working for Mpaulo. If he had been giving it to him, he [Mpaulo] would not have failed to introduce him to the headmen. The judgment of the court of Musaale is confirmed.

If it were possible for me to speak from within the Soga legal system, I should say that Malagala had been wronged—that these were "bad" or "incorrect" or "biased" decisions, for it is hard to see why Malagala's argument concerning acquiescence should not carry the day, as similar arguments have in similar cases. One is tempted to see in the case an injustice to a landless youth, forced by poverty to hire himself out to earn his bananas and his taxes. Some other courts, I think, would have reasoned: the fact that Malagala was allowed to cultivate a banana garden shows that a regular allotment was in fact

35. The village headman, however, became so contradictory in his testimony that he was charged, in a separate action, with perjury.

made to him by Mpaulo and the acting headman. "The bananas," Malagala says, quite brilliantly, "are my contract." Now, having enjoyed his labor for two years, Mpaulo is trying, wrongfully, to go back on the bargain. In any case, what is of primary interest from the point of view of the aims of this study is the manner in which the judges arrive at their decisions. From this point of view, even "bad" decisions may be "good" data. Whether justly or unjustly, the judges here have reasoned differently and I am inclined to see in this difference evidence of a change toward greater recognition of "lending" as a legally protected transaction in land.

The change (or at least difference) comes out clearly in the county court's decision: "If he had been giving [the land] to him, he would not have failed to introduce him to the headmen." The burden of proof has shifted from the lender to the borrower. In the cases previously discussed, it was for the person who claimed to have just lent to show that he had not, in allowing the alleged borrower to behave like a full tenant (by planting bananas, etc.), accepted that he was such. In this case, the court says such acquiescence (which is never explicitly challenged) is insufficient; it is instead for the person who claims to have received full rights as a tenant to show by direct evidence that a regular contract of allotment was entered into with a headman. Malagala's bananas will *not* serve as his contract.

Swaliki Balita v. *Zadoki Mugalya: contractual specificity upheld*

Finally, in *Swaliki Balita* v. *Zadoki Mugalya* (Busoga district court, 1950), one finds a decision based squarely and explicitly upon the specified terms of a written contract. Significantly, the case comes from Butembe-Bunya, the area in which land rights have become most individualized and commercialized, and in which litigation over land is most common.[36] Even so, there is much evidence, as the case is appealed through the whole Soga court system, of judicial reluctance to break with the received conceptual structure.

The land in question belonged to the late Yusufu Balita and is located in the village of Sikiro, where a small trading center has grown up. Yusufu allowed a number of shopkeepers, including Zadoki, to put up shops on his land. Now, however, Yusufu has died and he is survived by two sons: Dausoni Magumba, the elder, and a younger son, Swaliki, who claims to have inherited the land occupied by Zadoki's shop (see fig. 19).

Zadoki has recently begun to build a "permanent" building (that is,

36. See table 8.

one made of bricks instead of the more common wattle-and-daub) on the plot and both Swaliki and the headman have tried to stop him. When Zadoki persists, Swaliki takes him to court for "building a building by force on my land, which was only lent to him by my father." He fears that if Zadoki is allowed to build in brick, he will become more than a mere borrower. Responding to Swaliki's accusation, Zadoki gives his account of the transaction to the subcounty court:

> The land was given to me on July 8, 1945. I first went to Dausoni and told him I needed a plot on that land. He then took me to his father and his father told him to give me the land I wanted. He said I should first pay a fee, so I gave him twenty-five shillings to be handed on to Yusufu. Yusufu told Dausoni that after giving me the land, he should make a contract with me. So after showing me the land . . . he made out a contract.

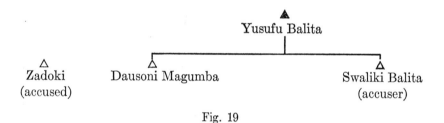

Fig. 19

When Dausoni appears to testify the court wants to hear from him the nature of this contract:

Q: Were you sent by Yusufu Balita to give Zadoki the land?
A: I was sent to lend it, not to give it.
Q: What did you do in lending it?
A: I marked a boundary so he wouldn't encroach on the garden of Babirye, Yusufu's wife.

(Dausoni does not want the establishment of the boundary to solidify Zadoki's claim, so he explains it simply as a protection—presumably temporary—for Babirye's garden.)

Q: How long was he to use it?
A: No definite time was agreed upon, but he said that he had a shop at Nakivumbi and wanted to try out his luck here, too. If it went well, he would find a holding of his own [a regular allotment].
Q: Was Swaliki in charge of the land?
A: Yusufu was the owner, but after his death Swaliki took over. . . .
Q: Do you admit that you wrote this letter [the contract, which Zadoki has shown to the court] allowing Zadoki to build his building . . . ?
A: Yes. . . .

Before coming to a decision, the court questions Swaliki:

Q: Is this land in dispute really yours, or do you just claim it because it belonged to your father?
A: It is mine; he gave it to me while he was still alive.
Q: If he gave it to you, why did he lend it to Zadoki? Where were you?
A: I was staying in Jinja [37]. . . .
Q: What did you do when you heard the land had been lent to Zadoki?
A: Yusufu told me he had lent it to him for only a short time while he looked for a holding of his own. . . .
Q: Why did you not accuse your father when he gave the land?
A: . . . because he told me Zadoki would stay for only a short time.

Notice that the judges have laid the groundwork for two alternative ways of viewing the case. On the one hand, in questioning Swaliki they have begun to build up a case for Zadoki on the basis of acquiescence. If Yusufu, before his death, had already indicated that Swaliki was to have the land, why did Swaliki not take steps to stop the transfer to Zadoki? If he did try to stop it, and failed, does this not show that Yusufu meant Zadoki to have the land? This way of viewing the case presupposes the received framework of concepts. Land must be either *kitongole* or else someone's *butaka*—in this case either that of Zadoki and his descent-group or that of Swaliki and his descent-group. Evidence of acquiescence is customarily used to decide among these alternatives. On the other hand, the judges have shown much interest in the contract, as if its terms were to be of crucial significance. This is, in fact, the path the judges choose. The document does not appear in the case file, but in the decision it is paraphrased:

It is obvious that the land is not Zadoki's. He calls upon the testimony of Dausoni Magumba, the emissary of Yusufu Balita, but Dausoni's testimony differs from his. Dausoni states that the land was only lent to [Zadoki]. . . . Zadoki produced a paper which he considers to be a contract given him by Dausoni, [but this] allows him to put up only a temporary building, though [it may have] a corrugated iron roof.[38] Therefore, Zadoki has no evidence to support him. . . . He hasn't the right to erect a permanent building without the permission of Swaliki Balita.

Having chosen to regard the terms of the contract as decisive, the judges have, for purposes of this case, rejected the acquiescence argument, and with it the received framework to which it belongs. They have accepted "lending" as a transaction—as a form of tenure. They have broadened the scope for contractual specificity in the law of tenancy.

---

37. Jinja is the nearest substantial urban area with employment to offer.
38. Corrugated iron is very popular as a roofing material because, unlike the traditional thatch, it is fireproof.

It is, however, instructive that this does not occur without a struggle. Zadoki, of course, is dissatisfied as, in terms of expectations based upon the existing legal culture, he has every right to be. In his appeal to the county court, he stresses the acquiescence argument: for four years after he took possession of the plot (1945–49), Swaliki "did nothing." As a second line of defense he argues that, assuming the land was only "lent," it is up to the lender to show that a definite time was specified in the contract: "[Dausoni] was asked [by the lower court] how long I was to be allowed to occupy the land, but he answered that no specific time was given." These arguments convince the county court and the decision is reversed:

> Swaliki took his complaint to his father, but he was not heard. This shows that Yusufu Balita gave Zadoki the land. Swaliki should have tried to settle this matter with his father before he died.

A classical judgment on traditional grounds, but of course Swaliki, having tasted victory in the lower court, does not easily yield. He in turn appeals to the district court arguing, as he had successfully done before, that "Dausoni . . . was only empowered to lend the land, not to give it out [permanently]." And the district court again reverses the decision:

> Dausoni Magumba admits that a contract was given to Zadoki, but says that the land was not given, but only lent. There is evidence for this, for the period for which he was to use the land was not specified.

Zadoki's argument about the burden of proof has been turned against him: in a lending transaction, it is for the *borrower* to show how long his rights run; otherwise, presumably, he occupies the land at the pleasure of the lender. Zadoki tries once more, petitioning the British district commissioner for revision. But, as usually happens, the D.C. upholds the judgment of the last Soga court, defeating Zadoki and accepting the district court's view of the importance of the terms of the contract and the locus of the burden of proof:

> Documentary evidence was . . . produced in the form of a letter permitting the petitioner to build a temporary structure only on the piece of land at issue. I am not satisfied that the petitioner has proved conclusively that any specific agreement was made transferring the land to him . . . for an unspecified period.

If the Soga courts were expected, and equipped, to operate under a system of precedent, a new departure in the Soga law of tenancy would have been established here. There would be no more decisions like those in *Kaluna Mukungu* v. *Musa Bin Juma* and *Asupasa Kibalya* v. *Kaligya Nume*. In the absence of such a system, however, the lower courts will not be expected to conform to *Swaliki Balita* v. *Zadoki Mugalya;* they will, in fact, be very unlikely even to hear of it. Similar decisions may well have been made before and incompatible ones will doubtless continue to be made. Without the directional guide of precedent (or legislation), legal change must proceed haltingly and uncertainly.

RECAPITULATION: THE EVIDENCE OF CHANGE

What, indeed, is the evidence that any real change at all has taken place? Although I have given this chapter the subtitle "The Growth of a Law of Tenancy" and have arranged the discussion of cases in such a way as to suggest a directional development, I must make it clear that this suggestion does not rest upon any direct historical evidence of trends in judicial thought and behavior. All the cases here discussed were decided within the same two-year period: 1949–51. But these contemporaneous cases do exhibit a significant range of variation in the way in which land rights are viewed by litigants and judges, and I suggest that the hypothesis of a trend toward greater individualization, commercialization, and contractual specificity is the best explanation for this range. In the light of other evidence of change in the socioeconomic environment of the law of land, one may legitimately view contemporary differences in legal ideas as ranging from the conservative to the avant-garde. One may say that the thinking of the judges in *Swaliki Balita* v. *Zadoki Mugalya* is in advance of that of their colleagues in *Kaluna Mukungu* v. *Musa Bin Juma,* and not merely different from it.

One might, of course, argue that these differences in legal thought merely reflect long-standing regional variations in landholding and land use within Soga society. There certainly is good evidence of regional variation in the frequency of land litigation [39] today and more than a little to suggest correlative variation in landholding arrangements and patterns of dispute.[40] But these regional differences themselves may, I think, be regarded as differences in the degree to which common processes of socioeconomic change have thus far affected the various parts of the country. What Butembe-Bunya is today, Bulamogi seems likely to become. As for the judges, although their early experiences of land disputes in their home counties may perhaps give

39. Table 8.
40. I was told by both Basoga judges and British administrative officers that the newer, often "illegal," kinds of land transactions are much commoner in Butembe-Bunya than elsewhere.

them different initial perspectives on their work, the frequency with which they are transferred about tends to expose them to the full Busoga-wide range of ideas and practices in land matters. Though it lacks the homogenizing effect of a precedent system, the possession of a single corps of highly mobile judges effectively makes of Busoga a single legal jurisdiction. If some judges, at a particular point in time, are more advanced in their views than the majority of their brethren, there is every reason to believe that these views will be shared at some time in the future by a majority of their successors.

Let me recapitulate, then, the development in Soga land law that seems to have occurred since the establishment of British administration in the nineties of the last century.

The basic concepts in the law of land—both that part of it which is concerned with headmanships and that part which pertains to individual holdings—are *butaka* and *kitongole*. These concepts are grounded in two leading institutional features of Soga society: the corporate, patrilineal descent-group and the dyadic relationship between superior and subordinate. These notions seem to have been used both politically and legally in the nineteenth century, but legally only with respect to headmanships; there is no evidence of their legal use in connection with individual holdings until quite recently, for cases of this sort have not, until recently, come before the A.L.G. courts. The reason for this, I have suggested, is that so long as the headmen were full members of the political hierarchy, sharing in its rewards through the *bwesengeze* and tribute systems, there was a community of interest between headman and peasant in the peasant's security of tenure. With the destruction of this community of interest, both headmen and peasants have tended to pursue their economic interests in land at each others' expense.

In this context, as litigation over individual holdings has increased, the courts have developed, out of received ideas applied to the experience of new conditions, a "general law of tenancy"; the scope of *butaka* and *kitongole* rights has been defined, with the aid of new subsidiary concepts. While this law is generally understood by most Basoga as defining the proper way of handling land, disputes continue to arise for two reasons: first, because there *is* real conflict of interests with respect to land, and hence persons seek to profit by behaving contrary to the law; and second, because the increasing individualization and commercialization of interests in land continues to lead to novel transactions whose "legality" or "illegality" is genuinely problematical.

In chapters 4 through 7, I have tried to illustrate, with reference to the two areas of Soga life which have been left most completely to "customary law," the manner in which the Soga courts develop and apply legal concepts. In the final chapter which follows, I shall review the findings of this study in the light of some anthropologists' and lawyers' ideas about the nature of the legal and will attempt a brief glance into the probable future of the Soga courts and their law.

As the verdicts (in English jury trials) intermingled issues of law with questions of fact, it was only to the extent that the judges freed the properly legal from the factual portions of the verdict and articulated the former as legal principles, that these verdicts could become part of a growing body of law.
—Max Weber

8 Soga Law Considered

I began this book with a comparative discussion to which I promised to return after presenting an analysis of the Soga courts and their law. In this final chapter I shall, first, reexamine the Soga material in the light of my earlier discussion of the nature of the legal, drawing out what seem to me the characteristic features of Soga law. Second, I shall compare this law, and the institutions through which it operates, with the relevant institutions and law in some other African societies. Africa is not, of course, the only source of potentially relevant comparative data, but the inquiry must have some limits and the African comparisons are particularly inviting because of the underlying similarity in attitude toward litigation which seems to pervade much of the continent. If one is interested particularly in law, and not in social control in general, it is more fruitful to compare data from societies in which relatively litigious and legalistic modes of social control are prominent and highly regarded. I shall be especially concerned here with the institutional concomitants of the varying degrees of legalism exhibited by societies within a generally legalistic cultural region. Finally, I shall say what I think can usefully be said, in this unsteady world, about possible alternative futures open to Soga law and its counterparts elsewhere in Africa.

THE NATURE OF SOGA LAW

Legal reasoning was defined in chapter 1 as "the application to the settlement of disputes of categorizing concepts that define justiciable normative issues" which must be decided by "inclusion or exclusion." Chapters 4 through 7 will, I hope, have vindicated my argument that Basoga judges and litigants engage in legal reasoning in this sense. They operate with a finite repertory of concepts of wrong which sets limits to the normative issues that may be litigated; only those bundles of rights and obligations which are recognized (in Hart's sense) by being embodied in concepts of wrong are justiciable. Other normative notions drawn from popular morality are often appealed to in litigants' arguments and judges' questions, and these may influence the severity of a sentence or the amount of an award, but the process remains relatively legalistic. The question of the reach of the concept of wrong with respect to the "facts" must be answered "yes" or "no." The participants in the courtroom dialogue also make use of subsidiary concepts—those of credibility, by means of which the "facts" are "found," and those of applicability, by means of which the outer boundaries of concepts of wrong are extended or withdrawn to include or exclude the "facts" of cases not covered by their core meanings.

Thus far Basoga litigants and judges resemble Anglo-American ones and perhaps others, wherever legal reasoning comes into use. This latter is no more than a suggestion, for which I have offered no real support, of the more general comparative usefulness of a conception of law arrived at by applying Hart's and Levi's notions to the Soga case. It is offered at this point simply as a contribution to the continuing comparative dialogue between conceptualization and empirical investigation in this field.

But here, for the most part, the resemblance between the conception of the legal process sketched by Hart and Levi and that process as it appears in the A.L.G. courts ends. The legal systems with which they, as students of Western jurisprudence, are concerned make use of devices for communicating rules or conceptual applications, both among courts and between courts and litigants, which are essentially absent in the Soga system. Thus Hart writes:

If it were not possible to communicate general standards of conduct, which multitudes of individuals could understand, without further direction, as requiring from them certain conduct when occasion arose, nothing that we now recognize as law could exist. . . . Two principal devices, at first sight very different from each other, have been used in communicating such general standards of conduct in advance of the successive occasions on which they are to be applied. One of them makes a maximal and the other a minimal use of general classifying words. The first is typified by what we call legislation and the second by precedent. We can see the distinguishing features of these in the following simple non-legal cases. One father before going to church says to his son, "Every man and boy must take off his hat on entering a church." Another baring his head as he enters the church says, "Look: this is the right way to behave on such occasions." [1]

Levi, also assuming that such communication is essential to the legal process, is concerned to point out the similarities in these devices:

Reasoning by example brings into focus the similarity and difference in the interpretation of case law, statutes, and the constitution of a nation. There is a striking similarity. It is only folklore which holds that a statute if clearly written can be completely unambiguous and applied as intended to a specific case. Fortunately or otherwise, ambiguity is inevitable in both statute and constitution as well as with case law. Hence reasoning by example operates with all three.[2]

The Soga system lacks these devices for communication, and yet judges and litigants work with a conceptual apparatus which is coherent and not uncomplex. Of course communication does take place. Young Basoga males acquire a self-advocate's command of the system in the process of growing up by attending court and listening to their elders' out-of-court legal conversation, which is considerable; and those who man the bench acquire a somewhat fuller command as parish chiefs, court clerks, and then as judges. But neither courtroom argument nor out-of-court discussion makes the conceptual structure of the law very explicit. To be sure, the concepts of wrong themselves are quite explicitly stated and manipulated; accusations must be lodged and decisions given in terms of them. But the subsidiary concepts with which, as Levi notes, the crucial work of a court in deciding the reach of concepts of wrong is done [3] remain, for the most part, quite unstated. My analysis of cases has consisted in large part of uncovering them by inference from the arguments, questions, and decisions of those who participate in the trial process. Although those who take part in the legal process learn them, they are not the vehicles for overt communication between the courts and the public or between different courts.

It is this latter sort of communication that Hart and Levi have in

1. H. L. A. Hart, *The Concept of Law,* p. 121.
2. Edward H. Levi, *An Introduction to Legal Reasoning,* p. 5.
3. Ibid., p. 6. Levi calls them "satellite concepts."

mind when they speak of legislation and precedent as the two devices for communicating with and about legal concepts. They consider these essential, I suggest, because they work with legal systems in which change is particularly prominent. Without explicit means of communicating about the law it would be impossible to maintain order within a rapidly changing legal system. The communication of precedent-setting decisions by appeal courts notifies lower courts that the ambiguity presented by a particular set of new circumstances will until further notice be resolved in only the one way indicated, among those possible. Legislation establishes new concepts, which then embark upon similar careers of interpretation by the courts with the aid of subsidiary concepts. Both Hart and Levi would say that a legal system without these means of orderly change is defective—indeed, Hart uses that language.[4] But this is essentially the situation of the A.L.G. courts in Busoga. With respect to the "secondary rules" (of recognition, adjudication, and change) that Hart finds essential to a legal system in the full sense, each court in the Soga system is on its own and each sitting represents a fresh start—in the sense that there is no formal, explicit authority outside that particular court for deciding what rules are justiciable, how such rules are to be applied, and how they are to be changed. (I ignore here the legislative powers of the protectorate government and the district council; the former stands outside the Soga legal system, setting limits to it without really participating in it, while the latter has never been exercised.) A "wrong" decision may be overthrown on appeal, but most other courts are unlikely to hear of such an event and the decision is unlikely to be presented in terms that make clear, conceptually, what has been decided.

Of course, as I have said, in another sense the courts are not autonomous of each other and of the past. There is a coherence in their conceptual equipment because Basoga share a common culture, both a common general culture and a common legal subculture. *The interest of the Soga material for comparative legal studies, I suggest, is that it shows how legal a system of social control can be without overt communication about the application of legal concepts—without precedent or legislation.* When the society and the law are relatively static, litigation and adjudication can consist for the most part of a repeated "unpacking" of the same concepts in response to stereotyped conflicts, and this can be done quite covertly, much as experienced bridge or poker players can play for hours without ever mentioning a rule. (The rules of card games are, of course, more readily explicitized than those

4. Ibid, pp. 89–96.

of Soga law, perhaps because they are explicitly taught; the situations would be more similar if all players learned by watching their elders, without overt tuition.) Such a system can even engage in orderly change provided it is gradual, as the development of the law of tenancy demonstrates, though I suspect that today the demands of change are pressing upon the limits of this capacity. Again, however, it is important to stress that the difference in these respects between the Soga courts and modern Anglo-American ones is a matter of degree. Soga courts are *relatively* implicit in their communication, modern Anglo-American ones *relatively* explicit. Modern Anglo-American legal communication, for all its carefully drawn statutes, briefs, and *ratio decidendi*, involves a vast body of unstated assumptions which function as implicit subsidiary concepts in the application of concepts of wrong—particularly at the lower levels in the court system.[5]

What, then, are some of the distinguishing features of law without precedent, Soga style? It is, first of all, *popular* in the sense that knowledge of the legal subculture, explicit and implicit, is widely shared, as is appropriate in a system in which the litigant must be his own advocate. The language of the law is mostly everyday language. The litigant is, on the average, only somewhat less expert than the bench, which itself in turn is a kind of judge and jury combined; the chief-chairman is, on the average, only somewhat more expert than his colleagues. This is not to say that there are no significant differences in expertise. If Soga law has no barristers, it clearly does have solicitors of an amateur sort. In at least two of the cases discussed, *Tonda Nandabi* v. *Walwendo* and *Nasani Beka* v. *Kibikyo*, it seems very likely that litigants received advice from persons legally more sophisticated than themselves during adjournments or in the intervals between trials and hearings on appeal. Letters of appeal, also, are often not the unaided products of appellants; the appellant in *Mpaulo Wakaze* v. *Malagala Musenero* probably had help from someone. I do not know who these particular amateur solicitors were, but I have known chiefs and headmen to give such help to kinsmen and friends.

Soga law is also *accessible* in the sense that the machinery for its application is readily available to all. It is cheap—fees amount to a few shillings—but more than this the courts are permissive with respect to grounds for action or appeal. This is perfectly compatible with the insistence upon accusation in terms of one of the recognized concepts of wrong. A person with a grievance, having exhausted the possibilities for settlement to his satisfaction in the unofficial tribunals

5. Karl Llewellyn, *Jurisprudence: Realism in Theory and Practice*, pp. 136–37.

of headmen and parish chief, carries his complaint to the subcounty chief, who hears what he has to say and may make a final attempt at out-of-court settlement. If this fails, the chief will place the complaint on the docket, always in terms of one of the recognized concepts of wrong. If the accuser has a poor case, the chief will so advise him, but if he is adamant, he gets his day in court. Similarly, there is no real scrutiny of grounds for appeal; leave to appeal seems always to be granted upon request, though I have heard a chief remonstrate with an intransigent litigant for wasting his time and money on fruitless appealing. Finally, the Soga version of *res judicata,* if one may call it that, does not keep a cause off the docket; if it comes out in the course of argument that the issue has been decided before, this merely defeats the argument of the litigant who would reopen it on the merits. The substance is not subject to reconsideration, but it may require some argument in court to determine just what the substance is. In *Aminsi Waiswa* v. *Sajjabi Kibba,* Aminsi is allowed to argue out his case at length, though it is clear almost from the start that the courts have already settled the matter. Yet another expression of accessibility is the practice of litigating in order to protect rights already enjoyed against counterclaims, as in *Alamanzani Zirabamuzale* v. *Magola Kinyaga.* Verbal assertion of an unacknowledged claim is as much a cause for action as is its attempted exercise.

The accessibility of Soga law is related to its implicitness. Since the grounds of decisions are so little spelled out, and since crucial subsidiary concepts are so little open to overt statement, everything must be put to the test of courtroom argument. There is a real sense in which Basoga do not know what to think about a case until they have heard what they have to say about it. The use of writing serves to improve record-keeping with respect to "facts," but it does not—at least not yet—increase the explicitness of communication with and about legal concepts.

Logic, Function, and Legal Order

The popular character and the accessibility of Soga law are procedural characteristics. I have also characterized the substantive side of the law as orderly—as a system of legal concepts—and I must now explain and defend this characterization.

One may look for two kinds of order in a body of legal ideas. On the one hand, legal ideas are about the norms of social relations—the rights and obligations of persons toward each other. Not all social norms are legal, but all legal ideas are normative—are used for normative inquiry. This means that legal ideas are deeply involved with the social order—with whatever degrees and kinds of order the society possesses. I do not mean to suggest here any assumption of social harmony or consensus. As I suggested in chapter 3, societies exhibit characteristic patterns of strain and conflict that are themselves part of the social "order" and that indeed, among other things, provide the occasions for the operation of the legal system, without which it would have no work to do. Keeping this in mind, one may say that in one sense the orderly or systemic character of a body of legal ideas is a sociological one; it "reflects" the structure of social relations whose rights and obligations it is law's "function" to guarantee.

Involvement in the social order is not, of course, peculiar to *legal* ideas. As writers on the "sociology of knowledge" from Marx forward have argued (sometimes too persistently), any cultural or subcultural system is "rooted" in the social structure, if only because those who create and use it play roles in the social structure which constrain the way they think as well as the way they act. But since law is concerned with the very norms of society, its relationship with society is particularly intimate—more intimate than, say, that of religion, whose "practice" (in the sense of ritual) so often involves withdrawal from social relations of an everyday sort. Even in a legalistic religion such as Islam the principal ritual makes use of cleansing and separation from daily social concerns; it affirms submission to a law-giving God, but does not itself apply the God-given law to actual conduct. The principal occasions for the "practice" of law, on the other hand, (including Islamic law) consist of inquiries into the normative status of actual, everyday social events. Law is thus the most normative part of culture.

But it also remains *part* of culture—the subculture of the legal institution—and thus ought to exhibit order, or system, or coherence of a "logicomeaningful" kind.[6] Similar conceptual themes should be encountered in parts of the law concerned with quite different institutional sectors of society—in the case of Busoga, in the law of sexual relations and the law of land, for example. In addition to concepts pertaining peculiarly to these and other institutional sectors, one should be able to discover concepts common to them all. One should not expect to find perfect consistency, for, again, the subject matters of the law in different institutional fields differ in ways that have consequences for legal ideas. Women are different from cattle and both are different from land, both "objectively" and by Soga cultural definition. Therefore, although concepts pertaining to transactions in all three

6. See discussion in chapter 1.

may be expected to have something in common, because they are all transactions in Soga law, they may also be expected to differ.

Before applying these notions to the case material presented in chapters 4 through 7, let me restate in more general terms, as clearly as I can in a few sentences, the view of human social action they imply and that I have attempted to follow throughout this study. Since man is radically dependent upon learned symbols and upon social cooperation for the patterning of his behavior and the accomplishment of his purposes,[7] "human nature" is such that there is in cultures a strain toward conceptual consistency or logical integration, and in social systems a strain toward functional integration in the sense that normatively governed patterns of interaction complement each other. For the relationship between social and cultural systems, this view has a double consequence. On the one hand, since the same persons inhabit and use both systems—are both "conditioned" or "programmed" (as the saying now goes) with the culture and involved in the complex of social expectations—some substantial congruence between them is to be expected. Indeed, in a concrete sense they are "the same thing." Both "society" and "culture" are abstractions from the same phenomenon—social action. As Ryle puts it, ". . . the styles and procedures of people's activities *are* the way their minds work and are not merely imperfect reflections of . . . the workings of minds. . . ."[8] But the requirements of cultural consistency and of functional integration are somewhat different. Putting one's thoughts in order and putting one's affairs in order are rather different activities for either a person or a community. They proceed along different lines, but tend to react upon one another so as to produce not a one-to-one matching of ideas and social relations, but rather a continuing process of mutual adjustment and challenge.

I merely state this view here, without attempting a full-scale defense of it, as the frame of reference within which my analysis has proceeded. There is nothing new in it; it is essentially the view that Talcott Parsons, in *The Structure of Social Action,* found in the work of Max Weber and that has inspired the work of many contemporary anthropologists, sociologists, psychologists, and philosophers. It is basically at variance, however, with either a functional-equilibrium or a cultural-structural model of human social life, *taken alone.* I would not find it as enlightening to view Soga law as *only* or *basically* either a mechanism for reestablishing social harmony or an expression of

7. Clifford Geertz, "The Impact of the Concept of Culture on the Concept of Man," pp. 106–14.
8. Gilbert Ryle, *The Concept of Mind,* p. 58.

unconscious intellectual structures—which is not, of course, to say that analyses in those terms cannot be revealing.[9]

The substance of Soga law, then, should reveal tendencies both toward conceptual consistency and toward differentiation in relation to different subject matters. Two examples stand out particularly clearly in the cases I have analyzed. One—the more simple and obvious—is the Soga notion of contract—*ndagaano*—as it operates in landholding and in marriage. The two applications of the concept have much in common: in both cases the contract is entered into by individuals, but its consequences extend to other members of their descent-groups. A husband's agnates succeed to his rights in his wife; a father-in-law's agnates succeed to his responsibilities toward his daughter and son-in-law. Likewise, headmen's and tenants' agnates succeed to their respective rights and responsibilities. Similar procedures are followed in establishing the contractual relationship: there must be a formal introduction (*kwandhula*) of the parties to each other and each must have his agent (*mukwenda* or *mubaka*) to act as go-between and witness. In both cases the contractual element is limited, and in a similar way: only the amount of the consideration and the identity of the woman or holding contracted for vary (I ignore here the recent development of greater contractual specificity in land transactions); beyond this the rights and obligations of the parties toward each other are matters of general law—the law of tort. There is clearly, here, a common and coherent conceptual scheme which Basoga make use of when they enter into contracts, whether the subject matter is land or women.

But Basoga do not view women as things, like land, or use them in the same way; hence conceptual consistency must make way for difference in subject matter. Failure to complete bridewealth payments does not excuse harboring [10] (though it is grounds for an action for bridewealth debt), but failure to complete payment of the allotment fee for land does give the headman cause to withdraw the land.[11] "Eating two hens" is a serious crime carrying severe penalties,[12] while contracting twice for the same land is a civil matter, settled by

9. Gluckman presents the most persuasive argument for the equilibrum model of which I am aware in *Politics, Law, and Ritual in Tribal Society*, chapters 5 and 7. The cultural-structural view is best presented in Lévi-Strauss' *Structural Anthropology*, especially chapters 2 and 15. He has not, to my knowledge, applied it to law, but Leopold Pospisil has done something broadly similar with law in his "A Formal Analysis of Substantive Law: Kapauku Papuan Laws of Land Tenure."

10. *Kayambya* v. *Kakokola.*

11. *Sitanule Gowa* v. *Kisubi Mwokyeku.*

12. *Mikairi Magino* v. *Ntumba.*

restitution.[13] Dissolution of a marriage (except through the death of the wife) always leaves the husband with a claim for return of the bridewealth, even if the wife and her father have sufficient grounds for divorce, [14] a headman, however, need not refund the allotment fee if he has grounds for repossessing the land as *kitongole*.[15]

These differences have a theme. The relationship established by the contract is a good deal more asymmetrical between the two parties in the case of marriage than it is in the case of land. In marriage, the law comes down heavily on the side of the husband, while with respect to land, rights and obligations are more nearly balanced between headman and tenant. The obvious explanation for the difference is the functional one. The heavy stress Basoga give to unilineal descent and male dominance places severe strains upon marriage, and particularly upon the wife. In order to hold marriages together at all, the law must support husbands' authority rather rigidly and harshly. Landholding, too, is beset by conflicts of interest, but of a rather different kind. While land is, to be sure, of more than economic value, it remains inert —something contracted for and contested *about;* whereas women, although marriages are contracted for them, are themselves social beings whose own social relations with the parties to the contract lie at the heart of the conflicts that arise and whose actions help to bring the law into play. Furthermore, I have presented evidence to suggest that conflicts of interest between headmen and tenants, at least in their present form, are relatively recent—the result of an increasing commercialization of land rights in which both headmen and tenants have participated. The law of tenancy is a response to this process and is itself in the process of further development. There is every indication, on the other hand, that the instability of Soga marriage and the law governing it are much as they have been since the nineteenth century. Thus the social trouble spots that I have called "the headman's dilemma" [16] and "the patrilineal puzzle" [17] present Soga law and its users with rather different problems in the application of its common concept of contract, and these differences are provided for in the legal subculture.

The other clear example of differentiation in legal subculture in response to differentiation in subject matter is provided by the notion, encountered again and again in the case material, that failure to assert

13. *Aminsi Waiswa* v. *Sajjabi Kibba.*
14. *Maliyamu Kyazike* v. *Samwiri Wakoli.*
15. Information from interviews with judges.
16. See above, p. 215; also Lloyd A. Fallers, *Bantu Bureaucracy,* pp. 175–79.
17. Appendix A.

a claim in time by litigation invalidates the claim. In the field of landholding, I have called this the concept of acquiescence. Acquiescence in someone else's planting of bananas, or burying his relatives, or allotting to a third party destroys a claim; [18] with respect to harboring, it appears in the necessity for a father to protect himself from the charge by accusing the husband of refusal to grant a divorce; [19] in the law of adultery, it appears in the requirement that a man assert his claim to inherit his husband's widow before she marries someone else.[20] Again, the continuity among the applications of the notion in the various fields is clear. In each case the claimant must act within a reasonable time or, more importantly, before certain critical events occur. In each case, the application of the concept by the judges and litigants is signaled by the same questions: "Why did you wait?" "What did you do then?"

But the difference in subject matter influences the application. Again, harboring and adultery are crimes, while violations of rights founded upon *butaka* and *kitongole* are not. And Basoga themselves seem to reason differently in applying the concept to the different subject matters. A man who waits too long to assert his claim to land is "just waiting for important witnesses to die; [21] his waiting indicates that his claim was *never* sound. There is a similar element in the way Basoga talk about the father-in-law who does not act soon enough to accuse his son-in-law of refusal to grant divorce: it perhaps indicates that he lacks sufficient grounds, but there is also an explicitly recognized element of the need to hold the woman's tie with her own people rigidly in check to protect marriage. With respect to wife-inheritance, in the only case I have cited the court explicitly accepted that the claim had originally been sound, but ruled that it could not be lawfully asserted after the claimant and his lineage had acquiesced in the widow's marrying someone else—presumably because a woman cannot have two legitimate sexual partners at the same time.

FACT-MINDEDNESS

There is, then, order of both a sociological and a cultural kind in Soga law. But it is, as I have said so often, very largely an implicit order, and there is more to be said on this point. The reasoning of Basoga judges and litigants is not equally implicit in all aspects of their law or from case to case. Some kinds of arguments are commonly

---

18. *Kaluna Mukungu* v. *Musa bin Juma; Gwampiya Kire* v. *Erifazi Birobire.*
19. *Gabudieri Gukina* v. *Waibi Butanda.*
20. *Zakaliya Yande* v. *Amadi Simola.*
21. *Tito Nantamu* v. *Kisubi Mwokyeku.*

stated quite overtly and plainly, while others are not; some cases seem
to call forth more explicit statement than others, and some litigants
and judges seem habitually to argue more explicitly than others. These
variations are important because it is its relative implicitness that
constitutes what Hart and Levi would see as the "defect" in Soga law
in relation to the requirements of more rapid change. An analysis of
the variations in explicitness that exist in Soga law as it is today may
help one to think about its capacity to become more explicit and hence
more adaptable.

Arguments and decisions in Soga law tend very strongly toward a
kind of "fact-mindedness." [22] To put it quite simply, Basoga in court
very seldom talk about the law—about the reach of the concepts of
wrong. They talk instead about the "facts"—about what happened—
without articulating the legal significance of these events. Consider
Alamanzani Zirabamuzale v. *Magola Kinyaga,* which is quite typical
in this respect. Magola, the accused, defends himself by recounting a
chain of events. His father received a holding from the village headman, and when the father died, Magola inherited it; then the subvillage headman took it back and allotted it to Alamanzani; Magola
accused the subvillage headman before the headman and was awarded
the holdings. Alamanzani also argues in narrative fashion. The subvillage headman allotted him the holding; but prior to that event, five
successive individuals had held the land since Magola's father relinquished it; Alamanzani once litigated with Magola before the parish
chief and was awarded the holding. The court's investigating commissioners say that the holding belongs to Alamanzani because five persons beside Alamanzani had held the land since Magola's father, while
the father was still living. After hearing all this the court concludes,
again with a chain-of-events argument: the land was taken from
Magola's father before he died and was left empty; thereafter it was
allotted successively to five tenants with no complaint from Magola's
father; the holding therefore belongs to Alamanzani.

Now I, viewing the case from the standpoint of legal analysis, find
in all this an argument and decision about the reach of the concepts
butaka and *kitongole,* with the aid of the subsidiary concept of acquiescence: the unchallenged assertion of *kitongole* by a headman
defeats a claim based upon earlier inheritance. But neither litigants
nor judges say anything of the sort. They say: "because x, y, and z
occurred, the land belongs to so-and-so." To anyone used to thinking
of legal argument as containing an element of explicit discussion of

22. I owe this phrase to Professor Alexander Nekam.

rules or concepts of wrong, the transcripts of Soga trials read like one non sequitur after the other.

Sometimes the non sequiturs are interlarded with apparent contradictions, as in the cases in which the reach of kinship concepts is in dispute. In *Sabasitiano Gavamukulya* v. *Bumali Mawa*, Bumali both "is" and "is not" the late Bikaba's "brother." The problem, as I analyzed the case, is whether or not they are brothers for purposes of the inheritance of land, but none of the participants ever says that— which is doubly remarkable in view of the fact that the decision involves recognition of "siblingship" within a group that is a descent group only by legal fiction. The case is not unique, but Basoga believe that the phenomenon is a recent one, the result of the scrambling of the population by the sleeping-sickness epidemics. Thus a relatively recent legal fiction, involving a novel use of the term "brother," is applied without overt discussion. Sabasitiano never says *why* he rejects Bumali's "siblingship" with Bikaba, and neither Bumali nor the court says why it should be accepted.

Of course neither the non sequiturs nor the contradictions really are such; the participants understand each other because they make implicit use of legal concepts which fill in the missing steps and resolve the contradictions.

But sometimes conceptual issues do come to the surface. This seems to happen when cases are closely contested, either because they are inherently difficult, involving the margins of legal concepts, or because litigants are particularly intransigent or articulate. The dialectic of courtroom argument provides a stimulus to legal creativity which may then yield greater explicitness. Thus Yowasi's appeal to the county court in *Yowasi Maliwa* v. *Genatio Magino* quite explicitly tests the margins of the concept "sister" with respect to the law of adultery:

> The [lower] court bases itself on the argument that the girl is not a relative to me, but it forgets the custom [*mpisa*] of the nation. It is well known that there is not just one kind of relationship . . . between people. And it is a mistake to think that because I am not of the same clan as a woman or of the same maternal parentage, I can marry her . . . blood brothers become clansmen and call each other "real brothers."

Yowasi, however, fails to draw the *court* into explicit statement, and it concludes with an utterly fact-minded decision: "there is no true evidence that Matama is a sister. For that reason he is defeated." Here the issue is not a difficult one, for "everyone knows" that step-siblings are not siblings for purposes of the law of adultery. Although the accused is unusually persistent and lucid, the court is not really challenged.

Occasionally, however, the impulse toward greater explicitness comes from the bench, as in *Salimu Waiswa* v. *Eria Wambi*:

The fact that [Salimu] has no house nor banana garden in the subvillage does not prove that it is not his. In Busoga a person may own three or four subvillages without having a house in any of them. For example, [Eria] has no house or banana garden in the village of Kiboyo . . . but he is still regarded as its owner.

This, too, is a rather plain case, but here the chairman of the court, the subcounty chief, whom I knew well, was of an unusually analytical turn of mind. His decisions were usually more fully spelled out, if not always more conceptually explicit, than those of his colleagues.

In *Maliyamu Kyazike* v. *Samwiri Wakoli,* however, greater explicitness clearly is at least in part a product of the difficulty of the issue—whether or not an arranged childhood marriage is binding upon a woman. Here, after recalling that Maliyamu had been given to Omw. Wakoli while very young, the court declared: "If the court gives her to him he will take her by force. But it is not the custom [*mpisa*] of the court to do this." Interestingly enough, the word "custom" is here used in connection with what is clearly an innovation in law. Such marriages have certainly been binding in the past, and the court splits, four to two. For two members of the bench, it still is, or should be, "the custom of the court to do this." The difficulty of the case and the disagreement concerning its disposition are the result of cultural change.

However, the difficult, innovating case is not always marked by such explicit statement of the innovation. This is quite strikingly shown in the series of cases, analyzed in chapter 7, in which land transactions involving "lending" come before the courts. I have argued that formal leases—contracts for the use of land for determinate periods and purposes—violate the received conceptual scheme in which land must be either *butaka* or *kitongole* and in which the notion of acquiescence is applied to determine which of these is appropriate in the particular instance. Since leases are in fact increasing, and when challenged increasingly result in litigation, the courts are under pressure to recognize and regulate them by appropriate conceptual innovations. However, although the courts find these cases difficult, as evidenced by the frequency of appeals and split decisions in connection with them, I found in my (admittedly very limited) sample of cases no indication of explicit recognition of the conceptual issues involved. Even in *Swaliki Balita* v. *Zadoki Mugalya,* in which the courts accept as binding a lease for a determinate purpose, there is no overt suggestion that a major legal departure has been urged and accepted. The issue is handled in entirely factual terms. In the subcounty court's words:

> Zadoki produced a paper which he considers to be a contract given to him by Dausoni, [but this] allows him to put up only a temporary building. . . . Therefore, Zadoki has no evidence to support him.

—as if a lease for a determinate period were the commonest thing in the world! And following a reversal by the county court, the district court concurs: "Dausoni Magumba admits that a contract was given to Zadoki, but says that the land was not given, but only lent. There is evidence for this. . . ." Again, no hint of change.

Why do the district court and the litigants in *Maliyamu Kyazike* v. *Samwiri Wakoli*—the child marriage case—recognize and state more clearly what they are doing than the same court and the litigants in *Swaliki Balita* v. *Zadoki Mugalya*—the land-leasing case? Both involve changes of substantial magnitude. The difference, I suggest, is that the marriage case involves the legal recognition of change which has been primarily cultural in its genesis, while in the land case the new feature which is accepted is the result of a primarily social development. The marriage case arises from a difference of view regarding the status of women in which the accused and a minority of the court uphold the older attitude pervasively institutionalized in Soga society, while the accuser, supported by a majority of the court, adopts a newer one which has been actively promoted by religious groups, schools, and women's associations. It is primarily a *view*, a *conception*, which is at issue. The land-leasing case, on the other hand, concerns a *social transaction* which must appear to those who undertake it as only a slight extension of social practice, involving no new ideas: the contract, which is a recognized part of the general law of tenancy, is simply modified to specify a particular use.

It is essential to be clear about what, precisely, is being said here, both concerning the changes that are the subject matter of the legal process in the two cases and about the legal process itself. I do not mean to say that the one change is completely cultural, the other completely social, for in my view of these matters all actual, concrete, changes in human patterns of life involve both kinds. Persons can engage in social interactions—actions based upon mutual expectations —because they share beliefs and values embodied in common symbols; indeed, they can only engage in meaningful conflict or dispute because they at least partly understand each other. At the same time, common beliefs and values are acquired and used in social interaction. The divergent views of women in marriage held by Maliyamu Kyazike, her

supporters, and her adversaries are learned and lived out in daily
social life, while the transaction in land that gave rise to *Swaliki
Balita* v. *Zadoki Mugalya* presupposed common understandings about
land and its uses. All this concerns the patterns of thought and action
that are the subject matter of the two cases; in addition, the legal
process which works upon this subject matter is itself both cultural
and social. The law, in the narrow sense of a system of legal concepts,
is a conceptual system, hence in both the cases under discussion the
legal change involved is conceptual—cultural—change. But those who
use the concepts and innovate with them operate within the social-organizational framework of the court.

What I am suggesting, then, is simply that while all change, either
in the law or in its subject matter, is ultimately both social and
cultural—involves both social and cultural innovation—the two aspects of change often do not proceed precisely together because, as I
argued earlier, they have different kinds of system or order—one
logicomeaningful, the other sociofunctional. Maliyamu and a majority
of the court in her case are convinced that arranged childhood marriages are incompatible, in a logicomeaningful sense, with the conception of women's status to which they are committed. The issue thus
comes to the court as a conceptual one, already half-explicit. The
court, in deciding the issue, is therefore more readily brought to
explicit formulation of what it is doing.

This is much less true of the land-leasing case. What is tested in that
case is the binding nature of a kind of contract which has developed
imperceptibly out of previous practice in accord with the increasing
commercialization of Busoga's economy. Informal, short-term lending
already existed, as did the general contract of tenancy. But the lending
is now for a new purpose: the erection of a shop. Basoga are increasingly entering shopkeeping, following the example of the Asian shopkeepers in the trading centers, where customary law does not apply.[23]
In previous practice, lending was for a season or two of cultivation and
the borrower would not be allowed to plant bananas—a perennial crop
—but only annuals, lest he establish a heritable interest through the
acquiescence concept under the general law of tenancy. A shop built of
permanent materials is also a long-term investment, albeit of a rather
different kind. What could be more natural than a stipulation in the
contract that only temporary materials should be used? But the difference in use is significant: a holding without bananas is of only tempo-

23. These are on Crown land; plots are leased for forty-nine and ninety-nine
years.

rary value as a *pied-à-terre*, while the borrower looks for a regular holding. A shop—even of temporary materials (which can be repaired) —may serve a useful function for some years. In basing its decision upon the specific terms of the contract, rather than upon the general law of tenancy, the court is making new rules to suit a functionally new kind of transaction. Since this particular contract does not specify a time, Zadoki apparently can stay as long as he likes, though he cannot build in brick. The court in fact accepts a new function for land and a new kind of headman-tenant relationship, but because the elements in the situation all seem familiar, the conceptual issue may remain disguised as a factual one.

I do not, of course, mean to suggest that cultural change is always more explicit than social change. Slow, long-term cultural change commonly occurs without overt recognition. Within time-spans of the magnitude involved here, however, I think it is true that major changes in beliefs and values present the legal institution with more conceptually explicit issues than do those changes which have proceeded mainly through the establishment of new kinds of social relations.

These differences aside, communication with and about legal concepts generally remains relatively covert in the Soga courts. Under present-day conditions, when both social and cultural change may be expected to press in upon the courts ever more insistently, this doubtless constitutes a defect, for there is nothing to prevent different courts in Busoga from responding to these challenges in conflicting ways. To be sure, there is a great deal to prevent them from responding in *randomly* different ways: Their shared general and legal subculture predisposes them to respond similarly to similar novel situations, and the mobility of the chief-judges tends to iron out differences. Weber's statement quoted at the head of this chapter is too strong, at least in relation to the Soga experience: with very little differentiation between "properly legal and . . . factual" portions of either arguments or decisions, the Soga courts *have* produced a "growing body of law" respecting land. Implicit legal reasoning is more powerful and more coherent than Weber recognized. But the processes traced in chapters 6 and 7—the "legal-ization" of the *butaka* and *kitongole* concepts and their development into a general law of tenancy—took place rather slowly and involved no sharp breaks with the past. Issues such as those presented by *Maliyamu Kyazike* v. *Samwiri Wakoli* (child marriage) and *Swaliki Balita* v. *Zadoki Mugalya* (land-leasing) are much more radical, and as such issues multiply, the body of common understandings will wear thin. Without some more explicit means of coordination, the law experienced by Basoga subject to different courts will begin to diverge to an unacceptable degree.

These considerations raise the question of the future of Soga law. Before taking up that question, however, I shall turn to a brief comparison between Soga law and legal institutions and those of some other African societies for which studies are available.

SOME OTHER AFRICAN SYSTEMS

Perhaps just because litigation looms so large in the lives of most sub-Saharan African peoples, the social anthropology of the region has produced a disproportionate share of the best legal ethnography. I shall choose here for brief comparison with Busoga three societies: The Lozi (or Barotse) of Zambia, as reported by Gluckman; [24] the Tiv of Nigeria, described by Bohannan; [25] and the Arusha of Tanzania, whose legal affairs have been analyzed by Gulliver.[26] There are other excellent studies, but these are most suitable for my purposes because their authors are most concerned with the sorts of problems I have taken up in my analysis of Soga legal institutions.

I think it is appropriate to say here that one important reason for the convergence of interest has been the wide influence of Gluckman's Lozi work, which set a new standard of sophistication in the social anthropological study of law. Whatever disagreements and differences of interest there may be among us—and these are by no means insignificant—Bohannan, Gulliver, and I are all "Gluckmanian" in the sense that Gluckman's writings have posed analytical problems and set standards of craftsmanship which have deeply influenced the work of all of us and will doubtless continue to dominate the field for some time to come.

First of all, the Barotse, the Tiv, and the Arusha are all, like the Basoga, litigious in the sense that they very readily resort to the public litigation and adjudication of disputes. Bohannan writes that "the Tiv are a litigious people and enjoy listening to and participating in *jir* (courts, moots)." [27] Gulliver says that he was drawn to an interest in litigation among the Arusha by "the large number of disputes occurring over land matters; [28] his description of a moot makes it clear that

24. Max Gluckman, *The Judicial Process among the Barotse.*
25. Paul Bohannan, *Justice and Judgement among the Tiv.*
26. P. H. Gulliver, *Social Control in an African Society: A Study of the Arusha: Agricultural Masai of Northern Tanganyika.*
27. Bohannan, *Justice and Judgement,* p. 13.
28. Gulliver, *Social Control,* p. x.

articulate argument is much appreciated.[29] The Barotse, "like all Africans," writes Gluckman, "appear to be very litigious." [30] And he remarks: "I agree with them that they have a true genius in law." [31] Thus, although they live in widely separated areas and are linguistically quite diverse,[32] all four peoples consider litigation a proper means of dealing with human conflict and admire those skilled in its practice.

They are not, however, equally legalistic in the sense outlined in chapter 1: their tribunals do not, to the same degree, oversimplify disputes in the interest of submitting them to a regime of rules.[33] At one extreme, the indigenous dispute-settling gatherings (*engigwana*) of the Arusha are morally quite holistic and also relatively political. Norms are brought to bear, but there is little attempt to limit consideration to a single, narrowly drawn cause of action or concept of wrong, and there is an important element of frank bargaining.[34] Arusha dispute settlement is "the result of a positive consent rather than passive acquiescence." [35] At the other extreme are the Basoga, whom I have described as relatively legalistic. A "case," for them, is a proceeding to decide whether or not a particular set of "facts" falls within the reach of one particular concept of wrong. All sorts of other issues may be raised in argument, but only those relevant to the reach of the particular concept of wrong enter into the decision; and the latter is delivered quite unilaterally, with little attempt to elicit consent.[36]

The Tiv and the Barotse fall between the Arusha and Soga extremes. In a Tiv tribunal (*jir*) it is important to reach agreement between the parties,[37] but the complainant must have a valid cause of action.[38] The *jir* may extend its inquiries to the actions of persons other than the principals,[39] but it is believed that there is always a correct decision to be found and that this decision will determine that the fault lies predominantly on one side.[40] The Barotse are more legalistic still. Again, the accuser must have a "dispute" (*muzeko*) which founds a

29. Ibid., p. 224.
30. Gluckman, *The Judicial Process*, p. 21.
31. Ibid., p. 6.
32. According to Greenberg (*Languages of Africa*), Basoga and Lozi are Bantu and Tiv Bantoid. Arusha are Nilotic.
33. See above, p. 11.
34. Gulliver, *Social Control*, chapter 10; chapter 11, pp. 296–302.
35. Ibid., pp. 232–33.
36. Occasionally the judges ask a litigant: "Now do you agree?" However, he rather seldom does so.
37. Bohannan, *Justice and Judgement*, p. 64.
38. Ibid., p. 17.
39. Ibid., pp. 65–66.
40. Ibid., pp. 61–64.

legal claim (*mubango*) [41]—a notion that seems very similar to what I
have called in Busoga a "concept of wrong." Lozi pleading and judgement seem more closely bound to particular concepts of wrong than
those of the Tiv—and certainly more than those of the Arusha. There
is no suggestion of bargaining. Conciliation enters, but only when
necessary to preserve permanent relationships.[42] Even then "the *kuta*
(court) should not achieve a reconciliation without blaming those who
have done wrong."[43] Reconciliation "does not lead to a sacrifice of
legal or moral rules, since wrong-doers are upbraided and punished
when they have failed to conform to these."[44] But Soga courts are even
less concerned with reconciliation—even in the case of "permanent
relationships." And Lozi litigation and adjudication are morally more
holistic than Soga in another respect. The Lozi *kuta* has administrative as well as judicial authority. "The judges are reluctant to support
a person who is right in law, but wrong in justice, and may seek to
achieve justice by indirect, and perhaps administrative, action."[45] In
"the case of the dog-in-the-manger headman," the judges upheld the
headman's claim; but since he had acted ungenerously, they threatened to dismiss him if he exercised it.[46] Soga courts lack administrative
authority of this kind, which resides in the hierarchy of chiefs as
administrators. They can dismiss a headman, but only for violation of
a specific concept of wrong; they always limit a case to consideration
of a particular charge against a particular person. They apply concepts of wrong one at a time—one per case. Barotse judges, Gluckman
says, "have great discretion in applying the laws in varied combination to particular circumstances. Different laws can be stated with
great certainty. When they are combined in application to particular
situations, various laws are given different weight, in order to achieve
justice."[47] In my language, more than one concept of wrong may be
applied to a single case.

There is, I think, a continuum here from the less to the more
legalistic legal subculture. To what, outside the various subcultures
themselves, may these differences be related? I suggested earlier that
the necessity for the legal process to oversimplify moral situations
required that the judges enjoy substantial respect and authority to
allow them to handle the resulting strain between law and morality.[48]

41. Gluckman, *The Judicial Process*, p. 233.
42. Ibid., p. 78.
43. Ibid., p. 22.
44. Ibid., p. 78.
45. Ibid., p. 22.
46. Ibid., p. 186.
47. Ibid., p. 202.
48. See chapters 1 and 3.

My analysis has, I think, shown that in Busoga, where litigation and adjudication are relatively legalistic, the bench does indeed enjoy such respect and authority. The Lozi, Tiv, and Arusha materials provide an opportunity for a modest comparative test of the proposition that the relationship is a more general one.

I take my hypothesis here from the work of Max Weber—from his work on the sociology of law and more generally from his theory of status groups, of which the sociology of law is a particular application.[49] In general, his notion is that social and cultural differentiation are interacting processes. Functionally differentiated groups tend to develop distinctive subcultures and to pursue "interests" defined by these subcultures, all the while further elaborating and refining ("rationalizing") them. On the largest scale, whole new classes sometimes emerge and achieve both functional and cultural dominance in society, but Weber also applied this analysis to occupational groups, including specialists in law. He showed, for example, that in the West the development of rationalized legal subcultures had proceeded along two quite different social routes. In England and the other common-law countries it was the work of a guild of lawyers in the service of private clients, while on the continent it was the creation of university-based scholars charged with training officials for state bureaucracies.[50]

Of course the legal institutions of none of these African societies exhibit the degree of either social or cultural differentiation characteristic of modern common-law or civil-law systems. The legal subculture is widely shared and there are only the beginnings of professionalization. But the four societies are by no means the same in these respects, and among them there appears to be a quite clear correlation between the differentiation of the bench, in terms of authority, and the legalism of the proceedings, in the sense of differentiation between law and popular morality.

At one extreme, again, stand the Arusha. In precolonial times, they had no chiefs. Their society and polity were organized around age- and descent-groups within which there were persons of influence and leadership, but no office-holders. During the colonial period, headmen, chiefs, and magistrates, the last being men of some education but no legal training, were introduced. The magistrate, with his clerk, sits with a bench of elders, much as the subcounty chief does in Busoga. In his court, the proceedings involve finding a "yes or no" answer to a particular charge, as in Busoga, but by no means all litigation—or

49. Max Weber, *The Theory of Social and Economic Organization*, pp. 428–29; *idem, From Max Weber: Essays in Sociology*, part 4.
50. Max Weber, *Max Weber on Law in Economy and Society*, chapters 7, 8.

perhaps even the most important—takes place there. The concilatory proceedings I described earlier take place in assemblies and moots in which there is no judge and in which litigants are supported by age and lineage mates. (One might, of course, say that the whole assembly is the "judge," but the point is of course that there is no *differentiated* bench—no differentiation between bench and litigant. Judicial authority, such as it is, lies in the whole assembly.) These, the precolonial institutions, stand parallel to the magistrates' courts. Disputes are sometimes appealed from them to magistrates' courts, but Arusha seem to disapprove of this and for the most part the two systems deal with different kinds of disputes. The magistrates' courts are largely occupied with offenses against modern legislation and with disputes between persons too distant from each other, spatially or socially, to be encompassed by age- or descent-group gatherings.[51] Thus the differentiated legal institution exists, by colonial fiat, but it is regarded as an evil, necessitated by modern conditions.

The more legalistic procedures are thus sufficiently alien to the Arusha that they continue to support an entirely separate set of institutions for a more congenial kind of dispute settlement. The precolonial Tiv, too, lacked officials of any kind; theirs was a patrilineal, segmentary society of the classical sort.[52] But this society appears to have been more receptive to differentiation, for here precolonial and colonial legal institutions have to a much greater extent merged to form a single system. The Tiv have more readily accepted chieftainship and the judicial function given it by the colonial government, though they have modified it to suit their own egalitarian conceptions of legitimate leadership. They continue to hold moots which are not recognized by the colonial government, and to some extent these deal with matters different from those considered by the courts,[53] as among the Arusha. The decisive difference, however, is that the chief is both a civil servant and a man of influence in the segmentary political system. In his efforts to achieve an agreed-upon settlement, he may manipulate the system from within and he has sufficient authority to declare one side right.[54] The existence of a differentiated judge, albeit one held on short rein by segmentary politics, is sufficient to allow a greater degree of legalism.

In Barotseland, as in Busoga, the customary courts are indigenous institutions which have been recognized, supervised, and supported by

51. Gulliver, *Social Control,* chap. 9.
52. Laura Bohannan, "Political Aspects *of Tiv Social Organization.*"
53. Paul Bohannan *Justice and Judgement,* pp. 208–24.
54. Ibid., p. 61.

the colonial authorities. As in Busoga, the courts were part of a state structure comprising a ruler and a hierarchy of chiefs with great authority, who were also the judges. The much more legalistic nature of proceedings in both Lozi and Soga courts, as contrasted with Tiv courts and Arusha moots and assemblies, is clearly related to the greater political differentiation.

But Lozi proceedings, as noted, are less legalistic than Soga ones and this difference also has an institutional correlate. Present-day Soga courts are purely judicial bodies. The chief-chairman, to be sure, is also an administrator and politician, but not while he is serving as a judge. The Lozi *kuta* is a more multipurpose body; administrative, political, and judicial structures are not differentiated. This difference is not, I think, entirely modern. While in the old Soga states administration and adjudication rested in the same structure—the *lukiiko*— the two were more differentiated from politics than was the case in Barotseland. The Soga states were more bureaucratic, the Lozi kingdom more conciliar. The Musoga chief was thought of—and thought of himself—as receiving authority from the ruler (or, in colonial times, from the A.L.G. and the colonial government), and in turn exercised it over his people in a relatively unilateral way. There was politics, of course, but it was the politics of kinship within the bureaucracy—the palace politics of appointment and dismissal.[55] The Lozi chief, while he held great authority, seems in addition to have had a more representative character on behalf of his people vis-à-vis the king.[56] Gluckman stresses the checks-and-balances character of the Lozi state. Its politics were more open and conciliar, conducted to a substantial degree within the *kuta*. In Busoga important political moves were made elsewhere, with the result that the courts have been freer of political functions.

If the Soga courts are more legalistic, however, the Lozi ones are clearly more explicit in legal argument. They have an explicit concept of law, embodied in the word *mulao*, and they use it in talking about "laws" and "the law." [57] They talk much more in court about what a person should, and should not, do. When I first read Gluckman's account, I suspected, under the influence of my experience in Busoga, that *mulao* was simply a Bantuization of the English "law"—a recent borrowing (*mu-lao;* the *mu-* is a nominal prefix). He has convinced

---

55. I have described this briefly in *Bantu Bureaucracy,* chapters 6 and 7, and at greater length—for Buganda, which is similar in the relevant respects—in *The King's Men,* chapter 4.

56. Max Gluckman, *Ideas in Lozi Jurisprudence,* chapter 2.

57. Gluckman, *The Judicial Process,* pp. 164 ff.

me, however, that the word is indigenous,[58] and in any case it is clear
that the Barotse are generally more explicit in their handling of legal
concepts. One reason for this difference, I suspect, may be found in the
precolonial histories of the two societies. The other peoples with whom
the Basoga have had intimate contact—principally the Baganda and
the Banyoro—have institutions very like their own. The Barotse,
however, were for thirty years around the middle of the last century
ruled by a southern Bantu people, the Kololo, whose institutions were
substantially different.[59] Today they themselves rule over a number of
minority peoples.[60] The sense of difference which such contacts must
have stimulated, and the conflict-of-laws problems with which they
must have confronted the Barotse, may perhaps have contributed to
their greater legal self-consciousness.

THE FUTURE

These legal systems, in both their precolonial and colonial manifestations, are surely among Africa's greatest cultural achievements.
Without written records, they produced regimes of law, tempered by
justice, whose centrality to African life, and whose success in ordering
the affairs of millions of people, is perhaps difficult for persons not
closely familiar with African communities to appreciate. They surely
will not simply disappear; whatever legal systems ultimately emerge
from present-day processes of postcolonial rearrangement will owe
something substantial to their precolonial and colonial ancestors—if
only the view that law and legal institutions are matters of high
importance.

Beyond this, however, prediction would be quite foolish, and I shall
therefore conclude this study with a brief outline of developments in
Busoga and Uganda since 1950–52 as these bear upon the local courts.

Most importantly, of course, Uganda became independent in 1962,
just one hundred years after J. H. Speke discovered—for Europe—the
source of the Nile at Jinja. The independence constitution was a
semifederal one, with the Bantu kingdoms of southern Uganda receiving greater autonomy than other areas. Busoga, with its elective
presidency, was given the same status as the Western kingdoms (Bunyoro, Toro, Ankole), while Buganda received a still more autonomous
position.[61] In the politics of the immediate preindependence and post-

58. Personal communication.
59. Gluckman, *Ideas*, p. 37.
60. Max Gluckman, "The Lozi of Barotseland in Northwestern Rhodesia," pp.
14–19.
61. C. J. Gertzel, "Independent Uganda: Problems and Prospects."

independence periods, the political groupings described in chapter 6 continued to function, now linked with political parties. The Bulamogi and Bugabula pretenders have each served as Kyabazinga once again.[62] In the period immediately following independence the then Kyabazinga, leader of the Bugabula faction, aligned himself with the Uganda Peoples' Congress which, with the Ganda ethnic party, *Kabaka Yekka* ("the king alone"), formed the national government under the U.P.C. leader, Mr. Milton Obote. However, the U.P.C.–K.Y. alliance soon broke down and relations between Buganda and the central government worsened, culminating in 1966 in the elimination of Buganda's autonomy and the exile of the Kabaka. Busoga, which appears to have in some sense identified itself with Buganda in this crisis, as it had so often before, also lost its lesser autonomy, becoming an ordinary district. In 1967 further constitutional changes, involving still greater centralization of authority, were being debated.[63]

With respect to the courts, the drift of policy during this period has been toward the absorption of the local courts into the national judicial system and toward restriction of the sphere of customary law. Until independence, things remained essentially as I have described them. Already in 1952 the first steps had been taken toward separation of administration and judiciary with the appointment of A.L.G. magistrates, though the appointees were men of the same type as the existing chiefs—indeed many of them had served as chiefs. Their appointment was designed mainly to relieve chiefs of the growing burden of litigation. The African Courts Ordinance of 1957 took a first step toward unification by providing for application of the national code of criminal procedure to criminal proceedings in the A.L.G. courts and by directing that whenever an offense similar to a customary one was found in the national criminal code the latter should be applied. Failure to follow these provisions would not, however, be grounds for acquittal or reversal of a court order.[64] Under the African Courts Ordinance of 1962, the county courts were abolished, leaving a two-tier system of subcounty and district courts.[65]

In the Magistrates' Courts Act of 1964, however, much more substantial changes were introduced. The separate A.L.G. courts were abolished, as were all customary criminal offenses, leaving customary civil law to be applied by the new unified magistrates' courts.[66] This

---

62. L. P. Mair, "Busoga Local Government."
63. A. W. Bradley, "Constitution-making in Uganda."
64. A. N. Allott, *Judical and Legal Systems in Africa*, p. 114.
65. Eugene Cotran, "Recent Changes in the Uganda Legal System."
66. Eugene Cotran, "The Place and Future of Customary Law in East Africa."

legislation would, for example, eliminate the offense of harboring—or at any rate would prevent its treatment as a criminal offense. A woman might, presumably, be returned to her husband and damages might be awarded to him under a "civil" treatment of the concept. As a concession to customary law, an adultery statute was enacted—none had previously existed in the national law; but one wonders what Basoga (and doubtless other peoples of Uganda) will make of it. It reads: "Any man who has sexual intercourse with any married woman not being his wife. . . ." Will the courts now have to prove actual sexual intercourse? Furthermore, "wife" is defined as "wife by monogamous marriage." [67] As Morris notes, a man who has sexual intercourse with his secondary wife by customary marriage will now be an adulterer!

Uganda has in all this adopted toward customary law a policy quite different from those followed by neighboring Kenya and Tanzania, both of which, while unifying the court systems, have acted to preserve customary law by turning it into written law.[68] In Kenya, "restatements" of the various bodies of customary law are being prepared for the guidance of the courts in civil matters and for the development of a uniform customary criminal law. In Tanzania, customary criminal law has been abolished, as in Uganda, but a uniform customary civil law, based upon the recording of existing customary law, is being developed for the whole county, or at least its Bantu-speaking areas. (In view of the cultural differences that exist in Tanzania—the country embraces matrilineal as well as patrilineal peoples—a good deal of outright legislation would seem to be involved here.) Cotran, the organizer of the Kenya restatements, remarks that in Uganda, in contrast, "the official view . . . seemed to be that one should leave the customary law alone and allow it to wither away." [69]

One may question, however, whether codification is really a more effective means of adapting the customary law to contemporary needs than "leaving it alone." As important as the substantive content of the customary law, at least from the point of view of its users in the rural communities that contain the vast majority of East Africa's peoples, is its popular character. Understanding of its concepts and their uses is widely diffused, and these concepts are intimately connected with the idiom of local life. Once removed from the matrix of local culture by

67. H. F. Morris, "Uganda: Changes in the Structure of the Courts and in the Criminal Law They Administer."

68. Cotran, "The Place and Future"; William Twining, *The Place of Customary Law in the National Legal Systems of East Africa*. Mrs. Shirley Castelnuovo has given me useful observations on these efforts.

69. Cotran, "The Place and Future," p. 76.

restatement in national languages (English in Kenya and Uganda, Kiswahili in Tanzania), the substantive rules embodied in the codifications, even if ultimately derived from the various bodies of customary law, are likely to prove almost as unfamiliar—and unmanageable —to local self-advocates as the parts of the national law derived from English sources. The example of "adultery," the one customary offense which has been codified in Uganda, is suggestive. "Adultery" and *"bwenzi"* simply do not have the same meanings. To prosecute only for "adultery" would in Busoga open a chasm of major proportions between law and morality. An alternative means of modernizing customary law would be to equip it with the tools for orderly development. These would include, most importantly, a reporting system by means of which appellate decisions might be monitored and precedent-setting ones reported to the lower courts. Where it is desired to lead, rather than follow, endogenous cultural change, the task might better be approached as a frankly legislative one.

Both codification and precedent-reporting are, of course, means toward greater conceptual explicitness, the increasing need for which under modern conditions is undeniable. Perhaps the most interesting question is how far this process, however induced, can proceed while maintaining in the law the popular quality and the accessibility that allow rural Africans to make such free use of litigation in resolving their conflicts. In this regard I suspect that more important than policy toward the law itself is policy toward professionalization of bench and bar. All three East African countries seem to be moving toward unified judiciaries with transferable personnel throughout and toward the admission of advocates to the local courts. At present, however, there are far too few lawyers to even begin to supply rural areas, and most local magistrates still seem, in Uganda at least, to be local men. So long as these conditions obtain, easy communication—much of it implicit—will be possible between bench and litigant and even the most alien rules will be applied with some regard for local structures of social relations and the systems of meaning that inform them.

Appendix A

Soga Kinship: A Patrilineal Puzzle

The discussion in this study of the Soga law of landholding and of relations between the sexes involves frequent reference to institutionalized relations of consanguinity and affinity in Soga society. As background for this discussion, I shall provide here a more connected account of Soga kinship than would have been appropriate in the body of the book.

The accompanying diagrams, showing the terms Basoga use in referring to kinsmen of various types, form a useful point of departure. In general, the terminology "makes sense" in terms of the institutionalized relations among kinsmen in Busoga; that is, kinsmen whom a person refers to by the same term are similarly related to him and to third persons in terms of mutually expected behavior. The terminology does not, however, make perfect sense in these terms. I try to show in the body of the book that kinship terms do not always have the same legal significance—a man may not, legally, behave in the same way toward all the women he calls "sister," for example—but the point applies more broadly to many aspects of institutionalized kinship relations not governed by law. A Musoga calls "mother" women with whom he has several different kinds of social relationship. Most sets of kinship terms, I suspect, and particularly those which recognize unilineal descent, represent compromises in the sense that institutionalized relationships among kinsmen are more differentiated than the terminology.

There is little that is novel in this account. Soga kinship terminology belongs to a familiar type known as the "Omaha," from the American Indian society for which it was first described. There is an extensive literature on the subject, of which the most important items are the discussions by Tax, Radcliffe-Brown, Murdock, Lévi-Strauss, and

Lounsbury.[1] Beattie has analyzed a very similar system among the Banyoro, who are neighbors of the Basoga to the northwest and greatly resemble them socially and culturally.[2] I shall not discuss here the various attempts to "explain" the Omaha-type terminology, which seems so exotic to English-speakers, but instead will simply expound it in relation to institutionalized kinship in Soga society. The general problem of relations among language, concepts, and social action, in both kinship and nonkinship contexts, is taken up in a more analytic way in chapter 8.

The most common term for "kinship" in Lusoga/Luganda is *luganda*. The word tends to be particularly associated with agnatic kinship, but when inquiring into the relationship between two people, as courts often have occasion to do, this is the term used. If they turn out to be matrilaterally or affinally related, the answer is given in those terms; one does not say, in such cases, "there is no relationship" (*luganda*). "Clan" (*kika*) and "lineage" (*nda*), in contrast, are strictly agnatic in meaning. Basoga think of clans and lineages as being made up of persons biologically related in the male line.

Closest to the English "family" is *maka*, "household," which, as explained in chapter 6, most often consists of a man, his wife or wives, and their minor children. In one sense the term includes everyone who happens to live in the household, but its connotations are less strictly residential than the English "household"; it tends to connote "spouses and their children." The first diagram (fig. 20), then, gives the terms for persons with whom a Musoga, in the course of his life, is most likely to share a household. *Lata* is "father" and *mukaire* "mother" for an ego of either sex. Both a man and a woman call a son *"mutabani"* and a daughter *"mughala,"* while "husband" is *iba* and "wife" *mukazi*. Sibling terms are differentiated by the sex of the speaker in relation to that of the one spoken of, and are reciprocal. A brother and sister call each other *mwanhina*, while *muganda* refers to a woman's sister and a man's brother. The two terms thus mean "sibling of the same sex" and "sibling of the opposite sex." "Step-" and "half-" kin take the same terms as "full" or "real" (in the English sense) kin and are distinguished, when necessary, by speaking of who begat or bore (*kuzala*) whom. Polygyny and frequent divorce make relations of these kinds common in Soga households and despite the broad extension of terms

1. Sol Tax, "Some Problems of Social Organization"; A. R. Radcliffe-Brown, "The Study of Kinship Systems"; George Peter Murdock, *Social Structure,* chapters 3 and 7; Floyd G. Lounsbury, "The Formal Analysis of Crow- and Omaha-type Kinship Terminologies"; Claude Lévi-Strauss, "The Future of Kinship Studies."
2. J. H. M. Beattie, "Nyoro Kinship"; *idem,* "Nyoro Marriage and Affinity."

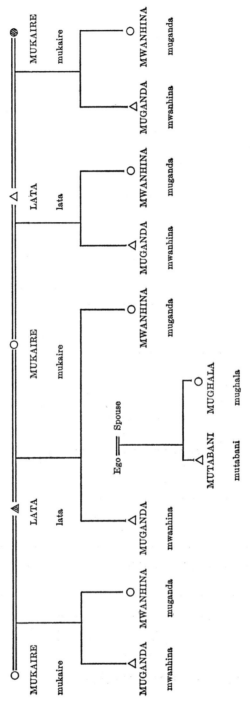

Fig. 20. Terms for household kin (man's terms in capitals, woman's terms in lower case)

for parents, siblings, and children, it often *is* important to establish precise biological relations, as several of the cases discussed show.

Households are cross-cut by the agnatic groups which play such a prominent role in Soga life. Since these groups are exogamous, and since children belong to the lineages of their begetters, the wife is commonly the only member of her lineage within the houschold, though through sororal polygyny she may be joined by a co-wife who is her sister. Furthermore, there is a tendency, especially in the demographically more stable areas, for the household to be located within the husband's natal community and at some distance from the wife's.[3] The second diagram (fig. 21), showing the terms men and women use for members of their own lineages, should be read with this in mind. A man is much more likely to have lineage mates among his neighbors than is his wife. From the man's point of view, the lineage may be visualized as importing wives and mothers and exporting sisters and daughters; from his sister's standpoint, she is one of the women exported; the lineage is a group with which her ties are never broken, but in whose company she will spend very little time during her married life.

The diagram shows only one line of grandparents, parents, siblings, children, and grandchildren, but the terms for these kinsmen are extended collaterally to the limit of the clan. One may distinguish father's brother from father (in the English sense) with the term *lata omuto*, "little faher," but this usage is rather uncommon; when it is important to locate a person's begetter among his other "fathers," the verb *kuzala*, "to beget," is usually used.

Lineage members are strictly differentiated by generation—a reflection of the authority relations that obtain between adjacent generations. Thus all members of the grandparental generation are *dhadha*, "grandparent"; all members of the parental generation are *lata*, "father," or *songa*, "father's sister"; all members of ego's generation are "siblings." In the first and second descending generations, all are "children" and "grandchildren," *baidhukulu* (singular: *mwidhukulu*), respectively. For all these kinsmen—members of the lineage—men's and women's terms are the same (except, of course, for the reciprocal sibling terms). The same is true of the terms for the wives of lineage males ("grandparent," "mother," etc.)—with one exception: a brother's wife cannot be "wife" to a woman and so there is a special reciprocal term—*mulamu*. With respect to the husbands and children of lineage females, however, men's and women's terms sharply diverge.

3. Lloyd A. Fallers, *Bantu Bureaucracy*, p. 103.

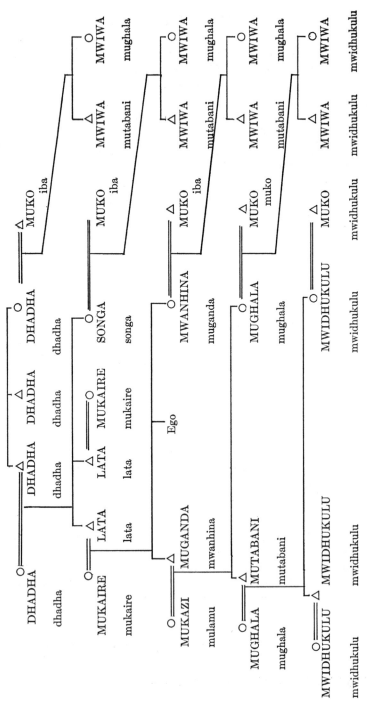

Fig. 21. Terms for lineage kin, their spouses and children

For a man, the spouses of all the exported women are *bako* (singular: *muko*), which I have throughout the book translated "in-law." Their children are all *baiwa* (singular: *mwiwa*). Thus, while the women of the lineage are differentiated by generation, their husbands and children are not. This neat pattern does not, however, fit the terms used by a woman. Since she herself is one of the exported women, she calls the husbands of the others in her own and ascending generations "husband," *iba.* Thus far she is speaking as a lineage member. Her sister's husband is in fact potentially her husband through sororal polygyny or wife inheritance. She is not a potential co-wife to her father's sister, her *songa,* or to her father's father's sister, *dhadha,* but she and they are in a similar position vis-à-vis the men of the lineage: her husband is the men's *muko,* "in-law," and her children their *baiwa.* Similarly, she speaks of the children of these other women of the lineage, children of men who are "husband" to her, as "son" and "daughter." In the descending generations, however, the pattern is broken: The husbands of her brother's daughter, and of her own daughter (both are "daughter" to her) are not her "husbands," but rather "in-laws." I shall comment further on this usage in connection with the terminology for affines, but note here simply that Basoga would feel it quite against the order of nature that a woman should address her own and her "daugher's" husband by the same term. As the defendant in *Genatio Magino* v. *Yowasi Maliwa* says: "Would I not fear to add a daughter to her mother?" Finally, a woman uses the term *mwidhukulu,* "grandchild," for all members of the second descending generation, both those within the lineage and those who are children of lineage women. Women thus have no *baiwa,* though they may *be baiwa,* and they have *bako* only in their daughters' generation.

These differences are consistent with the very different positions in the lineage occupied by men and women. The men hold corporate authority over both the women and the land of the lineage. Men act as individuals in controlling the marriages of their daughters and in managing their land, but when they die the lineage exercises corporately its residual authority to choose heirs to their property and successors to their guardianship over their children. In all this the women have no part, except as objects of the men's authority and affectionate concern. Normally, they are dispersed, as they reach maturity, to become wives of men of other lineages, often in other communities. They look back to the lineage for support against mistreatment by their husbands, and their children, the *baiwa* of the men of the lineage, look to the lineage for a kind of affection unencumbered by authority which is unavailable to them at home.

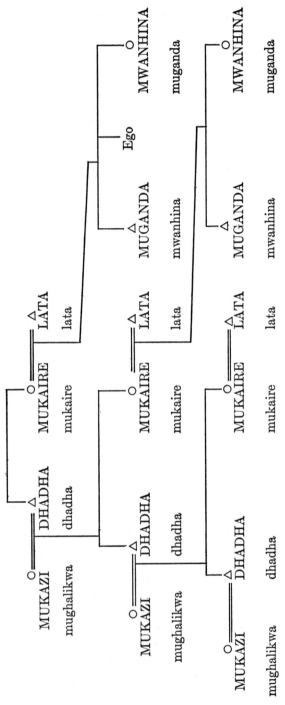

Fig. 22. Terms for kin in mother's lineage, their spouses and children

The diagram (fig. 22) showing the terms for kinsmen in ego's mother's lineage reverses the point of view. Ego, who in the previous diagram looked out toward those connected with his own lineage through the marriages of its women, now looks back at the lineage from the standpoint of a *mwiwa*, a child of one of its women. From this standpoint, the members of the lineage are differentiated only by sex, since the intergenerational authority relations which obtain among them are irrelevant to the *mwiwa*. All are "mother," *mukaire*, or "mother's brother," *dhadha*, from the standpoint of both male and female *baiwa*. I said earlier that there is some ambiguity with respect to the inclusion of matrilateral ties within the general category "kinship" (*luganda*). The source of this ambiguity, I believe, is the fact that the *mwiwa-dhadha* relationship is a close one, but yet carries rather little institutional load. There are, to be sure, mutual expectations: a *dhadha* should help a *mwiwa* assemble his bridewealth; a *mwiwa* has ritual duties at the funeral of his *dhadha*. But generally the relationship is a much more open one than are relations between lineage mates. One can to a much greater extent choose what sort of relationship to have with one's *mwiwa* or *dhadha*—or indeed whether or not to have much of a relationship with him at all. In contrast, one is "stuck" with one's place in the lineage. This comes out in the political use that is often made of the *mwiwa-dhadha* tie. The appointment of a *mwiwa* to office gave the ruler of earlier times a particularly loyal ally against his brothers and the pattern persists in the politics of the A.L.G.

The husbands of all the "mothers" in the mother's lineage are called "father," which makes for terminological consistency, though a person's relations with his mother's brother's daughter's husband and his mother's brother's son's daughter's husband have little in common with his relationship to his own father—an excellent example of the sort of terminological compromise I spoke of earlier. The easy, affectionate relationship between mother's brother and sister's child is reflected in the terms for mother's brother's wife: a man calls her *mukazi*, "wife"; a woman, *mughalikwa*, "co-wife." The same is true, incidentally, of grandparents. *Dhadha* means "grandparent" of either sex, as well as "mother's brother" (and mother's brother's son, etc.) and all grandparents may be spoken of by grandchildren as "husbands" and "wives." Like mother's brothers, grandparents do not exercise authority over their grandchildren; this role falls to the parental generation. Both grandparents and mother's brothers are believed to "spoil" children. A child brought up in a mother's brother's household or by grandparents, it is said, lacks firmness of character (*bugumu*).

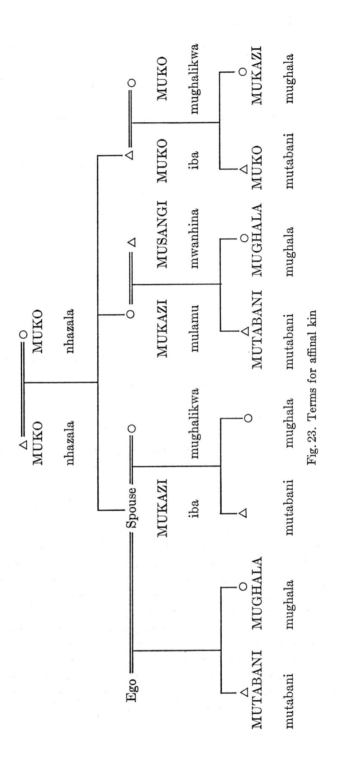

Fig. 23. Terms for affinal kin

The final diagram (fig. 23) shows the terms for affinal kin, and here again the male and female viewpoints differ. A man is related through the marriage contract to a lineage whose male members and their wives are all "in-laws" (bako), and whose female members are all "wives," bakazi. The husbands of these wives are called by ego basangi (singular: musangi), a term whose meaning would be "co-husband," if the Basoga had polyandry as well as polygyny. It is the male analogue of mughalikwa, "co-wife," since a man uses it for men whose wives he calls "wife" (or some of them; within the lineage such men are "brothers"; in the mother's lineage they are "mother's brothers"!). The wives of bako are called "bako"; that is, they are assimilated terminologically with their husbands.

The woman's view of her affines is very different. Her husband's parents are referred to by a special term, nhazala; his brother is "husband" and the brother's wife is "co-wife"; the husband's sister, as noted earlier, is mulamu, and her husband is "sibling of the opposite sex." All her husband's siblings' children are "son" and "daughter." Unlike a man's, the woman's terminology, in short, does not relate her in an undifferentiated way to the line of agnates to which her spouse belongs. Her husband looks at the lineage with which he is linked through his marriage from the outside, as a contracting party; she is much more inside the lineage into which she marries, bearing children for it, and yet she is not fully of it. In only one situation does a woman approach the position of a muko in the sense of wife-giver or party to a marriage contract: that is with respect to her daughter (she is not, of course, a party to her own marriage; that status is held by her male agnates, who contract for her). When her daughter marries, the bride-wealth contract is a matter for the men of her husband's lineage and it is heritable and returnable; but she receives a special personal gift of a goat "for bearing and rearing" her daughter—something which men, of course, cannot do. Thus alongside the lineage element there is, in Soga society, a recognition of the nuclear family—a recognition that these two individuals produced this girl from their bodies and thus, as a conjugal unit, are concerned in her marriage. Thus a woman, like her husband, calls her daughter's husband "muko," and he reciprocates; and a man uses muko in referring to the wives of his bako.

Many of the classificatory compromises in Soga kinship terminology are associated with the ambiguous position of the woman with respect to the lineage. Born into one lineage, with which she retains throughout her life profound emotional and residual legal ties, she must bear children for another. In the system of lineages, which structures so much of social life in Busoga, does she stand with her father and brothers or with her husband and children? Both positions cannot be consistently recognized and so the terminology makes compromises. As a member of her own lineage, the husbands of other women of the lineage are like husbands to her, but as a "member" (though of a very different kind) of her husband's group, her daughter's husband is her in-law, and so she calls "in-law" the husbands of women she calls "daughter," whether in her own or her husband's lineage. Again, like her brother, she is a *mwiwa* to the men of her mother's lineage, but since her brothers' children are members of her own lineage, she cannot have *baiwa;* her brothers' children, like her own, are "sons" and "daughters," but, again, of very different kinds.

All systems of unilineal descent face problems with respect to marriage, for the solidarities it establishes cut across descent-group solidarities. Not all such systems have terminologies which recognize the unilineal element as strongly as does the Soga one; other terminological compromises are possible.[4] But terminology aside, the position of the in-marrying spouse seems always to be problematical. Much attention has been given to the "matrilineal puzzle" in societies in which the husband is the in-marrying spouse.[5] In such societies, the problem is posed in terms of the strain between the husband's ties with his own lineage and his ties with his children, who belong to his wife's lineage. Since men always hold formal authority, in both matrilineal and patrilineal systems, matrilineal lineages must either retain some of their males to manage their affairs, in violation of the descent rule, or else must turn these affairs over to in-marrying males, who are not members, and whose ties with their own group tend to subvert their loyalties to their wives' groups. The situation in patrilineal societies like Busoga is not, of course, a simple mirror image of the "matrilineal puzzle." The women, who in this case are the foci of strain, are not holders of authority, though they, like the husbands in matrilineal societies, are members of different lineages from the one for which they produce children. The problematic character of their position is therefore not reflected in political affairs (or not to the same degree; the mother's brother-sister's son relationship *may,* as in Busoga, become a political resource to be used against the lineage). The effects of what I should like to call the "patrilineal puzzle" appear, rather, in the kinds of domestic strife and tragedy described in chapters 4 and 5 of this study.

4. Murdock, *Social Structure;* Lounsbury, "The Formal Analysis," p. 354.
5. A. I. Richards, "Some Types of Family Structure amongst the Central Bantu"; David M. Schneider, "Introduction: The Distinctive Features of Matrilineal Descent Groups."

Appendix B

The Case Records

The case records cited in this study are drawn from a larger body of cases collected between November 1950, and July 1952, while I was engaged in a field study of administration and politics. The records are kept in Luganda, the language of government in Busoga. At first, I naïvely told my field assistants to translate the records directly into English. I quickly discovered, however, that this was unsatisfactory, since the assistants, for all their intelligence and diligence, were not sufficiently sensitive to the importance of the phrasing of key concepts used by litigants in their arguments and by judges in their questions and decisions. Translation, I learned, was in fact an integral part of the analysis and one which I had to carry out for myself. Most of the material, therefore, was taken in Luganda and then carefully translated at leisure over the following several years, with the help of assistants at the East African Institute of Social Research.

The clerk of each court keeps a case register, in which the names of the litigants, the charge, and the disposition of each case are recorded (See fig. 24), as well as a complete transcript of the testimony. From the register it is possible to select cases of a particular kind, and the filing system is efficient enough that the transcripts of cases chosen can be found reasonably quickly. The practice of sending the transcripts of appealed cases to the appellate court, where they are incorporated into the record, requires this, of course, but it is a measure of the impressive efficiency of the system that it almost always works! Insects and fire take their toll in the flimsy, thatched buildings in which records are often stored, with the result that it is often impossible to find files more than fifteen years old. The case described in chapter 6, in which a litigant was able to cite a decision from almost three decades earlier, would hardly be typical. Clerks, however, seldom "mislay" files; if they have not been burned or devoured by termites, they can generally be produced on demand.

Case 63/50, Mutuba VII, Bugabula   N.A. 11

Date of complaint ___16-6-50___   *Adultery*

No. of case ___91/50___

Plaintiff ___Kibikyo Bireza of Bugulumbya, Mutuba VII___

Court fee receipt ___#1462   shs. 4/-, Mutuba VII___

Defendant ___Lukiio of Mutuba VII and Nadani Beka of Mutuba II___

Account of case ___For imprisoning him 3 months at hard labor and fining him shs. 160/-, including shs. 120/- compensation, alleging that he married the woman Kafuko, wife of N. Beka, whereas she is his sister.___

Witnesses ___For the court:___   ___For the appellant:___

___Nadani Beka___   ___Nabuti___

Decision of the Court ___11-7-50: The appellant, Kibikyo Bireza, has won the case. It appears that he did not marry the woman Kafuko as charged, but that he just visited her as a brother. Her husband seized him and accused him falsely.___

Sentence of the Court ___Therefore the decision of Mutuba VII is altered. The appellant Kibikyo has no fault and is released. He has been repaid his shs. 4/- fees.___

___L. Wakiso___ for County chief *Bugabula*
                    President of the Court

___N. Beka is not permitted to appeal because he is only a witness of the court.___

Remarks by the District Commissioner ___ A.B.___

Fig. 24. A page from the register of the county court of Bugabula (translation).

The records remain in the hands of the court rendering the final decision. At the lowest level, that of the subcounty courts, therefore, one finds the records of cases that have not been appealed. The records of cases appealed to the county courts and to the Busoga district court—the highest Soga court—remain in the hands of their respective clerks. An effort was made to sample cases at each of these levels. Most of the cases selected were heard between 1949 and 1951, so that the material would relate to the period of my own observations. In order to detect possible changes in law or in the frequencies of particular types of cases, however, some cases were selected from earlier periods.

The samples of cases collected are as follows: from the subcounty court of Ssaabawaali, Kigulu, 7 cases from 1949, 30 cases from 1950, and 33 cases from 1951; from the county court of Bulamogi, 25 cases from 1950; from the county court of Bugabula, 25 cases from 1950; and from the Busoga district court, 12 cases from 1950. In addition, the records of 90 cases from the subcounty court of Ssaabawaali, Kigulu were taken from the period 1920–23. These last are often no more than one-page summaries of the cases which do not provide the materials for detailed analysis, but they have proved useful for certain purposes. Finally, I discovered in one area a "clan court," operating outside the official system, whose records I was permitted to examine and copy. The 25 case records thus secured are also very brief, though again valuable for certain purposes. The main body of this study, however, rests upon the complete transcriptions of the 132 contemporary cases from the official courts, from which the fifty-odd cases actually cited have been selected.

How accurate are these transcriptions? How conscientiously and successfully does the court clerk do his job? Of course not every word spoken in court gets onto paper. There are exchanges of words that go unrecorded and there is some condensation by a clerk hard-pressed to keep up in his laborious longhand. Nonverbal communication goes completely unrecorded. More seriously, there are common understandings as to the "facts" that remain unspoken. It is sometimes impossible, for example, to determine precisely from the record the kinship relations among the parties, although everyone present clearly understands these. Ideally, in a study of this kind, the investigator should supplement the record of each case with intensive interviewing to determine the history and circumstances of the dispute, the relationships among the parties, and the like. This was possible in only a few cases. But, as much as these materials may fall short of the ideal, I offer two arguments for considering them sufficiently complete to be worthy of analysis.

First, these records are the working data of a remarkably efficient system of justice, one that clearly holds the respect of the people served by it. The system of appeals, which people use and trust, depends upon the adequacy and accuracy of the lower court records. Very rarely indeed does a litigant in an appellate court object when, as is the practice, the record of his testimony in the lower court is read out and he is asked to approve it. To achieve this result, the clerk works with great care and the bench paces the proceedings at a rate that allows him to make a reasonably complete record—a record far more complete, of course, than anything an outside observer might obtain by any means other than mechanical recording equipment. Equipment of this kind was not, in any case, available to me. And the very condensation of the testimony at the hands of the clerk doubtless tends to highlight the material that he, with his trained sense of relevance, considers essential. Thus the transcripts do have the merit of presenting what Basoga themselves consider an adequate representation of the trial process. Second, while I was unable to follow up most cases with extracourtroom investigation, I do have the knowledge that comes from extended field research in Busoga, much of it focused upon those areas of Soga life relevant to the case material. The institutions that form the social matrix of these disputes were investigated with some care. Without this, of course, the case records would have remained essentially unintelligible.

CASES CITED

Bibliography

African Population of Uganda Protectorate: Geographical and Tribal Studies. Nairobi: East African Statistical Bureau, 1950.

Allan, William. *The African Husbandman.* London: Oliver and Boyd, 1965.

Allen, C. K. *Law in the Making.* London: Oxford University Press, 1927.

Allott, A. N. *Essays in African Law.* London: Butterworth's, 1960.

Allott, A. N. *Judicial and Legal Systems in Africa.* London: Butterworth's, 1962.

Apter, David. *The Political Kingdom in Uganda.* Princeton: Princeton University Press, 1961.

Barton, Roy Franklin. *Ifugao Law.* University of California Publications in American Archaeology and Ethnology, 15. Berkeley, 1919.

Beardsley, Richard K.; Hall, John W.; and Ward, Robert E. *Village Japan.* Chicago: University of Chicago Press, 1959.

Beattie, J. H. M. "Nyoro Kinship." *Africa* 27 (1957): 317–40.

Beattie, J. H. M. "Nyoro Marriage and Affinity." *Africa* 28 (1958): 1–22.

Bell, Hesketh. *Correspondence Relating to the Famine in Busoga District of Uganda.* Cd. 4358. London: H.M.S.O., 1908.

Black's Law Dictionary, 4th ed. St. Paul: West Publishing Co., 1951.

Bohannan, Laura. "Political Aspects of Tiv Social Organization." In *Tribes Without Rulers*, ed. John Middleton and David Tait. London: Routledge and Kegan Paul, 1958.

Bohannan, Paul. *Justice and Judgement Among the Tiv.* London: Oxford University Press for the International African Institute, 1957.

Bohannan, Paul. "Law and Legal Institutions." *International Encyclopedia of the Social Sciences* 9:73–77.

Bradley, A. W. "Constitution-Making in Uganda," *Transition* 7 (August–September, 1967): 25–31.

Cotran, Eugene. "The Place and Future of Customary Law in East Africa." In *East African Law Today.* British Institute of International and Comparative Commonwealth Law Series no. 5 (1966), pp. 72–92.

Cotran, Eugene. "Recent Changes in the Uganda Legal System." *Journal of African Law* 6 (1952): 210–15.

Cross, Rupert. *Precedent in English Law*. London: Oxford University Press, 1961.

Eggan, Fred. "Social Anthropology and the Method of Controlled Comparison." *American Anthropologist* 56 (1954): 743–63.

Elkan, Walter, and Fallers, Lloyd A. "Labor Mobility and Competing Status Systems." In *Labor Mobility and Social Change in Developing Areas*, ed. Wilbert E. Moore and A. Feldman New York: Social Science Research Council, 1960.

Fallers, Lloyd A. *Bantu Bureaucracy: A Study of Conflict and Change in the Political Institutions of an East African People*. Chicago: University of Chicago Press, 1965.

Fallers, Lloyd A. "Changing Customary Law in Busoga District of Uganda." *Journal of African Administration* 8 (1956): 139–44.

Fallers, Lloyd A. "Customary Law in the New African States." *Law and Contemporary Problems* 27 (1962): 605–16.

Fallers, Lloyd A. "Ideology and Culture in Uganda Nationalism." *American Anthropologist* 63 (1961): 677–86.

Fallers, Lloyd A., ed. *The King's Men: Leadership and Status in Buganda on the Eve of Independence*. London: Oxford University Press for the East African Institute of Social Research, 1964.

Fallers, Lloyd A. "Societal Analysis." *International Encyclopedia of the Social Sciences* 14:562–72.

Fallers, Lloyd A. "Some Determinants of Marriage Stability in Busoga: A Reformulation of Gluckman's Hypothesis." *Africa* 27 (1957): 106–23.

Fallers, Lloyd A., and Fallers, Margaret C. "Homicide and Suicide in Busoga." In *African Homicide and Suicide*, ed. Paul Bohannan. Princeton: Princeton University Press, 1960.

Fallers, Margaret C. *The Eastern Lacustrine Bantu*. Ethnographic Survey of Africa, East Central Africa 11. London: International African Institute, 1960.

Fei, Hsiao-Tung. *Peasant Life in China*. New York: Oxford University Press, 1946.

Frank, Jerome. *Law and the Modern Mind*. New York: Brentano's, Inc., 1930.

Geertz, Clifford. "The Impact of the Concept of Culture on the Concept of Man." In *New Views of the Nature of Man*, ed. John R. Platt. Chicago: University of Chicago Press, 1965.

Geertz, Clifford. "Ritual and Social Change: A Javanese Example." *American Anthropologist* 59 (1957): 32–54.

Gertzel, C. J. "Independent Uganda: Problems and Prospects." *Africa Report* 7 (October, 1962): 7–9.

Gluckman, Max. *Ideas in Lozi Jurisprudence*. Storrs Lectures on Jurisprudence, Yale Law School, 1963. New Haven: Yale University Press, 1965.

Gluckman, Max. *The Judicial Process among the Barotse.* Manchester: University of Manchester Press for the Rhodes-Livington Institute, 1955.

Gluckman, Max. "The Lozi of Barotseland in Northwestern Rhodesia." In *Seven Tribes of British Central Africa,* ed. Elizabeth Colson and Max Gluckman. London: Oxford University Press for the Rhodes-Livingstone Institute, 1951.

Gluckman, Max. *Politics, Law and Ritual in Tribal Society.* Chicago: Aldine Publishing Co., 1965.

Goodrich, Carter. "Arbitration, Industrial," *Encyclopedia of the Social Sciences* 2:153–56.

Greenberg, Joseph H. *The Languages of Africa.* The Hague: Mouton & Co. for Indiana University, 1966.

Gulliver, P. H. *Social Control in an African Society: A Study of the Arusha: Agricultural Masai of Northern Tanganyika.* Boston: Boston University Press, 1963.

Gutkind, Peter C. W. *The Royal Capital of Buganda.* The Hague: Mouton & Co., 1963.

Hailey, Lord. *Native Administration in the British African Territories.* London: H.M.S.O., 1950.

Hart, H. L. A. *The Concept of Law.* London: Oxford University Press, 1961.

Haydon, E. S. *Law and Justice in Buganda.* London: Butterworth's, 1960.

Johnson, Frederick. *A Standard Swahili-English Dictionary.* London: Oxford University Press, 1959.

Kagwa, Sir Apolo. *Ekitabo Kye Mpisa Za Baganda* (Customs of the Baganda). London: Macmillan & Co., 1905.

Kroeber, A. L. *Anthropology.* New York: Harcourt, Brace and Co., 1948.

Larimore, Ann Evans. *The Alien Town: Patterns of Settlement in Busoga, Uganda.* University of Chicago Department of Geography Research Papers, 55. Chicago, 1958.

Levi, Edward H. *An Introduction to Legal Reasoning.* Chicago: University of Chicago Press, 1948.

Lévi-Strauss, Claude. "The Future of Kinship Studies." Huxley Memorial Lecture 1965. *Proceedings of the Royal Anthropological Society of Great Britain and Ireland for 1965* (1966), pp. 13–22.

Lévi-Strauss, Claude. *Structural Anthropology.* Translated by Claire Jacobson and Brooke Grundfest Schoepf. New York: Basic Books, 1963.

Llewellyn, Karl. *Jurisprudence: Realism in Theory and Practice.* Chicago: University of Chicago Press, 1962.

Llewellyn, K. N., and Hoebel, E. Adamson. *The Cheyenne Way.* Norman: University of Oklahoma Press, 1941.

Lobingier, Charles Sumner. "Customary Law." *Encyclopedia of the Social Sciences* 4:662–67.

Lobingier, Charles Sumner. "Limitation of Actions." *Encyclopedia of the Social Sciences* 9:474–80.

Lounsbury, Floyd G. "The Formal Analysis of Crow- and Omaha-type Kinship Terminologies." In *Explorations in Cultural Anthropology: Essays in*

Honor of George Peter Murdock, ed. Ward H. Goodenough, pp. 351–94. New York: McGraw-Hill, 1964.

Low, D. A. "The Northern Interior 1840–84." In *History of East Africa,* ed. Roland Oliver and Gervase Matthew, 1:297–351. London: Oxford University Press, 1963.

Low, D. A. and Pratt, R. C. *Buganda and British Overrule.* London: Oxford University Press, 1960.

Mair, L. P. "African Marriage and Social Change." In *African Marriage and Family Life,* ed. Arthur Phillips. London: Oxford University Press for the International African Institute, 1953.

Mair, L. P. *An African People in the Twentieth Century.* London: Routledge and Kegan Paul, 1934.

Mair, L. P. "Busoga Local Government." *Journal of Commonwealth Political Studies* 5 (1967): 91–108.

Maitland, F. W. *Doomsday Book and Beyond.* London: Fontana Library, 1960.

Malinowski, Bronislaw. *Crime and Custom in Savage Society.* London: Routledge and Kegan Paul, 1926.

Morris, H. F. "Marriage and Divorce in Uganda." *The Uganda Journal* 24 (1960): 197–206.

Morris, H. F. "Uganda: Changes in the Structure and Jurisdiction of the Courts and in the Criminal Law They Administer." *Journal of African Law* 9 (1965): 65–73.

Mulira, E. M. K. and Ndawula, E. G. M. *A Luganda-English and English-Luganda Dictionary.* London: Society for Promoting Christian Knowledge, 1952.

Murdock, George Peter. *Social Structure.* New York: Macmillan Co., 1949.

Nader, Laura, ed. *The Ethnography of Law. American Anthropologist,* 67, special publication, 1965.

Parsons, Talcott. *The Structure of Social Action.* New York: McGraw-Hill, 1937.

Parsons, Talcott, and Shils, Edward A. eds. *Toward a General Theory of Action.* Cambridge: Harvard University Press, 1951.

Pospisil, Leopold. "A Formal Analysis of Substantive Law: Kapauku Papuan Laws of Land Tenure." American Anthropologist, Special publication, 1965; pp. 186–214.

Pospisil, Leopold. *Kapauku Papuans and Their Law.* Yale University Publications in Anthropology, 54. New Haven, 1958.

Potter, Pitman B. "Mediation." *Encyclopedia of the Social Sciences* 10: 272–74.

Pound, Roscoe. "Rule of Law." *Encyclopedia of the Social Sciences* 13: 463–66.

Radcliffe-Brown, A. R. "The Study of Kinship Systems." *Journal of the Royal Anthropological Institute,* vol. 71 (1941); reprinted in A. R. Radcliffe-Brown, *Structure and Function in Primitive Society.* London: Cohen and West, 1952, pp. 49–89.

Redfield, Robert. *Peasant Society and Culture.* Chicago: University of Chicago Press, 1956.

Richards, A. I. "Some Types of Family Structure amongst the Central Bantu." In *African Systems of Kinship and Marriage,* ed. A. R. Radcliffe-Brown and Daryll Forde, pp. 207–51. London: Oxford University Press for the International African Institute, 1950.

Roberts, A. D. "The Sub-Imperialism of the Baganda," *Journal of African History* 3 (1962): 435–50.

Roscoe, John. *The Baganda.* London: Macmillan & Co., 1911.

Ryle, Gilbert. *The Concept of Mind.* New York: Barnes and Noble, 1965.

Schapera, I. *A Handbook of Tswana Law and Custom.* London: Oxford University Press for the International African Institute, 1938.

Schneider, David M. "Introduction: The Distinctive Features of Matrilineal Descent Groups." In *Matrilineal Kinship,* ed. David M. Schneider and Kathleen Gough, pp. 1–35. Berkeley: University of California Press, 1961.

Schurmann, Franz. *Ideology and Organization in Communist China.* Berkeley and Los Angeles: University of California Press, 1966.

Schutz, Alfred. *Collected Papers,* vol. 1. Edited by Maurice Natanson. The Hague: Martinus Nijhoff, 1962.

Sofer, Cyril and Sofer, Rhona. *Jinja Transformed.* East African Institute of Social Research, East African Studies, 4. Kampala, 1955.

Southall, A. W. "On Chastity in Africa," *Uganda Journal* 24 (1960): 207–16.

Tax, Sol. "Some Problems of Social Organization." In *Social Anthropology of North American Tribes,* ed. Fred Eggan, pp. 3–34. Chicago: University of Chicago Press, 1937.

Thomas, H. B. and Scott, Robert. *Uganda.* London: Oxford University Press, 1935.

Thomas, H. B. and Spencer, A. E. *A History of Uganda Land and Surveys and of the Land and Survey Department.* Entebbe: Government Printer, 1938.

Twining, William. *The Place of Customary Law in The National Legal Systems of East Africa.* Lectures delivered at the University of Chicago Law School in April–May, 1963. Chicago: University of Chicago Law School, 1964.

Uganda Protectorate. *Annual Report of the Department of Agriculture for the Year Ended 31st December, 1935.* Entebbe: Government Printer, 1936.

Uganda Protectorate. *Annual Report on the Eastern Province, Western Province, Northern Province and the Kingdom of Buganda for the Year ended 31st December, 1950.* Entebbe: Government Printer, 1951.

Uganda Protectorate. *Annual Report on the Eastern Province, Western Province, Northern Province and the Kingdom of Buganda for the Year ended 31st December, 1955.* Entebbe: Government Printer, 1956.

Uganda Protectorate. *Report of the Agriculaural Productivity Committee.* Entebbe: Government Printer, 1954.

United Kingdom. *Withdrawal of Recognition from Kabaka Mutesa II of Buganda.* Cd. 9028. London: H.M.S.O., 1953.

Von Hentig, Hans. *The Criminal and His Victim: Studies in the Sociology of Crime.* New Haven: Yale University Press, 1948.

Weber, Max. *From Max Weber: Essays in Sociology.* Translated and edited by H. H. Gerth and C. Wright Mills. New York: Oxford University Press, 1946.

Weber, Max. *Max Weber on Law in Economy and Society.* Edited and annotated by Max Rheinstein. Translated by Edward Shils and Max Rheinstein. Cambridge: Harvard University Press, 1954.

Weber, Max. *The Theory of Social and Economic Organization.* Translated by A. M. Henderson and Talcott Parsons. New York: Oxford University Press, 1947.

Index

For topics discussed in connection with particular cases in the Soga courts, see the table of cases cited, pp. 351–53.